Growing a Soul for Social Change

Building the Knowledge Base for Social Justice

a volume in
Teaching<~>Learning Indigenous, Intercultural Worldviews:
International Perspectives on Social Justice and Human Rights

Series Editor:
Tonya Huber-Warring
St. Cloud State University, Minnesota

Praise for *Growing a Soul for Social Change*

The editorial style of Tonya Huber-Warring, PhD, includes a much-needed and much-awaited modification to APA guidelines. User-friendly and nonhegemonic, full names of authors and editors are cited in this series. For those interested in the identities of originators of the work being cited, this newer tradition assists the ardent researcher as well as the casual reader. Such attention to detail honors the authors and editors, as well as their readers. Thank you for ending countless hours of searching for complete names and references, by including this documentation in the original manuscript!

Michele Periolat Dahl
Doctoral Candidate in Critical Pedagogy
University of St. Thomas, Minneapolis, Minnesota, USA
Religion Coordinator and Teacher
Oak Knoll School of the Holy Child, Summit, New Jersey, USA

Tonya Huber-Warring's *Growing a Soul for Social Change*, which contains 20 chapters with good quality illustrations, highly descriptive figures and tables through an international perspective by 33 authors from Australia, Botswana, Canada, China, Guatemala, Hong Kong, Nigeria, South Africa, and the USA, is one of the best works for those who seek for a reliable resource on Peace Education, especially, on antiracist positionalities and methodologies.

Dr. Ismail Hakki Mirici
Associate Professor, Head of the Foreign Languages Teacher Training Department
Akdeniz University, Antalya, Turkey

Tonya Huber-Warring has put together a wide and deep collection of voices, which focuses collaboratively on social justice in classrooms around the world. The authors, who represent many countries and perspectives, join to create a call for peace in local and global classes, through the application of the principles of culturally responsive teaching and curriculum development. Based on the premise that education has primacy in the struggles for human rights, the text encourages intercultural communication to expand traditional notions of teaching and learning. The multiple voices within the text are linked together by the ties of diversity, especially inclusive of indigenous worldviews. Huber-Warring and authors brilliantly combine their pedagogical perspectives and shine a very bright light on peace.

Dr. Joan Wink
Professor, College of Education
CSU Stanislaus, Turlock, California, USA

I know more than one person who by reading Barbara Wind's glorious essay decided they must visit that inspiring place in the mountains of Tennessee, Whitwell Middle School. It is there you can make a quiet pilgrimage and sense the will of the people who shared their inspiration and their support of the Children's Holocaust Memorial. And if you are truly blessed, you will meet Principal Linda Hooper and some of her dedicated students and staff.

Michele Periolat Dahl
Doctoral Candidate in Critical Pedagogy
University of St. Thomas, Minneapolis, Minnesota, USA
Religion Coordinator and Teacher
Oak Knoll School of the Holy Child, Summit, New Jersey, USA

Growing a Soul for Social Change

Building the Knowledge Base for Social Justice

edited by

Tonya Huber-Warring
St. Cloud State University, Minnesota

Information Age Publishing, Inc.
Charlotte, North Carolina • www.infoagepub.com

Library of Congress Cataloging-in-Publication Data

Growing a soul for social change : building the knowledge base for social justice / edited by Tonya Huber-Warring.
    p. cm. — (TeachingLearning indigenous, intercultural worldviews)
    Includes bibliographical references.
    ISBN 978-1-59311-887-7 (pbk.) — ISBN 978-1-59311-888-4 (hardcover) 1. Critical pedagogy. 2. Multicultural education. 3. Social justice—Study and teaching. I. Huber-Warring, Tonya.
    LC196.G76 2008
    370.11'5—dc22   2008000869

ISBN 13: 978-1-59311-887-7 (paperback)
ISBN 13: 978-1-59311-888-4 (hardcover)

Copyright © 2008 IAP–Information Age Publishing, Inc.

All rights reserved. No part of this publication may be reproduced, stored in a retrieval system, or transmitted in any form or by any electronic or mechanical means, or by photocopying, microfilming, recording or otherwise without written permission from the publisher.

Printed in the United States of America

Dedication

*For the Giants
who have shouldered us like Tolkien's Treebeard ...*

*and for the visionary Leaders
like Dr. Kate Steffens
who make this work possible.*

CONTENTS

Preface: Growing a Soul for Social Change—
The Trees We Have Planted: An Introduction
Tonya Huber-Warring xi

PART I: FOUNDATIONS OF INDIGENOUS, INTERNATIONAL, AND GLOBAL EDUCATION

1. An Introductory Reflection—Excerpt From "An Angel Behind the Camera, Filming *Angels in the Dust:* An Interview With Activist Filmmaker Louise Hogarth"
   Tonya Huber-Warring 3

2. Can There Be a Postsecular Education for Peace?
   Danielle Celermajer 11

3. Narratives of Experience: Crossing Cultures, Crossing Identities
   Betty C. Eng 27

4. Fuel Efficient Stoves and Community Development in San Lucas Tolimán, Guatemala
   John D. Abell 45

5. Evolution or Revolution? The Forces of Internationalization and Technology on Higher Education in the U.S.
   Patricia Aceves 79

PART II: PRINCIPLES OF CULTURALLY RESPONSIVE TEACHING AND CULTURALLY RESPONSIBLE CURRICULUM DEVELOPMENT

6. An Introductory Reflection—An Essay on Reconceptualizing Democracy Education
   Larry Hufford 103

7. Language, Culture, Identity, and Power: Immigrant Students' Experience of Schooling
   Ming Fang He, Elaine Chan, and JoAnn Phillion 119

8. The Relationship Between Reading and English Composition Writing: Implications for Community Junior Secondary School Teachers in Botswana
   Deborah Adeninhun Adeyemi — *145*

9. Developing Multicultural Sensitivity Through International Student Teaching: The Challenges Faced by a Southern University
   Judy C. Davison and Terrence K. McCain — *163*

PART III: SOCIOCULTURAL IDENTITIES AND CONTEXTS OF HUMAN GROWTH AND DEVELOPMENT

10. An Introductory Reflection—Science and Spirituality: A Synergy Made in Heaven
    Clay M. Starlin — *179*

11. Experiencing Tribes: Perceptions of Teacher Education Students
    Richard G. Berlach and Annette Sanders — *193*

12. A Sense of Purpose and Mission: Graduate Students' Perceptions of Writing Their Ethical Belief Statements
    Ilene L. Ingram and Kevin H. Brockberg — *209*

13. Identity Development for Holistic Global Interconnectedness
    Douglas F. Warring — *225*

14. Emotional Intelligence in the Classroom: A Behavioral Profile of an Effective Teacher
    Melinde Coetzee and Cecelia A. Jansen — *247*

15. Women and Development: The Case of Women in Military and Police Barracks in Nigeria
    Eno Edem — *269*

PART IV: EXPERIENTIAL KNOWLEDGE

16. An Introductory Reflection—Paper Clips: A Holocaust Survivor Remembers
    Barbara Wind — *289*

17. Seeking Solidarity Through Global and Indigenous Service Learning
    Kelly C. Weiley — *295*

18. Helping Beginning Teachers Shape Their Personal Practical
    Knowledge: An Essential Process in Teacher Education.
    Chun-kwok Lau, Wai-ming Yu, and Francis Nai-kwok Chan   *345*

19. Promise and Perils of Study Abroad: White Privilege Revival
    *JoAnn Phillion, Erik Malewski, Eloisa Rodriguez,
    Valerie Shirley, Hollie Kulago, and Jeff Bulington*   *365*

20. Sowing Seeds of Social Justice Through Performative Pedagogy:
    Middle School Students Explore Genocide
    Mary Ann Reilly and Rob Cohen   *383*

About the Contributors   *399*

Recognizing Reviewers   *409*

PREFACE

Growing a Soul for Social Change— The Trees We Have Planted

Tonya Huber-Warring

> *The finest thing we can do in life is to grow a soul and then use it in the service of humankind.... We writers may not live to see the changes that we work for, but readers will enjoy the shade of the trees we have planted.*
>
> —Mary Pipher (2006, p. 241)

The journey to this premiere volume of *Teaching<~>Learning Indigenous, Intercultural Worldviews: International Perspectives on Social Justice and Human Rights* has been a rather long one. Many trees have been planted along the way.

The present journey travels in the warm shadow of my first experience editing an international publication. As founding editor of the *Journal of Critical Inquiry Into Curriculum and Instruction* (JCI<~>CI) in 1998, I was committed to building richer understandings of the knowledge bases for diversity, just as I was passionate about hearing and sharing the stories that make a difference in the teaching<~>learning of indigenous worldviews. The JCI<~>CI carried a unique feature of its mission on the front cover: "a refereed journal committed to publishing educational scholarship and research of professionals in graduate study." When the sixth edition of *Cabell's Directory of Publishing Opportunities in Educational Curriculum and Methods* (Cabell, English, & Guarnieri, 2002) was released, the editors informed me that JCI<~>CI was the only journal in the directory specifically targeting the voices of professionals exploring issues of curriculum and instruction with the submission requirement that manuscripts "are the result of the graduate-level studies of the first-listed author" (p. 505). Why such a requirement? Because I had seen two patterns in my years in higher education that deeply troubled me; first, that graduate students frequently took second or even third or fourth authorship on their own theses and dissertations while chairs and committee members were listed first and, secondly, that research at the master's level was seldom dignified with publication, while doctoral research was expected to be published but without institutionalized strategies and mentoring practices for many new doctorates. The scenarios have always struck me as endemic of the institutionally hegemonic and elitist structure of much of higher education as I have experienced, observed, and studied it. Here, I would be remiss in not acknowledging the powerfully positive modeling that Drs. Ed Fagan, Jim Nolan, Bernie Badiali, and Kieth Hillkirk provided for me as my mentors at the Pennsylvania State University and the dynamic leadership of Principal Bill Padamonsky (during my years as a high school teacher) and Dean Kate Steffens (in my current professorial role). My vision and commitment are only because I have stood on the shoulders of these giants.

We are like dwarfs on the shoulders of giants, so that we can see more than they, and things at a greater distance, not by virtue of any sharpness of sight on our part, or any physical distinction, but because we are carried high and raised by their giant size.

—Bernard of Chartres, c. 1130 (Merton, 1965, p. 178)

The giant most influential to the knowledge base format of this premiere volume is Professor G. Pritchy Smith. As the author of *Common Sense About Uncommon Knowledge: The Knowledge Bases for Diversity*, Smith (1998) chiseled the content he had been presenting at conferences for more than a decade into what many of us have considered the "knowledge base (K-Base) Commandments"—though Pritchy himself has always been horrified at the idea that his work would become frozen in time and not be perceived as malleable to the ongoing development of diversity.

Proving that we needed to be ever cognizant of the need to continually re-examine the knowledge bases and expand to address diversity topics, Smith added two more knowledge bases in academic year 2000-01, just a few years after the seminal work had been published. The 15 K-bases, as they are currently configured, are identified in Table 1.

Table 1. **Smith's Knowledge Bases for Diversity**

	Parameters	Guiding Principles
1.	Foundations of multicultural education	A review of international, legal, and historical, theory, research, and practice undergird the study and practice of multiculturalism
2.	Sociocultural contexts of human growth and development in marginalized ethnic and racial cultures	Child-rearing, social interaction, gender role identification, parenting, responsibility, cultural/developmental scripts, and other psycho-socio-cultural patterns affect the way people learn and respond to reading
3.	Cultural and cognitive learning style theory and research	Cultural cognitive styles and multiple intelligences research, combined with a thorough understanding of learning style theory, enables the teacher to maximize instruction
4.	Language, communication, and interactional styles	Recognizing cultural styles related to speech patterns, verbal and nonverbal interactions, and inter-relationship patterns
5.	Essential elements of culture	Studying ancient through contemporary history of cultures highlights common features and distinctive differences of deep culture characteristics that help the educator better understand the individual child or student
6.	Principles of culturally responsive teaching and culturally responsive curriculum development	Analyzing the language, concepts, principles, practices, theory and research on teaching responsive to, and responsible for cultural issues in the explicit, implicit, and null curricula including cultural synchronicity, congruity, continuity, correspondence and cultural scripts
7.	Effective strategies	Strategies, policy, and practice can produce positive effects for previously low-achieving students
8.	Foundations of racism	Issues of racism, slavery, genocide, prejudice, bias, stereotyping, and discrimination and their effects on micro- and macrocultures
9.	Effects of policy and practice on culture, race, class, gender, and other categories of diversity	Determining the impact of the differential effects of policy and practices on race, class, gender, and culture regarding such issues as teacher expectations, ability grouping and curriculum tracking studies, desegregation and integration studies, discipline, and suspension/expulsion and drop out/push out factors

(Table continues on next page)

Table 1. Continued

Parameters	Guiding Principles
10. Culturally responsive diagnosis, measurement, and assessment	*Replacing* of the traditional view of intelligence as a physical substance, a measurable, entity, and a subsequent focus on measurable, easily quantifiable constructs focusing on linguistic and logical-mathematical intelligences and culture-specific norms
11. Sociocultural influences in subject-specific learning	Planning with recognition of cultural influences on specific school subjects
12. Gender and sexual orientation	Knowledge about gender differences and the impact of sexual orientations, both the students' own and those of family members, on students
13. Experiential knowledge	Lived and supervised clinical experiences that include personal cross-cultural and multicultural lifestyle experiences and supervised demonstration of culturally responsive teaching in clinical school settings with culturally diverse student populations and professional knowledge about how teachers teach effectively and responsibly in multicultural classrooms representing diversity issues, particularly from action research, ethnography, case studies, and educational anthropology
14. Foundations of identifying and teaching special needs students	Preparation of regular education teachers to identify and respond sensitively and appropriately to students' special needs, an aspect of teacher education that typically occurs only for those candidates certified as special education
15. Foundations of international and global education	Analyzing global and international education beyond introductory comparative education which often contributes to the provincialism of teachers in the United States

Adapted from Smith, 1991, 1998, 2000-2001 (Huber, 2002, p. 42).

Education brings daybreak; ignorance a long, long night.

—Maya Angelou

Authoring the summative "Afterthought" for JCI<~>CI, *2*(3), Smith (2000-2001) evaluated the journal publication through Maya Angelou's metaphor.

When JCI<~>CI burst on the educational landscape like the first light of daybreak ... it was visionary not just because it was and remains the only refereed journal committed to publishing educational scholarship and research of professionals in graduate study, but also because of the forum it would provide for defining and understanding important relationships among the knowledge bases for diversity in teacher education, critical pedagogy, critical inquiry, and story. (p. 26)

For readers new to the field of multicultural education and human relations education, the recency of these publications heralded as seminal may be confusing, for certainly the concepts building the field of multicultural education and human relations education have been around much longer. True. But, for the first time, we found the conceptual framework, guiding principles, and critical works across disciplines and fields in Smith's encyclopedic organization. Because of the comprehensive nature of Pritchy Smith's knowledge bases, they have been employed as the organizing themes for this volume. I would clarify that I have not burdened authors to study Smith's analysis and then apply it to their works; the categorization is my own. And, as is true of any topic, the interpretation and application may be broadly applicable.

One of my major goals in founding this series has been to further develop the knowledge bases with voices from those in the trenches (literally and figuratively) and at the chalkface—while proverbial for some parts of the world, chalk remains a teaching staple in many regions of the world. The pages of the *Teaching<~>Learning Indigenous, Intercultural Worldviews: International Perspectives on Social Justice and Human Rights* book series will be used to build the knowledge bases for diversity concerning places and peoples, philosophies and positionalities not commonly appearing in the professional literature on education.

To survive is to co-exist with other peoples. Learning to exist collectively demands a conscious attempt to redress multiple forms of oppression as they play out within and among communities.

—George J. Sefa Dei (2005, p. 15)

Though I had taught previously, my first licensed full-time teaching position started with the fall semester of 1982; thus, as this book has evolved and gone to press, I am in my 25th year of teaching, having taught every semester since beginning the best professional career on Earth. This book is, in part, a response to every time I have worked with a student minoring in human relations or a student teacher or a master teacher or a doctoral candidate who has told me that they find nothing in the professional data bases concerning the topic they are studying. This book is dedicated to the many and varied voices that I have heard in my years of teaching with an earnest prayer that their words will be heard and their stories located in the professional literature. This passion was first realized in my early thesis work concerning the dearth of indigenous literature by native peoples. As my research skills sharpened, so did my dismay—where were the studies of the experiences about which my students were seeking, speaking, enduring, and struggling to survive?

Given the role of education in the universal struggle for the realization of human rights, the purpose of this book series is to encourage intercultural communication concerning the parameters of education among pedagogists, practitioners, and policy makers worldwide, promoting critical understanding of diversity through multiple perspectives. The series is dedicated to publishing authors who represent and topics concerned about all aspects of diversity, particularly those inclusive of indigenous worldviews. And, once again, I am committed to seeking and supporting the new voices engaged in our dialogue from thesis and doctoral students committed to making a difference in their work on these issues.

Since I am seeking to provide pages for the full range of difficult and challenging issues facing teachers-learners in social justice and human rights work, words and ideas of the authors that appear on these pages do not necessarily reflect the positions of the editors or Information Age Publishing. Having said this, I will make no apologies for the many communications with our authors to invite reconsideration of word choice and/or phrasing and I invite readers, reviewers, and potential authors to continue to engage with us in the essential dialogue about words and language. From the smallest descriptor to the choice of naming and categorizing, our words carry power and, therefore, they can liberate, but they can—and often do—oppress. The history of colonialism and hegemonic oppression includes re-naming peoples, tribes, nations, and places. In an anti-colonial, anti-racist, indigenous, and liberatory positioning to *reject* this practice, as the Editor, I require full names (whenever available) with the initial introduction of people in and in all references. This small sign of respect for the meanings in people's names is a step in the journey of reparation for all the names taken, lost, changed, anglicized, or stolen in the generations of global movement. I remain hopeful that this seed will grow a tree with a long shadow.

> *As a teacher, before you walk into your classroom, you should have a bamboo tree fully grown in your chest.*
>
> —Ming Fang He (1999, p. 15)

In the 15 issues of my founding editorship of JCI<~>CI (1998-2004), I invited critical pedagogy, critical inquiry, and narrative story—epitomized in the second issue of the journal in the borders crossed by Ming, Shiao, and Wei as collective identities flowing somewhere between China and Canada. Written by Ming Fang He from her doctoral research at the Ontario Institute for Studies in Education, the article was the outcome of days of writing-intensive communication between the author and myself. The investment of time during that winter *break* was rewarded—the article continued throughout the journal's history to be a favorite that many came to associate with the journal (so much so that many people would refer to the journal when they met me at conferences as the one that featured the Asian art that they removed from the centerfold and framed!). Ming Fang's research would then be published by George Johnson, publisher and president of Information Age Publishing (see He, 2003, *A River Forever Flowing: Cross-Cultural Lives and Identities in the Multicultural Landscape*). Another tree had been planted and its many branches would include some of the authors and reviewers who worked on this volume.

A complete list of reviewers follows the About the Authors section of this volume. For all the authors' work, without the reviewers' critically reflective considerations, pages of feedback, and detailed track changes, these chapters would not be possible. Finally, no work of this magnitude is accomplished without synergy. To the two graduate student colleagues with whom I worked, I am indebted. Lisa A. Holtan joined the journey with little editorial experience and tackled a huge learning curve to become an impeccable technical editor, investing tremendous energy in reviewer composites and the difficult task of integrating edits and author's feedback.

The associate editor on this volume was not new to the experience, nor to working with me. Many of the reviewers and authors who responded to our invitation immediately recognized the name of Aneesh Joshi as the managing editorial assistant of the *Journal of Critical Inquiry Into Curriculum and Instruction* during its last 2 years. He would go on from there to work in a parallel position with guest editor Tony Ambrosio on the fall 2005 issue of the *Journal of Thought*. Aneesh's e-communication interpersonal skills are only rivaled by his command of the formidable American Psychological Association (2001) guidelines and British English. He is irreplaceable as an editor. I am indebted for the selfless support of both Aneesh and Lisa on this premiere edition. Ultimately, however, the decisions and the outcomes of this volume are mine as the editor, and for the missed e-communications, delays, and uncorrected errors, I take full responsibility. For all of us engaged in this publication journey, may we find in the process and in the words crafted for these pages the *conscientização* that Paulo Freire (1968/1970) challenged us to seek in "the deepening of the attitude of awareness characteristic of all emergence" (p. 101) that we may grow our souls to plant more seeds for the social change needed in the world.

Throughout this volume, authors explore and research their own discoveries on this journey—narratives of crossing cultures and developing communities, reconceptualizing democracy and reinterpreting traditions, seeking solidarity and sowing the seeds of social justice. In the shade of these giant trees, the critically reflective reader may glimpse another butterfly, plant a tiny seed in a world where forests and the people who depend on them are desecrated and destroyed, and discover a *bamboo tree fully grown* in place of being hollow.

REFERENCES

American Psychological Association. (2001). *Publication manual of the American Psychological Association* (5th ed.). Washington DC: Author.

Cabell, David W. E., Deborah L. English, & Nancy A. Guarnieri. (Eds.). (2002). *Cabell's directory of publishing opportunities in educational curriculum and methods.* Beaumont, TX: Cabell.

Dei, George J. Sefa. (2005). Critical issues in anti-racist research methodologies. In George J. Sefa Dei & Gurpreet Singh Johal (Eds.), *Critical issues in anti-racist research methodologies* (pp. 1-27). New York: Peter Lang.

Freire, Paulo. (1968/1970). *Pedagogy of the oppressed* (Myra Bergman Ramos, Trans.). New York: Continuum. (Original Portuguese work published 1968)

He, Ming Fang. (2003). *A river forever flowing: Cross-cultural lives and identities in the multicultural landscape.* Greenwich, CT: Information Age.

Huber, Tonya. (2002). *Quality learning experiences for ALL students.* San Francisco: Caddo Gap Press.

Merton, Robert K. (1965). *On the shoulders of giants: A Shandean postscript.* New York: The Free Press.

Pipher, Mary. (2006). *Writing to change the world.* New York: Riverhead Books.

Smith, G. Pritchy. (1991). *Toward defining a culturally responsible pedagogy for teacher education.* Paper presented at the annual meeting of the American Association of Colleges for Teacher Education, Atlanta, GA.

Smith, G. Pritchy. (1998). *Common sense about uncommon knowledge: The knowledge bases for diversity.* Washington, DC: The American Association of Colleges for Teacher Education.

Smith, G. Pritchy. (2000-2001). Relationships among knowledge bases for diversity in teacher education, critical pedagogy, critical inquiry, and story. *Journal of Critical Inquiry Into Curriculum and Instruction, 2*(3), 26-30.

PART I

FOUNDATIONS OF INDIGENOUS, INTERNATIONAL, AND GLOBAL EDUCATION

CHAPTER 1

AN INTRODUCTORY REFLECTION ...

EXCERPT FROM "AN ANGEL BEHIND THE CAMERA, FILMING *ANGELS IN THE DUST*: AN INTERVIEW WITH ACTIVIST FILMMAKER LOUISE HOGARTH"

Tonya Huber-Warring

AIDS has orphaned more than 14 million children worldwide—the equivalent to every child under five in America with no one to watch over them.[1]

South Africa, a country with the highest incidence of rape and child rape in the world,[2] has the fifth highest prevalence of HIV in the world, with 1.1 million AIDS orphans.[3] The UNAIDS Global Report determined 370,000 AIDS related deaths in South Africa in 2003.[4] Given the numbers of people infected and dying, South Africa is regarded as having the most severe HIV epidemic in the world. This pandemic is estimated to be several years away from peaking in terms of the numbers of projected AIDS related deaths with a projection of 75-100 million affected by 2010.[5]

Against this statistical background, nearly 60 children are raped every day in South Africa and the age range of the child rape victim is significantly found to begin at six or younger.[6] A growing body of medical and research evidence suggests the problem is much larger and more pervasive than the already staggering numbers would suggest. While 21,000 child rapes were reported in 2001, for instance, according to the South African Police Service, only 1 in 35 child rapes is reported suggesting the number could actually be closer to 735,000.[7]

What does a teacher committed to culturally responsible pedagogy do with such overwhelming data?

Multiculturalist G. Pritchy Smith (1998) in *Common Sense about Uncommon Knowledge: The Knowledge Bases for Diversity* details theory and research relevant to preparing teachers for effectively educating *ALL* students. As Smith admonishes:

> If preservice and inservice teachers study the appropriate bodies of literature, they will understand that norms for human growth and development vary from culture to culture and that much of the traditional knowledge base studied in the psychological foundations courses is Anglocentric or Eurocentric and not necessarily appropriate for interpreting and understanding the behavior of culturally diverse pupils of color. (p. 27)

Counseling research affords a rich, if often untapped, source of information on the sociocultural contexts of human growth and psychological development beyond the western tradition. Unparalleled, however, are the most recent issues evolving in South Africa for victims of child rape surviving in a nation spiraling out of control in the HIV/AIDS stranglehold. Teachers have a dual responsibility in this regard: (a) to authentically educate their students about the HIV/AIDS pandemic and (b) to be prepared to work with students and families impacted by the two-headed snake of HIV/AIDS and child rape.

What does a critically conscious citizen do with such overwhelming data?

Activist filmmaker Louise Hogarth decided it wasn't enough to send money. With her camera and commitment to nurture positive change, Louise went to *Botshabelo*[8] (a Tswana word meaning "place of safety") for children who have been orphaned by AIDS, starved, raped and, often, forgotten. Opened in December 1990, by wife and husband partnered team Marion and Con Cloete, Botshabelo has become an island of compassion and humanity in a country struggling under the weight of apartheid's legacy: poverty, violence, lack of education, and inadequate health care. Encompassing the orphanage, a school and an organic farm (though they lack the water to maintain the farm), Botshabelo provides food, education, hope, and therapeutic healing for hundreds of children of whom more than 90% are rape victims and more than 25% have HIV/AIDS.[9] While nearly 200 children stay at Botshabelo, as many as 400 other children come to the orphanage on a daily basis for education and food.

Huber-Warring: The challenge seems monstrous, Louise, what do you hope to accomplish?

Hogarth: Awareness of the AIDS orphan crisis; promotion of Marion's therapeutic work with these children; interruption of the victim-perpetrator cycle; consideration of the spiritual dimensions of death and dying; and a testament to the difference one person, Marion, makes when spiritual choices are followed over material possessions and gain.

Huber-Warring: When I was reviewing the program description, I was surprised to see a picture of elephants and a segment devoted to these creatures. The connection amazed me—would you please explain it.

Figure 1.1. The children learned social skills from the story of the orphaned elephants.

Hogarth: I've filmed a segment about a famous incident in South Africa. A culled herd of young orphaned elephants became uncharacteristically violent during their *teen* years, rampaging and killing each other and other animals at a sanctuary until adult elephants were placed with them to teach them how to relate to each other and their world. The elephants became peaceful and behaved more appropriately. The message is recognized by these children when they visit the elephant sanctuary. Like all the therapeutic activities at the orphanage, the children learn how to journey along the road to healing and break the cycle of abuse.

Huber-Warring: Your film trailer captures the plight of these fragile victims—these "angels in the dust" as Marion calls them. Their stories would be too painful to listen to, but as I watch your film and listen to their stories, I realize with what horrors they must cope, so how can I turn away because it is too painful for me to bear the anguish they must endure daily.

There is Little Lebo who was brought to the orphanage by her grandfather. She had been gang raped by three men who then carved their initials in her head, threatening all the while to return and fetch her if she ever told anyone. Marion had to work for a year and a half to be able to touch Lebo's head with a comb; therapy helping her to sleep at night without fear of the rapists coming for her.

Then, there is tiny Bafana who at 3 was raped so violently that the attack tore his rectum and caused his "whole anus to come out when he went to the toilet" (from the documentary). The pain was so severe that at 5 years of age he had just started to walk again.

These young children have not only endured the trauma of rape, but physical, violent, perverse abuse, as well. Then, one in four is discovering she or he has been infected—at birth or through rape—and is HIV positive, as well.

Hogarth: These are deeply wounded children. Marion and her husband and daughters are working miracles. I believe Marion's approach to healing can provide a model for other communities struggling to reclaim children from violence. I love Marion's work because she is breaking the cycle of perpetrator, victim, perpetrator—a central theme I am trying to address in my work.

Huber-Warring: Your documentary captures the poignancy of the situation and the Cloete family's response. Can you explain Marion's model for those who haven't yet had the benefit of seeing the trailer for the documentary?

Hogarth: Marion reports her original thinking that the angels at Botshabelo were the caretakers, but she came to realize that the small children, face down in the dust and needing to be helped to their feet, were the real angels. Anyone who has been raped feels dirty all over. So part of her counseling approach is to help the child find the one place the rapist didn't get to—a little toe, an ear—to find the place that isn't dirty. Another part of her approach is sound and feeling modality therapy. The children are asked to go the place that hurts and find a sound that comforts them. In the documentary Little Lilian shares her sound and healing movement—she explains it is "Mommy's sound"—the sound she associates with her deceased Mother that takes her to her "place of safety."

Many of these children have already been orphaned by HIV/AIDS and then are additionally traumatized by rape. To then discover that the rapist or rapists infected them epitomizes the severity of the victim/perpetrator/victim cycle exponentially escalating out of control in South Africa. Consider that in 2005 AIDS had already orphaned 14 million children. The estimate is that by 2010 in South Africa alone 26 million children will be orphaned by AIDS.

Another issue that people need to be made aware of is the failure of prevention around the world. I read last week that Zimbabwe received an award for their campaign: *It's not negative to be positive.* I'm sorry, but it is negative to be HIV positive. The *Love Life Campaign* (huge in SA), funded by the Kaiser Foundation, is a splendid example of this failure. The campaign's "Love Life—Get Attitude" billboards appear everywhere in South Africa, but many people admit to having no idea what the message is about.

The Dream Out Loud Films Web site (http://www.dolfilms.org) provides links to hosting fundraisers to finance the documentary (http://www.dolfilms.org/angels/host.html). I see the events as opportunities for people to come together to learn more about the orphans of AIDS, but the bigger picture is people coming together in cross-cultural dialogue to promote global citizenship and action.[10] Marion says it best: "Do you have something better to do with your life than to help children survive what has happened to them on this continent?"

ACKNOWLEDGMENT

Grateful acknowledgement is made to Editor and Publisher Alan H. Jones for permission to reprint from the author's 2007 article "An Angel behind the Camera, Filming *Angels in the Dust:* An Interview with Activist Filmmaker Louise Hogarth," appearing in *Multicultural Education* (Vol. 14, No

3, pp. 22-26). Modifications have been made for the purpose of this printing.

NOTES

1. Apathy is lethal. United Nations Foundation. Retrieved September 28, 2005, from http://www.apathyislethal.org/index.asp
2. Earl-Taylor, M. (2002). HIV/AIDS, the stats, the virgin cure and infant rape. In *Science in Africa, Africa's first on-line science magazine*. Retrieved September 27, 2005, from http://www.scienceinafrica.co.za/2002/april/virgin.htm
3. Global Aids Program. Department of Health and Human Services, Center for Disease Control and Prevention CDC. Retrieved January 22, 2007, from http://www.cdc.gov/nchstp/od/gap/countries/south_africa.htm
4. Ibid.
5. Joseph Edelheit. (2007, January 16). AIDS in India. PowerPoint presented at Faculty Workshop Days. St. Cloud State University, St. Cloud, MN.
6. Earl-Taylor, Ibid.
7. Ibid.
8. The orphanage and community complex has recently changed its name to the local name of *Boikarabelo* and work under the definitive title of "Poverty Alleviation Research and Development Village" (Con Cloete, personal communication, April 23, 2007).
9. *Sex with virgins to cure AIDS*. Retrieved October 9, 2005, from http://www.truthorfiction.com/rumors/a/aids-virgins.htm. The Johannesburg, South Africa, city council conducted a 3-year study of about 28,000 men. They found that one in five believed in the virgin-AIDS cure. The fallout from that is a rise in assaults of women and children, some of whom contract AIDS themselves. The belief in the virgin-AIDS cure is not restricted to Africa. According to a Knight-Ridder report from Mark McDonald in January of 2000, it is also helping fuel an increase in child prostitution in Cambodia. McDonald says there are many Asian men who believe that having sex with a virgin will cleanse their AIDS. The same is true for India, according to the fall 1995 *Harvard AIDS Review*, and Jamaica, according to the Ministry of Health in Jamaica. The belief in curing AIDS by having sex with a virgin is apparently an outgrowth of a long-standing belief in many cultures, including Europe, in the restorative and healing powers of virgins and having sex with virgins. See, also, *Women and Children in Portions of Africa are Being Sexually Violated by Men Who Believe That Sex With a Virgin will Cure Their AIDS-Truth!* Retrieved January 22, 2007, http://www.truthorfiction.com/rumors/a/aids-virgins.htm
10. Examples of the cross-cultural dialogue and efforts being made can be found at St. Cloud State University (SCSU), Minnesota, where students from the Organization for the Prevention of AIDS in Africa (OPAA) have been working to educate about the AIDS pandemic and raise funds for dif-

ferent nations in Africa. In 2006, OPAA members provided more than US $1000 for the children of Botshabelo orphanage after viewing Louise Hogarth's documentary trailer for *Angels in the Dust*. In 2007, a service-learning cohort of students at SCSU would again raise more than U.S.$1000 for the children. The same group would go on to found the organization Synergy of Solidarity whose members have committed ongoing support to the orphanage. Charter leadership for the organization included Amy M. Harris, Stacy Brown, Kelly C. Weiley, Tebra D. Petersen, and Tonya Huber-Warring. Synergy of Solidarity members continue to work with Linda Cullen, cofounder of Fifty Lanterns International (www.fiftylanterns.org), to provide solar lighting and other life-changing, earth-friendly, renewable energy sources for vulnerable people around the world who are affected by poverty, conflicts, and natural disasters.

REFERENCES

Smith, G. Pritchy. (1998). *Common sense about uncommon knowledge: The knowledge bases for diversity*. Washington, DC: The American Association of Colleges for Teacher Education.

CHAPTER 2

CAN THERE BE A POSTSECULAR EDUCATION FOR PEACE?

Danielle Celermajer

At a time when local and global violence increasingly speaks with a religious accent and, indeed, when the most significant conflicts in the world might well be characterized as a clash of triumphalist religious discourses, many people argue that in the name of global peace, religious discourses, and faith commitments should be relegated to a safely remote location (Dawkins, 2006; Hitchens, 2007; Onfray, 2007). In much the same way as the liberal solution to the insurmountable religious conflicts of seventeenth century Europe was to establish a common public sphere in which citizens bracketed their religious commitments (and thereby their religious differences), this line of argumentation insists that the social and political realties of today provide renewed reasons for reasserting a strong border between the secular and the sacred.

RELIGION IN A TIME OF RELIGIOUS VIOLENCE?

This principle of separation, applied most conspicuously in the sphere of politics, would seem to apply at least equally to the field of education.[1]

Indeed, when we speak about education, particularly educating our children, we are not simply speaking about managing the shared lives of differently committed people, but about creating the citizens of the future and shaping the consciousness of those who will decide the fate of their world. In an already conflict ridden century, it is thus especially incumbent upon those who wish to argue that there is a place for religious ideas or practices in education to justify their stance and elaborate their visions of an appropriate role for religious thought. In this chapter, I take up this challenge, both by engaging with some of the theoretical challenges and illustrating how religious resources might be brought into educational settings by looking at some Biblical text and my own experience in interfaith text interpretation.

A New Type of Public Religion

In recent years, a number of religious leaders and scholars of very different political persuasions, from the Dalai Lama (the spiritual leader and head of government in exile of Tibet) to Pope Benedict XVI (the head of the Roman Catholic Church) to Jonathon Sachs (the Chief Rabbi of Great Britain), have sought to promote the continued relevance of their religious traditions in the public sphere, albeit in very different ways. Sensitive to the social and value pluralism that characterizes modernity, their vision is not, however, one where public religion implies religious supremacy or political domination. Rather, in the face of what they see as the limits of modernity's adulation of instrumental rationality, they offer their own religious traditions as sources of moral and social principles vital for addressing contemporary challenges. In this sense, they are not speaking only to their co-religionists, and urging them to deepen their religious identities and commitments, but suggesting to all of us, including self-professed secularists, that religious traditions may have valuable resources to offer in our attempts to equip ourselves to solve the unprecedented challenges of the twenty-first century.

Three key arguments have been developed to provide a general justification for an expanded role for religious discourses in the public sphere, one defensive, one moral and proactive, and the other as a diagnosis of the deficits of modernity and liberal secularism. The first, defensive argument is that human beings of good faith cannot simply remain silent when the God in whose name they orient their lives is invoked to justify and sanction violence and hatred. As Sachs (2002) so eloquently phrased it, "We must withhold the robe of sanctity when it is sought as a cloak for violence and bloodshed" (p. 9). Sachs' argument, founded on something like Jonathon Swift's (2003) famous aphorism, "We have just Religion enough to make us hate, but not enough to make us love one another," (para. 1) is that we must meet religion with religion until we have true holiness. The challenge, of course, is to differentiate *good* or peaceful religious discourses and identities from *bad* or intolerant ones, a challenge made even more difficult by the fact that anyone who claims to know where to draw that line is unlikely to receive universal endorsement from his or her radically divided co-religionists.

The second, moral and proactive argument is that the world's religions are a source of key moral principles concerning, for example, the intrinsic dignity of human beings and the sanctity of life. This view of religions' contribution was dramatically illustrated by one of the participants at the Parliament of the World's Religions in Barcelona in 2004, who spent the seven days of the meeting walking around with a poster displaying the various versions of the Golden Rule articulated in different religious traditions and languages. Again, the argument has its obvious merit conceptually; the difficulty is in translating what are often abstract principles into lived realities. Ample historical experience should be more than enough to convince us that general moral principles about love and respect alone are not sufficient to alter the actual praxes of human beings whose identities, social and economic status, and embodied beliefs about self and other are often structured around deep divisions. Something more than an abstract principle will be required to engage actual human beings in a different sense of themselves and those who seem so radically *other*.

The third, related but more pointed argument is that because of its explicit and primary focus on moral concerns and ethics, the field of religion provides a desperately needed supplement to the cold utilitarian thrust of modernity. Religious worldviews can bring humanity's moral capacities back into a disenchanted world (as Max Weber, 1918/1946 observed it), where reality has come to be interpreted solely within a scientific paradigm and human beings have come to see themselves and each other as components of an ever more efficient mechanism, rather than as active subjects who create their own moral universe.[2]

Thus, Father Richard Neuhaus (1984), Catholic priest and president of the Institute of Religion and Public Life, challenges the Enlightenment assumption that throwing off religious systems would be a modern Exodus and liberal secular humanism would be the promised land. Perhaps in ideal theory, a space where individuals could contract without constraint sounded like a formula for freedom; but this projection ignored the very real human need for a sacred canopy that imbues the public square with grace and meaning (pp. 80-82). More pointedly, though, it is arguable that there is a necessary link between secularism and the form of late modern capitalism at which we have arrived, in the contingent world of actual history (which is the only one we actually have), liberal secularism has ushered in an era where progress for its own sake and the accumulation of material wealth have a monopoly over all other values, even the Enlightenment's most beloved value of critical evaluation.

It was in this vein that the great twentieth century Rabbi Abraham Joshua Heschel (1977) reflected on the gaps in his own education, reflections that might provide food for thought as we reflect on contemporary educational choices. Heschel came out of the pious and closed Shtetls of Eastern Europe and went to study with the great German philosophers in Berlin. Although he had come with a view to integrating the Jewish approach and this Greek German tradition of thought, he found, as he wrote in his reminiscences, that the professors did not even recognize the types of questions he brought: "They were fettered in categories which presupposed certain metaphysical assumptions that could never be proved. The questions I was moved by could not even be adequately phrased in categories of their thinking" (p. 135).

With Heschel, one might ask, what are the questions we do not even allow ourselves, or our students, to think about? How are we fettered by a desiccated reason that is excellent at producing technology, but apparently poor at sustaining an ethic of respect? An education that worships the God of reason is also a dogmatic monotheism when it shuts out all new questions or perspectives, like those that speak in the language of wonder and awe and unreason. Sometimes, unreasonableness, or the refusal of the answers our reason currently gives us, is just the quality that we need, especially given that our standards of reason are given by what we already know, not by what we are on the verge of learning. As Einstein is said to have observed, the knowledge that got us into our current problems will not be sufficient to get us out of them.

ENGAGING RELIGIOUS TEXTS: THE BOOK OF RUTH

To explore how one might pursue this alternative path, I want to look briefly at the Book of Ruth. This text, I suggest, can be read in a way that enriches the moral reflections of the readers, without demanding that they accept any metaphysical or dogmatic claims that are usually associated with religious education. My brief engagement with Ruth is intended as an illustration of how other texts might be engaged in this way.

The book of Ruth is the text that Jews read on the night of Shavuot, when they commemorate the giving of the Torah at Sinai. Perhaps, surprisingly, given this context, the book makes no mention of Moses, to whom the Torah was initially given, nor the laws that one associates with the Torah, but rather tells the story of two women, Naomi and Ruth. The story begins with two Hebrews, Naomi and Elimelech, moving from Bethlehem to Moab, with their two sons. Ruth and Orpah, both Moabites (a people much reviled by the Hebrews) marry the two sons, but some time later both Elimelech (the father) and the two sons die. Without her husband or sons, Naomi sets out to leave Moab and return to Bethlehem, and Ruth and Orpah, now also widowed, try to follow Naomi. But Naomi puts to them that their choice is entirely unreasonable, telling them that there is no future for her, and none for them if they come with her; whereas in Moab, they can marry again and have families. Orpah, acting reasonably, remains in her home town. Ruth, *unreasonably*, cleaves in love to her beloved Naomi and accompanies her to the place where Moabites are not welcome.

What transpires when this stranger enters Bethlehem gives rise to what is most powerful about this story. The two women arrive, without the economic and social support of fathers, brothers, husbands, or sons. Naomi approaches this situation by advising Ruth to go and glean in a certain field, where she might make herself known to one of Naomi's relatives, Boaz. She does so, and through a series of events choreographed by Naomi, Boaz falls in love with Ruth, they marry, and they give birth to a son, Obed. This son, it will transpire, will become the grandfather of King David, thereby making Ruth and Obed's union the beginning of the line of the Messiah. In other words, not only does Ruth's unreasonable action not fail; it is the catalyst for the generation of the Messiah. *Redemption*, in other words, the *ultimate hope of peace*, begins not with what was reasonable, but with what *defied* reason. Moreover, redemption begins when the stranger, the *other*, breaks through the boundaries of a particular community. Embracing Ruth's act and perspective does not, of course, mean that we should banish reason from our educational toolkit; in fact, it was in part Naomi's deployment of instrumental reason that brought about the union from which the Messianic line arose. Rather, the modification is that *reason* should not be a despotic ruler.

This third argument thus contends that religious perspectives, often defying *reason*, have a redemptive force that one needs the courage to introduce, even when the lenses of reason ridicule them, or when this means breaking through with another type of identity. As a response to the very obvious gap between the promises of rationalized modernity and the desperate, violent, and radically unequal world in which we find ourselves, this argument certainly has significant rhetorical force. At the same time, however, it is an argument that one must approach with significant care. The ability to observe a gap is not the same as the ability to fill it. Just as communitarian critics of liberalism's tendency to atomize individuals must themselves envision forms of community that do not suppress difference or persecute dissenters, so too, critics of the excesses of the Enlightenment must answer a list of legitimate objections to traditional religious values and forms of organization and, most seriously, the excesses of unreason. The challenge that this poses is to find ways of opening ourselves to the possibility of wonder, to what has traditionally been called the miraculous, and to religions' sacred canopy, without sacrificing the enormous benefits that a reasoned epistemology has brought to bear.

Principles for Introducing Religious Discourses

Thus, if one accepts the legitimacy and force of these arguments, the all-important practical question becomes, what is it that educators can draw from religious traditions as they seek to create learning environments and curricula for the twenty-first century? Quite clearly, certain answers to that question, and indeed some traditional arguments that may be derived from the third argument in particular, will be ruled out. That is, the shifts we associate with modernity may have had unanticipated and negative consequences from the point of view of human dignity and human and planetary well-being, but the antidote cannot be an uncritical return to an idealized space of monolithic, anthropocentric, dogmatic religious systems and monochrome communitarian social contexts. Rabid critics of all things religious like Richard Dawkins (2006) might well be providing a caricatured vision of religion in order to discredit it wholesale, but their observations are not without merit.[3] As I noted above, anyone seeking to fight religious fire with religious fire will have to find a way of differentiating the former from the latter, lest they add to what is clearly a world-threatening conflagration.

Moreover, the religious resources we call upon today as part of the toolkit for facing contemporary social, political and, vitally, environmental challenges will have to be ones appropriate to the context in which our learners have already developed their subjectivities. That is, we are all moderns now, with a high stake in our individualism and the lights of our own reasoning minds, and we are all steeped in social contexts with a diversity of cultural perspectives, as well as a supermarket of belief systems. If they are to be meaningful and respectful, religious discourses have to speak to such individuals, recognizing their deep and necessary enmeshment in an enlightened world. This is of course a significant intellectual challenge. On the one hand, part of the justification for the reinvocation of religious teachings is the failure of liberal secular discourses to provide the intellectual and moral resources necessary to sustain a decent society; on the other, certain dimensions of this late modern social and intellectual space are either inevitable or invaluable. There is no recipe for working out which of our late modern perspectives, methodologies and values we need to suspend, and which we need to engage.[4]

As a general methodological (rather than prescriptive) rule of thumb, one might suggest that every time we move toward engaging religion in our educational processes, we must require of ourselves that we pass through the way station of an explicit conversation between the (multiple) perspectives, values, and methodologies of religious and secular systems. In other words, this enterprise cannot be a return to an idealized enchanted world of faith and moral grandeur, but must be understood as forging a genuinely novel engagement with the religious and the secular or faith and reason. More substantively, we can specify several orienting principles that must be a sine qua non of an engagement with religious discourses in educational settings. Here, I specify three: critical reflection, deep diversity, and world (not human) centeredness.

First, irrespective the excesses of reductive rationality, the Enlightenment value of critical engagement or reflexivity is not one that can be discarded. In other words, uncritical acceptance of text or teachings, or more malignly the expectation of uncritical acceptance among our students, is no longer (if it ever was) ethically acceptable. Undoubtedly one of the dangers of religious teachings is their tendency toward what Hannah Arendt (1990) called the Absolute—that force of capital "*T*" Truth that kills all plurality and human spontaneity and, irrespective the fine ethical content of the teaching, turns human beings into automata who would (ideally) simply enact the program of divine law or mandate. Arendt's point, and it remains critical for us, was not simply that religious teachings can contain morally repugnant prescriptions, and that if we enact them (as per the caricatured cult member), we can commit grave wrongs. Rather, it was that when religious teachings are taken as Truths that stand over and above us, derived from a metaphysical realm with which we have no relationship, they deprive human beings of the creative and moral faculties that are ultimately the most potent defenses against evil or the denigration of human dignity.

Even the value of love, she argues, recalling Herman Melville's (Arendt, 1990) character Billy Budd, when taken as a religious Absolute, can lead to the commission of wrongful acts, because the person enacting the principle relinquishes his capacity to see the world that is actually in front of him, in all its particularity (Arendt, 1959, pp. 83-88).[5]

Thus, responsibility entails that we engage religious teachings and texts in a living and active dialogue, as if it was truly up to us how they would be rewritten in this world; as if we were in the position of the prophets, or the redactors, or the Apostles, rather than those who receive truth after the fact. As the Haggadah, the text Jews read on the festival of Passover teaches, we might read the text as if it actually concerns us here and now, not as if it drops down like manna from some time out of history where absolute truths were set in place for us to imitate.

And yet, to echo my general theme of a creative dialogue between religious world views and methodologies and those of secular reason, this critical engagement must not be interpreted as a swing to the other extreme where anything goes: I take on board only what *I* deem as convenient or appropriate to me now. In other words, critical engagement is not equivalent to atomistic individuals unhinged from any system of values visiting the religious shelf in the supermarket of ideas.

Again, there is no formula for finding a point of equilibrium between these tendencies. One might take as a guiding (though ideal) model a certain style of engaging text in the Jewish tradition, where whoever is now reading (or hearing) the text enters into a conversation with a history of interpretations of that text.[6] Of course, she reads it from the particularity of her own historically and socially located position, but not as a free-floating individual who need justify her reading to no one and can assert her position without consideration of other perspectives. Indeed, this engagement with the minds of others does not take place only across time, but also occurs in the present; for she will always (ideally) read and discuss with others, and the development of her own understanding will occur in the context of others' developing and testing theirs. Again, Arendt (1959) made a not dissimilar point, though in an entirely secular context, when she insisted that political thinking or action should always take place in a context of plurality, where free and equal subjects speak with each other and cannot remain sovereign over their own thoughts or truths.

In this vein, Franz Rosenzweig (1961), writing as a self-consciously modernist and Jewish thinker in the early twentieth century suggested what he called *the New Thinking* as a model of critical engagement conducive to both freedom and ethics. His suggestive remarks might well guide us today:

> In the new thinking, the method of speech replaces the method of thinking maintained in all earlier philosophies. Thinking is timeless and wants to be timeless. With one stroke it would establish a thousand connections. It regards the last, the goal, as the first. Speech is bound to time and nourished by time, and it neither can, nor wants to abandon this element. It does not know in advance just where it will end. It takes its cue from others. In fact, it lives by virtue of another's life, whether that other is one who listens to a story, answers in the course of a dialogue, or joins in a chorus; while thinking is always a solitary business, even when it is done in common by several who philosophise together.... I do not know in advance what the other will say to me because I do not even know what I myself am going to say. (pp. 198-199)

This raises the question of who is invited into this circle of interlocutors and suggests my second orienting principle for thinking about how to engage with religious texts and thought. One of the characteristics of much traditional religion is that there are strong identity-based strictures concerning both who can authoritatively interpret text or doctrine and who is considered a legitimate partner in conversation. Thus, for example, in virtually all religions, being a male has been a basic entry ticket for interpretive authority, if not for being able to study at all. Similarly, authority has been conditional on certain types of education. People whose lives were taken up with the practicalities of survival (their own and others) tended to be de facto excluded, and relegated to the position of recipients of others' wisdom, rather than recognized as sources of a different dimension of wisdom.

Today, however, where one of the most serious moral issues we face is increasing and deeply structural inequality, often itself based on gender, class and educational differences, the readings of those who have been excluded along these lines are perhaps those that most urgently need to be included. When base communities in Central and South America took the Bible into their own hands, we know that they found in Exodus both a critique of their oppression and a narrative of possibility (Dussel, 2003). Today, as they (along with others) are reading Genesis, they are finding a mandate for care for and partnership with the earth. In the former case, their reading was the occasion for liberation movements; in the latter, it is the occasion for a re-evaluation of agricultural practices and how we use natural resources.

What has perhaps been missing, however, is a context in which those on the other side of the class fence are engaged in the same conversation, rather than observing it from a distance, or feeling themselves the objects of an alien critique. The tremendous and unique potential here is that people can walk and talk around shared texts and generate very different understandings and commentaries on life, thus creating a context where there is commonality and significant difference. In contradistinction to those cases where different political visions are sourced in very different traditions of political thought, and those in different camps do not recognize the legitimacy of each other's source texts (Marx vs. Burke), here, the thoughts are not derived from alien soil, but interpretations of a text that they all consider holy—a point of commonality through which they might be able to recognize each other as humans struggling to make sense of enigma. It would be naïve to suggest that broadening the interpretive circles would dissolve profound structural conflicts; but allowing those differences to be refracted through a common text or tradition, or moral commitment, and insisting that those interpretations traditionally excluded get a hearing in the conversation seems a fruitful way of opening those profound structural divides to a different and perhaps more generous type of conversation.[7]

Staying with the issue of exclusion, still more absolute has been the exclusion of people from different religions. Even religions that teach tolerance and coexistence have not, traditionally, considered the possibility, let alone the value, of discussing teachings and doctrines with members of other faith communities. This has changed to some extent with the burgeoning of interfaith dialogue but, even then, we tend to close the door when it comes to interpretive authority or voice. With the exception of the few new interfaith seminaries, our seminaries are almost the exclusive territory of our co-religionist teachers and our students, and then we might meet those belonging to other religions after hours.[8] Yet, in a world where an ever-decreasing number of actual communities remain religiously or culturally homogenous, and where an ever-increasing number of people are engaging (even if at a distance, or via their representatives) with people steeped in different texts and traditions, can we afford to confine our interpretive conversations to a religiously homogenous membership?

Importantly, my suggestion here is not that teaching religion means teaching synchromism or dissolving differences. It is rather than in the face of massive misunderstandings about each other's sacred beliefs and, more proactively, in the face of the undeniable problems that our own religious traditions have in resourcing us to live in a world of deep value diversity, opening ourselves to the perspectives of those with different texts and traditions marks a wise, as well as a courageous move.

Indeed, one might even argue that this hermeneutic movement towards the other, the stranger, is continuous with a principle at the heart of the Bible. The Biblical commandment repeated more often than any other in the entire Hebrew Bible is to care for the *ger*, the stranger, the one who is not like you and does not naturally belong to your community. The text enjoins its readers (or listeners) to observe this principle more often than any other, including those setting out what they should eat, how they should pray, who they should have sex with and what words or prayers they should speak. And they are told to do this because this is what God did for them. This, and not standing still looking at our glorious ritual, or at our self same image, is acting in the image of God.

I would suggest, however, that the authentic care for the *other* demands, as Emmanuel Levinas (1969) insists, far more than that we treat her well because we see her as an image of ourselves (pp. 194-201). Authentic recognition of the *other* means that we do not reduce her to an object of our own consciousness or projections, viewing her solely through the lens of who we believe she is and what we think she believes. Genuine care rather demands that we make the space for her to appear before us as an independent subject and source of wisdom. We can only truly care for her when she also has a voice in creating what it means to care and act morally. Irrespective whether this was the dominant reading of the Biblical text when it was received in the past, it must surely be how we read it in the context of our pluralistic world.

Finally, a third, and somewhat different guiding principle for educators drawing on religious ideas or practices concerns the place that the natural world plays in the theologies on which we draw. Traditionally, environmental and theological concerns have been seen as conceptually distinct; or, even worse, religious systems have promoted a vision where only human beings truly mattered, and the natural world figured only as a background, something to be dominated and controlled. Placing human beings at the ontological center, the rest of nature has been seen as our dominion, to be manipulated for our own edification and progress, but with no independent worth as part of holy creation. Indeed, indigenous spiritualities that place the natural world at the center and recognize human beings as part of an integrated system of being have historically been disparaged as primitive, not worthy of the status of higher order religion. At this point of history, where human beings' instrumental relationship with the natural world has brought us to a point where we are faced with the truth of interdependence in the form of interdependent destruction, theologies that encode this hierarchy are among the aspects of our lives that are unsustainable.

Fortunately, there are a plethora of figures in a number of religions reinterpreting their traditions in a manner that places respect and love for the natural world at the heart, rather than as an occasional afterthought.[9] To recognize the centrality of ecological concerns in the religious enterprise requires, however, that one embrace the deeper and more challenging contention that the essential and most important concerns of God, or the divine (however one conceptualizes it) may alter as history brings new dimensions of human morality and creation itself to light.

WOMEN ACROSS DIFFERENCE

The ways in which educators and students might take up these principles and delve into religious resources to develop the perspectives and capabilities they need to face their world will no doubt be as various as they are numerous. In these closing pages, I offer one experience, not as a model, but as a possible point of reflection.

In the years 2001-2004, I participated as a member of a group of three women, one Jewish (me), one Muslim, and one Christian, who together and publicly, read certain stories about women in our sacred texts. The stories we focused on, chosen in part because women were protagonists in each of them, and in part because women's relationship with water was prominent in most of them, were the stories of Sarah and Hagar, Ruth and Naomi, Miriam and Pharaoh's daughter (saving Moses) and the Samaritan woman. With the exception of the latter, all three appeared in at least two, if not all three of the traditions and, in our readings, we presented them as they were told by our own traditions. We also reflected on both our own and each other's stories, the traditional interpretations of those stories and our responses to them as we re-experienced them in each other's presence.

Two aspects of this rereading of sacred texts were exceptional. First, the interpreters were all women; and second, three women from three religious traditions were reading their stories with each other. What developed in this process was remarkable and requires a far lengthier reflection than I will conduct here, but I want to remark on three particular outcomes. First, and most obviously, we learned that each other's traditions told the same stories, but often in very different ways. Thus, for example, I learned that Muslims also tell the story of Sarah and Hagar but, for them, Abraham simply had two wives, in two houses, and two sons, one with each of them. Hagar is not a slave of Sarah but another wife. Similarly, the daughter of Pharaoh not only features in the Koran, but is said to have a place in Paradise because of her good works. Being taken on a walk outside the traditional narrative in this way, and considering the possibility that an entirely other perspective on events has informed another world religion was not only a deeply humbling experience, but one that placed each of us in a very different position in relation to our own traditions. For now, the assumption of certain archetypes of identity was decentered, and with this, a space was created for looking anew at ourselves, at our stories, and at each other.

Second, and building on this, telling our own stories in the presence of women to whom we were committed, but who came from different traditions, induced a level of humility and at times shame one may not have when reading the stories in the company of those who have always read the same stories together, and who are portrayed as the winners in our own narratives. Thus, for example, when I had to read about Sarah's banishment of Hagar and her son Ishmael into the desert without adequate food and water, a story I had read before, but now in the presence of my Muslim sister, I simply could not but feel troubled and ashamed. Similarly, when I read the authoritative commentaries of my own forebears vilifying Hagar and lionizing Sarah despite the latter's cruel actions, my sense of responsibility for how we would continue to read the story took on a new dimension.[10] Certainly, Jewish women have long struggled with aspects of that story, but when one reads it face to face with the child of Hagar (in the tradition), a different level of ethical responsibility is invoked. There is a difference between being self critical in the safety of a self-same hermeneutic circle and standing in front of the one who is the object of our violence or vilification (albeit hermeneutic). Indeed, the same story was used in medieval Christianity but transposed onto Christianity and Judaism, with Sarah now the Christian and the reviled Hagar now the Jew, thus drawing our Christian sister into a similar critical engagement with her own tradition.

Third, the actual process of our reading these stories as we did, openly and with each other, had a profound and powerful effect not only on us, but also on those who were present while we did it (the audience). There seemed to be something profoundly liberating about the process of opening borders that are traditionally closed. It seemed to me that the act of witnessing our struggles with traditions we clearly loved and embraced gave those who were present some type of permission to engage with those traditions themselves in a more open and empowering way. In this sense, the plurality of the reading and our willingness to give up our sovereignty over the teachings mimicked what educators know is true of the best teaching: it provides a space for the learners to go further than the teachers themselves.

Indeed, it is perhaps the struggle with the text that is the finest form of religious action and a paradigm for how we might approach religious resources in the process of education. By way of an offering, in my tradition, one interpretation of the identity of those who can be called Israel is precisely this—God wrestlers. The name *Israel* was first given to Jacob, Abraham's grandson, after he had fiercely wrestled with an angel all night. This angel, we should be clear, was not a cherub, but a fierce and to-the-death opponent. Israel, then, on this reading is not, as the Greek Jew Philo interpreted it, *the one who sees God* (*ish*–man, *ra-ah*–sees, *El*–God)—for to see God is to fix a Truth that all must thenceforth obey. And the ideal of being Israel is not to see the true God as an image one might know and show others. Rather, Israel is one who wrestles with what comes to us at night, with what we would rather not see, with what we relegate to the other side of consciousness, to our not-selves. Israel is the one who calls out this not self and faces it as part of the truth of daylight. And anyone who wrestles with his or her angels belongs to Israel. This does not mean that they belong to an identity group, Jewish or any other. It means that they belong to an ethic of engaged and courageous action. I have no doubt that other religious traditions have their own models for the engagement with religion that is active, empowering, and challenging. Inviting them in as methodologies for education might be a powerful starting point.

NOTES

1. Throughout this text, I use the term *education* without specific reference to the level or formality of the educational setting. I deliberately keep this definition open as it is with principles of education that I am engaging, and those principles would be applicable to all levels, from early childhood to higher education, in both formal and informal settings.

2. One might locate this strategy within a broader problematic that theorists of the early Frankfurt school identified as the negative side of the Enlightenment and modernity. For the most part, we associate their solution (through the work of Theodoro W. Adorno) with the appearance of a radical aesthetics, but others, notably Max Horkheimer (in his later work), thought religion had an indispensable role to play in overcoming modernity's reductive tendencies (see Mendieta, 2005).
3. Compare Dawkins (2006). Dawkins' book is actually one of a number of similar books to have come out in a short space of time, including Harris (2004, 2006), Hitchens (2007), and Onfray (2007).
4. For a rich discussion of this interpenetration of Enlightenment and religious approaches, see Browning and Fiorenza (1992).
5. The Jewish philosopher Emmanuel Levinas (1994), in fact, suggests just the opposite definition of *God*, when he writes: "God is perhaps nothing but this permanent refusal of a history which would come to terms with our private tears" (p. 20).
6. The association of this hermeneutic with Judaism should not be taken to imply that it is not also one adopted by other religious traditions in general, and Biblical traditions in particular. My reference is rather to the particular dialogical quality of Jewish interpretive texts, so well illustrated by the Talmud, where every page is filled with trans-historical arguments and multiple voices.
7. This is not deny the hostility that can be generated in intra-religious disagreements, which can, in fact, be worse than any other. Such a process would thus have to include some type of contract of basic commitment.
8. For a discussion of contemporary interfaith movements, mainly in the United States, including a discussion of interfaith seminaries, see Kirkwood (2007).
9. For a comprehensive bibliography of Jewish sources see Jacobs' Judaism and ecology bibliography; for Christian sources see Bakken's (n.d.) Christianity and ecology bibliography; for Islam, see Foltz's (n.d.) Islam and ecology bibliography; for Buddhism, Williams' (n.d.) Buddhism and ecology bibliography; for Hinduism and Jainism, see Chapple's (n.d.) Hinduism and ecology bibliography.
10. I have written about Sara and Hagar in this context in greater detail in Celermajer (2006).

REFERENCES

Arendt, Hannah. (1959). *The human condition*. Chicago: Chicago University Press.
Arendt, Hannah. (1990). *On revolution*. London: Penguin Classics.
Bakken, Peter. *Christianity and ecology bibliography*. Retrieved October 22, 2007, from http://environment.harvard.edu/religion/religion/christianity/bibliography.html
Browning, Don S., & Francis Schlüssler Fiorenza. (1992). *Habermas, modernity and public theology*. New York: Crossroad.

Burke, Edmund, & Conor Cruise O'Brien. (Eds.). (1969). *Reflections on the revolution in France*. Harmondsworth, England: PenguinGroup.

Celermajer, Danielle. (2006). A post-secular human rights framework; Religions facing the challenge of universalism. In Toh Swee-Hin & Virginia Carwagas (Eds.), *Cultivating wisdom, harvesting peace* (pp. 137-152). Brisbane, Queensland: Australia: Multifaith Centre, Griffith University.

Chapple, Christopher Key. (n.d.). *Hinduism and ecology bibliography*. Retrieved October 22, 2007, from http://environment.harvard.edu/religion/religion/hinduism/bibliography.html

Dawkins, Richard. (2006). *The God delusion*. Boston: Houghton Mifflin.

Dussel, Eduardo, & Enrique Mendieta. (Eds.). (2003). *Beyond philosophy: Ethics, history, Marxism, and liberation theology* (New critical theory). Lanham, MD: Rowman & Littlefield.

Foltz, Richard. (n.d.). *Richard Foltz's Islam, an ecology bibliography*. Retrieved October 22, 2007, from http://environment.harvard.edu/religion/religion/islam/bibliography.html

Harris, Sam. (2004). *The end of faith: Religion, terror, and the future of reason*. London: W. W. Norton.

Harris, Sam. (2006). *Letter to a Christian nation*. Toronto: Bantam Press.

Heschel, Abraham Joshua. (1977). Toward an understanding of Halacha. In Seymour Siegel (Ed.), *Conservative Judaism and Jewish law, Studies in conservative Jewish thought*. New York: The Rabbinical Assembly and KTAV.

Hitchens, Christopher. (2007). *God is not great: How religion poisons everything*. Sydney, Australia: Allen and Unwin.

Horkeimer, Max. (1987). *Dawn and decline: Notes 1926-1931 and 1950-1969* (Michael Shaw, Trans.). New York: The Seabury Press.

Jacobs, Mark. *Judaism and ecology bibliography*. Retrieved October 22, 2007, from http://environment.harvard.edu/religion/religion/judaism/bibliography.html

Kirkwood, Peter. (2007). *The quiet revolution: The emergence of interfaith consciousness*. Sydney, Australia: ABC Books.

Levinas, Emmanuel. (1969). *Totality and infinity: An essay on exteriority* (Alphonso Lingis, Trans.). Pittsburgh, PA: Duquesne University Press.

Levinas, Emmanuel. (1994). *Nine Talmudic readings* (Annette Aronowicz, Trans.). Bloomington: Indiana University Press.

Mendieta, Eduardo. (Ed.). (2005). *The Frankfurt School on religion; Key writings of the major thinkers*. New York: Routledge.

Neuhaus, Richard. (1984). *The naked public square: Religion and democracy in America*. Grand Rapids, MI: William B. Eerdmans.

Onfray, Michel. (2007). *The atheist manifesto* (Jeremy Leggatt,Trans.). New York: Arcade.

Rosenzweig, Franz. (1961). The new thinking. In Nahum H. Glatzer (Ed.), *Franz Rosenzweig, his life and thought* (pp. 190-208). New York: Schocken.

Russell, Bertrand, & Albert Einsten. (1955, July). Retrieved September 24, 2007, from www.pugwash.org/about/manifesto.htm

Sachs, Jonathon. (2002). *The dignity of difference*. London: Continuum.

Swift, Jonathan. (2003). *Thoughts on various subjects*. Retrieved September 24, 2007, from http://etext.library.adelaide.edu.au/s/swift/jonathan/s97th/

Weber, Max. (1918). Science as a vocation. In H. H. Gerth & C. Wright Mills (Eds. & Trans.), *From Max Weber: Essays in sociology* (pp. 129-156). New York: Oxford University Press. (Original work published 1918)

Williams, Duncan Ryuken. (n.d.). *Buddhism and ecology bibliography.* Retrieved October 22, 2007, from http://environment.harvard.edu/religion/religion/buddhism/bibliography.html

CHAPTER 3

NARRATIVES OF EXPERIENCE

Crossing Cultures, Crossing Identities

Betty C. Eng

This research study explores teacher development and teacher knowledge through the autobiographical narrative of an Asian American woman who is a teacher educator in Hong Kong. Crossing cultures, identities, languages, places, and time, the chapter explores how experience is central to informing and shaping teacher knowledge. Captured through narrative inquiry and grounded in the scholarship of John Dewey and the values of a Confucian philosophy, the experiences take place in the United States, Hong Kong, and China. Positioned within an educational and curricular context, the research puzzle explores how experiences of identity, culture, and sense of belonging shape a personal practical knowledge. The research contributes to the discourse of intercultural relations that empowers personal understanding and global connectedness.

THEORETICAL FRAMEWORK: EXPERIENCE AND EDUCATION

This chapter is grounded in the scholarship of John Dewey (1938) and the values of a Confucian philosophy. Dewey recognized the importance of developing a philosophy of experience in education. He believed that to study education and life is to study experience. Dewey also believed that experience, education, and life are essentially intertwined and that to understand why teachers do what they do is to understand their experiences. Educating a child is centered on a development of their experiences (Dewey, 1971). Moreover, Dewey held that the connection between education and personal experience is organic because it is fluid, changing, relational, and interactive. For Dewey (1934), "an experience is a whole and carries with it its own individualizing quality and self-sufficiency" (p. 35). When the material or event experienced runs its course to consummation or fulfillment, we have an experience. Dewey believed an experience has a unity and flows freely from something to something in a continuous merging.

Dewey (1916, 1938) encouraged a respect for all sources of experiences from the teacher and to develop experience as a mean and a goal in education. But he also cautioned that not all experiences are educative and that there is a need to be discriminating about the quality of the experience. Experience exists in continuity or an experiential continuum where some experiences are educative and others are mis-educative. While Dewey believed that all genuine education comes about through experience, not all experiences are genuinely or equally educative. Experiences can be mis-educative if they, for instance, prevent growth of further experience. "An experience may be such as to engender callousness; it may produce lack of sensitivity and responsiveness. Then the possibilities of having richer experiences in the future are restricted" (Dewey, 1938, p. 25-26).

Dewey's thinking resonates with a Confucian philosophy or a Confucian-heritage culture. That Confucianism has an enduring and profound effect on Chinese culture is well established, even with its controversial history of being alternatively revered, deified, vilified, and rehabilitated over the years. The Chinese saying: *Knowledge and wisdom are gained through the experience of elders* suggests that the accumulated experience one gains with age makes one not only knowledgeable, but also wise. The expression acknowledges a valued and revered place of authority accorded elders in a traditional Chinese society that permeates social status and economic class. "The old man" is how Olga Lang (1946) in her classic study of Chinese family and society, characterizes the importance of age. Lang wrote:

> The very fact of age evoked reverence. Confucius and his disciples made a special point of this reverence. Respect and devotion were due to parents all their lives, but the feelings of children toward aged parents were especially stressed. Indeed, a respectful attitude was demanded toward all old people,

even those who did not belong to one's own family. Teachers, for instance, were venerated not only for their learning but for their age. By preserving and developing the institution of ancestor worship, Confucius still further strengthened the position of the old man. This rule of the old made a young man of Confucian China a rather weak and insignificant figure. (pp. 10-11)

Dewey's philosophy of experience and education and the Confucianism reverence for experience and wisdom gained with age suggest implications for teacher development.

TEACHER DEVELOPMENT AND PERSONAL PRACTICAL KNOWLEDGE

Teacher development, for the purposes of this discussion, is the experience of becoming or being a teacher. F. Michael Connelly and D. Jean Clandinin propose a study of teacher knowledge as opposed to knowledge for teachers. They argue that it is more important in a teacher education program for preservice students to understand their own education than it is to understand how to educate others (Clandinin & Connelly, 2000). Thinking narratively, they describe and study personal stories that reflect a person's social and historical life. Following the thinking of Dewey and the curriculum specialist Joseph Schwab (1973), Connelly and Clandinin (1988) state that teachers possess a personal practical knowledge. Clandinin (1985) writes:

> By knowledge in the phrase "personal practical knowledge" is meant that body of convictions, conscious or unconscious, which have arisen from experience, intimate, social, and traditional, and which are expressed in a person's actions.... "Personal practical knowledge" is knowledge which is imbued with all the experiences that make up a person's being. Its meaning is derived from, and understood in terms of, a person's experiential history, both professional and personal. (p. 362)

This experiential and practical knowledge is embodied and based on the narrative of experience and it is through narrative that experience can be best represented and understood.

NARRATIVE INQUIRY

Kathy Carter (1993) describes storying ones personal experiences as a mode of knowing that provides a source of personal knowledge. Narratives are also "narratives of the self" that are highly personalized and revealing about the author's lived experiences. They are a form of writing that engages the voice of the narrator in the research. Such writings are also reflective, reflexive, and summon collaboration between the researcher and participant (Cole & Knowles, 2000; Schn, 1983).

Ming Fang He and JoAnn Phillion (2000) describe narrative inquiry as an approach that offers possibilities for a "fluid and experiential way of understanding" (p. 48). He and Phillion view the qualities of narrative as a way of thinking that is fluid rather than fixed, as being in the midst of lives or seeing research as living in the daily realities of participants. Making meaning of experiences is developed in a relational knowing.

Moreover, narrative inquiry as a research approach provides the theoretical framework that invites and supports social justice, equity, and democracy in the classroom (Ayers, 2004; Phillion, He, & Connelly, 2005). By providing an experiential, participatory, and shared classroom community of learners and teachers, narrative inquiry provides us the opportunity to hear the voices of its participants. The narratives of its participants become central to the curriculum.

Narratives of experience provides the possibilities of blending and merging the boundaries of power and role between learner and teacher to enhance a reciprocal exchange of teaching and learning that is defined by all participants. Schwab provides a constructive framework that elaborates on what he viewed as the essential participants in curriculum deliberations.

Schwab (1973) recognized the importance of experience and translated Dewey's thinking into the "commonplaces" that served as agents or bodies of experience in curriculum deliberations. Schwab identified the four *commonplaces*—the teacher, learner, subject matter, and milieu as essential participants to the discourse of curriculum planning and development. According to Ellen Lagemann (2000), Schwab, like Dewey, held that these commonplaces should form a "partnership between and among many different people—a wide range of scholars and citizens as well as teachers, administrator, and parents" (p. 50). These participants in curriculum deliberations would take on a collaborative approach to education rather than a hierarchical relationship.

Autobiographical Narrative

The voices of the commonplaces can be forcefully expressed through autobiographical narrative or life writings. Autobiography is life writing of the self and is a reconstruction of one's narrative (Edel, 1989; Kerby, 1991; Olney, 1980). Of the autobiographical method, William Pinar (1981) believes that "life-histories are not liabilities to be exorcised but are the very precondition for knowing. It is our individual and collective stories in which present projects are situated, and it is awareness of these stories which is the lamp illumining the dark spots, the rough edges" (p. 184). Autobiographies serve as a type of field text and are a "way to write about the whole context of a life" (Clandinin & Connelly, 1994, p. 421). In educational studies, Berk (1980) and Connelly and Clandinin (1991) write that autobiography was one of the first methodologies used to study *what it meant for a person to be educated*. However, they continue, with the shift of inquiry to *how are people educated*, the use of autobiography for the study of education disappeared. (For more information on this transition see, Berk, 1980, who states in a discussion of the history of the uses of autobiography/biography in education, that autobiography was one of the first methodologies for the study of education. Shifting inquiry from the question "What does it mean for a person to be educated?" to "How are people, in general, educated?" appears to have led to the demise of autobiography/biography in educational studies.)

One's particular reconstruction of narrative suggests there could be other reconstruction. Such reconstruction involves complex issues and tensions of memory, self-deception, and truth and reality. The purpose of narrative research method is to reveal something about the person. With the study of personal practical knowledge, the narrative focuses on how people know the classroom. For Clandinin and Connelly (1994), an autobiography is a research text. Autobiographical narrative uses reflective journals, interviews, participant observations, informal conversations, oral histories, archival search, and artifacts as sources of data.

Narratives of Experience: Asian American Community

As an autobiographical narrative, this chapter explores my life experiences centered on identity, culture, and sense of belonging. Writing *self* is also an act of writing *nation* according to Elaine Kim and Norma Alarcon (1994). This means that my experiences as a Chinese American woman are not isolated experiences. When these experiences are placed in their social context, they are played out and resonated in the experiences of many other Asian American communities.

Kim (1994) describes her writings of self as part of *lifetime* stories that are integral to her understanding of her Asian culture and history. Leila Fu, the heroine in Fae Myenne Ng's (1993) book, *Bone*, says: "Family exists only because somebody has a story, and knowing the story connects us to a history" (p. 36). These stories are not just a part of a narrative to be inserted into mainstream America but are a distinct narrative that is in the "process of being lived, contested, and constructed in the flux of U.S. culture and society" (W. Ho, 1999, p. 211). Wendy Ho's study of Chinese mother-daughter relationships characterizes it as a highly complex and evolving women's culture of *talk-story*. Ho invites us to rethink the potential in such mother-daughter stories rather than "summarily dismiss them as nostalgic Orientalist fare" (p. 109) intended for mainstream audiences. An exciting and growing body of literature by Asian American writers traces the cultural tradition of *talking stories* and folklore that form an indigenous Asian oral tradition of conveying and recording the history of the Asian American community.

Acts of Empowerment: Rediscovery and Reclaiming

Narrative inquiry offers opportunities for rediscovering and reclaiming Asian American history. This history, for various social and political reasons, has been lost to the Asian American community and the acts of rediscovering and reclaiming are acts of social justice and equity. Autobiographies have the power to give voice to a community that has been made invisible or silenced (Kim & Alarcon, 1994; Smith, 1994). By rediscovering and reclaiming the experiences of Asian Americans, we are not only *adding on* to the landscape of the American experience but also transforming the very framework that guides the whole of our understanding of the United States' past, present, and future.

Stanley Sue (1999), the educator and psychologist, states that there continues to be a dearth of research and literature on diverse ethnic cultures and calls for more support and funding for such efforts. Sue urges researchers to not limit our "ways of knowing" to science. He suggests we broaden our research to embrace qualitative research to discover deeper and fuller meanings to the understanding of cultures. A linear and scientific approach of cause and effect may not capture the spirituality of a culture which can be best understood through lived realities. Narrative provides an empowering mode of inquiry in which the experiences and voices of a community can be rediscovered and reclaimed.

A Hong Kong Classroom

Hong Kong's highly competitive educational system has been strongly criticized as one that is examination driven. The teaching and learning experience is dominated by rote learning and memorization of facts that hinders creativity and critical and reflective thinking (Sweeting, 1990). At the very beginning stages of children's education, their placement and advancement to the next grade is determined by examinations at the end of each school year. Hong Kong schools are ranked by a banding of 1 to 3, with 1 as the most prestigious, to indicate their status. Whether a student is placed in a Band 1 school, or pursues a mathematics or science program that increases the likelihood of future university admissions, or is given the opportunity to enroll in a school that uses English as a medium of instruction is dictated by the results of the examinations (Cheng, 1997).

For Hong Kong, narratives of experience provide potent possibilities for reconstructing the curriculum by rediscovering and reclaiming the voices of its participants. However, tensions to its use arise as expressed by these statements by two of my first-year preservice teacher education students:

> But, teacher, I have no experiences to tell. I am just a recent secondary school [high school] graduate in my first year as a preservice student and not a qualified teacher. How can my personal experiences matter?
>
> Teachers talk, students listen. Teachers are supposed to tell us how to be a teacher by giving us solutions and answers. It is the student's role to listen, follow, and obey the teacher. This is what I have been taught by my teachers in primary and secondary school. (Eng, 2005a, p. 98)

These students claimed they had no experiences of value to share in a curriculum determined primarily by policy makers and dominated by a *how are people educated* perspective. The responses by my students express an absence of authority to recognize the significance of their experiences and how they are connected to shaping a professional identity and personal practical knowledge. Their personal experiences did not have a "legitimate" voice or place in the classroom since decisions about the curriculum are determined by a governmental process of what has been referred to as a "consultative autocracy," according to Kai-ming Cheng (1997), a Hong Kong educator.

But, my students *do* have experiences that are genuinely and positively educative. When asked to recall their favorite teacher and to reflect on what it was about the teacher that was special, most of the preservice students have rich experiences and stories to retell. Even those students who emphatically declare that they did not have a favorite teacher have an experience that serves to educate. Reconstructed here, their stories are ones of care and sustained bonding with their favorite teacher:

> My favorite secondary school teacher spent time after the school day tutoring me in the subjects I was experiencing difficulty. She organized special outings on the weekends to go hiking or trips to the surrounding islands. *Missee* invited me to her home for dinner with her family and regularly telephoned me to ask me about my studies and my personal life. She listened to me talk about my difficulties communicating with my father, my relationship with my boyfriend, and my career plans. Knowing that she cared for me motivated me to be a better student and a better person. Even after all

these years, she still calls and writes me to ask about my progress in my teacher training and gives me advice on my assignments. I am grateful and indebted to her and am deeply touched by how she cares for me like an older sister or mother. It is a relationship that I treasure and one that will endure a lifetime. (Eng, 2005b, p. 194)

My student's personal experiences with her favorite teacher are a part of her personal practical knowledge that shapes her development as a teacher. From these experiences, she possesses an understanding of the care and nurturing a teacher can provide for her students. The student's story becomes a part of my personal practical knowledge as I relate and interact with her experiences. Her experiences serve to educate me as I strive to understand the Hong Kong cultural context. The student's story challenges me to reflect on my own values, beliefs, and experiences as a westernized Chinese American woman. Reflecting on my student's story, I write in a journal,

Having been raised in the United States and completing my teacher training there, I was taught to maintain a professional distance from my students. I am nervous about *crossing the line* to enter into the personal lives and homes of my students. I worry over the possible repercussions of conflict of interest and ethical issues when one becomes *like a mother* to a student. Can I view my students as a member of an extended family? If I become their friend, can I maintain professional objectivity in grading their assignments? Would there be disapproval or reprimand for getting too close to a student or the looming threat of litigation for behavior perceived *unbecoming* of a professional?

These puzzles lead me to my journey for self-identity and culture. Like my students who have been displaced as British subjects with the return of Hong Kong to China, I question: "What is a Chinese American?" "What is Chinese and Chinese culture?" and "What are the beliefs I value from my Westernized self that blends and merges to being a woman of multiple cultures?" "Are my students and I both *pseudo-Chinese* or corruptions of the original?" My students' questions parallel and resonate in my journey in a quest for self-understanding and identity (Eng, 2002, 2005b).

My student's story of her favorite teacher presents me with her version of the qualities and role of a Chinese Hong Kong teacher. To provide the educative and positive growth that Dewey describes in his experiential continuum, I need to consider extending my understanding of what is meant by education and my care for students beyond the confines of the classroom (Noddings, 1992). I can see that my student's personal practical knowledge and teacher development are connected to her past experiences that are reflected and retold in her present context as a student preparing to become a teacher.

Narratives as a form of inquiry in Hong Kong have limited precedent and are markedly absent from the research and literature in teacher education. Narratives of experience have been lost and are generally not an acceptable form of learning in Hong Kong education. Educators David Yau-Fai Ho, John A. Spinks, and Cecilia Siu-Hing Yeung (1989) described the research in Hong Kong in the discipline of psychology as limited and dominated by a quantitative approach that is a thoughtless replication of Western studies and urged Hong Kong researchers to be more imaginative in their research designs. While Ho, Spinks, and Yeung focused on the discipline of psychology, their findings have implications for all research in Hong Kong. Narrative inquiry provides possibilities that can create the scholarship for an alternative way of knowing for Hong Kong.

LIFETIME STORIES

Using the narratives of experience, I now provide selected significant life experiences that connect and relate my cross-cultural autobiographical narrative to teacher development and teacher knowledge. I situate these experiences from my life by using Schwab's (1973) commonplaces of the teacher, learner, subject matter, and milieu as central bodies of experience to understanding the curriculum and education. For Schwab, the commonplaces represent the bodies of experience that serve to translate the practical into the curriculum. Ideally, the commonplaces share equal power and work together collaboratively in curriculum deliberations.

Teacher Commonplace: *Living in the Margins*

I am a Chinese American woman, born in China, raised and educated in the United States. For over fifteen years, I have been living and working in Hong Kong as a counselor and educator. Making Hong Kong my home is part of the journey in search of identity, culture, and sense of belonging. At times I view myself as a sojourner who seeks to establish a sense of belonging for my changing and evolving sense of self. I often find myself living in the margins of multiple identities and cultures, situated in the space between cultural boundaries. I am not a Hong Konger, yet I am not an American expatriate living in Hong Kong. I am a daughter of China, yet am not accorded citizenship by the People's Republic of China. At times, I discover points of commonalties in the cultures; at others, I encounter puzzles, contradictions, and tensions.

My identity and culture is a blending of the East and the West. I am not Chinese *and* American but Chinese American. The values, beliefs, and cultures of the two merge and blend to form a *new* identity that represents, for instance, the individualism held in western thought and the collective spirit of the Chinese (Atkinson, Morten, & Sue, 1989). I readily move from my fundamentalist Christian church to paying homage to the spirits in the Buddhist temple. Living in the margins provides a source of diversity and richness of life experiences as well as conflicts. The values and beliefs of my dual cultures are connected to the roots of my birth in my village in China, growing up in the United States, and my present role as a teacher educator in Hong Kong to shape who I am to become in the future. These experiences become embedded in my personal practical knowledge that shapes my teacher development and my place within the curriculum.

Learner Commonplace: "I Forgot My Eyes Were Brown"

For me, identity is defined as who I am or how I see myself, and how I became who I am. "I forgot my eyes were brown" encapsulates how I had been taught to strive for the American dream and the compromises that were exacted along the way. I grew up in a culture that idealized the blonde and blue-eyed, Barbie-doll standards of beauty. Looking into the mirror, many Asians contrived to achieve those standards by bleaching and straightening our hair, cosmetic surgery to "de-slant" our eyes, and contact lenses to colorize our eyes ("Asian Women," 1971; Eng, 2005b). Seeking to obtain such standards, we rejected and subsumed our Chinese identity and culture.

I perceive my school experience as one that taught me to fit in and adapt. I was fulfilling the expectations of Asians as a model minority, who, despite race and economic hardships, serve as exemplars to other minorities of how to be successful. When I was growing up, the message for me was that if one worked diligently, persevered, and obeyed the rules, one could become successful in the melting pot of the America. America, I was taught, was a land of opportunity for all. Only those who were lazy and irresponsible were not successful.

Achieving the American ideals meant speaking proper American English instead of Chinese, and getting better than good grades, especially in math and the sciences. I learned to favor mayonnaise and boloney as ingredients for school sandwich lunches instead of my mother's rice box, and to forget my eyes were brown in a blonde, blue-eyed, Barbie-doll culture. It was also my first experience being hugged by my first-grade teacher. I come from a culture where physical contacts are not a commonly practiced form of expression. My teacher's embrace surprised me, and I was bewildered by the meaning of her touch. Her warm and enthusiastic embrace was inviting but also exacted, I discovered, its conditions. Its conditions meant I embraced and fulfilled the expectations of a model minority student. I was hard working, obedient, and excelled in school to graduate early from high school to be accepted to the university of my choosing. I completed my university studies to become an elementary school teacher, a profession that is regarded as a respectable and secure career for a Chinese woman, and continued with graduate studies to obtain a Master of Science degree in counseling.

I learned from my working-class parents through the examples they set that it was a necessary and good thing to labor in the cannery, sewing factory, and grocery store for 12 hours a day, and 7 days a week. I learned through them to go to work though one is sick, to practice filial piety or respect for my elders and ancestors, to *save face* to ones family and community by not bringing them shame, and about duty and loyalty to the family. They taught me to value education as a means to escape hard labor, and of humility, dignity, and courage.

Growing up, I was chastised by my mother for being a *hollow bamboo*. The interior of the bamboo is empty and commonly associated with Asia. My mother's use of the bamboo metaphor was her way of pointing out to me that I was devoid of culture on inside even though I appeared Chinese on the outside. My identity today as a Chinese American was discovered through a journey of self-exploration, self-awareness, and self-acceptance. A pivotal moment in my journey was the experience of the Civil Rights Movement and student activism of the 1960s and 1970s in the United States. In higher education, student strikes occurred across the country to demand the inclusion of the diverse cultures of third-world people in the curriculum. It was through the efforts of the Civil Rights Movement and the student movements that programs in ethnic studies developed. Ethnic studies provided students the opportunity to study their own cultures and histories. It was through the experience of my participation in the student movement that I came to explore my identity as a Chinese in America. I realized that throughout my schooling, I had been taught a curriculum that excluded the lives and experiences of my Chinese community. This realization was profound and empowering, and I continue to feel its reverberations today.

Through rediscovering and reclaiming my history, I learned of the systematic exploitations of Chinese laborers who died working on the railroads as a result of the hazardous dynamiting work along mountainous terrains, of murders of Chinese miners, and burning of Chinatown campsites by racist prospectors during the gold rush in the 1800s (Liu, 1963; Sung, 1967; Wu, 1972). Chinese were not allowed to purchase property, unlike the European immigrants, and could only work as laborers on farms, laundries, and saloons which were meager paying and labor-intensive jobs that other immigrants did not want (Chen, 1980; Takaki, 1979; Wong, 1982). A generation of Chinese men led the lives of bachelors because immigration laws prohibited women and wives from coming to the United States.

I had been ignorant of such exploitations in the history of my people. I had been taught the praises of the American *melting pot* that welcomed its people and provided opportunities and success for all who were willing to work for it. As a learner, I was rediscovering and reclaiming my past, present, and future to develop my identity, culture, and sense of belonging in America. These experiences as a learner became embedded in how I perceived myself as a teacher and shaped my development.

Subject Matter Commonplace:
Curriculum as Community/Community as Curriculum

Shortly after university graduation, I was invited to teach at the university in the newly established Asian American Studies program. With a bachelor's degree and my teaching credential, and not much older than most of my students, I had only the experiences and personal understanding of becoming a Chinese American to prepare me for university teaching. Asian American studies was part of ethnic studies, composed of Afro-American studies, Chicano studies, and Native American studies. Asian American studies had the ambitious task of studying the lives and experiences of the Chinese, Japanese, Koreans, Filipinos, Vietnamese, and Pacific Islanders. We offered courses entitled, "The Asian American Experience," "Asian American Women," and "Asian American Community."

This was a historical period of the 1970s that taught me the power of students and political activism. In Asian American Studies classes, student autobiographies, interviews with parents, journal writing, and tracing family trees and histories formed the curriculum. Sharing our stories, we developed the first written textbooks for an emerging discipline (Asian Women, 1971; Hong, 1993; Sue & Wagner, 1973). In this way, teacher, learners, and community were empowered as the planners and makers of the curriculum.

My students shared their stories of experience. They were stories of parents working in the laundries (Siu, 1987), of *paper sons* who circumvented immigrant laws to gain passage to the United States, of arranged marriages, and family pressures to succeed (Chen, 1980; Daniels, 1988; Lyman, 1974; Takaki, 1993, 1998; Wu, 1972). By telling and retelling these stories of experience, we were developing a richer, clearer, and deeper understanding of our identity, culture, and place in the United

States. And in this way, the experience of the community became curriculum and the curriculum became community.

Experience was the beginning point and foci of the early developments in Asian American Studies. After all, as neophytes in academics, all we had were our experiences. We did not enter the classroom armed with social theories or historical analysis in which to teach our subjects. There were few research studies or textbooks about our people or our communities that we could use as a source of reference. Fewer still, were there authors of Asian descent that represented what we considered an *authentic* voice. The students and I began writing and sharing our own personal narratives of experience that became stories for the curriculum. These were *raw* stories drawn from our experiences growing up, expectations, pressures from our parents and community, and our hopes for our futures.

But the vision of Asian American Studies intended to go beyond experience to evolve into a process of theory-making that genuinely reflected our communities. Going beyond experience would somehow *elevate* Asian American Studies for acceptance into mainstream academics. While experience was an acceptable beginning point for Asian American Studies, its next step would be a *theorization* of our experiences. While creating theories and new knowledge that truly reflect our communities is a valuable scholarly endeavor, this was often done with uneven success. Most efforts relied on established theoretical frameworks in traditional academic disciplines of sociology, psychology, economics, and history. *Fitting in* our experiences within a prescribed conceptual framework to understanding our communities often proved incongruent and just did not make sense. Three decades later, experience continues to be the foci of my research to understanding my experiences as an Asian American woman and the experiences of my students in Hong Kong.

Milieu Commonplace: *One Country, Two Systems*

Finally, Schwab's milieu provides the context of my storied experiences. My journey in search of identity and sense of belonging has taken me to Hong Kong. Hong Kong becomes the social and cultural milieu in which I now continue my autobiographic narrative. Until recently, I was a teacher educator with an institute in Hong Kong that provides training for preservice students and experienced teachers. The subjects I taught were in the areas of personal and social education and counseling. These subjects provided the opportunity for students to explore their personal and professional identities through writing life experiences and reflective journals.

Hong Kong was a British colony for about 150 years until 1997 when the Peoples' Republic of China (PRC) regained sovereignty and Hong Kong. Hong Kong now functions as a Special Administrative Region (SAR) under a "one country, two systems" policy (Postiglione, 1992). This means that while Hong Kong is now a part of China, it continues to operate under social and economic systems distinct and separate from China. In this milieu or context, the issues of identity and culture are raised. No longer British subjects, students in my classes question whether they are Chinese, like their counterparts in the PRC, or *Hong Kongers*. Their discussions raise such puzzles as,

- What is Chinese?
- What is Chinese culture?
- Who is it that I wish to become?
- Who or what determines who I am to become?

Their questions mirror and parallel the experiences of self-exploration that I encountered in my own personal journey and with my Asian American students in the United States. And while the Chinese in China and the Chinese in Hong Kong appear to be monolithic and are of one country, we are of complex and diverse identities and cultures. These experiences resonate over space and time and the Hong Kong milieu becomes embedded in my personal practical knowledge.

This is a challenging period in Hong Kong's history that presents possibilities for transformation. There are calls from the community to make the classroom a more democratic one to recognize the essential place of teachers, learners, subject matter, and milieu in collaboratively defining the curriculum (Postiglione & Lee, 1997). Instead of recording the history of Hong Kong as one limited to policies and political systems, there is an opportunity to seek out the experiences and stories of its people. Translated into the classroom and the curriculum, these experiences become my Hong Kong students' personal practical knowledge that informs and shapes their teacher development.

UPON REFLECTION

These significant events in my life, composed as an autobiographical narrative, are a curriculum story. Through seeking my personal self-understanding, I am better prepared to facilitate and collaborate in my students' journey of self-awareness. My personal journey of seeking identity, culture, and a sense of belonging informs my personal practical knowledge and becomes integral to my professional development that empowers my place as a planner and maker of curriculum.

This paper to explore and understand teacher knowledge through an autobiographical narrative demonstrates how experience is central to understanding teacher development and teacher knowledge. The qualities of narrative inquiry forcefully capture the rich complexities of *lived experiences*. By thinking narratively, I can rediscover and reclaim the Asian American community's experience and history. Narrative inquiry provides an empowering and expansive way of knowing that is fluid, relational, and not confined by conventional terms. I intend that my theoretical analysis has provided an understanding of experiences that cross cultures, identities, places, and time to contribute to understanding our practice in creating a new form of scholarship in teacher education.

REFERENCES

Asian Women. (1971). *Asian Women's Journal*. Berkeley: University of California Press.
Atkinson, Donald R., George Morten, & Derald Wing Sue. (1989). *Counseling American minorities: A cross cultural perspective*. Dubuque, IA: W.C. Brown.
Ayers, William. (2004). *Teaching toward freedom: Moral commitment and ethical action in the classroom*. Boston: Beacon Press.
Berk, Leonard. (1980). Education in lives: Biographic narrative in the study of educational outcomes. *The Journal of Curriculum Theorizing, 2*(2), 88-153.
Carter, Kathy. (1993). The place of story in the study of teaching and teacher education. *Educational Researcher, 22*(1), 5-12, 18.
Chen, Jack. (1980). *The Chinese of America*. San Francisco: Harper & Row.
Cheng, Kai-ming. (1997). The policymaking process. In Gerald A. Postiglione & Wing On Lee (Eds.), *Schooling in Hong Kong* (pp. 65-78). Hong Kong: Hong Kong University Press.
Chang, Leslie. (1999). *Beyond the narrow gate*. New York: Penguin.
Clandinin, Jean D. (1985). Personal practical knowledge: A study of teachers' classroom images. *Curriculum Inquiry, 15*(4), 362-385.
Clandinin, Jean D., & Michael F. Connelly. (2000). *Narrative inquiry: Experience and story in qualitative research*. San Francisco: Jossey-Bass.
Clandinin, Jean D., & Michael F. Connelly. (1994). Personal experience methods. In Norman K. Denzin & Yvonna S. Lincoln (Eds.), *Handbook of qualitative research* (pp. 413-427). Thousand Oaks, CA: SAGE.
Cole, Ardra L., & Gary J. Knowles. (2000). *Researching teaching: Exploring teacher development through reflexive inquiry*. Boston: Allyn & Bacon.
Connelly, Michael F., & Jean D. Clandinin. (1988). *Teachers as curriculum planners*. Toronto, Canada: The Ontario Institute for Studies in Education.
Connelly, Michael F., & Jean D. Clandinin. (1991). Narrative inquiry: Storied experience. In Edmund C. Short (Ed.), *Forms of curriculum inquiry* (pp. 121-152). New York: State University of New York Press.

Connelly, Michael F., & Jean D. Clandinin. (2000). Teacher education: A question of teacher knowledge. In John Freeman-Moir & Alan Scott (Eds.), *Tomorrow's teachers: International and critical perspectives on teacher education* (pp. 89-105). Christchurch, New Zealand: Canterbury University Press in association with Christchurch College of Education.

Daniels, Roger. (1988). *Asian America: Chinese and Japanese in the United States since 1850*. Seattle: University of Washington Press.

Dewey, John. (1916). *Democracy and education*. New York: Macmillan.

Dewey, John. (1934). *Art as experience*. New York: Capricorn.

Dewey, John. (1938). *Experience and education*. New York: Simon & Schuster.

Dewey, John. (1971). *The child and the curriculum*. Chicago: University of Chicago Press.

Edel, Leon. (1989). *Writing lives: Principia biographica*. New York: W. W. Norton.

Eng, Betty C. (2002). Unpublished journal entries.

Eng, Betty C. (2005a). Hong Kong's shifting classroom narrative. In Paul Chamnes Miller (Ed.), *Narratives from the classroom* (pp. 89-107). Thousand Oaks, CA: SAGE.

Eng, Betty C. (2005b). *Exploring teacher knowledge through personal narratives: Experiences of identity, culture and sense of belonging*. Unpublished doctoral dissertation, The Ontario Institute for Students in Education of the University of Toronto, Canada.

He, Ming Fang, & JoAnn Phillion. (2000). Trapped in-between: A narrative exploration of race, gender, and class. *Journal of Race, Gender & Class, 8*(1), 47-56.

Ho, David Yau-Fai, John A. Spinks, & Cecilia Siu-Hing Yeung. (Eds.). (1989). *Chinese patterns of behavior: A sourcebook of psychological and psychiatric studies*. New York: Praeger Press.

Ho, Wendy. (1999). *In her mother's house: The politics of Asian American mother-daughter writing*. Walnut Creek, CA: AltaMira Press.

Hong, Maria. (Ed.). (1993). *Growing up Asian American*. New York: Avon Books.

Kerby, Anthony Paul. (1991). *Narrative and the self*. Bloomington: Indiana University Press.

Kim, Elaine, & Norma Alarcon. (1994). *Writing self, writing nation*. Berkeley, CA: Third Woman Press.

Lagemann, Ellen Condliffe. (2000). *An elusive science: The troubling history of education research*. Chicago: The University of Chicago Press.

Lang, Olga. (1946). The *Chinese family and society*. New Haven, CT: Yale University Press.

Liu, Kwang-Ching. (1963). *Americans and Chinese: A historical essay and a bibliography*. Cambridge, MA: Harvard University Press.

Lyman, Stanford M. (1974). *Chinese Americans*. New York: Random House.

Ng, Fay Myenne. (1993). *Bone*. New York: Hyperion.

Noddings, Nel. (1992). *A challenge to care in schools: An alternative approach to education*. New York: Teachers College Press.

Olney, James (Ed.). (1980). *Autobiography: Essays theoretical and critical*. Princeton, NJ: Princeton University Press.

Phillion, JoAnn, Ming Fang He, & Michael F. Connelly. (Eds.). (2005). *Narrative and experience in multicultural education*. Thousand Oaks, CA: Sage.

Pinar, William F. (1981). "Whole, bright, deep with understanding": Issues in qualitative research and autobiographical method. *Journal of Curriculum Studies, 13*(3), 173-188.
Postiglione, Gerard A. (Ed.). (1992). *Education and society in Hong Kong: Toward one country and two systems.* Hong Kong: Hong Kong University Press.
Postiglione, Gerard A., & Wing On Lee. (1997). *Schooling in Hong Kong: Organization, teaching and social context.* Hong Kong: Hong Kong University Press.
Schön, Donald A. (1983). *The reflective practitioner: How professionals think in action.* New York: Basic Books.
Schwab, Joseph. (1973). The practical 3: Translation into curriculum. *School Review, 81,* 501-522.
Siu, Chan Pang Paul. (1987). *The Chinese laundryman: A study of social isolation.* New York: New York University Press.
Smith, Louis M. (1994). Biographical method. In Norman K. Denzin & Yvonna S. Lincoln (Eds.), *Handbook of qualitative research* (pp. 286-305). Thousand Oaks, CA: SAGE.
Sue, Stanley. (1999). Science, ethnicity, and bias. *American Psychologist, 54*(12), 1070-1077.
Sue, Stanley, & Nathaniel N. Wagner. (Eds). (1973). *Asian-Americans: Psychological perspectives.* Palo Alto, CA: Science & Behavior Books.
Sung, Betty Lee. (1967). *Mountain of gold: The story of the Chinese in America.* New York: Macmillan.
Sweeting, Anthony Edward. (1990). *Education in Hong Kong pre-1841 to 1941: Fact and opinion, materials for a history of education in Hong Kong.* Hong Kong: Hong Kong University Press.
Takaki, Ronald T. (1979). *Iron cages: Race and culture in nineteenth-century America.* New York: Knopf.
Takaki, Ronald T. (1993). *A different mirror: A history of multicultural America.* Boston: Little Brown.
Takaki, Ronald T. (1998). *A larger memory: A history of our diversity with voices.* Boston: Little Brown.
Wong, Bernard P. (1982). *Chinatown: Economic adaptation and ethnic identity of the Chinese.* New York: Holt, Rinehart, and Winston.
Wu, Cheng-Tsu. (1972). *"Chink!": Documentary history of anti-Chinese prejudice in America.* New York: World.

CHAPTER 4

FUEL EFFICIENT STOVES AND COMMUNITY DEVELOPMENT IN SAN LUCAS TOLIMÁN, GUATEMALA

John D. Abell

Nearly half of the world's peoples cook over open fires. A variety of problems are associated with such cooking: exposure to toxic fumes, deforestation, and the cost of obtaining firewood, all of which place great stress on families' health and budgets, as well as on the environment. Open fire cooking, however, is only a *proximate* cause of these problems. I argue that these stressors are *ultimately* the result of more insidious factors such as inequality, poverty, malnutrition, discrimination, human rights violations, as well as lack of access to education, credit, land, water, and other resources. Fuel efficient stoves are necessary to correct the proximate problems, but insufficient to correct the ultimate causes. This study analyzes the fuel efficient stove program of San Lucas Tolimán, Guatemala. It is shown that the stove program *in conjunction with* a number of other community development programs (education, job skills apprenticeship, forestry, and land development) is actually capable of significantly reducing stress in the three problem areas: health, environment, and family

Growing a Soul for Social Change: Building the Knowledge Base for Social Justice
pp. 45–78
Copyright © 2008 by Information Age Publishing
All rights of reproduction in any form reserved.

economy. This is because of the way the programs work together in a coordinated manner to reduce inequality, poverty, discrimination, and the other ultimate causes.

INTRODUCTION:
OPEN FIRE COOKING AND FUEL EFFICIENT STOVES

It was daybreak on a cool March morning in the *Caqchiquel* Mayan community of Panamaquip in the Guatemalan central highlands. The year was 1997. Four-year-old Brenda Chocho was warming herself beside the fire in her family's one-room house. Water was boiling away in a large kettle resting precariously over the fire supported by three rocks. Without warning, one of the rocks gave way, causing the kettle to spill its scalding contents onto the startled child. Brenda was wounded badly and in agonizing pain with third-degree burns over 35% of her body. To the extent there was anything fortunate about her accident, it was that it took place in the catchment area of the parish of San Lucas Tolimán. Brenda was rushed to the parish clinic for immediate attention, where doctors, after addressing her immediate discomfort, determined that she would need specialized attention, including skin grafts, in a major hospital in Guatemala City. A hospital stay of 20 days, followed by twice-a-week follow-up visits for 6 weeks (covered financially by the parish) led to enough healing that Brenda and her family could begin to think about the process of long-term recovery and the eventual diminution of her scars (personal communication with San Lucas Tolimán, Guatemala parish priest Father Greg Schaffer, 2004, along with unpublished parish archives).

The analysis that follows draws on 15 years of travel (1993-2007) to the community of San Lucas Tolimán in the central highlands of Guatemala. I have visited for periods as short as a week and for as long as a month as a participant in study seminars, as a leader of a student group, as a researcher, observer, writer, and volunteer. As a volunteer, I have worked in the majority of the parish development programs that will be described below. All stories and analyses of San Lucas Tolimán, from the accident of Brenda Chocho, to the start-up of the fuel efficient stove program in response to Brenda's accident, and to the descriptions of the other development programs of San Lucas, are based upon personal reflections and observations, parish archives, formal interviews and informal conversations with parish priests, parish staff, community leaders, program leaders and employees, citizens, and *campesino* families. While the majority of the citizens of San Lucas are *Caqchiquel* Maya, most of those I have come in contact with speak Spanish, as well as the *Caqchiquel* language. The parish priests speak English and Spanish. Father Greg Schaffer, in particular, has been an invaluable source of information.

Regrettably, Brenda Chocho's experience is not uncommon in Guatemala and throughout the developing world. It is estimated that nearly half of the world's 6 billion-plus people rely on biomass fuels—including wood, charcoal, crop waste, and animal dung—as energy sources for their food preparation (Bruce, Perez-Padilla, & Albalak, 2000; Manuel & Dooley, 2003; McCracken, Smith, Diaz, Mittleman, & Schwartz, 2007). In rural Guatemala, the percentage is even higher, 86%, according to Winrock International (2004). A typical cooking arrangement consists of three stones, an open fire, and a metal cooking surface or kettle placed on top of the stones, not unlike that used by the Chocho family. For many who have accidents like little Brenda Chocho, the scarring and disfigurement leave permanent reminders of the dangers of cooking over an open fire. In Brenda's case, there was fortunately a happier ending than most accident victims experience in the developing world. Because she received immediate, as well as long-term medical care, today she is a happy, healthy teenager exhibiting no visible scarring at all.

Burns and scalding are only the most obvious problems associated with open fire cooking; there are other problems that are more insidious. They fall into roughly three categories: human health, environmental, and family economy, with the harshest impacts being borne disproportionately by women and children.

At first glance, the solution to all of these problems appears both simple and relatively affordable—the introduction of fuel efficient stoves.[1] In fact, in Guatemala, since at least the early 1980s, there have been a variety of stove building programs throughout the country carried out by both governmental agencies and nongovernmental organizations (NGOs), with thousands of stoves constructed. For a detailed list of such programs, and for an analysis of the evolution of fuel efficient stove technology, see Winrock International (2004, p. 2). Also, there is overwhelming and well-documented evidence of the benefits of fuel efficient stoves. In addition to the Winrock International analysis, see, for example, Albalak, Bruce, McCracken, Smith, and de Gallardo (2001); Boy, Bruce, Smith, and Hernandez (2000); Bruce et al. (2004); McCracken and Smith (1998); and McCracken et al. (2007).

While cooking with open fires might be the proximate cause of the aforementioned problems of human health, environment, and economy for Guatemala's rural families, the ultimate cause(s) surely must be more complex.[2] One might attempt to pass off the problem as simply one of cultural resistance or barriers to the adoption of new technologies like fuel efficient stoves. In fact, such barriers may exist (see, for example, Gill, 1985; Pandey & Yadama, 1992; & Winrock International, 2004)—yet, surely, they are also proximate rather than ultimate causes for these problems. In the literature on health, environmental, and family economic problems *associated with open fire cooking*, the focus is generally on the improvements associated with the use of stoves, especially through fuel switching (see, for example, Edwards & Langpap, 2005, or Elias & Victor, 2005). There is less said, though, in that same body of literature, of the connections between the three problems of health, environment, and family economy, and systemic factors like inequality, poverty, malnutrition, discrimination, human rights violations, or lack of access to education, credit, land, water, and other resources; factors that may well be the *ultimate* causes of the problems in the first place.[3] Den Ouden (1995) is an exception. He states that, "Technology can play a constructive role in addressing environmental problems. However, in situations of incredible need and overwhelming poverty a number of criteria must be met. Technological solutions must be simple, sustainable, and extremely inexpensive" (p. 1). He suggests that families in the developing world need not only appropriate technology such as fuel efficient stoves, but access to land and resources, as well, and the confidence that their possessions won't be confiscated arbitrarily (p. 2). A few other studies have noted that there is an *intersection* of problems attributed to open fire cooking and factors such as inequality, poverty, malnutrition, human rights violations, and so on (see, Ferring, 2003; Heltberg, 2003). Heltberg, for example, suggests that, "Improving access to and use of clean and efficient energy is ... an important part of the struggle against poverty and underdevelopment (p. 2).

With the exception of den Ouden (1995), in the literature related to open fire cooking with which I am familiar, few writers are asking what appears to me to be the most important question; the question that gets to the heart of ultimate, rather than proximate causes of health, environmental, and economic suffering of rural Guatemalans. And that question, albeit somewhat rambling, goes something like this: "Suppose we convince poor *campesino* families of the need to switch from cooking over open fires to using fuel efficient stoves, or even using liquefied petroleum gas. And suppose further that we offer these new technologies to them at subsidized prices or even for free. If we do so, will that truly lead to a broad-based improvement in their lives? Or, might other systemic factors like inequality, poverty, malnutrition, discrimination, human rights violations, or lack of access to education continue to work in the opposite direction, reducing significantly their quality of life?" It seems to me that technological solutions, even if they are "simple, sustainable, and extremely inexpensive," as den Ouden suggests, can be effective only if they are pursued *in conjunction with* solutions to the above problems of inequality, poverty, malnutrition, discrimination, human rights violations, lack of access to education, credit, and so on. And, the effectiveness is increased, if, as den Ouden suggests, the people on the receiving end of new technology and other programs are *enfranchised* in the process (p. 4).

There is, in fact, a community in the central highlands that is attempting to address problems of health, environment, and family economics, not only by providing fuel efficient stoves—in a program that was begun in the immediate aftermath of Brenda Chocho's accident with her family's cooking fire—but also through a comprehensive human-centered approach to communitywide development. The community is San Lucas Tolimán. Its parish has had a partnership with the Diocese of New Ulm, Minnesota, for over 40 years. From this partnership a wide variety of development programs have evolved focusing foremost on education, along with job skills, forestry, land development, fuel efficient stoves, and more (Abell 1997, 2002a). With this comprehensive focus, the community is addressing the health, environmental, and family economic problems, not only from the perspective of the proximate cause (open fire cooking), but also the ultimate causes (inequality, poverty, malnutrition, discrimination, human rights violations, lack of access to education, and so on). In the context of all of San Lucas' development programs, the fuel efficient stove technology is *necessary* to help relieve the suffering, but, by itself, not *sufficient*.

The education and job skills apprenticeship programs, programs traditionally not accessible to anyone but the privileged in Guatemala, form the backbone of San Lucas' approach to development. In the case of the fuel efficient stove program, I will show how the program works with the education and apprenticeship programs to pull troubled youth off the streets and provide them with opportunities to learn skills that could sustain them for life.

I should note that in the analysis that follows, I am not offering another scientific analysis that measures particulate matter or hemoglobin levels or incidents of chronic lung obstruction, for example. Analyses that have carried out such investigations are detailed in the next section. The stove technology employed in San Lucas is not revolutionary—the program is simply using its own version, with modifications, of the so-called *plancha* stove that is the industry standard. What I am offering in this analysis instead is a personalized look at the way in which the stove program works with all of the other development programs to provide a human-centered approach to health, environment, and family economic problems.

I will first review the many problems associated with cooking over an open fire. Next, I will examine the problems of health, environmental, and economic problems of rural Guatemalans in the context of proximate and ultimate causes. Next, I will provide an overview of the development programs of San Lucas focusing especially on the educational and apprenticeship aspects of those programs. The next section will cover the details of the fuel efficient stove program, explaining first, how it got started, second, how it works with the job skills apprenticeship program to provide opportunities for troubled youth, third, how the program works to address the immediate suffering associated with open fire cooking, fourth, how the program affects the local economy, and fifth, how the program can be seen as an investment in the long term public health of the region. The paper concludes with a discussion and analysis of the general applicability of the fuel efficient stove program.

PROBLEMS ASSOCIATED WITH COOKING OVER AN OPEN FIRE

In an agrarian society like Guatemala, maize (corn) is not only a primary source of nourishment, but it is part of the cultural history and identity. It is generally consumed in the form of tortillas, which are cooked over an open fire. Girls are taught by their mothers at an early age how to carefully prepare and then slap the *nixtamal* (maize dough) into perfectly round, flat tortillas using only their hands. The tortillas are placed on a metal cooking surface, known in Guatemala as either *planchas* or *comals*. The *planchas* or *comals* oftentimes sit balanced on as few as three large stones with an open wood fire in the center. Since a significant number of hours out of every day are devoted to the preparation and cooking of tortillas—not to mention the collecting of the wood for the fire—this whole process becomes part of the social fabric. Cooking, in addition to providing nourishment, provides an opportunity for chatting with friends, neighbors, and family, as well as for educating daughters. It would not necessarily occur to the women and their families to seek out alternatives to a cooking process that is thousands of years old. The dangers associated with it are as much a part of life as the process of cooking itself.

Burns and scalds provide the clearest evidence that open fire cooking is, in fact, dangerous. Blowing on a fire, to keep it burning, occasionally results in hair catching on fire or eye injuries when the fire pops. Standing too close to the fire can result in clothes catching on fire, as well. Little children have been known to accidentally stick their hands in the fire, touch a hot boiling pot, or kick one of the supporting stones causing a pot of boiling water to tip over and scald them. Díaz et al. (2007) point out that back pain is another outcome of using open cooking fires, the result of constant stooping, occasionally with an infant tied to the mother's back.

While burns and scald injuries sometimes create catastrophic problems for the families involved, they are experienced less frequently than other health-related problems that are on-going and more insidious. A number of analyses suggest that acute respiratory infections are the leading cause of death and disease in Guatemala, with pneumonia accounting for as much as 36% of infant deaths. See, for example, Boy et al. (2000), Pan-American Health Organization (2007), and Winrock International (2004). Open fire cooking, of course, is thought to be a major contributor. Such cooking takes place generally in small, poorly ventilated kitchens where one simply cannot escape inhaling fumes that consist of particulate matter such as carbon monoxide, nitrous oxides, formaldehyde, polycyclic organic matter, and carcinogens such as benzopyrene (Manuel & Dooley, 2003, pp. 2-3). According to Whitfield (2007), living in the presence of such conditions is the equivalent of smoking as much as *20* packs of cigarettes per day. Human lungs simply were not made to process such toxic matter on a daily basis. The result of such exposure is a long list of health problems. In addition to obvious diseases like pneumonia and bronchitis, there are problems such as chronic obstructive lung disease among adults, high blood pressure, elevated hemoglobin concentrations, low birth weight, still-births, increased risk of tuberculosis, childhood asthma, nasopharyngeal, laryngeal, and lung cancers, headaches, and more (Boy, Bruce, & Delgado, 2002; Boy et al., 2000; Bruce et al., 2000; Díaz et al., 2007; McCracken et al., 2007; Nuefeld, Haas, Ruel, Grajeda, & Naeher, 2004; & Schei et al., 2004). Nor are eyes supposed to be subjected to such volumes of toxic smoke. Long-term exposure results in eye problems such as cataracts or even partial or total blindness (Bruce et al., 2000; Manuel & Dooley, 2003).

As a frequent traveler to Guatemala who is rather finicky about the air I breathe, it is always overwhelming to visit the home of a family that cooks with an open fire; the air is typically so dense with smoke that it practically takes my breath away and makes my eyes water. I am always polite and engage the family members in pleasant conversation knowing that my time there is but for a handful of minutes, but well aware that for the females in the family, especially, along with babies tied to their backs, a significant portion of their lives will be spent close to those toxic fumes. According to Bruce et al. (2000, p. 3), as many as 7 hours a day may be spent breathing such polluted air. In colder or mountainous regions, or during the rainy season, such exposure may approach 24 hours.

In Figure 4.1, the family has elevated their cooking fire using a metal tub, an improvement over using three rocks on the ground, but the support for the cooking pot is rickety. The air is filled with fumes and the walls are blackened.

Practical Action (2006, June; formerly Intermediate Technology Development Group), founded in 1966 by the economist E. F. Schumacher (more on him and his influence on the San Lucas stove program will be

Figure 4.1. Typical open cooking fire (2005).

discussed later in the chapter) forecasts that the number of people in the developing world who rely on firewood and other biomass fuels for their cooking and who are thus subjected to these potential health problems will grow by 200 million to 2.6 billion by 2030 (p. 5). This expected growth in the use of firewood comes on top of an 80% increase occurring between 1961 and 1998 according to estimates from the United Nations Food and Agriculture Organization (as cited in Manuel & Dooley, 2003, p. 5). Not surprising, then, is the fact that there is evidence that the practice of cooking with firewood in open fires is having harmful effects on the environment. Deforestation, with its associated problems of erosion, diminished rainfall, global warming, loss of animal and plant habitat, and loss of food and medicinal plant sources, is the primary concern. In Guatemala, in particular, firewood use is widespread according to Edwards and Langpap (2005) with almost 75% of households relying on it for cooking. They note further that the use of firewood for cooking is not limited to just the poorest households, who use it nearly exclusively (99.5% and 98% in bottom two quintiles), but is also used by both middle (91% and 76% in third and fourth quintiles) and upper classes (46% in the upper quintile), as well (p. 572).

Fuel Efficient Stoves and Community Development in Guatemala 53

Figure 4.2. Young *Caqchiquel* woman carrying 75-100 pounds of firewood (1993).

In the highlands of Guatemala, a frequent image in any rural community is that of *campesinos* with stacks of freshly cut firewood on their backs heading back home after a trip to the mountain forests. Typically, this task falls to the women of the house, so those images more accurately might be young girls carrying on their backs as much as 50 pounds or their mothers carrying nearly 100 pounds (see Figure 4.2). In Guatemala, whose *Nahuatl* name means "land of trees," the forests appear to be under assault. In 1950, two thirds of the country was still covered with forests, but by the end of the 1990s, the forested area had fallen by half, with a deforestation rate of 2% per year. Given the extensive use of firewood for cooking mentioned above, it seems clear that this is a major source of not only deforestation, but also top soil erosion, and river silting (Edwards & Langpap, 2005; Reding, 2000).

To obtain a local perspective on the use of firewood for cooking, I interviewed three *campesinos* living in the San Lucas area (personal communication, May 2004). Each man owned a small parcel of land of about two *cuerdas* (about 40% of an acre) each. My initial questions were designed to get a sense of the magnitude of firewood use in the community. They informed me that a typical tree to be cut for firewood would be a 16-foot hardwood tree—a likely candidate would be a *gravilea* tree—with a one and a half foot diameter trunk. It would yield two to three *tareas* of firewood. In Guatemala a *tarea* is an all-purpose word that refers to one's task, such as the amount of a day's workload, or the amount of a harvested crop one might carry, or in the case of firewood, it refers to an amount of wood that might last a family 18-20 days when used for open fire cooking. Working through the math reveals that a single family—and I'm assuming an average family size of six to eight individuals, at least in rural areas—would consume an entire tree over the course of one and a half to two months time for firewood alone. This works out to seven to eight trees per family per year. For the community in this analysis alone—San Lucas Tolimán, with a population of approximately 40,000—the impact of open fire cooking results in the annual loss of nearly 50,000 trees. Multiply this result across all of the other rural communities of Guatemala and it is not hard to imagine that cooking with firewood, especially using nonimproved stoves, is a major source of deforestation.

Next, I asked the *campesinos* about the physical and economic hardships of using firewood in such volumes. They suggested that it would take approximately 4 days of difficult labor to take down a 16-foot tree using machetes and cut and split it into firewood consisting of individual pieces that are about 22 inches long. They added that 4 days is a significant amount of time out of the working life of a rural family. Furthermore, they noted that not all families would actually have access to or own a stand of trees. For families without access to trees or the ability to chop them down, their only recourse is to buy firewood in the marketplace. The most economically efficient way to make such a purchase would be to buy an entire *tarea* at once for a price of 150 quetzals (approximately U.S.$20). For most rural families, however, having such a sum of money all at once would be an impossibility, regardless of how financially efficient the bulk purchase might be. Thus, they are faced with the prospect of doling out their hard-earned income Q10 (U.S.$1.33) at a time for firewood sold by the *manejo*, by the handful. A family would need about two *manejos* to get through the day, so their daily cost would be Q20. Working through the math reveals a significant economic hardship for those having no choice but to buy the firewood by the *manejo*. That annual cost is over Q7000 or nearly U.S.$1,000. Since that amount exceeds the typical rural annual income by at least a couple hundred dollars, one can assume that most families are forced to scrimp, conserve, or perhaps go without in order to make ends meet. For those able to make purchases one *tarea* at a time, their outlays are dramatically less—nearly Q3000 or U.S.$400—but still a sizeable portion of their annual incomes. There is also the matter of time, energy, and bodily effort of carrying bundles of wood from market or forest to home, a chore that a number of studies suggest is increasingly being undertaken by women and children (see, for example, Elias & Victor, 2005; Kaarlsson, 2007). Finally, there is the problem that as firewood supplies become depleted—as deforestation progresses—a vicious circle sets in, whereby women mostly, have to travel ever farther in search of firewood. Elias and Victor (p. 18) note that these longer distances pose risks of falls, fractures, bites and bee stings, along with the additional economic burden of increased time devoted to this task. There is, of course, also the potential for physical assault.

HEALTH, ENVIRONMENTAL, AND ECONOMIC PROBLEMS OF RURAL GUATEMALANS: PROXIMATE AND ULTIMATE CAUSES

Given the fact that acute respiratory infections are the leading cause of morbidity and mortality in Guatemala, the proximate cause, of course, being cooking with open fires, the next logical step is to begin thinking of technical fixes such as the introduction of fuel efficient stoves. But what about the ultimate causes? A quick perusal of the Pan American Health Organization's health indicator data base for Guatemala (2007, pp. 5-6) reveals a witches brew of preventable diseases that affect the population, especially the rural and indigenous population. In addition to the obvious acute respiratory infections (pneumonia and bronchitis), there are also vector-borne diseases (malaria, dengue), diseases preventable by immunization (acute flaccid paralysis, measles, tetanus, pertussis, tuberculosis meningitis), intestinal infectious diseases (acute diarrhea, cholera), chronic communicable diseases (tuberculosis), zoonoses (rabies, HIV/AIDs), malignant neoplasms (cancer of the reproductive system, breast cancer), and nutritional and metabolic diseases (chronic protein-energy malnutrition, global malnutrition, vitamin A deficiency, iron deficiency, anemia). The last of these problems—nutritional and metabolic diseases—most likely moves us a step closer to uncovering the ultimate causes of health problems in the country.

The World Bank (2003) notes that the extent of malnutrition in Guatemala is worse than in any other country in the Latin America and Caribbean region, with an overall stunting rate of 44% of all children under age 5 (p. 14). It further reports a strong connection between poverty and malnutrition, observing that the majority of malnourished children (80%) are poor. Furthermore, these malnourished children are mostly indigenous and living in rural parts of the country. In recent years, the World Bank has also begun to recognize the problem of *inequality* as a stumbling block to poverty reduction (see for example, its *World Development Report 2000/ 2001* devoted to the topic of poverty, especially chapters 2 and 3). While the bank still insists on economic growth as the best method for a country to reduce poverty, it acknowledges that inequality in the distribution of income inhibits the transmission of economic growth into poverty reduction (pp. 31-59, particularly 35 & 55).

Inequality in Guatemala is extreme. According to the United Nations Human Development Report (2006), the top 20% of the population earns 60% of the nation's income, while the bottom 20% does not quite earn 3%, one of the most skewed income distributions in the world. It is even worse with regard to land. According to a special UNHDR study of Guatemala, 2% of the population own 72% of agricultural land, producing cash crops such as sugar, coffee, and bananas, rather than food for domestic consumption (Krznaric, 2005, pp. 3-4). As a result, 72% of the rural and indigenous population live in poverty, with 31% falling into the extreme poverty category (pp. 3-4). Also, according to the UNHDR, Guatemala is near the bottom of the list of Latin American countries in nearly every single category of human development; categories such as life expectancy, illiteracy, access to improved water, and more.

So, finally, we arrive at what is likely the ultimate cause of health, environmental, and economic problems for Guatemala's rural families; inequality. The inequalities in this country are endless. For the vast majority of Guatemala's citizens, there is a lack of access to land, education, income, health care, credit, clean water, transportation, and communication. Furthermore, all of these inequalities are compounded by violations of human rights. This especially was the case during the war years, 1961-1996.

Inequalities in education are of particular concern. United Nations Educational, Scientific, and Cultural Organization (2001), for example, suggests that, "The role of education in poverty eradication, in close co-operation with other sectors, is crucial. No country has succeeded if it has not educated its people" (p. 1). The World Bank (2000/2001) goes even further to suggest that, "the rights of men and women are flagrantly unequal" and that "closing the gender gap in schooling more rapidly would boost economic growth" (pp. 118-119).

It is difficult to read any account of Guatemala, historical or otherwise, that does not touch upon these problems (see, for example, Handy, 1984; Jonas, 1991; Lovell, 2000; Menchú, 1984). Policies that contribute to inequalities result from a small oligarchy (with a supportive military) that frames public policy in such a way that results in poverty on a scale that most of us can't imagine. Guatemalan scholar, George Lovell, in a presentation at a National Endowment for the Humanities conference (July 28, 2006) in Guatemala City suggested that this state of affairs has been part of the social fabric for centuries. There was, of course, the formal Spanish conquest of 1524 that brought war, disease, loss of land and, ultimately, subjugation to the crown. But the conquest did not stop there. Independence in 1821 brought little relief for the indigenous Maya, with control of most of the country's resources simply passing from the crown to the landed oligarchy. In 1871, under the "liberal" regime of Justo Rufino Barrios, the poor and indigenous lost thousands more acres of land to the elite and also to foreign investors in the name of economic modernization. Following an aborted 10-year experiment with democracy and agrarian reform from 1944-1954 under the presidencies of Juan José Arévalo and Jacobo Arbenz, Guatemala entered into a 4 decades-long period of state-sponsored terror peaking in the late 1970s and early 1980s under the military regimes of Generals Lucas García and Efraín Ríos Montt.[4] During this period at least 200,000 people, mostly indigenous Maya, were killed or disappeared, as many as 1.5 million were displaced, and as many as 700 villages were wiped off the Guatemalan map (Commission for Historical Clarification, 1999). Peace accords were signed in 1996, bringing the awful conflict to an end, yet the oligarchy and military remain firmly in control. Guatemala's indigenous, meanwhile, still struggle to put food on the table. The country is full of beauty and abundant resources, but it can't feed its own people. Lovell refers to this strange contradiction that survives even in the postpeace accords period as *A Beauty That Hurts*, the title of his 2002 book.

COMMUNITY DEVELOPMENT PROGRAMS IN SAN LUCAS TOLIMÁN: AN OVERVIEW

In the central highlands, no more than 60 miles or so from the epicenter of the "scorched earth" policies of the 1970s and 1980s, nestled along the southeast corner of Lake Atitlán, lies the predominantly *Caqchiquel* Mayan community of San Lucas Tolimán. On the Saturday before Palm Sunday, 1964, Father Greg Schaffer, a young Catholic priest from Minnesota barely out of seminary, assumed the duties of parish priest of the *parroquia* of San Lucas. He barely had a grasp of the language or of the civil unrest that was brewing in the country. The agrarian reforms of 1952 had barely touched San Lucas, thus leaving the majority of its citizens landless and desperately poor. Many were living under serflike conditions in *colonias* that were attached to the giant coffee *fincas*. To Father Greg, as he is called by most of his parishioners, one of the worst aspects of the situation at that time was that there was little hope for improvement on the part of the citizenry. Like most rural Guatemalans, they had been excluded from formal education or job skills training. Such things weren't necessary for a people who the oligarchy assumed were on Earth for one purpose only; to harvest their coffee. This attitude is long standing. According to the postpeace accords truth commission, the Commission for Historical Clarification (1999),

> The proclamation of independence in 1821, ... saw the creation of an authoritarian State which excluded the majority of the population, was racist in its precepts and practices, and served to protect the economic interests of the privileged minority. (Conclusions, chap. 2, p. 1).

The Commission for Historical Clarification found that 170 years later, racism was still an important part of the State's "doctrine of superiority" (p. 7).

The prospects of serving effectively as priest to a community in the highlands of Guatemala in 1964 could not have been more daunting.[5] But, Father Greg had at least three things working for him. One, he knew better than to come into a new foreign parish and attempt to dictate how they might do things—he simply didn't have the language, expertise, or inclination. However, he was an especially good listener. Listening carefully to the concerns and needs of his parishioners would be the only way for him to accomplish anything in this community in which he was totally out of his element. Very early in his tenure, Father Greg was befriended by an older man named Max; known to most people as *Don Max*. Don Max kept asking him why he was in San Lucas. Greg would always respond that he was there to "serve the people." Apparently, to Max, Greg appeared impatient to get on with the business of organizing or improving the parish. Max quietly told him one day that he simply had to be patient with himself. As their relationship progressed, this message of patience was repeated often. However, Max was old and ready to die. On Don Max's last night he called Greg to his bedside and asked for his blessing. When Greg was finished, Max then offered his own blessing for Greg. He said, "God, teach this young man to be patient with himself and with my people." And with that, he passed away. For Greg, Don Max's message of patience was one that would help shape his ministry for all time to come; a message that powerful policymakers in multilateral lending and development organizations who offer one-size-fits-all economic growth solutions to the developing world would be wise to listen to.

The second thing Father Greg had working for him in 1964 was that winds of change were blowing strong in the Catholic Church in the form of the openings associated with the Vatican II meetings in Rome (Foley, 1993). A few of the changes in areas such as ecumenism, liturgy, role of the laity, and an expanded view of the church's missionary role allowed his young ministry in a mostly Mayan community to flourish. In addition to carefully listening to his parishioners, he could involve them in church and community development activities that might have been unthinkable a few years earlier. One lasting result of those early changes was that, rather than employing top-down decision making, a committee of parish and community leaders was established which, to this day, makes all decisions regarding projects or programs associated with the parish. The ecumenism, especially, allowed for a tolerance of and occasional blending of Mayan traditions and customs with those of Christianity that generated trust among the people and thus facilitated the expansion of a variety of meaningful parish projects.

Greg also brought with him to San Lucas an appreciation for the newly expanded missionary role of the church as well. In the past this role was essentially limited to the preaching of the gospel and administering of the sacraments. After Vatican II, that role now included a focus on social justice, peace, and the provision of social services to the sick, poor, and needy (McBrien, 1998). Other strong influences that helped to shape his ministry came from his readings of Mhatma Ghandi, Dorothy Day and, a few years later, E. F. Schumacher.

The final thing that Father Greg had working for him was that the diocese of New Ulm, as part of its outreach to its new sister parish in San Lucas, wished to establish a school in the community, something that was quite rare in the highlands of Guatemala in those days. As noted earlier, educating Mayan children was simply not a priority of the oligarchy. To get things started, the diocese intended to send down to San Lucas two Catholic sisters who would organize and teach classes to elementary-age children. While this was an exciting first step toward educational development, it immediately posed a serious problem. Given the lack of community infrastructure, there were no hotels or other buildings sufficient to house the Sisters. The Diocese was sending them anyway though, and they needed a place to stay. Thus, Greg was forced to take a good hard look at what infrastructure, resources, and finances did exist. A new housing unit constructed with expensive professional architects, contractors, and imported resources was out of the question. A building of the quality Greg had in mind for the Sisters using only local resources was somewhat of a leap into the unknown. Despite the uncertainty, a decision was made to start building a new church annex building—*Casa Madre*."

The manner in which this building was constructed would influence all future development projects. One day in the spring of 1964, Father Greg was standing in front of the church deliberating where on the property a new building might go when a man from town, Bartolo Juárez, came up and asked Greg what he was doing. They chatted for awhile, discussed the dilemma regarding the building, and, out of the blue, he offered to help. Greg recalls Bartolo's remarks, "You have come to help here. I, too, would like to help. I can work with you getting men to work and directing them." As Greg puts it, "It was like having someone sent directly by God" (unpublished parish archival document).

Construction started on June 6, 1964. Bartolo identified a local stonemason—one of only a tiny handful in town—to head up the project, as well as a student willing to learn how to read a blue print. A decision was made to use volcanic rock from around the San Lucas area. It was essentially free, and could be cut from any number of places on the mountainsides or corn fields. A handful of volunteers eager to earn a modest paycheck—including young Lucas Xiruc, now a master stone mason and head of the parish apprenticeship program—comprised the remainder of the work crew. The volunteers' experience over the course of the project proved to be valuable both individually and for the parish. The workers learned not only new job skills, which they were quick to share with others, but they also gained a significant measure of hope, pride, and dignity; feelings had been absent for a long time in this little part of Guatemala. The sturdy little building, by the way, is still a prominent feature on the front property of the church grounds.

Over the years, this skill building was transformed into a formal apprenticeship program, thus filling a sizeable gap in the technical and trades education in the central highlands. Today, there are opportunities in stone masonry, stone cutting, carpentry, welding, plumbing, and electricity, with 12 master tradesmen—themselves, graduates of the apprenticeship program—providing supervision. If someone in the community is out of work and would like to learn a trade, the application process is streamlined. One simply needs to go over to the church around 8:00 a.m. on any weekday when the parish committee is meeting and ask to speak to Lucas Xiruc. Once Lucas determines what kind of work skills the inquirer would like to learn, he will direct the person to one of a number of parish construction projects underway. There have been hundreds of graduates of the apprenticeship program over the years, resulting in a stream of skilled workers being channeled into the community and surrounding region.

Over time, the parish development programs acquired a rather sophisticated philosophical grounding, based in part on the principles espoused by E. F. Schumacher. Father Greg attended a conference back in the United States in the early 1970s where Schumacher was promoting the ideas in his 1973 book, *Small is Beautiful: Economics as if People Mattered*. In addition to attending formal presentations and seminars, he had the good fortune of finding time for informal conversations with Schumacher on topics that we know today under labels like *sustainability* and *subsidiarity*.

In *Small is Beautiful* he notes that the products of sophisticated technology are not normally an urgent need of the poor. "What the poor need most of all are simple things—building materials, clothing, household goods, agricultural implements—and a better return for their agricultural products. They also most urgently need ... trees, water, and crop storage facilities. Most agricultural populations would be helped immensely if they could themselves do the first stages of processing their products" (p. 186). These three sentences—especially the final one—are among the most important ever written regarding advice for sustainable economic development. Father Greg took these ideas seriously and the parish programs have been influenced by them ever since. You can see Schumacher's ideas interspersed with ideas unique to the circumstances of San Lucas Tolimán in the following list of formal goals the parish laid out for its parish development programs (unpublished parish archival documents).

- To develop area resources for the service of the needs of its people, and not for the profit of a few.
- To make all work areas be as labor intensive as possible—respecting the trilogy of participation, creation, and responsibility.
- To introduce technology that does not cut the labor force, but only serves the person in working more completely.
- To become self-sufficient as possible in terms of food production.
- To bring outside money into the area through processing a given product as far as possible before it meets a wholesale or retail market.
- To introduce only new technology that is ecologically sound and with low or medium combustible energy needs.

In previous analyses, I have described the construction of the community's first hospital (completed in the early 2000s) as an example of a project that applied Schumacher's principles and, as well, made extensive use of the apprenticeship program (Abell, 1997, 2002a). The coffee program, described in Abell (2004), makes extensive use of Schumacher's principles, as does the fuel efficient stove program, the details of which will be described later.

Education and job skills training have formed the supporting structure of all the other programs that have evolved over the years. Here is how Father Greg views the parish's role with respect to education: "The object of the educational program is to give unawakened and unchallenged minds the opportunity to learn, to think for them selves." Elsewhere, he adds,

> As part of this evolutionary process we came to see that as foreigners we will never be able to effect real change in the attitudes of the people. It will be

up to us then to provide an opportunity for this growth and change to take place. This will have to be done from many angles, but the most important of these is education" (unpublished parish archival documents).

From the single elementary school started by the Catholic Sisters in the 1960s, there has been remarkable progress in education. Parish-related schools today educate over 700 students per year, most of whom attend at least through sixth grade. Since the educational program doesn't discriminate on the basis of ethnic identity, the schools are helping to reduce a serious educational attainment gap between indigenous and Ladinos that plagues the country as a whole. According to the World Bank, overall educational attainment for indigenous Guatemalans is only 3.5 years of schooling while it is 6.3 years for Ladinos (Hall & Patrinos, 2005). There are over 50 teachers employed these days, serving 23 schools in both San Lucas (the city proper) and the *aldeas* (outlying communities), all but two of which the parish had a direct hand in creating. In Figure 4.3, school children from the community of Santa Teresita—former *colonia* residents of the *finca* Santa Teresa—are shown outside their new temporary school house. The parish helped with the construction of the school as a stopgap measure until more a permanent living arrangement for the community could be secured.

Figure 4.3. Temporary school house built with parish assistance for families displaced from the *finca* Santa Teresa (1999).

As the parish schools have flourished over the years, reaching out to ever more distant communities, the government has stepped into the picture to assist with funding. Most highlands communities are lucky to have a single functioning school, much less 23. A study conducted by local teachers in the early 1990s estimated a literacy rate in San Lucas of 85% (unpublished parish archival document). This statistic stands in sharp contrast to the national average of only 61% in 1991, or even 69% from the most recent data of 2004 (United Nations Human Development Report, 2006). What is even more impressive about the 85% literacy rate of the 1990s, is that in the 1960s there was a 97.5% *illiteracy* rate in the region (unpublished parish archival document). In a recent conversation with Father Greg, he suggested to me that he suspects that the literacy number is actually a bit higher than 85% these days (personal conversation, September 6, 2007).

As the educational programs were unfolding over the course of the mid 1960s and 1970s, a number of other disturbing trends or problems were becoming apparent, all of which eventually resulted in the creation of a forestry program. First, Father Greg heard again and again from local farmers that something appeared to be going wrong with the regular weather patterns. The traditional rainy season (May to early December) was being shortened, and the limited, but historically predictable January rains that preceded *maize* planting had all but stopped. The general consensus was that deforestation—obvious to anyone willing to stand for a moment and look up at the bare hillsides and volcanoes—was affecting the hydrologic cycle.

Another obvious problem was that the citizens of the San Lucas area were living in substandard and oppressive housing arrangements. Few of the indigenous not living in the *finca colonias* had property they could call their own. The parish addressed this by initiating a home building program (for more on this, see Abell, 1997). Home construction, of course, at least in those days, required lumber, and lots of it, something that was in especially short supply given the deforestation.

There was another trend yet that was becoming apparent in Guatemala whereby *finca* owners (*finqueros*) were realizing that it was more profitable to evict the permanent work force from their *colonias*—thus saving the expense of having to provide housing and a year-round wage—and simply hire the workers back at harvest time. Hundreds of families at a time found themselves suddenly without homes. People had no choice but to search for land and resources farther and farther into the forests and up the hillsides in a non-sustainable effort to eke out a living. All of these trends remind us of the concern that Schumacher (1973) expressed regarding the general mismanagement of the global economy contributing to the consumption of our natural resources at an unsustainable rate (p. 14).

Achieving sustainability would imply reorganizing society in ways such that human activities could be carried out within the bounds of the earth's *carrying capacity*. The upper limit of resources that can be sustained for a region (or possibly for the entire world) defines its carrying capacity (Beazley, 1993). An economic system such as that of Guatemala whose best lands are set aside for the production of chemical-intensive cash crops such as coffee or sugar is not sustainable. A system that displaces indigenous peoples from their lands, who then have no choice but to seek out ever more distant and disagreeable plots on which to carry out their family farming activities is not sustainable. Likewise, a system that throws people off their lands and forces them to sell their labor at starvation wages is not sustainable. Finally, a system that clear cuts its forests with the resulting negative effects of erosion and loss of vegetative transpiration is not sustainable.

To address the problems of housing and environmental non-sustainability in the region, the parish committee initiated a forestry program. The project had two goals: (a) to provide lumber for local construction needs and (b) to assist in the reforestation of the region. Experimentation with crossbreeding over the years has resulted in a strain of fast-growing cypress trees that are capable of producing mature trees in 15 years. Fuel efficient stoves would have been another logical approach, but this program was still a number of years off. Trees and lumber, however, without land would be of little use. The lack of land to meet the basic needs of the population was the most vexing of all the many sustainability-related problems facing San Lucas, a problem facing nearly every community in the country. Many analysts conclude that land, or rather, the unequal distribution of it, is the number one problem facing the country, and that social justice and a lasting peace cannot prevail until this problem is addressed (see Handy, 1984; Lovell, 2000).

San Lucas is hemmed in, in practically every direction; giant coffee *fincas* lie to the south and west, Lake Atitlán to the north, and a steep 2000 foot ridge to the east. The parish committee contemplated both short-term and long-term solutions to the land problem. In the short-run, it was necessary to determine the most efficient agricultural techniques and highest yielding crops that could be grown on the limited amount of land in the community. An experimental farm was started to explore such possibilities. A variety of plant and animal food resources were tried, including citrus, avocado, sheep, goats, pigs, chickens, and rabbits[6] (for more on this, see Abell, 1997).

The long-term aspect of the land problem, on the other hand, required a great deal of patience, something Father Greg had already been lectured about by his friend Don Max. Land, which confers wealth, power, and prestige, rarely, if ever, becomes available for sale in Guatemala. Occasionally, however, a family, many generations into the ownership of a *finca*, may find itself financially strapped or weary of the responsibilities of maintaining the operation. The parish committee has stepped in on many occasions to make a land purchase on behalf of various groups of families. The circumstances are always different with each purchase, but typically the families receiving the land are *campesinos* who have been displaced from their *colonias* for one reason or other. On one occasion in 1997, for example, 100 families were simply kicked off of the *finca Santa Teresa* because of a disagreement with a new owner over the details of the daily *tarea*. They had lived there for countless generations (Abell, 2002, pp. 63-64). More recently, two sizeable parcels of land were purchased for families who were the victims of natural disasters. The families of El Porvenir—former *colonia* residents—were washed off their land by a devastating mudslide on September 12, 2002 (see Abell, 2002b, for the details of this event). Seventy-six families have since been resettled (beginning in 2005) onto a new parcel of land just south of San Lucas with parish assistance. The families of San Andres—also former *colonia* residents—were washed out of their homes by Hurricane Stan in October 2005; 166 families have been resettled (beginning in 2006) onto a new parcel of land also south of San Lucas with parish assistance. In these two instances, and in others where large parcels of land are purchased, there is normally adequate acreage to allow for both housing and food production. I wrote in 2002, that approximately 2,100 families had received property through the parish land development program (Abell, 2002a). Since then, at least 500 additional families have received land, including the San Andres and El Porvenir families. Assuming an average family size of six, this suggests that over 15,000 formerly landless people can now carry themselves with the pride and dignity that come from owning their own homes, having a plot of land, and being in charge of their own destinies. There is a popular saying among the *Caqchiquel* Maya that seems apropos: "Tortillas from corn we ourselves have grown on our own land always taste better."

SAN LUCAS' FUEL EFFICIENT STOVE PROGRAM

As a result of the numerous people showing up at the doors of the parish clinic[7] over the years with respiratory problems, the need to address the problem of open fire cooking had become unavoidable. The incident with Brenda Chocho back in 1997 helped to rush fuel efficient stoves to the top of the parish's to-do list. Brenda's father Valentin was distraught and wanted to do something to prevent such a thing from ever happening to others. Coincidentally, at about this same time, a volunteer from the United States, Tom Benevento, was visiting San Lucas. He was experienced with the newer models of fuel efficient stoves—the so-called *plancha* stoves—being introduced throughout the country. In fact, he had come up with some modifications of his own. This new fuel efficient stove was far safer and sturdier than cooking over an open fire and had been proven to use up to two-thirds less firewood. Valentin Chocho was available to help. He had some experience as a stonemason and was currently out of work. He and Tom, along with experienced stonemason Lucas Xiruc, worked together to build the first fuel efficient stove in the community in Valentin's own home.

Neighbors watched with interest and word of the new stove spread quickly. Other families liked what they saw and heard of the new stove and wanted one of their own, including families from San Lucas. It didn't take much convincing for women to give up their traditional open cooking fires in favor of the new fuel efficient stoves. The cultural resistance to the adoption of this new technology, that apparently has been experienced elsewhere (Gill, 1985; Pandey & Yadama, 1992; Winrock International, 2004) was not a problem for families in the San Lucas area. I attribute this to the relatively high levels of education of the citizenry, and also to their repeated exposure to new ideas associated with the abundant parish programs throughout the community. At any rate, less than two months after little Brenda was burned so badly, experimental stove construction had turned into a full-scale stove program called the *Projecto Poyo Mejorado* (literally: improved stove project). It was soon turned over entirely to Valentin. He built slowly at first, but eventually he developed the skills, speed, and confidence needed to build stoves on a larger scale; a good thing, because the numbers of families wanting stoves was increasing day by day.

It became obvious that it would be difficult to make a dent in the waiting list of families if Valentin was the only builder. Others have been added along the way, many coming through the ranks of the parish job apprenticeship program. Currently, the stove program is headed by Julio Morales, who has four apprentices working under him.[8] Julio is a busy man. In addition to heading up the stove project, he runs the construction office for the parish construction projects, plus, he is also a youth counselor. On a daily basis, he encounters young men, boys, mostly, struggling with drug, alcohol, and gang-related problems. Where many in the community might have dismissed these youth as so troublesome as to be beyond salvage, Julio simply and quietly began taking them under his wings as a mentor. This might have involved guidance in the form of small group discussions or home visits on the one hand, and introducing them to the world of work and responsibility through the job apprenticeship program on the other hand.

While the stove program is one option for these young men, there are a variety of other job skills to be learned. I should add that there are no hand outs in this program. In the United States, as we all know, 16-year-olds can't just sign on with Papa John's Pizza, for example, as store managers; rather, they have to earn their way to the top by "slapping" or delivering pizzas for a few years. Likewise, youth in San Lucas might have to begin their apprenticeships with menial and difficult tasks like breaking boulders into smaller rocks to facilitate the construction of a sanitation drain field. Even with a *relatively* more glamorous job like fuel efficient stove construction, there are still a number of laborious tasks like mixing two hundred pounds of concrete, sand, and water, or hauling a wheelbarrow full of concrete blocks from the supply store across town to the worksite. Apparently, some of Julio's young apprentices have taken great pride in their work; so much so that they have even given themselves a name: *Generacion Juvenil-Nueva Vida* (The Young Generation New Life; Schaffer, 2007). Pride, dignity, job skills, and a life off the streets are what are being learned here.

During my most recent visit to San Lucas (April 2007), I found myself working alongside one of Julio's youths on a construction site. Luís was his name. He shared a story nearly exactly as I have depicted it above. He had been a drug abuser living on the streets, but thanks to the apprenticeship program, he was off the streets and learning both job and life skills. He was extremely appreciative of the opportunity that had been given him. He was a most interesting young man; smart, hard working, curious—he questioned me endlessly about how life in the United States compared to Guatemala—and eager to gain the skills needed to start his own construction business one day.

The overall stove project is demand driven, with stove builders and funding struggling to keep up with the list of those desiring new stoves. Families are provided stoves partly on a first-come, first-served basis, but also on a needs basis. In addition, there are the two new communities mentioned earlier, El Porvenir and San Andres; they need stoves as well. Construction is under way in El Porvenir. The population of the San Lucas area is large—40,000 or so—so the need for stoves seems endless. Plus, word of the program is spreading. For example, a stone mason in the nearby village of Panimaquip, Brenda Chocho's community, ironically, has requested funding to hire apprentices and to start building stoves. Given the tightness of the parish budget, at the moment, Julio only has funding enough to employ two stove builders and two apprentices.

The stove program is consistent with Schumacher's principles. This is seen in the manner in which resources are obtained and used. To maximize the economic impact on the local community, where possible, as many of the raw materials that go into each stove are made or purchased locally. If they are not available from local sources, then they are obtained from regional sources. If they are not available from regional sources, then they are obtained from as far away as Guatemala City. The materials themselves are very basic—cement blocks, bricks, a steel cooking *plancha*, tiles, sand, cement, and lime—making use of culturally appropriate resources and technologies. In some cases, where the nearby soil is of sandy consistency, the purchase of bagged sand can be avoided, and a screen sifter is used to clean the sandy soil for use in mixing the mortar.

Basic tools are used: machetes, hoes, buckets, trowels, wire cutters, tape measures, levels, corner squares, and pencils. Power tools are used only occasionally. In addition to the jobs associated with the construction of the stoves themselves, there are jobs associated with the provision of each of the building materials, and those jobs mean incomes that circulate locally or regionally. The actual construction of the stoves is a very detailed, labor intensive process. A more capital intensive approach would not maximize the relative labor abundance in the San Lucas area. In Figure 4.4, Dany Ajcalon, a former stove program manager, is shown cutting a concrete block with a machete. Having tried this myself a number of times with

Figure 4.4. Basic stove construction technology: cutting a concrete block with a machete (2005).

Fuel Efficient Stoves and Community Development in Guatemala 69

Figure 4.5.   Proud new stove owners in Tierra Santa (2007).

varying degrees of success, I can say with some authority that cutting a straight line on a concrete block with a machete requires skills and confidence. One cannot simply walk off the street and start building a stove.

The final product is sturdy—a permanent fixture in the kitchen (see Figure 4.5). It is easy to use, clean, and maintain. In comparison to an open fire, as noted earlier, it uses up to two thirds less wood because of the closed fire-box design and it emits virtually no smoke into the living space since there is venting to the outside. The firebox also helps to contain the fire and any associated pops or sparks. Because the unit is relatively tall— about hip height for most Mayan women—it is easier on the back and is beyond the reach of little children. The white tiles around the perimeter are a relatively new addition to previous models that, in addition to providing a pleasant aesthetic touch, adds to the safety of the unit by providing a place to set pots and pans away from the heat. The tiles also make this area of the stove easier to clean. The *plancha* itself consists of a large rectangle thin steel plate with concentric cooking rings. The rings allow the cook to adjust the amount of heat.

Other stove models have been considered and rejected. One that has superficial appeal is a prefabricated model consisting of poured concrete and a tin chimney. The appeal comes from its lower cost (U.S.$80) and its portability, but it has proved to not hold up over long periods of use due to the intense heat that is generated. The concrete tends to crack and the tin chimney is extremely hot to the touch. Also, it is too low to the ground for comfortable use, and there is no extra space for placing pots and pans before and after cooking.

The families that I have encountered as I have served as a volunteer in the stove program have been thrilled to receive their stoves. The women take to them immediately. They beam when you ask them to pose for photos in front of their stoves. The pride is evident. When I took the photo of the couple above in front of their stove, I had assumed that only the woman would want to be in the shot, but the man also wanted to be included. And he insisted that I wait while he went into the other room and put on a clean shirt. While I waited on him, I could not help but look with dismay at the pitiful little pile of cinders and stones that had constituted their former open fire cooking location.

You can tell just from watching the women cook that they appreciate its functionality. There is no stooping. Their pots and pans, when not cooking on the *plancha*, are placed around the tiled edge instead of on the ground as in the case of an open fire. Their tortillas can be stacked, as well, along the tiled edge. They acknowledge that they use less firewood and have to make fewer trips to the forests or market place. And, perhaps, most importantly, the air in kitchens with new stoves is decidedly easier to breathe. The program, so far, seems to be meeting the needs of the people.

The stoves that the program is currently building—like the one in Figure 4.5—cost approximately U.S.$130. Nearly two thirds of this cost is associated with the use of local resources (materials, labor, and transportation). Father Greg and Julio Morales estimate that approximately 1,200 stoves have been built in San Lucas proper and in the *aldeas* since the program's inception nearly a decade ago, averaging a little less than one and a half stoves per worker per week. This represents a sizeable injection of money into the local, as well as regional, economy. Using the estimate that two thirds of the cost of each stove represents payments to local resource providers, then one can calculate the direct economic impact on the community as being approximately U.S.$104,000 (2/3 × $130 × 1200 stoves). With one-third of the cost attributed to resource providers outside of San Lucas, that economic impact is approximately U.S.$52,000 (1/3 × $130 × 1,200).

Economists speak of *multiplier effects*. A conservative assumption would suggest a multiplier value of two, meaning that for every dollar spent directly on stove-related inputs, another dollar is spent (indirectly) in the community on related services or by employees spending their paychecks on goods and services. For example, the machine shop that fabricates the *plancha* uses special cutting tools to create the concentric rings. That machinery needs occasional maintenance and replacement. That creates a stream of payments into the community. Also, the employees actually carrying out the work on the *planchas* receive a wage that is due in part to the hours spent on fuel efficient stove-related business. They, of course, proceed to spend at least part of their paycheck in the community. For all these reasons, it can be assumed that the overall impact of the stove project on the San Lucas area, so far, has been approximately double the U.S.$104,000.00 direct impact, or $208,000.00, a tidy sum in a poor part of the world.

For the moment the parish is simply absorbing the cost of each stove and making them available to families for free as fast as they can be built. The Winrock International (2004) analysis suggests, however, that this approach creates market distortions. If stove recipients were to take a financial position in the ownership of their stove, being also responsible for the purchase of replacement parts and maintenance, then the market for both stove production and repair would be strengthened and a base for commercialization expanded (p. 37). When asked about this, Father Greg notes first of all that the program targets extremely poor people. They barely have the income to buy firewood, much less the start-up money to buy a stove; a reality that Winrock International acknowledges (p. 37). Regardless of the cost, the goal of the stove program, according to Greg, is for every single permanent house in the San Lucas area to have a fuel efficient stove. If a commercial market develops along the way and speeds along the process, then all the better, but the parish will continue to build them as fast as they can obtain funding and hire qualified stove builders, and give away every one of them.

Father Greg states that the church is simply making an investment into the health of the people and the community. The benefits appear almost immediately in the form of cleaner air to breathe, fewer accidents, and a family budget that stretches further due to fewer purchases of firewood. However, the benefits extend out over longer periods of time in the form of reduced pulmonary and other diseases and greater work productivity. The health benefits also extend to the environment in that far fewer trees need to be cut, thus reducing the problem of deforestation. The construction of the stoves can be viewed more broadly as investments in public health, something the Guatemalan government has generally refused to get involved with.

The authors of *Dying for Growth* (Kim, Millen, Irwin, & Gershman, 2000) make the point that countries like Guatemala that narrowly pursue the goal of economic growth, focusing on privatization and export-led expansion, tend to have poorer health outcomes for the least advantaged in their societies. They suggest instead that, "With the political determination to put health and equity before private and corporate interests, even poor countries with limited resources can achieve high health standards and excellent health outcomes" (p. 384). Since such political determination does not yet appear to exist in Guatemala in a meaningful or sustained way, then programs like that of San Lucas Tolimán are vital to fill in the gaps.

DISCUSSION

In this analysis, I have suggested that the problems associated with cooking over an open fire fall into roughly three categories: human health, environmental, and family economy, with the harshest impacts being borne by women and children. I refer to open fire cooking as the proximate cause of those problems and show that the fuel efficient stove program of San Lucas Tolimán, Guatemala, using a modified version of the *plancha* stove, quite capably is addressing the most immediately felt aspects—burns, scaldings, respiratory ailments, deforestation, stresses on family budgets of buying firewood, stresses on women who generally walk long miles carrying firewood, and so on. I further suggest that while the introduction of fuel efficient stoves is necessary to help relive such suffering, it is not sufficient to address deeper and more systemic problems in the San Lucas area such as inequality, poverty, malnutrition, discrimination, human rights violations, lack of access to education, credit, water, and other resources. These are most likely the ultimate factors contributing to the health, environmental, and family economic problems, and they require an approach that is much more broad-based than just fuel efficient stoves. Such an approach is, in fact, being attempted in San Lucas in the form of a number of human-centered, community-oriented development programs. The analysis provides an overview of the following programs, in addition to fuel efficient stoves: education, job skills apprenticeship, forestry, and land development. I have described these and other programs such as housing, health care, experimental agriculture, and coffee in greater detail in Abell (1997, 2002a, 2004). It appears that the stove program, *in conjunction with* the rest of the programs of San Lucas, is helping to make significant inroads into those systemic problems—the ultimate factors.

The majority of Guatemalans can't even begin to think of luxuries like a fuel efficient stove. Many are caught in a downward spiral whereby they lack land, resources, employment, income, food, and housing. Many are malnourished; their children suffering from stunting. They have had no access to education, and thus no way to improve their station in life. Living like a medieval serf in a *finca colonia*, most have no self-esteem or dignity. These are the first things to go when you live in poverty according to parish priest Father Greg Schaffer. They can't move beyond these problems to the next level where they might think about necessities like medicine and education. For most of the recipients of the new stoves in San Lucas Tolimán, however, they also have access, via the various parish programs, to all of these necessities.

Children are receiving an education. Attendance levels and literacy rates are well above the national averages. A job skills apprenticeship program is available to both youth and adults wanting to learn a trade. This provides a constant flow of human capital to the region, thus stimulating the economy. Families, even in the most remote locations of the San Lucas catchment area, have access to health care. The forestry and fuel efficient stove programs are helping to return trees to the hillsides, while providing at the same time, sufficient trees for use in construction projects. The stove program, as noted, is improving the health of women and children and relieving stress on family budgets. Land is slowly being returned to its former owners, the *Caqchiquel* Mayan people, thus helping to reduce inequality.

I have written elsewhere (Abell 1997, 2002a, 2004) that the development programs of San Lucas, with their focus on sustainability, could serve as role models for other communities. The fuel-efficient stove program is no different, and in fact, is probably the easiest to replicate. Making $130 stoves available to families is a lot easier than providing land, a house, or the ability to process export-quality coffee. Not all communities may have a benevolent church to assist in giving away stoves, but, in the interest of public health, governments (at any level; local, state, or national) could facilitate the process. They may not be inclined to give away stoves, but they could certainly sell them at subsidized prices and under concessionary terms; low interest rate loans with a long pay back period. A more visionary approach on the part of governments would be to recognize that if they made stoves available free of charge, they would be repaid many times over in the form of healthier and more productive citizens along with a healthier ecosystem. Lastly, governments should keep in mind that even under the least visionary perspective, where they view a stove program as a dead-weight loss of scarce tax payer monies, there is an additional payback above and beyond the public health benefits. A stove project can be used as part of a job skills training and a youth rehabilitation program. Employment in the community is enhanced, troubled youth are given a second chance in life, and the incomes received by the participants multiply throughout the community as monies are spent on resources, as well as on personal goods and services.

ACKNOWLEDGMENTS

The author wishes to thank Kathy Schaefer of Randolph College and anonymous reviewers for helpful comments on earlier drafts, as well as Frances Webb for valuable research assistance. Portions of this analysis are excerpted from Abell (2002a) with permission from the publisher.

NOTES

1. The English word *stove* translates into the Spanish word *estufa*. However, in the highlands of Guatemala, *estufa* usually refers to a propane stove. The sorts of stoves referred to in this chapter—those made of concrete, bricks, and mortar—are referred to in Spanish as *poyos*. Fuel-efficient *poyos* are referred to as *poyos mejorados* (improved stoves). Furthermore, much of the literature on fuel efficient stoves or improved stoves refers to the particular style of stove currently being built in San Lucas Tolimán as a *plancha* stove. But *plancha*, in the Spanish of the highlands of Guatemala, actually refers to the metal cooking surface of a stove. In an attempt to reduce confusion, I will refer to the *poyos mejorados* or *plancha* stoves simply as *fuel-efficient stoves* or sometimes just *stoves*.
2. The distinction between *proximate* and *ultimate* causation dates at least as far back as the teachings of Aristotle—*efficient* and *formal* were terms he actually used to refer to these concepts (Ackrill, 1981, pp. 36-37, New Advent Catholic Encyclopedia, 2008). This is a distinction that is important in a number of disciplines: philosophy, the sciences, and economics, among others. Generally speaking, a proximate cause of some event is one that immediately precedes that event. However, it may not be the actual reason an event took place. The actual or real reason underlying an event is referred to as the ultimate cause.
3. Outside of the literature addressing problems with cooking over an open fire, there are, of course, numerous studies that link factors like poverty and health, or discrimination and economic well being. See, for example Kim et al. (2000) or United Nations Human Development Report (2000), especially chapter 2.
4. The nearly 4 decades-long civil war began in 1961. For more on this episode in Guatemala's history, see Menchú (1984), Jonas (1991), or Commission for Historical Clarification (1999).
5. Father Greg was joined in 1967 by Father John Goggin whose focus then and now has been to serve the outlying *finca* communities (*colonias*).
6. An offshoot of the experimental farm has been the highly successful Juan-Ana coffee program. For more on this, see Abell (2004).
7. Prior to the completion of the hospital, the only effective health care available to ordinary citizens in the San Lucas area was the parish health clinic. Before the parish partnership with the diocese of New Ulm, health care was limited to visits to *curanderos* (faith healers). There have always been a handful of doctors available to people of means.

8. Valentin Chocho currently works with an assistant as an independent contractor building stoves.

REFERENCES

Abell, John D. (1997). Peace in Guatemala? The story of San Lucas Tolimán. In Jurgen Brauer & William Gissy (Eds.), *Economics of conflict resolution and peace* (pp. 150-178). Brookfield, VT: Ashgate.

Abell, John D. (2002a). Economic theory and reality: evidence from San Lucas Tolimán and the rest of the world. *Journal of Interdisciplinary Education, 5*(1), 41-69.

Abell, John D. (2002b, October 6). Mudslide at El Porvenir. *Lynchburg News and Advance*, A-4.

Abell, John D. (2004). Coffee production and sustainable development: San Lucas Tolimán, Guatemala. *Latin American Studies Association (LASA) Forum, 35*(2), 5-7.

Ackrill, John Lloyd. (1981). *Aristotle the philosopher.* Oxford, England: Clarendon Press.

Albalak, Rachel, Nigel Bruce, John P. McCracken, Kirk R. Smith, & Thelma De Gallardo. (2001). Indoor respirable particulate matter concentrations from an open fire, improved cookstove, and lpg/open fire combination in a rural Guatemalan community [Electronic version]. *Environmental Science & Technology, 35*(13), 2650-2655.

Beazley, Mitchell. (1993). *Caring for the Earth: A strategy for survival.* London: Reed International Books.

Boy, Erick, Nigel Bruce, Kirk R. Smith, & Ruben Hernandez. (2000, September). Fuel efficiency of an improved wood-burning stove in rural Guatemala: implications for health, environment, and development [Electronic version]. *Energy for Sustainable Development, 4*(2), 21-29.

Boy, Erick, Nigel Bruce, & Hernan Delgado. (2002). Birth weight and exposure to kitchen wood smoke during pregnancy in rural Guatemala [Electronic version]. *Environmental Health Perspectives, 110*(1), 109-114.

Bruce, Nigel, John McCracken, Rachel Albalak, Morten Schei, Kirk R. Smith, Victorina Lopez, & Chris West. (2004). Impact of improved stoves, house construction and child location on levels of indoor pollution exposure in young Guatemalan children [Electronic version]. *Journal of Exposure Analysis and Environmental Epidemiology, 14*, S26-S33.

Bruce, Nigel, Rogelio Perez-Padilla, & Rachel Albalak. (2000). Indoor air pollution in developing countries: a major and public health challenge [Electronic version]. *Bulletin of the World Health Organization, 78*(9), 1078-1092.

Commission for Historical Clarification. (2000, February). *Guatemala: Memory of silence.* Retrieved September 2, 2007, from http://shr.aaas.org/guatemala/ceh/report/english/toc.html

Den Ouding, Bernard. (1995, Fall). Poverty, human rights, and the consequences of deforestation. *Society for Philosophy and Technology, 1*(1-2), 1-6. Retrieved August 30, 2007, from http://scholar.lib.vt.edu/ejournals/SPT/v1_n1n2/ouden.html

Díaz, Esperanza, Tone Smith-Sivertsen, Dan Pope, Rolv T. Lie, Anaité Díaz, John McCracken, Byron Arana, Kirk R. Smith, & Nigel Bruce. (2007). Eye discomfort, headache and back pain among Mayan Guatemalan women taking part in a randomized stove intervention trial [Electronic version]. *Journal of Epidemiology and Community Health, 61*(1), 74-79.

Edwards, John H. Y., & Christian Langpap. (2005). Startup costs and the decision to switch from firewood to gas fuel. *Land Economics, 81*(4), 570-586.

Elias, Rebecca J., & David G. Victor. (2005). *Energy transitions in developing countries: A review of concepts and literature.* The Program on Energy and Sustainable Development (Working Paper #40). Retrieved August 30, 2007, from http://iisdb.stanford.edu/pubs/20910/energy_transitions.pdf

Ferring, Anya. (2003). Integrating environment and health with human rights. *AAAS Report on Science and Human Rights, 23*(2). Retrieved August 30, 2007, from http://shr.aaas.org/report/xxiii/hrenv.htm

Foley, Leonard. (1993, March). Vatican II: The vision lives on. *Catholic Update.* Retrieved September 2, 2007, from http://www.americancatholic.org/Newsletters/CU/ac0393.asp

Gill, Jas. (1985, December). *Stoves and deforestation in developing countries.* Paper presented at the United Kingdom-International Solar Energy Society Conference, Energy for development-what are the solutions? Reading University. Retrieved September 1, 2007, from http://www.odi.org.uk/fpeg/publications/greyliterature/fuelwood/gill/gill.pdf

Hall, Gillette, & Harry Patrinos. (2005, May 18). *Indigenous peoples, poverty and human development in Latin America: 1994-2004.* Guatemala highlights. Press release. Retrieved November 19, 2007, from http://web.worldbank.org/wbsite/external/ countries/lacext/0,,contentMDK:20505834~menuPK:258559~pagePK:146736~piPK:226340~theSitePK:258554,00.html

Handy, James. (1984). *Gift of the Devil: A history of the Devil.* Boston: South End Press.

Heltberg, Rasmus. (2003, June). *Household fuel use and fuel switching in Guatemala* [Electronic version]. Joint UNDP/World Bank Energy Sector management Assistance Programme.

Jonas, Suzanne. (1991). *The battle for Guatemala.* Boulder, CO: Westview Press.

Karlsson, Gail. (2007, July). Women's business? [Electronic version]. *World Conservation,* 1-2.

Kim, JimYong, Joyce V. Millen, Alec Irwin, & John Gershman. (2000). *Dying for growth.* Monroe, ME: Common Courage Press.

Krznaric, Roman. (2005) The limits on pro-poor agricultural trade in Guatemala: Land, labour and political power. *United Nations Human Development Report 2005,* Human Development Report Office Occasional Paper [Electronic Version].

Lovell, W. George. (2000). *A beauty that hurts: Life and death in Guatemala.* Austin: University of Texas Press.

Manuel, John. & Erin E. Dooley. (2003, January). The quest for fire: Hazards of a daily struggle. *Environmental Health Perspectives Online, 111*(1). Retrieved July 4, 2004, from http://ehp.niehs.nih.gov/members/2003/111-1/focus.html

McBrien, Richard P. (1998). For Vatican II, service to society is at the core of living the gospel. *National Catholic Reporter.* Retrieved September 7, 2007, from http://findarticles.com/p/articles/mi_m1141/is_n39_v34/ai_21139327

McCracken, John P., & Kirk R. Smith. (1998). Emissions and efficiency of improved woodburning stoves in Highland Guatemala [Electronic version]. *Environmental International, 24*(7), 739-747.

McCracken, John P., Kirk R. Smith, Anaité Díaz, Murray A. Mittleman, & Joel Schwartz. (2007). Chimney stove intervention to reduce long-term wood smoke exposure lowers blood pressure among Guatemalan women [Electronic version]. *Environmental Health Perspectives, 115*(7), 996-1001.

Menchú, Rigoberta. (1984). *I Rigoberta Menchú: An Indian woman in Guatemala.* London: Verso.

Neufeld, Lynnette M., Jere Douglas Haas, Marie T. Ruel, Rubén Grajeda, & Luke P. Naeher. (2004). Smoky indoor cooking fires are associated with elevated hemoglobin concentration in iron-deficient women [Electronic version]. *Pan American Journal of Public Health, 15*(2), 110-118.

New Advent Catholic Encyclopedia. (2008). Aristotle: Metaphysics. Retrieved January 16, 2008, from http://www.newadvent.org/cathen/01713a.htm

Pan American Health Organization. (2007). *Basic health indicator base for Guatemala.* Retrieved August 31, 2007, from http://www.paho.org/english/DD/AIS/cp_320.htm

Pandey, Shanta, & Gautam N. Yadama. (1992, December). Community development programs in Nepal: a test of diffusion of innovation theory [Electronic version]. *Social Service Review, 66*(4), 582-597.

Practical Action (formerly Intermediate Technology Development Group). *Smoke's increasing cloud across the globe.* Retrieved September 23, 2007, from http://practicalactionpublishing.org/?id=smoke_report_2

Reding, Andrew. (2000, January). *Guatemala: hardship considerations. Question and answer series.* Prepared for the Resource Information Center of the Immigration and Naturalization Service, U.S. Department of Justice. Retrieved September 20, 2007, from http://worldpolicy.org/globalrights/Guatemala/2000-guatemala-hardship.html#environment

Schaffer, Greg. (2007, August). Mission news. *Diocese of New Ulm Newsletter,* 1-4.

Schumacher, E. F. (1973). *Small is beautiful: Economics as if people mattered.* New York: Perennial Library.

Schei, Morten A., Jens O. Hessen, Kirk R. Smith, Nigel Bruce, John McCracken, & Victorina Lopez. (2004). Childhood asthma and indoor woodsmoke from cooking in Guatemala [Electronic version]. *Journal of Exposure Analysis and Environmental Epidemiology, 14,* S110-S117.

United Nations Educational, Scientific, and Cultural Organization. (2001, July 30-August 3, 2001). Report from International Workshop on Education and Poverty Eradication, Kampala Uganda. Retrieved September 7, 2007, from http://www.unesco.org/education/poverty/news.shtml

United Nations, *Human Development Report 2000.* New York: Oxford University Press.

United Nations, *Human Development Report 2006* [Electronic Version]. Retrieved September 7, 2007, from http://origin-hdr.undp.org/hdr2006/

Whitfield, David. (n.d.). Ecological cookers: An essential element in bettering household health. *Solar Cooking Archive*. Retrieved August 31, 2007, from http://solarcooking.org/Ecocookers.htm

Winrock International. (2004, October). *Household energy, indoor air pollution and health: Overview of experiences and lessons in Guatemala*. Prepared for the Partnership for Clean Indoor Air and the U.S. Environmental Protection Agency [Electronic version]. http://www.pciaonline.org/assets/Guatemala_Household_Energy_and_Health_Overview.pdf

World Bank. (2000/2001). *World development report: Attacking poverty*. New York: Oxford University Press.

World Bank. (2003, February). *Guatemala poverty assessment* (Report No. 24221-GU) [Electronic Version].

CHAPTER 5

EVOLUTION OR REVOLUTION?

The Forces of Internationalization and Technology on Higher Education in the United States

Patricia Aceves

The impact of globalization, internationalization, and technology on higher education systems in developing nations is examined from the historical perspective of higher education in the United States. Globalization and technology are key elements in strategic planning efforts in higher education today, and understanding the historical and cultural implications of expanding Western models to developing nations is critical to finding solutions to the hegemonic risks imposed. Framed in the discussion of significant educational milestones in American higher education, this essay reminds us of the need to allow systems to fit the culture and questions the intent and motive behind the development of new knowledge societies. Strategic solutions from the literature are presented for consideration when developing international, cross-border programs.

INTERNATIONALIZATION OF HIGHER EDUCATION

Why *internationalization* and not *globalization* as the term describing one of the themes that frame this essay? The context of this question begins in the late 1990s with the growing availability and popularity of the Internet, and the fact that our planet has suddenly become much smaller in terms of reaching out and *touching* people and organizations in parts of the world we never knew existed (Friedman, 2006). In the words of former U.N. Secretary General Kofi Annan, "It has been said that arguing against globalization is like arguing against the laws of gravity" (August 1, 2006). Globalization has become a household word, and is a key element in strategic planning for higher education in the United States (Douglass, 2005; Magrath, 2000; Scott, 1998). The term *globalization*, which has been the term du jour for the past decade, is associated with everything from cell phones, to big-box retailers, to trade agreements. As we read more about the impact of globalization on our daily lives and our educational realm, we come to understand that the true meaning of globalization may not have the same connotation that the media has led us to believe.

Jürgen Enders and Oliver Fulton (2002) define the term as "processes of increasing interdependence, and ultimately convergence, of economies, and to the liberalisation of trade and markets" (p. 6). The International Association of Universities (2003) describes globalization as "an economic process, bringing economies (and countries) closer together and exerting in this way influence on political, social, and cultural processes" (p. 3). Peter Scott (1998), a leading author on globalization in higher education defines "the radical processes which include not only round-the-clock, round-the-globe markets and new information technologies, but revolutionary conceptions of time and space" (back cover). And as a final example, Herman E. Daly (1999) describes globalization as "the global economic integration of many formerly national economies into one global economy, mainly by free trade and free capital mobility, but also by easy or uncontrolled migration. It is the effective erasure of national boundaries for economic purposes" (para. 1).

Internationalization, on the other hand, connotes, "the increasing importance of international trade, international relations, treaties, alliances, and so forth. International, of course, means between or among nations. The basic unit remains the nation, even as relations among nations become increasingly necessary and important" (Daly, 1999, para. 1). Given these descriptions, it is important to note that in globalization, the boundaries between nations in areas of economy, trade, and services are dissolved, whereas in terms of internationalization, the national boundaries remain intact, but cooperation between nations in the economic, trade and services sectors increases. For the purposes of this chapter, the term internationalization will be used in describing the phenomenon occurring in higher education. The changes occurring in higher education—in fact, the changes that are forcing us to reconsider the value that higher education plays in society—have much to do with the forces of internationalization (Enders & Fulton, 2002), and will force us to consider whether the education the United States wishes to *sell* is equally desired by consumers around the world. By understanding the systems of higher education and their historical underpinnings, as educators we have the opportunity to reflect on how the systems within which we interact and exchange ideas and knowledge, affect ourselves and our students. As Apple (2005) states,

> The history of higher education—from early mechanics institutes, to "people's universities," to the many attempts at creating closer cooperative connections between universities and culturally, politically, and economically dispossessed groups—suggests that there is a rich storehouse of knowledge on possibilities for doing this. But this requires the restoration of memory. Thus, historical work is absolutely essential if we are to go forward. (p. 25)

UNIQUELY POSITIONED: HIGHER EDUCATION IN THE UNITED STATES

The development of higher education in the United States has followed a similar path of democratization as the nation itself did in 1776. While the first universities were conceptualized from Anglican institutions in Britain (specifically, Emmanuel College at Cambridge University), Harvard University was founded in 1636 using the motto, *pro modo Academiarum in Anglia*, which literally means "according to the manner of universities in England" (Brubacher & Rudy, 2005, p. 3; Harvard University, 2006). Early colonial colleges in the United States were fashioned similarly, following standards set hundreds of years prior in England, with later influence from German research universities. This colonial model, founded in the Americas by the Puritans who required its ministers to hold a baccalaureate degree, instituted the Harvard charter which provided for "the advancement of all good literature, artes and sciences" and "the education of the English and Indian youth of this Country in knowledge and godliness" (Wertenbaker, 1947, p. 140).

Colonial Beginnings and Religious Overtones

Richard Hofstadter (1996) discusses how early colonial colleges began to separate from their European counterparts in distinct ways that foretell the future changes that were on the horizon for American academia. While established primarily as Christian Protestant denominational colleges seeking to educate future ministers and congregational leaders, the colleges were governed by boards of trustees made up of ecclesiastics and state supervisors. Not teachers or academics, the college overseers were lay persons from within the jurisdiction of the local community and colony (individuals who would have been in favor with the church or university president and who had influence over the curricula and administrative policies); a sharp departure from the European colleges which were overseen by academicians. Additionally, the U.S. colleges were geographically distributed rather than clustered into centers of academia. The diffusion of learning throughout the colonies and territories was brought about by the religious sects seeking to create their own denominational colleges in areas where they held concentrations of followers. Hofstadter writes,

> what is true is that the desire to educate a suitable, orthodox body of native clergymen could be plausibly asserted to be the most urgent and immediate reason for founding the majority of the colonial colleges. But their curricula were not those of divinity schools but of liberal arts schools. (p. 116)

For all of their religious underpinnings, the early colonial colleges began as much to educate clergy as to produce literate, educated citizens in the New World.

After struggling against colonial rule for nearly 150 years, the American Revolution of 1776 brought academic and religious freedom for sectarian colleges that including Harvard, William and Mary, Yale, Princeton, Brown, Queen's College (later Rutgers), and Dartmouth (Hoftstadter, 1996). The hardships and struggles these early American institutions faced—and overcame—were a model for those who would follow. The post-colonial collegiate expansion was about to begin.

Democratic Forces at Work

In 1816, Dartmouth College challenged the political forces of the State in defending its right to remain a privately controlled institution, against the wishes of the New Hampshire legislature, who wished to move the college to public control as a state university. In a landmark Supreme Court ruling, Dartmouth won the right to retain its private charter contract which had been sealed and approved by the Crown over 50 years earlier (Brubacher & Rudy, 2005). This tension between the private colleges and the desire of the States to create publicly controlled universities ultimately led to the efforts of John Morrill, a state senator from the neighboring state of Vermont.

One of the first major departures from the colonial, religious, private-school model came in 1862 with the Congressional ratification of the Morrill Act, which provided federal funding to create the land-grant college. This act established institutions specifically to teach the agricultural and mechanical industries, and allowed commoners to attain a university degree. As Brubacher and Rudy (2005) wrote,

> How shall we summarize the significance of the land-grant colleges? They fostered the emancipation of American higher education from a purely classical and formalistic tradition ... the early land-grant colleges represented the force of democracy working as a mighty leaven in the world of American higher learning. (p. 64)

The First Morrill Act was instituted in 1862, during the Civil War, and was applicable only to states that had not seceded from the Union. States were granted up to 90,000 acres of federal land within their boundaries, which they were to sell to fund the development of a new university dedicated to the study of agriculture, mechanical arts, and military tactics. Over 70 land grant colleges were created in this first step toward providing access to public higher education to the citizens of every state. In 1870, after the conclusion of the Civil War, the Second Morrill Act was passed, allowing Southern states the ability to create land-grant colleges, but only if they could prove that race was not a consideration in admission. If this was not shown to be the case, they were required to provide a separate-but-equal institution for People of Color (U.S. Department of State, 2007). At this moment in history, the path of American public higher education was forever changed and its ties to the colonial model were irrevocably severed. Access to education for the mass citizenry of the nation-state had been created and the nation's people were hungry for more.

Diversity Emerges:
Higher Education for Women and People of Color

The next step in the diversity of American higher education was the creation of the first women's college in 1836. By the late 1800s desegregation efforts began with the admission of men and women of color into public universities. Institutions were also influenced by the work of William Rainey Harper and Charles McCarthy in the development of continuing education programs for working adults (Brubacher & Rudy, 2005; Scott, 2006).

Harper, the first president of the University of Chicago (1890), quickly established his goals of realizing a university where citizens would have the opportunity to receive a high-quality university education: "I have a plan which is at the same time unique and comprehensive, which I am persuaded will revolutionize university study in this country" (Harper, 1880). This plan included his vision of a *multiversity*, an institution with multiple graduate and doctoral programs, medical and legal training, and evening and continuing education programs for the working-class person (University of Chicago, 2007). This concept of *open education* did not reach European higher education institutions until the mid-1960s, almost a century later (The Open University, 2007). Likewise, Charles McCarthy's experiment in Wisconsin changed the face of university extension services in ways that the founding fathers never dreamed.

McCarthy, quoted in his treatise of 1912, wrote:

> Under this new extension arrangement, professors of the highest rank are sent out into the villages, shops and factories as practically travelling teachers, meanwhile bringing the students in the field in touch with the university by means of correspondence studies. There are several centers or stations from which the work can expand into the surrounding localities established throughout the state for this work. (Wisconsin Electronic Reader, 2006)

The Wisconsin Idea of 1912 was revolutionary in that it placed into the hands of working farmers, laborers, and businessmen, the knowledge of the university. Extension services, up to then, had been poorly run, sloppy arrangements of universities pretending to consider the working man a serious student in his discipline (Wisconsin Electronic Reader, 2006). This concept provided tangible knowledge directly to the layperson in his or her home community. In the wake of these initiatives, higher education was on the verge of exploding: farmers, merchants, and tradesmen were being schooled at the university and it was but a matter of time before educational opportunities would truly, and irrevocably, be opened to everyone.

The Populace at the Crossroads

While the spread of educational access throughout the new nation in the nineteenth century supported the burgeoning Industrial Revolution, the twentieth century in the United States was a hotbed of social change that resonated within higher education. Specifically impacting the development of the United States as one of the first *knowledge societies*, it is important to note significant legislative acts that furthered the ability of men and women in the ability to pay for a college education. As World War II ended in 1944, the Government Issue (G.I.) Bill was passed:

> The law was originally designed as unemployment compensation for returning veterans, in case there weren't a lot of jobs available at the end of the war. A congressional committee threw in the idea that veterans should get money to go to college if they wanted to. Even the supporters of the bill didn't think very many G.I.'s would really want to go to college. Most of the soldiers came from working-class families, and there was no reason to think they wouldn't go back to those same working-class jobs on farms and in factories. (Keillor, 2007)

Over 1 million veterans applied for these educational benefits over the next 20 years, swelling the ranks of college students in every state of the nation, and nearly 15 years after the G.I. bill, the Higher Education Act of 1965 was passed. Access "embedded in federal legislation" was now provided for all citizens who were eligible for admission regardless of ability to pay (Eaton, 1997). The number and types of institutions multiplied: community colleges and vocational-technical schools provided open admission, and state universities with the capacity for thousands of students became the norm. Diversity was seen more often across campuses, but inequalities still existed. Judith Eaton states, "the rule of thumb that could be applied to access was that the less prestigious the institution, the greater the presence of women and minorities" (p. 238). Academic preparation leading to college admission and graduation was traditionally expected of rich, White men, but with the appearance of women and other minorities on campuses, the institutions found themselves in a quandary of how to best serve this new population, many of them with the ability to succeed, but without the preparation which had previously been expected of new students.

Additional features of the U.S. higher education system that are relevant to mention include the introduction of for-profit institutions in the twentieth century that added to the mix of public, private, and nonprofit institutions. Many of these for-profit institutions initially focused on teaching vocational and technical skills, but in the latter part of the 1900s, for-profit virtual universities began to appear. When we think of a *campus*, we tend to think of the traditional collection of brick-and-mortar buildings, not of a virtual campus, which is an innovation that began in the late 1980s, with the first colleges and universities that did not hold classes in a traditional classroom, only through the Internet, using e-mail, file transfer protocols (FTPs), and course management systems (Emmerson, 2004).

Our educational institutions have been the catalyst for societal changes and as such, remain flexible to meet the changing needs of our nation and world. While technology and internationalization are impacting the world's citizens on a daily basis, these changes are also impacting our formal educational systems and the missions they serve (J. C. Scott, 2006). It is equally important to stress that creating and moving forward on these internationalization missions cannot be successful without first confronting the hegemonic teaching and learning that is predominant in traditional U.S. higher education systems. We must continue to be vigilant in our acknowledgement that the curriculum of many higher education institutions in English-speaking countries is still based on the colonial model and it is vital for scholars to acknowledge that expansion of Western programs will, if not unintentionally also transfer Western "official knowledge" (Apple, 2005).

HIGHER EDUCATION'S MISSION: A WORLDWIDE PERSPECTIVE

John C. Scott's (2006) survey of the historical foundations of higher education world-wide highlights the six primary types of university missions: (a) teaching mission, identified in the Middle Ages; (b) research mission, a German contribution to higher education; (c) nationalization mission, meaning service to government—a movement never adopted in the United States; (d) democratization mission, meaning service to the individual—the primary mission of U.S. universities; (e) public service mission, including the Morrill Act; and (f) internationalization mission, the most recent contribution to higher education.

The internationalization mission focuses on service to not just one, but all nation-states, and is a mission that is actively promoted by the European Union, the World Bank, and the United Nations Educational, Scientific, and Cultural Organization. The internationalization mission of universities places the United States in the unique position of having a system with tremendous capacity, a history of utilitarian service to its citizens, and a multitude of providers, each with specialties that can literally provide education to anyone, anywhere. "Internationalization is contributing to, if not leading, a process of rethinking the social, cultural and economic roles of higher education and their configuration in national systems of higher education" (Enders & Fulton, 2002, p. 1). Nowhere is this rethinking of roles more important than beginning to conceptualize internationalization in our own classrooms, schools, and communities. In 2000 and again in 2006, the Kellogg Foundation commissioned a group of U.S. university presidents to study public higher education reform, an effort that was created out of the need to address change:

> Unprecedented problems confront our campuses. We face seismic shifts in public attitudes. We are challenged by new demographics and exploding technologies. We are beset by demands to act "accountably" toward students, parents, communities, and taxpayers. An increasingly skeptical press questions our priorities.... We must take charge of change. (Byrne, 2006, p. 1)

Issues confronting higher education in the United States are issues similar to those being faced by other Western-nation universities: declining government funding of free and low-cost student subsidies (decline of the welfare state), increased competition from for-profit providers (a market-driven industry), and the forecast of a decline in matriculating freshman by the year 2010 (Daniel, Kanwar, & Uvalic-Trumbic, 2006). In the United States, this translates to the need for action, and universities are moving in two directions to internationalize their missions: through curriculum changes and outreach efforts. Attracting international students to their campuses and globalizing traditional curriculum for U.S.-based students, and creating cross-border degree programs on foreign soil.

Competing International Missions

The internationalization pressure on higher education today is presenting itself on two ideological fronts: neoliberal globalization policies, including the General Agreement of Trade and Services (GATS) as put forth by the World Trade Organization, and internationalization policies, as put forth by United Nations Educational, Scientific, and Cultural Organization and the World Bank toward the reduction of poverty and the transference of developing countries from agricultural societies to knowledge economies. Given these contexts, which role does higher education in the United States (and other Western countries) play? That of the historically altruistic educator of the mass citizenry, or the capitalist entrepreneur, seeking new markets and enrollments abroad to boost declining domestic revenues? The literature tells us is that both of these scenarios are occurring.

Historically, universities in the United States served to prepare the nation's leaders, clergy, merchants, and farmers to support a growing citizenry (Brubacher & Rudy, 2005). Today, the United States has the world's highest rate of college enrollment; approximately 70% of all high school graduates will attend postsecondary education within 2 years of graduation (Haycock, Patte, Mitchell, & Wilkins, 1999); however, the United

States' 27% college graduation rate (of those earning at least a bachelor's degree) has fallen behind other Western nations (United States Census Bureau, 2003). The reality is that the U.S. higher education system has the capacity, experience, and utilitarian philosophy that support educating its own citizens, as well as those of other nations. Peter Magrath (2000) notes that nonprofit universities no longer dominate the educational market and are witnessing competition from for-profit higher education providers who have the flexibility and resources to mass-produce program offerings, often utilizing information communication technologies as a primary delivery mode to a non-traditional and international student market.

The arguments against globalization (and, in contrast, proponents for internationalization) include fears of capitalistic Westernism, Europeanism, consumerism, and cultural imperialism (Yang, 2002). Rui Yang (2002) also points out that "education as investment in human capital has become a key plan of official policy platforms in many countries" (p. 63). This trend toward creation of knowledge economies from transitioning agricultural and industrial economies is driving much of the developing world's policies. Peter McLaren and Ramin Farahmandpur (2001) implicate educational globalization as the aim of capitalism and neoliberal politics. From this perspective, they ask the question: "Dare schools build a new social order? For what purpose do schools serve and in whose interest?" (p. 271). These questions could certainly have been asked of the colonists in the early American education system as well as the authors of legislation such as the Morrill Act—which coincidentally, came on the eve of the industrial revolution (The Internet Modern History Sourcebook, 2001). Were the efforts of these great leaders working toward a Hobbesian vision of the future—or were they simply forecasting the need for better educated workers to lead the United States into the industrial revolution? These questions, and others, are being posed today by educational leaders worldwide, in an effort to determine whether the importance of internationalizing our higher education systems is more than a response to seeking new enrollments in other countries, but producing literate and informed citizens at home and abroad.

Technology Innovations Drive Internationalization Efforts

Most recently, the United States led development of computers and technology innovation has changed our higher education system in ways that we have yet to fully realize. Many of the earliest computers were developed in American universities or by the U.S. military (Oldehoeft, 2006), and the U.S. Department of Education later funded computer laboratories in schools from the primary to postsecondary level. Technology innovations captured more than just the computing market. In fact, distance education as a component of higher education latched onto the wave of technology as early as the transistor radio and television (Brubacher & Rudy, 2005). By the 1970s, universities were transmitting courses through public television and closed-circuit systems to reach students around the world. By the 1980s, faculty were experimenting with FTPs to disseminate information to colleagues and students by computer. And by the 1990s, the advent of the Internet and the World Wide Web transformed education unconditionally, allowing real-time transmission of voice, picture, and data instantaneously to individuals in their own homes (Brubacher & Rudy, 2005). "No other nation," John A. Douglass (2005) writes, "has such a variety of educational [sic] providers, public and private, as the U.S." (p. 18).

While the achievements of American higher education fill entire textbooks, it is important to note that many of these developments were evolutions to a system that had remained unchanged for centuries. While institutions in Europe and other industrialized countries have since followed suit in many of these initiatives, the movement and effects of the democratization of higher education is as *American* as baseball and apple pie.

INTERNATIONALIZATION AND TECHNOLOGY: CREATING GLOBAL KNOWLEDGE SOCIETIES THROUGH HIGHER EDUCATION

In a 2002 World Bank Report, *Constructing Knowledge Societies: New Challenges for Tertiary Education*, trends in trans-global higher education include the need for a holistic system of higher education which values learning not only in terms of increasing human capital, but also for the greater good. In this report, four messages for the development of knowledge societies are stressed:

1. Social and economic progress is achieved principally through the advancement and application of knowledge.
2. Tertiary education is necessary for the effective creation, dissemination, and application of knowledge and for building technical and professional capacity.
3. Developing and transition countries are at risk of being further marginalized in a highly competitive world economy because their tertiary education systems are not adequately prepared to capitalize on the creation and use of knowledge.

4. The state has a responsibility to put in place an enabling framework that encourages tertiary education institutions to be more innovative and more responsive to the needs of a globally competitive knowledge economy and to the changing labor market requirements for advanced human capital.

What the World Bank report fails to stress is that the development of knowledge societies does not extend only to developing nations, but that as countries learn to be producers of global knowledge, they must first be consumers of that knowledge. For the United States and other Western nations to be good stewards of education, it will be essential for our leaders and citizens to understand those cultures we seek to educate. In the words of Mahatma Gandhi, "Be the change you want to see in the world."

With the free-market expansion of higher education in the past 10 years, some entrepreneurs and legislators hold the opinion that higher education is a service to be negotiated and traded on the international market. This topic has come under intense debate in recent years with the latest round of GATS negotiations in trade and services (Green, 2004; Knight, 2002). While the Doha Round of trade negotiations (begun in 1995) was put on hold indefinitely in 2006, the opposition to the United States and other Western, developed nations to address the higher education trade liberalization is growing (Green). Several of the higher education policy trends currently on the table in this round of negotiations include (a) the increasing use of information communication technologies (ICTs) for domestic and cross-border delivery of programs; (b) the growing number of private, for-profit entities providing higher education domestically and internationally; (c) steadily increasing tuition fees and other costs faced by students of public and private institutions; (d) the need for public providers to seek alternate sources of funding; and (e) the questionable ability of government to fund the increasing demand for higher and adult education (Knight, p. 15).

GATS could certainly enhance these trends as opportunities, as well as promote the competitive edge for for-profit providers and ultimately, draw into question the quality and intent of the programs delivered. In 2000, specific mention of educational services was included in GATS talks, a service that has always been provided for in the trade agreement, but rarely utilized or noticed. The discussion of educational markets for *free trade* has generated heated discussion by government leaders, non-governmental organizations, economists, and scholars worldwide. The negotiating request put forth by the United States that specifies higher education trade in services states:

Properly regulated, increased trade in private higher education services opens the door to great economic, social, cultural and political benefits. Trade in private education complements public university systems by offering greater choice at global standards of quality, thereby helping to level the playing field in the knowledge-driven economy (Office of the United States Trade Representative, 2006, ¶12)

The four methods of cross-border education addressed in the GATS summary include distance learning, study abroad, branch campuses/physical presence, and faculty exchange (Academic Information Centre of Latvia, n.d.; Green, 2004). Part of the argument in support of higher education inclusion in GATS supports that in order to alleviate the higher education bottleneck in developing countries, efficiency models need to be incorporated, and only by opening up education to the marketplace can these efficiencies occur (Czinkota, 2005; Douglass, 2005). Douglass examines the forces of globalization on higher education and notes that information communication technologies are "perhaps the most significant source of a coming revolution in the HE sector" (p. 18).

Marjik Van der Wende (2002) stresses the risks involved in general trade agreements that appear to open the door to for-profit institutions with little control over quality. "Traditional higher education institutions," Wende states, "are most aware of the fact that transnational education and cross-border trade in educational services may endanger their position and market monopoly. They are therefore opposed to the further liberalization of the higher education market and the role of the World Trade Organization in this process" (p. 5). In a 2005 policy brief drafted by the International Association of Universities, the Association of Universities and Colleges in Canada, the American Council on Education, and the Council for Higher Education Accreditation, collective opposition was posed to the GATS talks on promoting for-profit higher education services in international trade. Their specific argument *against* the GATS proposition states:

1. Trade frameworks are not designed to deal with the academic, research, or broader social and cultural purposes of cross-border higher education.
2. Trade policy and national education policy may conflict with each other and jeopardize higher education's capacity to carry out its social and cultural mission.
3. Applying trade rules to complex national higher education systems designed to serve the public interest may have unintended consequences that can be harmful to this mission (p. 5).

Further, according to the International Association of Universities, higher education institutions should be familiar with and knowledgeable of the considerations of cross-border education. In order to engage in dialogue with local governments, institutions must initiate an approach to local communities in the host country that provides for economic well-being, remaining cognizant of social and cultural differences in the higher education systems. Equally important is the self-awareness which must occur—to ensure that our approaches do not reflect only the U.S. perspective on teaching and learning. As educational ambassadors entering a different culture, our internationalization models must be self-aware and culturally sensitive (Bennett & Bennett, 2002). Of critical importance is cooperation with local and national governments in the host country in obtaining permissions to offer educational services within their borders (many countries still pose difficulty in securing these permissions) which can appear insurmountable to institutions attempting to navigate foreign bureaucracies. In addition to offering support to local universities in the host country, our institutions should be providing opportunities and financial support on our own campuses (scholarships) for international students with demonstrated need. Perhaps most importantly, but often overlooked in the process of establishing cross-border educational programs, are the transparent quality assessment processes and procedures that provide governments, accrediting commissions, parents, students, and the general public with information on the institution's status, its authority to grant degrees, and its quality-assurance measures (p. 4).

A critical examination of the impact of globalization on higher education systems worldwide signals that GATS itself is not the problem, but rather a symptom of a paradigm shift that is occurring. For the International Association of Universities and cooperating organizations to be satisfied with removing the education provisions within GATS would be short-sighted. Higher education should ask the questions of how and why internationalizing benefits the institution and its local and global communities, and discussions surrounding these questions should unify "the efforts of all who are able to contribute" (Sadlak, 2000, p. 245). At this juncture in history, institutions must study internal, local, state, national and international interests in order to be certain that they are responding to the needs of their institution and local market before they prepare to expand into the international market (Marginson & Rhoades, 2002). Failing to provide an international perspective to students within the United States will seriously shortchange our students, communities, and ultimately our nation if we, as a citizenry are unprepared and uneducated the changes in the world around us. Institutions may go so far as to ask themselves: what does it mean for an institution to expand to the international market, and is this even a choice?

ICT Development in Higher Education

As technology has adapted for teaching and learning, the Internet is now a primary vehicle in transmission of education, and ICT use in the U.S. and other Western countries has exploded (Bright & Yang, 2005). China, as well as other developing nations are becoming knowledge economies and rely on the ICT industry to support their "economic and structural changes" (Meng & Li, 2001, p. 3). In 1998, for example, the Chinese Ministry of Education became dedicated to creating an educational society based on lifelong learning, and created the Modern Distance Education (MDE) program, and the E-Learning program:

> The term modern distance education means the provision of ICT-based distance education using multimedia computer facilities and the Internet as core technologies for off-campus learners. The term *e-learning* refers to the integration of ICT with curriculum reform and pedagogical innovation in teaching and learning for all sectors of formal education, continuing education, in-service training and lifelong learning. (Ding, Gu, & Zhu, 2005, p. 64)

To support this mission, the Ministry of Education granted 67 online education licenses to traditional universities and built 2,347 study centers (complete with computers and Internet access) (Ding et al., 2005). As the Chinese government implemented these initiatives, it also recognized its inability to provide sufficient resources for educating its citizens, and government leaders called upon U.S. and Western institutions to create joint ventures, partnerships, and private universities within its borders (Mooney & McMurtrie, 2006).

To understand the role of ICTs it is important to understand the development of educational programs in both the U.S. and developing or transition countries like China. The World Bank has been committed to assisting China and other developing countries with education projects aimed at reducing illiteracy and creating knowledge societies based on lifelong learning:

> ICT will only become an effective and mainstream tool of poverty reduction and sustainable development if the proponents of ICT for development can provide more rigorous evidence, strategies, benchmarks, indicators, and good practices that are directly relevant to the core poverty-reduction and development priorities of developing countries and their international partners. (Batchelor & Norrish, 2006, preface)

The role that the United States plays in the international higher education market is significant, given the history of the educational system previously described. Not only was the United States an innovator in higher education, it was an innovator in ICT development and expansion worldwide. Utilizing empirical research literature, ICT and education can be internationalized to effectively serve developing nations while minimizing the risks to native cultures, languages, and economies. Robin Middlehurst (2001) defines the external factors revolutionizing higher education systems as economic, social, intellectual, technological, and governmental policy changes and developments. U.S. institutions have witnessed unprecedented growth over the past century and have increasingly used ICTs to meet the learning and training needs of nontraditional, working adults. This "knowledge expansion, *and* specialization, *and* reconfiguration are a self-propelling phenomena" (Clark, 1998, p. 130). Similarly, China is expanding its ICT capacity at an unprecedented rate, becoming the fastest growing sector of the Chinese economy (Meng & Li, 2001); a tool that is increasingly used to serve growing numbers of postsecondary students, and provide needed training and education to rural areas (Zhiting, Xiaoqing, & Qiyun, 2003).

While these educational ICT expansions are generally serving the common good, there still exists controversy over Western educational ICT capitalizing on markets in developing nations. Concerns include (a) issues of access and equity, (b) the use of higher education as a commodity rather than a public good, (c) for-profit institutions dismantling the functions of the university, (d) quality and quality-assurance issues, (e) cultural and pedagogical issues (Van der Wende, 2002, p. 6); (f) linguistic barriers, and (g) restrictive legal and governmental policies (Fava-De-Moraes & Simon, 2000).

Higher education has traditionally been one of the most collaborative industries, sharing faculty, research, syllabi, and so on, and the innovations created through ICT are no different (Fuchs, 2004). The advantages for institutions to collaborate in international ICT projects, according to Fuchs, include efficiencies in cost and time; however there are disadvantages in collaborating which are even more exacerbated internationally. Security of intellectual property rights, obtaining copyright permissions, and overcoming security firewalls, differing network configurations, and bandwidth limitations are common frustrations for institutions (Fuchs, 2004; R. Wagenius, personal communication, September 22, 2006).

Critics of the ICT revolution argue that a *digital divide* is being created between the ICT-haves and have-nots, leading to greater gaps between rich and poor. Following what occurred in the United States, these *gaps* in the Western world are likely to become *chasms* in developing and transitioning nations (Bright & Yang, 2005; Gladieux, 2000). As technology and Internet use expanded in the late 1990s in publicly funded K-12 schools and wealthy and middle-class homes, the American Indians residing in mostly rural tribal communities and reservations had very little connectivity due to the lack of technology infrastructure in and near their rural communities (Casey, Ross, & Warren, 1999). "The lack of infrastructure and equipment is the greatest obstacle to tribes' attempting to achieve connectivity and networking systems in their communities" (National Congress of American Indians, 2001). The digital divide in the U.S. is still greatest among African Americans and Hispanics (Anderson, 1999), but American Indians, as the indigenous culture in America, should be considered important to the discussion on the impact of technology on indigenous cultures around the world.

While the chasm between the haves-and have-nots in the United States grew as Internet and wireless communications flourished, history has shown that the gap is widest at the initial introduction of the new technology (as was seen with telephone and television) and lessens as the technologies diffuse through society (Brescia & Daly, 2007). The creativity and ingenuity of the American Indians which had allowed their culture to prosper for thousands of years before the arrival of the Europeans, has shown promise in lessening this technology divide with forward-thinking and progressive programs being instituted on many reservations (National Congress of American Indians, 2001). William Brescia and Tony Daly's 2007 study of tribal leaders and businesses indicated that the technology skills and access most needed to assist their people and communities include the need for basic computer skills for the workplace (education and training opportunities), the ability to use *off-the shelf* computer programs to provide business and government technology solutions (rather than costly programming), the ability to troubleshoot business technology problems and solutions (problem-solving skills), further educate tribal government and business leaders about the safety and security of the computer and Internet, and perhaps most importantly, Indian leaders sought to create learning communities where their employees and community members could learn to use and become comfortable with technology. As technology infiltrates into other indigenous and aboriginal cultures worldwide, the American Indian's experience with integrating technology to better serve their communities is a valuable story to be told.

"Virtual space is infinite, but it does not promise universality or equity, nor is it appropriate for many students whose experience with technology is limited—and who might benefit far more from traditional delivery systems" (Gladieux, 2000, p. 353). University strategies focused on transnational programs will be highly dependent upon a number of key ingredients. "The strategic link between ICT or e-learning, and internationalization or global strategies, is worked out by institutions aiming to be 'global enterprises'" (Van der Wende, 2002, p. 12). Given the educational needs of developing countries, the risks that accompany the opportunities for higher education providers are crucial when considering developing international education programs that utilize ICT.

FUTURE OF INTERNATIONALIZATION IN HIGHER EDUCATION

If higher education in the United States and throughout the world continues on the internationalization path, made easier with ICT, it will be paramount for institutions in the United States and other Western countries to take into account the risks associated with introducing Western culture and the English language into another culture in the name of education. At the same time, these very institutions and nations cannot overlook the tremendous importance of introducing and integrating Eastern cultures and languages into the Western paradigm.

The technology gaps that may exist between urban and rural areas in developing nations can be extreme and the educational opportunities presented with ICTs can artificially create need for technology over that of the value of the education. Perhaps most importantly is the determination of the delivering institution to decide what their mission is in providing international education opportunities: is it to assist a people and a culture with positive societal change or is it to provide the institution with more enrollments and a more profitable bottom line? And, what is the cross-benefit attained for the home institutions' faculty, staff, and students, and what role does this play in the decision making process?

Providers of educational access should critically examine the development of their own nation's higher education systems as we have with that of the United States so that we might learn from the efforts of the past and ensure that the future is built on the highest ideals that education can offer.

REFERENCES

Academic Information Centre of Latvia. (n.d.). *GATS overview document*. Retrieved September 24, 2006, from http://www.aic.lv/rec/Eng/new_d_en/gats/ GATS_ovw.html

Anderson, R. (1999, October 14). Native Americans and the digital divide. *The Digital Beat, 1*, 1.

Apple, Michael W. (2005). Education, markets, and an audit culture. *Critical Quarterly, 47*(1-2), 11-29.

Batchelor, S., & P. Norrish. (2006). *Framework for the assessment of ICT pilot projects: Beyond monitoring and evaluation to applied research*. Washington, DC: World Bank Information and Development Program.

Bennett, Janet M., & Milton J. Bennett. (2004). Developing intercultural sensitivity: An integrative approach to global and domestic diversity. The Diversity Symposium, The American Institute for Managing Diversity.

Brescia, William, & Tony Daly. (2007). Economic development and technology—skill needs on American Indian reservations. *American Indian Quarterly, 3*(1), 23-43.

Bright, Larry K., & Jack Fei Yang. (2005). An East/West dialogue about universal technology access. *Asian Journal of Distance Education, 3*(2), 36-41.

Brubacher, John S., & Willis Rudy. (2005). *Higher education in transition: A history of the American colleges and universities* (4th ed.). New Brunswick, NJ: Transaction.

Byrne, John V. (2006, January). *Public higher education reform five years after the Kellogg commission on the future of state and land-grant universities*. A Report Issued by the National Association of State Universities and Land-Grant Colleges and the W. K. Kellogg Foundation.

Casey, James, Randy Ross, & Marcia Warren, (1999). Native networking: Telecommunications and information technology in Indian country. *Benton Foundation Communications Policy and Practice Program*. Washington, DC: Benton Foundation.

Clark, Burton R. (Ed.). (1998). *Creating entrepreneurial universities: Organizational pathways of transformation*. New York: Pergamon Press.

Czinkota, Michael R. (2005, April). *Loosening the shackles: The future of global higher education*. World Trade Organization symposium on cross-border supply of services, Geneva, Switzerland.

Daly, Herman E. (1999). *Globalization versus internationalization: Some implications*. Retrieved September 24, 2006, from http://www.globalpolicy.org/globaliz/econ/herman2.htm/

Daniel, John, Asha Kanwar, & Stamenka Uvalic-Trumbic. (2006, July/August). A tectonic shift in global higher education. *Change (Carnegie Foundation for the Advancement of Teaching)*. Retrieved October 13, 2006, from http://www.carnegiefoundation.org/change/sub.asp?key=98&subkey=1841

Ding, X., X. Gu, & Z. Zhu. (2005). The Chinese approach. In Christopher McIntosh & Zeynep Varoglu (Eds.), *Perspectives on distance education: Lifelong learning & distance higher education*. Vancouver, Canada: Commonwealth of Learning/UNESCO.

Douglass, John A. (2005). How all globalization is local: Countervailing forces and their influence on higher education markets. *Higher Education Policy, 18*(4), 445-473.

Eaton, Judith. (1997). The evolution of access policy: 1965-1990. In Lester F. Goodchild, Cheryl D. Lovell, Edward R. Hines, & Judith I. Gill (Eds.), *Public policy and higher education* (pp. 237-246). Needham, MA: Pearson.

Emmerson, Anne M. (2004). *A history of the changes in practices of distance education in the United States from 1852-2003*. Unpublished doctoral dissertation, Dowling College, Oakdale, NY.

Enders, Jürgen, & Oliver Fulton. (Eds.). (2002). Blurring boundaries and blistering institutions: An introduction. In *Higher education in a globalising world: International trends and mutual observations; a festschrift in honour of Ulrich Teichler*. Dordrecht, Netherlands: Kluwer Academic.

Fava-De-Moraes, Flavia. & Imre Simon. (2000). Computer networks and the internationalization of higher education. *Higher Education Policy, 13*(3), 319-326.

Friedman, Thomas L. (2006). *The world is flat: A brief history of the twenty-first century* (2nd ed.). New York: Farrar, Straus, & Giroux.

Fuchs, Ira H. (2004). Creating a collaborative information technology environment for higher education. In Maureen Devlin, Richard Larson, & Joel Meyers (Eds.), *The Internet and the university: Forum 2003* (pp. 129-167). Boulder, CO: Educause.

Gladieux, Lawrence E. (2000). Global on-line learning: Hope or hype? *Higher Education in Europe, 25*(3), 351-353.

Green, Madeleine F. (2004, Fall). GATS update. *International Higher Education, 37*. 3-5.

Harper, William Rainey. (1880). *Personal quote*. Retrieved July 22, 2007, from the University of Chicago Web site: http://www-news.uchicago.edu/president/history/harper.shtml

Harvard University. (2006). *Harvard university frequently asked questions*. Retrieved October 1, 2006, from http://www.harvard.edu/siteguide/faqs/faq14.html

Haycock, Kati, Barth Patte, Ruth Mitchell, & Amy Wilkins. (1999). Ticket to nowhere. The gap between leaving high school and entering college and high performance jobs. *Thinking K-16, 3*(2).

Hofstadter, Richard (1996). *Academic freedom in the age of the college: Foundations of higher education*. New York: Columbia University Press.

International Association of Universities. (2003, June). *Internationalisation of higher education: Trends and developments since 1998*. UNESCO Meeting of Higher Education Partners. Paris: Author.

Internet Modern History Sourcebook. (2001). *The industrial revolution*. Fordham University. Retrieved July 23, 2007, from www.fordham.edu/halsall/mod/modsbook14.html

Keillor, Garrison. (2007, June 18). Writer's almanac. *Minnesota Public Radio*. Retrieved July 25, 2007, from http://writersalmanac.publicradio.org/programs/2007/ 06/18/#Friday

Knight, Jane. (2002). *Trade in higher education services: The implications of GATS*. London: The Observatory on Borderless Higher Education.

Magrath, C. Peter (2000). Globalization and its effects on higher education beyond the nation-state. *Higher Education in Europe, XXV*, 251-258.

Marginson, Simon, & Gary Rhoades. (2002). Beyond national states, markets, and systems of higher education: A glonacal agency heuristic. *Higher Education, 43*(3), 281.

McLaren, Peter, & Ramin Farahmandpur. (2001). The globalization of capitalism and the new imperialism: Notes toward a revolutionary critical pedagogy. *The Review of Education/Pedagogy/Cultural Studies, 23*, 271-315.

Meng, Qingxuan, & Mingzhi Li. (2002). New economy and ICT development in China. *Information economics and policy, 14*(2), 275-295.

Middlehurst, Robin. (2001). University challenges: Borderless higher education today and tomorrow. *Minerva, 39*(1), 3-26.

Mooney, P., & McMurtrie, B. (2006, 2/17/06). The wild, wild East [Electronic version]. *The Chronicle of Higher Education*. Retrieved June 5, 2006, from Academic Search Premier database.

Office of the United States Trade Representative. (2006, March). *Trade in services policy brief.* Retrieved October 1, 2006, from www.ustr.gov/assets/Document_Library/ Fact_Sheets/2007/asset_upload_file846_10548.pdf

Oldehoeft, Arthur. (2006). *University of Iowa, department of computer science web page.* Retrieved October 1, 2006, from http://www.cs.iastate.edu/jva/jva-archive.shtml

The Open University. (2007). *Home page*. Open University Web site. Retrieved July 22, 2007, from http://www.open.ac.uk/

Sadlak, Jan. (2000). Globalization *versus* the universal role of the university. *Higher Education in Europe, 25*, 243-249.

Scott, John C. (2006). The mission of the university: Medieval to postmodern transformations. *The Journal of Higher Education, 77*, 1-39.

Scott, Peter. (Ed.). (1998). *The globalization of higher education*. London: SRHE and Open University Press.

United States Census Bureau. (2003). *Educational attainment in the United States: 2003*. United States Department of Commerce Economics and Statistics Administration.

United States Department of State. (2007). *Backgrounder on the Morrill Act*. Retrieved July 22, 2007, from http://usinfo.state.gov/usa/infousa/facts/democrac/27.htm

University of Chicago. (2007). *William Rainey Harper.* Retrieved September 16, 2007, from http://www-news.uchicago.edu/president/history/harper.shtml

Van der Wende, Marjik. (2002). *The role of U.S. higher education in the global E-learning market*. Research and Occasional Paper Series. CSHE.1.02. Berkeley: University of California, Berkeley.

Wertenbaker, Thomas J. (1947). *The Puritan oligarchy: The founding of American civilization*. New York: Grosset and Dunlap.

Wisconsin Electronic Reader. (2006). *The Wisconsin idea*. University of Wisconsin Library. Retrieved July 22, 2007, from http://www.library.wisc.edu/etext/WIReader/ Contents/Idea.html

Yang, Rui. (2002). *Third delight: The internationalization of higher education in China.* New York: Routledge.

Zhiting, Zhu, Gu Xiaoqing, & Wang Qiyun. (2003). A panorama of online education in China. *Educational Technology, 43*(3), 23-27.

PART II

PRINCIPLES OF CULTURALLY RESPONSIVE TEACHING AND CULTURALLY RESPONSIBLE CURRICULUM DEVELOPMENT

CHAPTER 6

AN INTRODUCTORY REFLECTION ...

AN ESSAY ON RECONCEPTUALIZING DEMOCRACY EDUCATION

Larry Hufford

If the role of civic education is to mold engaged, responsible citizens dedicated to creating a more just and peaceful nation and world, then educators must reevaluate the standard definition of *democracy*. Democracy comes from two Greek words: *demos* (the people) and *kratos* (authority or power). Definitions of democracy centered in Western political theory are variations of *government of, by, and for the people*. A survey of basic American government textbooks illustrates this point. Harvard University political scientist, Samuel Huntington, defines a democratic regime as one in which "the people elect their principal leaders in free, open, fair and periodic elections" (Jillson, 2002). Berman and Murphy state that "democracy is a system of government in which the people rule, either directly or through elected representatives" (Berman & Murphy, 2002). Other textbooks offer variations of these definitions (see Table 6.1).

Growing a Soul for Social Change: Building the Knowledge Base for Social Justice
pp. 103–117
Copyright © 2008 by Information Age Publishing
All rights of reproduction in any form reserved.

Table 6.1. Definitions of Democracy From Leading College Level Introductory Textbooks in American Government, Dictionaries, and Web Sites

"Elite Democracy: a theory of democracy that limits the citizens' role to choosing among competing leaders.... Pluralist Democracy: a theory of democracy that holds that citizen membership in groups is the key to political power.... Elite Democracy: a theory of democracy that limits the citizens' role to choosing." (Barbour, Wright, Streb, & Wolf, 2006, p. 15)

"Democracy: A system of government in which the people rule, either directly or through elected representatives." (Berman & Murphy, 2007, p. 9)

"America's commitment to democracy rests on a profound belief in an idealistic set of core values: freedom, equality, order, stability, majority rule, protection of minority rights, and participation." (Berman & Murphy, 2007, p. 13)

"Government by the people, either directly or indirectly, with free and frequent elections." (Burns, Peltason, Cronin, & Magleby, 2000, pp. 3-6):

Democracy as a System of Interacting Values:
- Personal liberty
- Respect for the individual
- Equality of opportunity
- Popular consent
- Democratic values in conflict

Democracy as a System of Interrelated Political Processes:
- Free and fair elections
- Majority rule
- Freedom of expression
- The right to assemble and protest

"According to our Founding Fathers, a democracy is a government by, for and of the people. This definition implies that the people are the main political force, demonstrated by their ability to vote officials into and out of office, engage in frequent and meaningful debates about relevant issues, and participate in *public life*–engaging in activities related to their community and possibly their country." (ACFnewsource, 1995)

"Liberal democracy is a representative democracy along with the protection of minorities, the rule of law, separation of powers, and protection of liberties (thus the name *liberal*) of speech, assembly, religion, and property." (Wikipedia, 2007)

Definitions of *Democracy*
1. Government by the people; a form of government in which the supreme power is vested in the people and exercised directly by them or by their elected agents under a free electoral system (*Dictionary.com Unabridged*, p. 1).

2. Government by the people, exercised either directly or through elected representatives (*American Heritage Dictionary*, p. 2).

3. The political orientation of those who favor government by the people or by their elected representatives (World Organization of the Scout Movement, p. 2).

(Table continues on next page)

Table 6.1. (Continued)

4. A system of government in which power is vested in the people, who rule either directly or through freely elected representatives (*American Heritage New Dictionary of Cultural Literacy*, p. 3).

5. A: Government by the people; *especially*: rule of the majority B: A government in which the supreme power is vested in the people and exercised by them directly or indirectly through a system of representation usually involving periodically held free elections. (*Merriam-Webster's Dictionary of Law*, p. 4)

"A meaningful definition of democracy must include the following ideals: recognition of the dignity of every individual; equal protection under the law for every individual; opportunity for everyone to participate in public decisions; and decision making by majority rule, with one person having one vote." (Dye, 2005, pp. 10, 12)

Minimum Requirements for a Country to be Defined as a Democracy:

- Control over government decisions about policy constitutionally vested in elected representatives
- Elected representatives chosen in frequent and fair elections
- Elected representatives exercise their constitutional powers without facing overriding opposition from unelected officials
- All adults have the right to vote in elections
- All adults have the right to run for public office
- Citizens have the right to express themselves on political matters, defined broadly, without the risk of state punishment
- Citizens have the right to seek out alternative sources of information, such as the news media, and such sources are protected by law
- Citizens have the right to form independent associations and organizations, including independent political parties and interest groups
- Government is autonomous and able to act independently from outside constraints (such as those imposed by alliances and blocs)

If any of these conditions is not present, experts argue that the country is not truly a democracy. (Graham, 2006, p. 3)

"Harvard political scientist Samuel Huntington defines a democratic regime as one in which the people elect their principal leaders in free, open, fair, and periodic elections." (Jillson, 2002, p. 16)

"The word *democracy* is nowhere to be found in the Declaration of Independence or in the U. S. Constitution, nor was it a term used by the founders of the Republic. It is both a very old term and a modern one. It was used at the time of the founding of this nation to refer to various undesirables: mobs, lack of standards, and a system that encourages leaders to gain power by appealing to the emotions and prejudices of the rabble.

The distinguishing feature of democracy is that government derives its authority from its citizens. In fact, the word comes from two Greek words: *demos* (the people) and *kratos* (authority or power). Thus democracy means *government by the people*, not government by one person (a monarch, dictator, or priest) or government by the few (an oligarchy or aristocracy)" (Magleby, 2006, p. 8).

(Table continues on next page)

Table 6.1. (Continued)

"Democracy today means representative democracy, or, to use Plato's term, a *republic*, in which those who have governmental authority get and retain authority directly or indirectly as a result of winning free election in which all adult citizens are allowed to participate." (Magleby, 2006, p. 9)

"Democracy: A system of rule that permits citizens to play a significant part in the governmental process, usually through the selection of key public officials." (Lowi, Ginsberg, & Shepsle, 2006, p. 5)

"Democracy provides opportunities for (a) effective participation, (b) equality in voting, (c) gaining enlightened understanding, (d) exercising final control [by the people—WR] over the agenda, and (e) inclusion of adults. The political institutions that are necessary to pursue these goals are (a) elected officials; (b) free, fair, and frequent elections; (c) freedom of expression; (d) alternative sources of information; (e) associational autonomy; and (f) inclusive citizenship." (Dahl, 1998, pp. 38, 85, in Reisinger, n.d.)

Democracy is "governance by leaders whose authority is based on a limited mandate from a universal electorate that selects among genuine alternatives and has some rights to political participation and opposition." (Danzinger, 1998, p. 159, in Reisinger, n.d.)

"Democracy is a form of government in which the policy decisions of the government are based on the freely given consent of the people and the people are guaranteed certain basic rights." (Volkomer, 2007, p. 4). "In a representative democracy (sometimes referred to as *republican government*), citizens transfer their decision-making power to people whom they elect to represent them.... The American social and economic theorist Joseph Schumpeter (1883-1950) once defined modern democracy as an 'institutional arrangement for arriving at political decisions in which individuals acquire the power to decide by means of a competitive struggle for the people's vote.'" (p. 5)

RECONCEPTUALIZING DEMOCRACY

If elections are the heart and soul of a democracy, then one would have to conclude that the United States was not a democratic society prior to the passage of the Voting Rights Act of 1965. Free and fair elections may demonstrate that a majority of voters support authoritarian rulers, such as Chavez in Venezuela or Putin in Russia. Does the fact that Iraq and Haiti have elected governments make them a democracy? Does the fact that the United States has an elected government make it a democracy? The answer lies in the definition of *democracy*.

The challenge to educators is to broaden the definition of democracy beyond the political realm. Democracy needs to be defined holistically if new generations of engaged citizens are going to create a more just and nonviolent community on the local, state, national, and global levels. Therefore, I propose that a holistic definition of democracy has four parts: political, cultural, economic, and ecological.

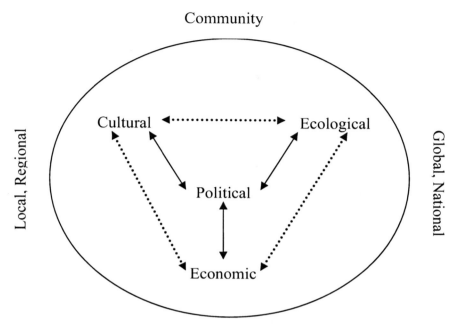

Figure 6.1. Holistic democracy.

POLITICAL DEMOCRACY

The generally agreed on minimal standard by which to judge whether a regime is politically democratic includes an electoral democracy constituted by the fundamental principals of representational government, constitutionalism, human rights, citizenship, civil society and a market economy (Dahl, 1998). Within this framework there are four components of civic education: (a) civic knowledge, (b) cognitive civic skills, (c) participatory civic skills, and (d) civic disposition (Patrick, 2003). Effective teaching of those components would emphasize the interconnectedness of all four, that is, to elevate one component over the other would be a pedagogical flaw that would impede an understanding of political democracy (Patrick, 2003).

According to Gandal and Finn (1992) the curriculum must cover four fundamental areas if students are to have a sufficient understanding of and appreciation for democracy.

1. Adequate attention must be paid to the roots and branches of the democratic idea as well as to the history of its expansion throughout the world.
2. The curriculum must help students explore how the ideas of democracy have been translated into institutions and practices around the world and through the ages.
3. The curriculum must explore the history of democracy in the students own nations.
4. The students need to understand the current condition of democracy in the world today.

The Gandal and Finn (1992) model is illustrative of the narrow emphasis on Western definitions of democracy as political. The danger of overemphasizing elections is that democracy can come to mean rule by a political or economic elite so long as it has been elected by popular vote. Joseph Schumpeter wrote that "the rule of the people is simply to produce a government. The people are sovereign only on election day. Once they have done their job, they should go back to their private affairs and leave governing to the elite they have selected" (Durand, 2006, para. 4).

There is much in Schumpeter's portrait that is descriptively accurate of the United States today. As Cliff Durand (2006) has written, "Citizens are absorbed in the concerns of private life and disengaged from politics" (para. 15). This leads one to question the strength of American democracy and, therefore, the role of education in teaching a narrow, compartmentalized view of democracy or empowering teachers to create an interdisciplinary, holistic democracy curriculum from Grades pre-K–12 on to introductory university courses in American government, economics, environmental science, and sociology/cultural anthropology. In holistic democracy, civil society consists of consensual social relationships citizens have with one another. Community, if it is to be healthy and whole, is participatory and relational. At the foundation, whether one is referring to the local, regional, national, or global community, there must be respect and trust rooted in shared values and positive interaction across racial, ethnic, sexual, class, and generational boundaries.

Civil society implies participatory democracy that is fundamentally dialogic. By this, one means that when individuals or groups speak they do so to be understood and that one, in turn, listens to understand. A holistic definition of *democracy* celebrates diversity and is not, in any way, about sameness. Holistic democracy is partly rooted in, "the Greek notion of *Isonomia*, meaning that all citizens are equal under the law and that political power should not be concentrated ... but should be distributed broadly among the members of the citizen body.... Isonomia is, therefore, equality *before* the law and *through* the law" (Hufford 1982, p. 124) To the Greeks, freedom and equality were attained by living and acting with others, in community. The law became formative power, the aim of which was to educate citizens to an ideal of character and action fulfilling the creation of a more just society. The task of educators today is to teach democracy in an interdisciplinary manner that enables and empowers students to understand that democracy with the end goal of a just society is far more complex than elections, civil liberties and civil rights.

In holistic democracy, individualism must be balanced by a strengthening of community. Individuals must learn to transcend *self-interest* narrowly conceived. The individual, in a holistic democracy, reaches her/his fullest potential as a member of a healthy community working towards a grassroots consensus based common good.

Pedagogically, at all levels, democracy education must emphasize the act of knowledge. By stressing the *act* of knowledge, educators can avoid a simplistic and overly idealistic compartmentalized, fragmented understanding of democracy. The key is to enable students to conceptualize the interrelatedness of political, economic, cultural, and ecological issues in the struggle to create more just communities.

Key values underlying an understanding of holistic participatory democracy are reciprocity, restraint and compassion. For example, reciprocity in a political, economic, cultural and ecological context resembles the Golden Rule of Life found in all major religions. It is participatory and relational and is at the core of healthy local, regional, national, and global communities. Restraint is a value that promotes the common good, especially in economic and ecological terms while compassion is the caring, sharing and giving that form the core of a just democratic society. Sharing also incorporates the democratization of political, cultural and economic power. These values are foundational to a healthy politically democratic process of determining the allocation of resources, protection of basic civil liberties and rights and preservation of the environment for future generations.

Economic Democracy

While political democracy is realized through an empowered, engaged, informed, active citizenry and is the key to respecting basic civil rights and liberties, economic democracy is basic to constructing a strong and healthy human society. Economic democracy, to be meaningful, implies that all citizens are guaranteed the minimum requirements of life: food, clothing, housing, education, and medical care (Sarkar, 1999).

Today, the global economy with institutional structures such as the International Monetary Fund, World Bank, and World Trade Organization, is experiencing a democratic deficit crisis. Globalization has positive and negative consequences, but the most serious issue is the absence of a transparent process of democratic decision making. Educators need to empower students to understand the implications of globalization and to effectively organize to ensure that global economic decision making process is more participatory, consensual and democratic. This explains the necessity to educate students to be responsible global citizens. Whether it is on the local, national or global level, patterns of citizen participation help define the nature of a democracy. Holistic democracy ought to have as a goal of global citizenship the transparency and accountability of decision making in transnational economic forces.

Economic democracy implies a market economy in which citizens function as responsible individuals concerned with the common good of the community. Holistic democracy promotes *economic self-management* which occurs when people have input into a decision proportional to the degree they are affected by it (Sarkar, 1999). For example, free market individualism often ignores the extent to which one's decision to emit a pollutant into the atmosphere might affect others (Shalom, 2006). If one returns to the Greek understanding of *demos* as the authority of the people in the political sphere, then *demos* could also imply the authority of the people in the economic sphere. Economic democracy not only removes decision-making power from an economic elite; it is the antithesis of a statist economic model. State central planning is undemocratic as is a system where a concentration of economic power corresponds to a concentration of political power. What educators must understand is that democratic participatory decision making is not simply a means of affecting goals; *it is an end in itself*.

Educators need to enable students to visualize the interconnectedness of political and economic democracy. For example, Gary Chartier (2001) documents that standard civil rights law textbooks address equal educational opportunity, public accommodations and housing, employment, the administration of justice, constitutional torts, the rights of linguistic minorities and people with disabilities, and affirmative action. However, only in chapters on voting is democracy discussed (Chartier, 2001). This, again, is a narrow view of democracy rooted in Western political theory. Chartier argues that a broader concern with economic democracy and economic justice grows naturally from an underlying concern for civil rights for three reasons:

1. Economic justice has always been a key goal of the civil rights movement.
2. The achievement of economic justice will contribute instrumentally to the achievement of the movement's noneconomic goals.
3. The underlying vision of the civil rights movement implies an understanding of community and human dignity from which a commitment to economic democracy flows.

This example illustrates the fact that educators need to be trained to conceptualize the connectedness of the component parts of holistic democracy.

Ecological Democracy

Ecological interdependence is becoming more apparent with a growing recognition of the depletion of the planet's single ozone layer, the threat of human-induced global climate change, the effects of pollution that cross international boundaries, the excessive use of renewable and nonrenewable resources on which many nations depend, and the declining populations of migratory species (Presbyterian Advisory Committee on Social Witness Policy, 1996). The thesis is clear: political, social, economic and ecological interdependence on a global scale is confronting humankind with extraordinarily complex problems. Holistic democracy rooted in the ecological crisis has two strategic principles:

1. Human solidarity is essential to an adequate response to interdependence. We are experiencing the moral reality of humanity's indivisibility.
2. Interdependence places a premium on coordinated thought and action. Everything is connected with every thing else ... new relational realities require new relational strategies (Presbyterian Advisory Committee on Social Witness Policy, 1996).

In the ecological and economic context, the issue is not growth but sustainable human development. Simply put, sustainability is living within the bounds of the regenerative, assimilative, and carrying capacities of the planet (Presbyterian Advisory Committee on Social Witness Policy, 1996). The concern for sustainability forces one to think holistically. Sustainable ecological and economic development is inextricably linked to human development. The Human Development Report of the United Nations describes human development as "development of the people for the people by the people." Human development theorist and practitioners meeting in Sri Lanka in 1986 observed that human development is an ethical concern that includes five dimensions:

1. an *economic* component dealing with the creation of wealth and improved conditions of material life, equitably distributed;
2. a *social* ingredient measured as well-being in health, education, housing and employment;
3. a *political* dimension including such values as human rights, political freedom, enfranchisement, and democracy;
4. a *cultural* dimension in recognition of the fact that cultures confer identity and self-worth to people; and
5. a dimension called the *full-life paradigm*, which refers to the meaning systems, symbols, and beliefs concerning the ultimate meaning of life and history (Goulet, 1991).

Enabling children and students to understand and live out their ecological interdependence with others and the natural world will require educators to enable and empower students to act collectively through a community based experiential curriculum. One consequence of such efforts would be that the line between school, home, workplace and the natural world would become less defined. Students' critical thinking, conceptual and analytical skills would be sharpened as they contextualized their interdependence within an understanding of holistic democracy. It is important for educators to understand that ecological democracy is a prerequisite for the establishment of sustainable human societies. There are many alternative programs/policies for solving the same environmental problems, so it is important for educators to remember that different solutions have different social, economic, cultural and political consequences. Once again, the practice of democracy is an end in itself. The process must be participatory and dialogic on all levels: local, regional, national and global.

Cultural Democracy

Teaching holistic democracy means teaching about an inclusive society. Inclusive democracy recognizes all citizens/members regardless of race, ethnicity, religion, gender, socioeconomic status and sexual preference. A basic human value to be promoted in democracy education is respect for human dignity. Teachers must sincerely practice this value on a daily basis. Educators must be exemplars of respect for human dignity.

Walter C. Parker (2002) agrees with Amy Gutmann that school education is a conscious social reproduction, arguing that education plays a critical role in learning democracy by teaching nonrepression and nondiscrimination and importing the values and confidence necessary for healthy civic participation. He also suggests that "cultural pluralism and equality are best served by nurturing the kind of democratic political community that in turn protects and nurtures cultural pluralism and equality, which in turn protect and nurture democratic political community." Educators can easily observe that cultural and political democracy are inseparable and that both are intertwined with economic and ecological democracy.

Parker (2002) proposes five practical tools with which educators can draw children creatively and productively into a multicultural democratic civic culture:

1. understand that democracy education is not a neutral project, but one that tries to predispose students (citizens) to principled reasoning and just ways of being with one another;
2. educators need simultaneously to engage in multicultural education and citizenship education;
3. the diversity that schools contain makes extraordinarily fertile soil for democratic education...dialogue across differences;
4. dialogue across differences plays an essential role education, moral development, and public policy; and
5. the access/inclusion problem that we face today is one of extending democratic education to students who typically are not afforded it (Parker, 2002; Singleton 2005).

Parker (2002) goes on to say in multicultural education tools of power should be shared with those who don't have them, while those who do have them must be educated to use them fairly and compassionately. "Democratic education is for everyone, and this includes those who (for now) have the most power, for they are in a position to do the most harm when they lack virtue" (Parker, 2002, p. xvii). Sacramento City College's Cultural Democracy Initiative (CDI) defines cultural democracy as "a philosophy of practice that recognizes and respects the diverse cultural paradigms. It is focused on transforming behavior to celebrate the richness that can be found in every culture" (Sacramento Community College, 2006). The CDI quotes Ralph Ellison:

> If you can show me how I can cling to that which is real to me, while teaching me a way into the larger society, then and only then will I drop my

defenses and my hostility, and I swill sing your praises and help you make desert bear fruit.

A nation that espouses political democracy yet demonstrates dubious concern for cultural democracy by showing little regard for the value and practices of diverse cultures, need educators committed to teaching and modeling holistic democracy. There is a need to promote a new global citizen-based cultural democracy movement. Brazilian sociologist Carlos Alberta Rabaca noted that key questions related to cultural democracy are (a) how to safeguard sovereignty and culture without fear of the advantages of international integration; (b) how to globalize without exclusion; (c) how to carry forth the advance of technology without killing humanism; (d) how to avoid citizenship becoming subordinate to dictates of the market; and (e) how to impede the monotheism of the market from transforming itself into an instrument of social control (Early, 2000).

Finally, in the context of cultural democracy, it is imperative that students today learn to respect, appreciate and understand the major religions of the world. With regard to teaching about the *religious other*, David Smock (2005) found that

1. One antidote to hatred between religious communities is to teach communities about the belief and practices of the religious other.
2. It is particularly important that teaching about the religious other be introduced in schools, universities, and seminaries.
3. In instructing about the religious other, instructors need to act as though they are in the presence of the other and to teach the religion as seen from the perspective of the believer.
4. Beyond studying scriptures, religious history, and theology, it is essential that students be exposed to rituals, worship, and music of the faith. This helps convey how believers of another faith actually live out their faith.
5. It is important to foster inter-religious dialogue at the academic level, at the grassroots level, and at the level of lived spiritualities.
6. Fears that studying about the religious other will undermine the religious convictions of students have generally proven to be unfounded.
7. Students are often better at studying other religions than at studying their own, because they usually approach the other faith with fewer preconceptions.
8. Some programs, particularly those geared toward younger students of one faith, have found it particularly effective to combine

learning about another religion with a shared service project that brings together adherents to both religions.

Regarding multi and interfaith dialogue, educators should step outside the classroom in search of a supportive learning community in which students can, in a safe, loving environment, have personal contact with the religious other. Learning how to engage in a meaningful sincere interfaith dialogue is a much-needed skill in our increasingly culturally diverse communities.

SUMMARY

It is apparent that the traditional Western approach to teaching democracy as only political is woefully inadequate in today's complex global society. Educators must teach democracy holistically, integrating political, economic, ecological and cultural democracy. This should be done by writing curriculum across disciplines where teachers complement one another, thus enabling students to understand and experience the interconnectedness of the four component parts of holistic democracy. The result will be more just and peaceful communities, from the local to the global. Learning and practicing holistic democratic values and principles will enable future generations to be more politically, culturally, economically and ecologically secure. The task of educators today is to affirm and extend measures in schools that demonstrate to children their attachment to one another and the world in which they live, that is, to teach and model holistic democracy.

REFERENCES

ACFNewsource. (1995, August 7). *Definitions of democracy*. Retrieved July 19, 2007, from http://www.acfnewsource.org/democracy/democracy_def.html

American heritage dictionary of the English language. (2005). Retrieved July 19, 2007, from http://www.bartleby.com/61/73/P0667300.html

American heritage new dictionary of cultural literacy. (2002). Retrieved July 19, 2007, from http://www.bartleby.com/59/13/democracy.html

Barbour, Christine, Gerald C. Wright, Mathew J. Streb, & Michael R. Wolf. (2006). *Keeping the republic: Power and citizenship in American politics*. Washington, DC: Congress Quarterly.

Berman, Larry, & Bruce A. Murphy. (2007). *Approaching democracy* (5th ed.). Upper Saddle River, NJ: Pearson Prentice Hall.

Burns, James M., Jack W. Peltason, Thomas E. Cronin, & David B. Magleby. (2000). *Government by the people: National version* (18th ed.). Upper Saddle River, NJ: Prentice Hall.

Chartier, Gary. (2001). *Civil rights and economic democracy*. Retrieved July 19, 2007, from http://washburnlaw.edu/wlj/40-2/articles/chartier-gary.pdf

Dahl, Robert. A. (1998). *On democracy*. New Haven: Yale University Press.

Dictionary.com (n.d.). *Democracy*. Retrieved July 19, 2007, from http://dictionary.reference.com/browse/democracy

Durand, Cliff. (2006). *Democracy and struggles for social justice*. Retrieved July 19, 2007, from http://www.globaljusticecenter.org/papers/durand1.htm

Dye, Thomas R. (2005). *Politics in America* (6th ed.). Upper Saddle River, NJ: Pearson Prentice Hall.

Early, James. (2000). *Towards a new cultural democracy: Artistic expression, culture, and sustainable development in the new global era*. Retrieved July 19, 2007, from http://www.folklife.si.edu/resources/center/cultural_policy/pdf/JamesEarly2000Towards.pdf

Gandal, Matthew, & Chester E. Finn, Jr. (1992). *Teaching democracy*. Retrieved August 17, 2007, from http://usinfo.state.gov/products/pubs/archive/freedom/freedom2.htm

Goulet, Dennis. (1991). Development: Creator and destroyer of values. *World Development, 20*(3), 469-470.

Graham, Paul. (2006, May 17). *Meaning of democracy*. Retrieved July 19, 2007, from http://aceproject.org/ace-en/topics/ve/vea/vea01

Gutman, Amy. (1987). *Democratic education*. Princeton, NJ: Princeton University Press.

Hufford, Larry (1982). Defining political equality: Modernizing *isonomia*. In Alacoque Power, Sr. (Ed.), *In words commemorated: Essays celebrating the centennial of Incarnate Word College* (pp. 119-155). Austin, TX: Best Printing.

Jillson, Calvin. (2002). *American government: Political change and institutional development* (2nd ed.). Toronto: Thomson Learning.

Lowi, Theodore J., Benjamin Ginsberg, & Kenneth A. Shepsle. (2006). *American government: Power and purpose* (9th ed.). New York: W. W. Norton.

Magleby, David. B. (2006). *Government by the people: Teaching and learning classroom edition* (6th ed.). Upper Saddle River: Pearson Prentice Hall.

Merriam-Webster. (1996). *Merriam-Webster's dictionary of law*. Retrieved July 19, 2007, from http://dictionary.reference.com/search?db=mwlaw&q=democracy

Parker, Walter C. (2002). *Teaching democracy: Unity and diversity in public life*. New York: Teachers College Press.

Patrick, John J. (2003). *Teaching democracy*. Retrieved August 17, 2007, from http://www.ericdigests.org/2004-2/democracy.html

Power, Alacoque, Sr. (Ed.). (1982). *In words commemorated: Essays celebrating the centennial of Incarnate Word College*. Austin, TX: Best Printing.

Presbyterian Advisory Committee on Social Witness Policy. (1996). *Hope for a global future: Toward just and sustainable human development*. Louisville, KY: Office of the General Assembly.

Reisinger, William M. *Selected definitions of democracy*. Retrieved July 19, 2007, from the University of Iowa Web site: http://www.uiowa.edu/~c030142/DefinitionsOfDemocracy.html

Sacramento Community College. (2006). *Cultural democracy*. Retrieved July 19, 2007, from http://web.scc.losrios.edu/cd/stories/storyReader$5.

Sarkar, P. R. (1999). *Requirements for economic democracy*. Retrieved July 19, 2007, from http://www.proutworld.org/ideology/ecdem/ecdemreq.htm

Shalom, Stephen R. (2006). *In search of economic justice*. Retrieved August 22, 2007, from http://www.wpunj.edu/newpol/issue40/Shalom40.htm

Singleton, Lianne. (2005). *Discovering democracy: Teaching democracy in the primary school*. Retrieved July 19, 2007, from http://www.abc.net.au/civics/democracy/pdf/td_primary.pdf

Smock, David. (2005) *Teaching about the religious other*. Washington, DC: United States Institute of Peace.

Volkomer, Walter E. (2007). *American government* (11th ed.). Upper Saddle River: Pearson Prentice Hall.

Wikipedia. (2007). *Democracy*. Retrieved July 19, 2007, from http://en.wikipedia.org/wiki/Democracy

World Organization of the Scout Movement. (2008). *Democracy—or a lack of democracy*. Retrieved July 19, 2007, from http://worldnet.scout.org/scoutpax/en/8/8_democracy_en

CHAPTER 7

LANGUAGE, CULTURE, IDENTITY, AND POWER

Immigrant Students' Experience of Schooling

Ming Fang He, Elaine Chan, and JoAnn Phillion

In this chapter we explore immigrant students' experience of schooling. We begin with a sketch of the increasingly diversified world landscape and describe the changing North American landscape. We briefly review research literature that addresses the experience of immigrant students and ethnic groups. We focus on *language, culture, identity,* and *power*—key terms that emerged in reviewing the literature on immigrant students' experience of schooling. We perceive language, culture, identity, and power as key issues in capturing the nuances of the schooling experience of immigrant students. One group of Asian American students and one group of Chinese Canadian students are the focal groups of the inquiries discussed in this chapter. We acknowledge that the terms *Asian American* and *Chinese Canadian* are contested and historically pejorative, and recognize diversity within this group in terms of ethnicity, language, culture, religion, and geographical areas. We employ these terms, however, since they are commonly used in the literature. We feature two major lines of inquiry and two specific studies to explore the interconnection between these key issues with a particular focus on how the dynamic interplay of language, culture, identity, and power impacts these immigrant students' experience of schooling. We conclude with a discussion of reasons we selected Asian American and Chinese Canadian immigrant students as the focus of this chapter. We extend our exploration of the schooling experience of Asian American and Chinese Canadian students to a discussion of the education of immigrant students in the United States, Canada, and the world landscape.

THE INCREASINGLY DIVERSIFIED WORLD LANDSCAPE AND NORTH AMERICAN LANDSCAPE

The world landscape is becoming increasingly multicultural and multilingual. United Nations Educational, Scientific, and Cultural Organization reported that more than 6,800 languages in 228 countries were in use in 2000. Approximately 185 million people worldwide live outside their countries of birth, up from 80 million 3 decades ago. The foreign-born population in 2004 represented 23.6% in Australia, 18.8% in New Zealand, 18.0% in Canada, 12.8% in the United States, 12.2% in Sweden, 10.6% in the Netherlands, and 7.8% in Norway (Organization for Economic Cooperation and Development, 2006).

This changing and diversified world landscape is reflected in the cultural and linguistic diversity in the United States and Canada, focal countries of this chapter. The foreign-born population of the United States (31.1 million) represented 11.1% of the total population in 2000 (U.S. Census Bureau, 2002). Latin America represented 52%, Asia 26%, Europe 16%, and other areas of the world 6.0% of the foreign-born population. In Canada, as of 2001, 18.4% of the total population, a total of 5.4 million people, were born outside the country. Of 1.8 million immigrants who arrived between 1991 and 2001, 58% came from Asia and the Middle East; 20% from Europe; 11% from the Caribbean, Central and South America; 8% from Africa; and 3% from the United States (Minister of Industry, 2003).

Immigrants coming to the United States and Canada are more diverse than ever. Not only do they arrive from a broad spectrum of countries, but they come from a wide range of linguistic, cultural, racial, and socioeconomic backgrounds (Statistics Canada, 2002b; U.S. Census Bureau, 2002). Previously, between 1890 and 1960, the majority of immigrants in the United States were from the British Isles and Northern and Southern Europe. Recent immigrants, however, tend to be from Asia, Central

America, and the Caribbean (U.S. Census Bureau, 2002). Similarly, immigrants arriving in Canada for the first 60 years of the past century tended to be from European nations such as the United Kingdom, Italy, Germany, and the Netherlands, as well as the United States. Since 2003, immigrants in Canada are more likely to be from Asian countries (Minister of Industry, 2003).

These changes in immigration patterns contribute to diversity in the United Sates and Canada. Over 500 ancestries were reported in the U.S. Census 2000 (U.S. Census Bureau, 2004) and over 200 ethnic origins were reported in the Canada 2001 Census question on ethnic ancestry (Minister of Industry, 2003). Immigration and migration have brought cultural and linguistic diversity not only to countries, but also to locales and, inevitably, schools.

The number of immigrant children aged 5 to 20 living in the United States grew from 3.5 to 8.6 million from 1970 to 1995, and will increase to 9 million by the year 2010 to represent 22% of the school-aged population. Currently, one in 15 schoolchildren was born outside of the United States, and one in seven speaks a language other than English at home (Ruiz-de-Velasco, Fix, & Clewell, 2000). In Canada from 1991 to 2001, there were 310,000 school children between the ages of 5 and 16 among the 1.8 million immigrants. For many of these children, the first language learned and used at home is neither English nor French, the two official languages in Canada (Minister of Industry, 2003).

Immigrant students in North American schools are learning to speak, read, and write in their new languages while their families often struggle with economic insecurity or poverty (Cummins, 1989, 2000, 2001). For these students, academic, physical, emotional, and social development challenges associated with economic insecurity are exacerbated by language barriers, migration and acculturation processes, and limited access to safety-net programs (Ruiz-de-Velasco et al., 2000). The educational system fails to meet the needs of this population (Cummins, 2001). Implications of this phenomenon for policy makers, school administrators, educators, students, and parents are enormous.

RESEARCH ON IMMIGRANT STUDENTS

Accordingly, researching issues of diversity in schooling has become of paramount importance in the United States and Canada. Educational research on immigrants addresses, among other issues, demographic research (Isajiw, 1999), immigration patterns and policies (Dentler & Hafner, 1997; Moodley, 1995); acculturation and enculturation (Brown, 1994; Herskovits, 1958; Schumann, 1978); voluntary and involuntary immigrants (Ogbu, 1978), bilingual education (Cummins, 1989, 2000, 2001; Ovando & McLaren, 2000); multicultural literacy (Courts, 1997; Well, 1998; Willis, García, Barrera, & Harris, 2003); and race, gender, and class issues (Grant & Sleeter, 1986). This work contributes to a theoretical understanding of the sociopolitical and cultural context of education of immigrant students. In addition, research in minority education by African American scholars (Banks & Banks, 1995; Delpit, 1995; Gay, 1988, 2000; Ladson-Billings, 1994) and scholars of Native American education (Deyhle & Margonis, 1995; Hermes, 2005; McCarty, 2002; Swisher, 1996) further informs policy making, pedagogy, and curriculum for immigrant education.

Within this large body of literature on immigrant students and minority students of color, there is less literature focused on their school experiences. Specifically, there is a need for more research addressing ways in which schooling shapes cultural and ethnic identity and sense of belonging in schools and communities; challenges of balancing affiliation to home cultures and participation in North American schools and communities (Lee, 1994; Rolon-Dow, 2004); and obstacles immigrant students encounter to achieving academic success when expectations, behaviors, and practices of school educators differ from those of families of immigrant and minority students of color (Valdés, 1996).

RESEARCH ON ETHNIC GROUPS

In addition to research on immigrant students, there is a wide array of research, primarily ethnographic, on ethnic groups. Much of this research is done by ethnic minorities or immigrants, and focuses on issues of language, culture, identity, and power within specific sociopolitical contexts. Addressing these issues, for us, is at the heart of understanding immigrant students' experience of schooling. There is a large body of research literature on the experience of African American and Black students inside and outside schools (Ladson-Billings, 1994; Thompson, 2002); a growing body of literature addressing the experiences of Hispanic students, including Mexicans, Mexican Americans, Puerto Ricans, Cubans, Chicanos, Latinos (Ada, 1988; Delgado-Gaitan, 1992; Noguera, 2003; Soto, 1997; Tapia, 1998; Valenzuela, 1999); Aboriginal and Native American students (Deyhle & Margonis, 1995; Hermes, 2005; Lomawaima, 1995); and Inuit students (Crago, Annahatak, & Ningiuruvik, 1993).

There is a developing literature on school experiences of Asian students (Lee, 1994, 2001; Kim & Chun, 1994; Pang, 1995; Lew, 2004); some highlights diversity between (Smith-Hefner, 1993) and within group differences (Lee, 1994). Research on the school and community experience of specific Asian groups such as Cambodian (Hornberger & Skilton-Sylvester, 2000), Hmong (Goldstein, 1985; Lee, 2001, 2005), and Vietnamese (Zhou & Bankston, 1998) is growing although research on the experience of some groups, such as Khmer (Smith-Hefner, 1990, 1993) and Tibetans (Phuntsog, 2000), remains relatively sparse.

Despite this growing body of literature on ethnic groups, there remains much we do not know about the experience of immigrant students of particular racial and language groups in North American schools. Much of the research examining the experiences of minority students in North American schools suggests that we may learn more about the complex ways in which identities are coconstructed and shaped in school contexts by acknowledging ways in which influences interact, rather than dichotomizing perceptions about schooling and identity among immigrant and minority students (Garcia, 1995; Hemmings, 1996; Lee, 1994; Rolon-Dow, 2004; Smith-Hefner, 1993).

LANGUAGE, CULTURE, IDENTITY, AND POWER

Key terms—*language, culture, identity*, and *power*—have emerged in reviewing literature on immigrant students' experience of schooling. These terms reflect the complexity of immigrant students' experience of schooling, and contribute to awareness of controversies in research, policy, and practice. Key *language issues* center on English language learning and heritage language maintenance (Cummins, 2000; Kouritzin, 1999; Wong-Fillmore & Meyer, 1992); English as a second language education and culturally incongruent curriculum and teaching (Au & Jordan, 1981; cf. Trueba, Guthrie, & Au, 1981); time needed to attain academic English proficiency (Cummins, 1989); and English proficiency and academic achievement (Valdés, 2001). Closely related to language issues are *culture issues* which include cultural discontinuity between homes, schools, and communities (Ada, 1988; G. Li, 2002; Vasquez, Pease-Alvarez, & Shannon, 1994; Valdés, 1996); cultural incompatibility in learning and teaching styles (Foster, 1995; Irvine & York, 1995); and race, gender, and class (Grant & Sleeter, 1986).

Issues of language and culture are at the center of controversy over identity. Key *identity issues* recognize identity as complex, fluid, and changing over time and place (He, 2003); developed in relationship with peers, teachers, parents, and grandparents (Chan, 2003, 2004; Lei, 2003); shaped by ethnic groups to which immigrant students belong and societal perceptions of specific ethnic groups (Lee & Zhou, 2004; Olsen, 1997); and impacted by sociopolitical and cultural contexts (Cummins, 2001; Nieto, 2000). The term power overarches and permeates research on language, culture, and identity (He, Phillion, & Roberge, 1999). Research on *power issues* includes the marginalization and disempowerment of minorities (Cummins, 2001; Darder, 1991), racism (McCarthy, 1990; West, 2001), poverty (Kozol, 1991), educational inequalities (Oakes, Ormseth, Bell & Camp, 1990), and critical pedagogy (Freire, 1970; Giroux, 1988; McLaren, 1989).

Language, culture, identity, and power are closely interconnected in immigrant students' experience of schooling. We now turn to specific studies to discuss this interconnection with a particular focus on how the dynamic interplay of language, culture, identity, and power impacts immigrant students' school success. Examining the impact of these factors in shaping immigrant students' school success is of paramount importance, given that significant numbers of immigrant students drop out of school. For instance, 39.4% of immigrant Hispanic students leave school without a diploma (National Center for Education Statistics, 2006).

Heritage language maintenance and bilingual education have been found to support English language acquisition (Cummins, 2001), which in turn enhances self-esteem and contributes to school success (Wong-Fillmore, 1991a, 1991b). In a rush to learn English in order to be accepted by their English-speaking peers, many North American-born immigrants in Kouritzin's (1999) study abandoned their heritage languages to overcome initial exclusion; these individuals, however, later felt excluded from their ethnic communities due to an inability to communicate in their heritage languages. Their English and heritage language proficiencies shaped their sense of identity and belonging in both their ethnic and North American communities.

Acknowledgment and inclusion of diverse cultures and languages in school contexts are crucial in promoting immigrant students' school success (Cummins, 2001; Wong-Fillmore, 1991a, 1991b). In a critical ethnographic study on the literacy development of immigrant children in her own classroom, Igoa (1995) found that the inclusion of home languages and cultures in classroom activities and lessons enhanced her students' sense of belonging in their U.S. classrooms and their sense of identity as members of their school and ethnic communities. Igoa argues that cultural resources children of diverse backgrounds bring into classrooms contribute to their social and academic development rather than hindering academic success and school adjustment.

Wong-Fillmore (1991a) addresses the detrimental effects of heritage language loss on families and ethnic minority communities when parents, who are not fluent in English, lose the ability to communicate with, guide, and teach their children. Wong-Fillmore (1991a, 1991b) examined the role of schools in contributing to the heritage language loss of children of immigrant and minority families. She highlighted the important role of educators in helping to prevent heritage language loss by supporting its maintenance. Cummins (2001) strongly advocates for the inclusion of ethnic cultures and languages in the classroom. He argues that heritage language proficiency is a distinct advantage as knowledge of language structures and components in the heritage language may be transferred to enhance the acquisition of English. This phenomenon, referred to as the linguistic interdependence principle, provides evidence against practices of encouraging ethnic minority families to abandon heritage languages in favor of English.

Cummins (2001) emphasizes the role of language and culture at school and home in shaping immigrant students' identities. Language, culture, identity, and power, for Cummins, are intertwined. Immigrant and minority students in his work feel that they do not have a sense of belonging when their heritage languages and cultures are not acknowledged in school. Their academic success and subsequent career success are jeopardized when schooling does not draw on the linguistic and cultural knowledge they bring to school. Other research demonstrates that immigrant students are more likely to succeed in school settings when they are not alienated from their cultural values (Heath, 1983; Ogbu, 1995). The lack of acknowledgement for home cultures was identified as contributing to the high dropout rate among Latino/Latina students (Zanger, 1994). Hertzberg's (1998) work with Mexican and Latino students further substantiated the positive impact of a nurturing school setting and a culturally flexible teaching approach where linguistic and cultural diversity were validated. Cummins (2001) concludes that incorporating immigrant students' linguistic and cultural knowledge in the curriculum creates an empowering school environment where immigrant students have a sense of belonging and feel proud of their heritage languages and cultures.

ETHNOGRAPHY AND MULTICULTURAL AND CROSS-CULTURAL NARRATIVE INQUIRY: IMMIGRANT STUDENTS' EXPERIENCE OF SCHOOLING

A large set of qualitative methodologies in educational research focus on experience, including autobiography (Grumet, 1992; Pinar, 1988), biographical method (L. Smith, 1994), cross-cultural narrative (Conle, 2000; He, 2002a, 2002b, 2002c), ethnography (Olsen, 1997; Valenzuela, 1999), hermeneutics (D. Smith, 1991), life history research (Hatch & Wisniewski, 1995), memoir (Neumann & Peterson, 1997), narrative multiculturalism (Phillion, 2002a, 2002b, 2002c, 2002d), oral history (Yow, 1994), personal narrative and narrative inquiry (Clandinin & Connelly, 2000), phenomenology (Van Maanen, 1990), and portraiture (Lawrence-Lightfoot &

Davis, 1997). Within this array of methods, we have identified two major lines of inquiry—*ethnography and multicultural and cross-cultural narrative inquiry*—that eclectically examine language, culture, identity, and power as key issues in immigrant students' experience of schooling.

The emergence of multicultural and cross-cultural phenomena in many disciplines has motivated the development of research approaches focusing on achieving in-depth understanding of diverse experiences of individuals, families, and communities. Much of the work was done by women, many are ethnographers and critical ethnographers, and some are narrative inquirers. Many are from the same ethnic background as those with whom they work, are fluent in the languages of the communities where they live and study, and advocate on behalf of students, parents, and communities (Carger, 1996; Feuerverger, 2001; Soto, 1997; Valdés, 1996; Valenzuela, 1999).

In the following sections, we review one ethnography and one multicultural and cross-cultural narrative inquiry that examine these interconnected phenomena. We demonstrate significant contributions these two lines of inquiry make to understanding the experience of schooling of Asian American and Asian Canadian students. We feature studies on one group of Asian American students and one group of Chinese Canadian immigrant students for reasons addressed in the previous section and further elaborated in the last section.

Ethnography

To foreground the lived experience of ethic and cultural groups (Tedlock, 2003), ethnographers ground research purposes and theoretical interpretations in the actual experience of their participants and embed inquiry in social, cultural, and political contexts. Ethnographers spend extensive time in the field, experience lives of the participants, and respect knowledge held by participants and their communities. Some ethnographers assume an advocacy stance as they develop a nuanced understanding of their experience in the field, critically examine experience, and search for opportunities to improve the lives of their participants.

Within the wide array of ethnographic research in the field of education, we refer to research focusing on issues of language, culture, identity, and power that, as elaborated above, are central to an understanding of immigrant students' experience of schooling (Delgado-Gaitan & Trueba, 1991; Feuerverger, 2001; Lee, 1996; Olsen, 1997; Soto, 1997; Toohey, 2000; Valdés, 1996, 2001; Valenzuela, 1999; Vasquez et al., 1994). In the next section, we feature Stacey Lee's ethnographic study (1996) as it represents the complexity of Asian American immigrant students' experience of schooling by eclectically exploring within-group diversity to challenge the model minority stereotype.

Stacey Lee—Unraveling the Model Minority Stereotype: Listening to Asian American Youth

Lee (1996) brought forward the voices of Asian American students silenced in the model minority stereotype in an American high school-based ethnographic study. She explored the impact of stereotypical perceptions of Asian Americans as model minorities on their school experience, relationships with non-Asian students, and sense of identity, and challenged this stereotype as inadequate in describing Asian American students' experience of language, culture, identity, and power. Among the small subset of Asian students in the school who acted as participants, the range of diversity in terms of language and culture, and commitment to, interest in, and success in academic endeavors varied immensely. One of her most significant findings was that these Asian American students developed their ethnic and racial identities within the context of interracial relationships in school (also see Olsen, 1997). Social and academic expectations corresponding to these students' membership in peer-labeled groups contributed to their academic performance and success, which in turn influenced their identities.

Drawing on knowledge gained through a six-month ethnographic study consisting of formal interviews, observations in and out-of-classrooms, informal conversations with faculty, students and staff, and participation in school activities, Lee (1996) examined social, cultural, and personal forces contributing to the formation of four Asian groups. Asian American-identified students were perceived as high achievers. The Korean-identified group attempted to accommodate to the White dominant group. The Asian-identified group developed a pan-Asian identity despite tensions and disputes carried over from their countries of origin. The new wavers represented a culture of resistance.

The students did not believe the labels accurately described them. High achieving Asian American-identified students, perceived as model minorities, felt strongly that the stereotype ignored challenges they had overcome in order to succeed and overlooked Asian Americans who were not doing well. Asian-identified students scorned students such as new wavers who displayed poor behavior and failed at school. New wave-identified students developed their identities in response to their negative experience with other groups and their marginalized position within Asian groups.

Although acknowledgement of similarities and differences within the ethnic group facilitates learning about the academic needs of an increasingly large Asian student population, the model-minority myth imposed expectations for the students based on sweeping generalizations rather than specific knowledge about individuals. Lew (2004) and Zhou and Bankston (1998) also elaborate on the negative effect of the model minority myth on Asian Americans who are at risk. The students recognize differences that set them apart from their Asian peers (Lee, 1996; Lee & Zhou, 2004) and need teachers and administrators to establish curricula that acknowledge their academic strengths and weaknesses rather than relying on stereotypes.

Lee explored interracial relationships among Asian American students and their non-Asian peers. She found that some White students and teachers used the success of Asian Americans as proof of a *color-blind* system where equal opportunity existed for students of all races. This perspective, sometimes used to silence claims of inequality among other minorities, fuels resentment toward Asian Americans' success. The extent to which Asian Americans themselves went along with stereotypes of other minority groups despite their own dislike of the model minority label further illustrated the power of stereotypes to influence interracial relationships negatively.

Lee identified structural barriers and hierarchy as factors contributing to these interracial tensions, and argued that tensions between members of ethnic and racial groups were rooted in structural positions in society. Lee referred to studies in which White students felt that their status was threatened when Asian American students succeeded academically. She found there was a direct link between a racial group's perceptions of their position in the system and their attitudes toward Asians/Asian Americans and Asian American success. More specifically, White and African American students' attitudes toward Asian Americans seemed to depend on their relative position in the system. These findings illustrate that although interracial tensions might not have originated in school, school policies, such as ranking top students in each grade, contributed to tensions through its culture of competition.

Identity, culture, language, and power are complex and interconnected phenomenon shaping Asian students' experience of schooling. Given the growing population in North America in recent years, the dearth of research examining these nuances is puzzling. Lee's study goes beyond the stereotype of Asian Americans as model minorities to reveal nuances of ways in which students develop ethnic and racial identities within the context of social expectations about their academic abilities and social preferences, and interracial relationships in schools. Lee has brought the study of Asian American students' experience into the discourse of mainstream scholarship and makes a significant contribution to the debate on the education of all immigrant students.

Multicultural and Cross-Cultural Narrative Inquiry

Narrative inquiry is another research methodology being used to gain knowledge and understanding of the school experience of immigrant and minority students. Researchers in different educational fields incorporate narrative, story, and experience into inquiries in education—Bell (1997), Carger (1996), and Valdés (1996) in language and culture issues; Ayers (2001), Foster (1997), and Michie (1999) in teacher narrative; Feuerverger (2001) and Soto (1997) in family and community narrative; Chan (2006, 2007), Elbaz-Luwisch (1997), Hollingsworth (1994), and Phillion (1999, 2002a, 2002b, 2002c, 2002d) in multicultural teaching and learning; Conle (2000), He (1999, 2002, 2002a, 2002b, 2002c, 2003), and Schlein (in press) in cross-cultural teaching and learning; and hooks (1991) in race, gender, and class. Narrative is also becoming prevalent as educational researchers draw upon critical race theory (Ladson-Billings, 1998). These researchers use stories to tell hidden and silenced narratives of suppressed and underrepresented groups to counter the preconceived meta narrative represented in 'scientific based research' that is often used to portray these groups as deficient and inferior.

Within narrative inquiry, there is a developing body of literature that explores language, culture, and identity as interconnected phenomena to contribute to a deeper understanding of immigrant students' experience (Carger, 1996; Chan, 2003; He, 2003; Kanno & Applebaum, 1995; X. Li, 2002; Phillion, 2002a; Xu, Connelly, He, & Phillion, 2007). Narrative inquiry may be distinguished from other forms of educational inquiry by its focus on understanding experience on its own terms rather than categorizing experience according to predetermined structures and theories (Phillion, 1999). In some forms of traditional educational research, experience is determined by theory, with the researcher using theoretically derived forms to interpret and write about experience. In contrast, experience represents the starting point in narrative inquiry, and is in the forefront at every stage of research (Clandinin & Connelly, 1994, 2000). As such, narrative inquiries arise from researcher and participant experiences rather than being formulated as abstract research questions, and they proceed by continual reference to experience as field texts are collected, analyzed and interpreted, and as meanings are crafted.

Fluidity is another quality of narrative inquiry. This notion of fluid inquiry is influenced by Schwab (Westbury & Wilkof, 1978), who refers to

> two kinds of inquiries: stable inquiry and fluid inquiry. Stable inquiry lends itself to fixed research phenomena, questions, purposes, objectives, methodologies, and outcomes ... ambiguity characterizes fluid inquiry ... focused on developing understandings of changing real-life situations and contexts,

rather than on the use of pre-established, often unfit, theory. (He, 2003, p. 80)

There is also a body of nonacademic literature, termed *life-based literary narratives* (Phillion & He, 2004), that explores nuanced life experience, in this case, of immigrant students. Life-based literary narratives include memories, autobiographies, and novels (Hoffman, 1989; Kaplan, 1993; Kingston, 1975; Rodriguez, 1982; Santiago, 1993; Tan, 1989). They portray in intimate detail language and culture learning and identity development from an insider perspective that highlights the temporal and existential dimensions of immigrant students' experience of schooling.

Multicultural and cross-cultural narrative inquiry (He, 2002a, 2002b, 2002c, 2003; Phillion, 2002a, 2002b, 2002c, 2002d) builds on Dewey's theory of experience (1938), Schwab's fluid inquiry (Westbury & Wilkof, 1978), Connelly and Clandinin's (1990; Clandinin & Connelly, 2000) narrative inquiry, multicultural perspectives (Gay, 1995; Ladson-Billings, 1994; Nieto, 2000; Sleeter & McLaren, 1995), life-based literary narratives (Hoffman, 1989; Tan, 1989), and ethnographic work (Soto, 1997). Multicultural and cross-cultural narrative inquirers explore the experience of language, culture, identity, and power by bringing personal, linguistic, cultural, and political experience to bear on inquiry; interpreting research as having autobiographical roots that are embedded in the life experience of language, culture, identity, and power; by thinking narratively and critically to view complex experience as a starting point for inquiry, as fluid and changing rather than fixed, as contextualized rather than decontextualized, as politicized rather than depoliticized; by being in the midst of changing lives and changing identities, seeing research as long-term, passionate, and cultural immersion in daily struggles of participants, rather than short-term, in and out, detached observation; and by making meaning of experience in relationships and contradictions, rather than making meaning in isolation and Hollywood stories (He & Phillion, in press; Phillion & He, 2001, 2007). Multicultural and cross-cultural narrative inquiry permits and encourages the study of human experience in the context of changing life and changing identity, and in the pursuit of broad educational questions in global contexts (He & Phillion, in press). It focuses on the complex and untold experience of marginalized and underrepresented groups and individuals played out in contested cultural, linguistic, and sociopolitical milieus.

Elaine Chan—Narratives of Ethnic Identity: Experiences of First- and Second-Generation Chinese Canadian Students

While Stacey Lee's (1994, 1996) work is an examination of the power of stereotypical perceptions of Asian American youth in shaping their identities, Elaine Chan's (2004, 2006, 2007) work is an exploration of the role of schooling experience in shaping students' sense of identity. Chan (2003, 2004), a second-generation Chinese Canadian, conducted a three-year narrative inquiry of the ethnic identity development of four first- and second-generation Chinese Canadian middle-school students in Toronto, Canada. She explored ways in which students' schooling experience interacted with their cultural experience of growing up in immigrant Chinese households to shape their ethnic identity as Canadian and Chinese.

Using a cross-cultural narrative inquiry approach, stories of the students' experiences were gathered through (a) long-term participant-observation, (b) informal interviews, and (c) the collection of documents, school notices, and communication between the students' families and teachers and administrators at their culturally-diverse, urban school. Chan examined the students' schooling experiences to identify ways in which participation in the curriculum and interaction with peers and teachers in school contributed to shaping their sense of identity as Chinese-Canadians. She focused in particular on challenges encountered by the students as they attempted to balance affiliation to their home culture and affiliation to Canadian culture.

Chan found that the students interpreted and expressed membership in their ethnic communities in relation to their knowledge of Chinese customs, English and Chinese language proficiency, physical appearance, academic performance, and length of residency in Canada. Examination of the interaction of culture and curriculum in this school context revealed personal and cultural tensions the four Chinese students encountered in their attempts to be accepted by their same-aged peer groups, while at the same time attempting to maintain maternal language proficiency and adherence to behavior standards of their parents and older members of their ethnic communities. Conflicts with peers revealed power differences among peer groups, with English-speaking students and earlier-arriving members of their ethnic groups setting standards for acceptance and belonging. Conflict with parents also became apparent as the students struggled towards academic success and adjustment to academic and social pressures to conform in school, while at the same time feeling compelled, pressured even, by their parents to assist in family businesses and to take responsibility for younger siblings and elderly grandparents. The students were often caught in the midst of these sometimes conflicting pressures. Chan's work also reveals nuances of ways in which immigrant Asian students' academic performance may be challenged by differences in expectations, behaviors, and practices between school educators and families of immigrant and minority students of color that G. Li (2002) also refers to in her work. In one instance, the homeroom teacher of one of the students, well-intentioned as he believed his student's academic performance was suffering due to a perceived over-commitment to responsibilities in the family business, called child protection officials to report her parents for negligence and a failure to support her future academic success.

Events and incidents observed in school highlight the imbalance of power that continues to persist despite claims to support diversity in schools and society through the existence of national multiculturalism policies (Minister of State Multiculturalism, 1988), school board educational equity policies (Toronto District School Board, 1999), and school-based practices that include the provision of ELL classes and translators to mediate between members of the school community and the families of immigrant and minority students. Learning about the students' experience also highlighted the extent of diversity within the ethnic group and provided insight into ways in which childhood school experience may contribute to ethnic identity development.

The students' experience featured in this research challenged the model minority myth (Kao, 1995; Kim & Chun, 1994; S. Lee, 1996; Stevenson & Stigler, 1992) in different ways and further confirmed its inadequacy in describing the complexities of identity development in ethnic minority students. The students' experience supports S. Lee's (1996) argument for the need to better understand diversity within the Asian community. The findings reveal nuances of ways in which achieving academic success is a challenge for these students as they balance affiliation to home cultures and participation in North American schools and communities. This study addressed Cook-Sather's (2002) statement of the dearth of research focusing specifically on examining students' experiences of schooling from their perspective (Erickson & Shultz, 1992; Schubert & Lopez, 1994), and Lee's (1996) call for more research examining ways in which schooling shapes cultural and ethnic identity and sense of belonging in Asian student communities.

The multicultural and cross-cultural narrative inquiry approach used in Chan's study allows for a deeper, more nuanced, understanding of the complexities of the interaction of culture, language, identity and power in an increasingly diverse global community. Examination of Asian immigrant students' experience of ethnic identity development and school curriculum contributes to our knowledge of the intricacies of building and sustaining vibrant ethnic communities while at the same time assisting immigrant students to integrate in meaningful ways into their new country.

WHAT DO INQUIRIES ENTAIL FOR THE FUTURE OF ASIAN AMERICANS, ASIAN CANADIANS, AND THEIR CHILDREN?

S. Lee's study shatters the stereotype of Asian Americans as model minorities and reveals nuances of ways in which students develop ethnic and racial identities within the context of social expectations about their academic abilities, social preferences, and interracial relationships in schools. Chan's study develops a deeper, more nuanced, understanding of the complexities of the interaction of culture, language, identity and power in Chinese Canadian immigrant students' experience of ethnic identity development and school curriculum. Lee and Chan's work, to some degree, brings the study of Asian American and Chinese Canadian immigrant students' experience of language, culture, identity, and power in schools and societies more firmly into the discourse of mainstream scholarship and public debate on education for immigrant students.

We have observed that these Asian Americans, Chinese Canadians, and their families, like many other immigrants, bring language, cultural, and ethnic diversity to North American communities, schools and classrooms. The linguistic heritage, cultural knowledge, and experience they bring to schools, however, are either ignored or overlooked, or not adequately or accurately represented in school curriculum, events, and activities. They are also by and large neglected in educational policy making in terms of funding programs, services, and educational resources (Yeh, 2002). This relative absence from the discourse in educational policy and practice, despite their growing presence in schools and society, are major reasons for featuring studies on Asian American and Chinese Canadian immigrant students in this chapter.

We have also found that the absence of their experiences and perspectives from school curriculum, policy making, and research literature are in stark contrast to their growing presence in schools and societies. More specifically, unprecedented numbers of Asian immigrants arrived in Canada and the United States in the past 2 decades (Statistics Canada, 2002a; U.S. Census Bureau, 2002). Of 31.1 million immigrants in the United States by 2000 (11.1% of the total population or 281.4 million people), 26% were Asian (11.9 million). In Canada, of 1.8 million immigrants who arrived between 1991 and 2001 (6.2% of the total population in 2001), 58% came from Asia. In contrast, immigrants from Asia represented only 47% of immigrants during the 1980s, 33% during the 1970s, and 3% before 1961.

We have also found that the ethnic and cultural diversity within Asian and Pacific American groups is often obscured and ignored in mainstream scholarship (Park, Goodman, & Lee, 2001). Asian and Pacific Americans are either excluded entirely from studies that focus on people of color or compared with European Americans and other minorities. Furthermore, Asian immigrant students are perceived as having "common experiences, backgrounds, aspirations, and stories" (Park, Goodman, & Lee, 2003, p. vii).

A number of educators have discussed the negative effects of the model minority myth (S. Lee, 1996, 1994; Park, Goodwin, & Lee, 2003). One of the major reasons supporting the exclusion of these students from the dominant discourse in education is "the stereotype that Asians do not have any problems (i.e., they are model minorities)" (S. Lee, 1996, p. 5). Yeh (2002) points out that misinterpretation of similar data have led to the stereotyping of Asian Americans as a group of high-achieving students who possess the skills and knowledge needed to succeed at all levels of education (also see Nakanishi, 1995).

The model minority image masks struggles and difficulties Asian students face. Thus, for us, Asian immigrants may be double-marginalized (Zhou & Gatewood, 2000)—they do not fit in the mainstream, dominant discourse nor do they fit in marginalized minority discourse. They may live in-between two worlds; not "Asian" enough to repatriate, and yet not "American" or "Canadian" enough to integrate. This perception masks the extensive amount of time and effort expended and overshadows the learning needs of those with limited English and a lack of resources and support (Xu et al., 2007). In addition, the model minority myth perpetrates resentment and hostility from members of the majority and other minority groups. This perception has even contributed to crimes being committed against Asians (Nakanishi, 1995).

We have also noticed that stereotypes of these groups shift dramatically as race relations change through history. Public images of an entire ethnic group may be threatened by a single catastrophe, such as the Virginia Tech tragedy, and are vulnerable to the acts of individual Asian students since they are viewed as a monolithic race category which is perceived to share common roots, backgrounds, experiences, and futures. Further, their voices are absent and quiet in the "public square—the common good that undergirds our national and global destinies" (West, 2001, p. 6).

As we live as Asian Americans or Asian Canadians or engage in research with these groups with shared concerns, we begin to realize that to understand Asian immigrant students' experience of schooling, we need to eclectically examine the nuances and complexities their experiences entail. The complex nature of experience that these immigrant students and their families bring to schools calls for approaches, such as ethnography and multicultural and cross-cultural narrative inquiry, that not only recognize diverse perspectives, but also draw on differences as a resource for interpreting immigrant students' experience to inform education policy and practice. We also recognize not only the importance of bringing the study of these groups to the forefront of mainstream scholarship and public educational debate, but also the significance of thinking further about what our inquires entail for the future of these groups.

We hope that Asian American and Asian Canadian scholars, educators, researchers, journalists, artists, and community activists will come together to bring issues of concern among Asian Americans and Asian Canadians to the forefront of educational discussion in the public sphere. Stacey Lee and Elaine Chan's studies demonstrate that the experience of one group of Asian American students and one group of Chinese Canadian students is a highly intricate combination of diverse experiences that go beyond traditional race relation theories, myths, and stereotypes. We hope that Asian Americans and Asian Canadians realize that "essentializing Asian American [and Asian Canadian] identity and suppressing our differences ... risks particular dangers: not only does it underestimate the differences and hybridities among Asians, but it also inadvertently supports the racist discourse that constructs Asians as homogeneous group" (Lowe, 1991, P. 24). We hope that they are not only able to accept the diversity among others but also within their own communities. We would urge them to speak out about their concerns with the education of their children and that of other people's children in the "public square" (West, 2001, p. 6). We also hope that they would "think globally and act locally" (Fong, 2002, p. 310)—join forces with other ethnic groups and immigrant and minority activists with shared concerns, and work together as allies in communities, schools, and societies to develop strategies to enact educational and social change that fosters equity, equality, freedom, and social justice. These joint efforts, for us, embody possibilities, create hopes and dreams, and invent spaces where Asian Americans, Asian Canadians, immigrants and disfranchised groups, and their children might live more robustly, equitably, and peacefully together in an increasingly changing and diversifying world.

REFERENCES

Ada, Alma Flor. (1988). The Pajaro Valley experience: Working with Spanish-speaking parents to develop children's reading and writing skills in the home through the use of children's literature. In Tova Skutnabb-Kangas & Jim Cummins (Eds.), *Minority education: From shame to struggle* (pp. 223-238). Clevedon, England: Multilingual Matters.

Au, Kathryn Hu-Pei, & Cathie Jordan. (1981). Teaching reading to Hawaiian children: Finding a culturally appropriate solution. In Henry Trueba, Grace Pung Guthrie, & Kathryn Hu-Pei Au (Eds.), *Culture in the bilingual classroom: Studies in classroom ethnography* (pp.139-162). Rowley, MA: Newberry House.

Ayers, William C. (2001). *To teach: The journey of a teacher.* New York: Teachers College Press.

Banks, James. A., & Cherry A. McGee Banks. (Eds.). (1995). *Handbook of research on multicultural education.* New York: Simon & Schuster Macmillan.

Bell, Jill Sinclair. (1997). *Literacy, culture, and identity.* New York: Peter Lang.
Brown, H. Douglas. (1994). *Principles of language learning and teaching* (3rd ed.). Englewood Cliffs, NJ: Prentice Hall.
Carger, Chris Liska. (1996). *Of borders and dreams: Mexican-American experience of urban education.* New York: Teachers College Press.
Chan, Elaine. (2003). OP-ED. Ethnic identity in transition: Chinese New Year through the years. *Journal of Curriculum Studies, 35*(4), 409-423.
Chan, Elaine. (2004). *Narratives of ethnic identity: Experiences of first generation Chinese Canadian students.* Unpublished doctoral dissertation, University of Toronto, Ontario, Canada.
Chan, Elaine. (2006). Teacher experiences of culture in the curriculum. *Journal of Curriculum Studies, 38*(2), 161-176.
Chan, Elaine. (2007). Student experiences of a culturally-sensitive curriculum: Ethnic identity development amid conflicting stories to live by. *Journal of Curriculum Studies, 39*(2), 177-194.
Clandinin, D. Jean, & F. Michael Connelly. (1994). Personal experience methods. In Norman K. Denzin & Yvonna S. Lincoln (Eds.), *Handbook of qualitative research in the social sciences* (pp. 413-427). Thousand Oaks, CA: SAGE.
Clandinin, D. Jean, & F. Michael Connelly. (2000). *Narrative inquiry: Experience and story in qualitative research.* San Francisco: Jossey-Bass.
Conle, Carola. (2000). Thesis as narrative: What is the inquiry in narrative inquiry? *Curriculum Inquiry, 30*(2), 189-213.
Connelly, F. Michael, & D. Jean Clandinin. (1990). Stories of experience and narrative inquiry. *Educational Researcher, 19*(5), 2-14.
Cook-Sather, Alison. (2005). *Education is translation: A metaphor for change in learning and teaching.* Philadelphia: University of Pennsylvania Press.
Courts, Patrick L. (1997). *Multicultural literacies: Dialect, discourse, and diversity.* New York: Peter Lang.
Crago, Martha B., Betsy Annahatak, & Lizzie Ningiuruvik. (1993). Changing patterns of language socialization in Inuit homes. *Anthropology & Education Quarterly, 24*(3), 205-223.
Cummins, Jim. (1989). *Empowering minority students.* Sacramento, CA: California Association for Bilingual Education.
Cummins, Jim. (2000). *Language, power and pedagogy: Bilingual children in the crossfire.* Clevedon: Multilingual Matters.
Cummins, Jim. (2001). *Negotiating identities: Education for empowerment in a diverse society* (2nd ed). Los Angeles: California Association for Bilingual Education.
Darder, Antonia. (1991). *Culture and power in the classroom: A critical foundation for bilingual education.* New York: Bergin & Garvey.
Delgado-Gaitan, Concha. (1992). School matters in the Mexican American home: Socializing children to education. *American Educational Research Journal, 29*(3), 495-513.
Delgado-Gaitan, Concha, & Henry T. Trueba. (1991). *Crossing cultural borders: Education for immigrant families in America.* London: Falmer.
Delpit, Lisa. (1995). *Other people's children: Cultural conflicts in the classroom.* New York: The New Press.

Dentler, Robert A., & Anne L. Hafner. (1997). *Hosting newcomers: Structuring educational opportunities for immigrant children.* New York: Teachers College Press.

Deyhle, Donna, & Frank Margonis. (1995). Navajo mothers and daughters: Schools, jobs, and the family. *Anthropology & Education Quarterly, 26*(2), 135-167.

Dewey, John. (1938). *Experience and education.* New York: Collier Books.

Elbaz-Luwisch, Freema. (1997). Narrative research: Political issues and implications. *Teaching and Teacher Education, 13*(1), 75-83.

Erickson, Frederick, & Jeffrey Shultz. (1992). Students' experience of the curriculum. In Philip Jackson (Ed.), *Handbook of research on curriculum: A project of American Educational Research Association* (pp. 465-485). New York: Simon & Schuster Macmillan.

Feuerverger, Grace. (2001). *Oasis of dreams: Teaching and learning peace in a Jewish-Palestinian village in Israel.* New York: Routledge Falmer.

Fong, Timothy P. (2002). *The contemporary Asian American experience: Beyond the model minority.* Upper Siddle River, NJ: Prentice Hall.

Foster, Michelle. (1995). African American teachers and culturally relevant pedagogy. In James A. Banks & Cherry A. McGee Banks (Eds.), *Handbook of research on multicultural education* (pp. 570-581). New York: Simon & Schuster Macmillan.

Foster, Michelle. (1997). *Black teachers on teaching.* New York: The New Press.

Freire, Paulo. (1970). *Pedagogy of the oppressed.* Baltimore, MD: Penguin Books.

Garcia, Eugene E. (1995). Educating Mexican American students: Past treatment and recent developments in theory, research, policy, and practice. In James A. Banks & Cherry A. McGee Banks (Eds.), *Handbook of research on multicultural education* (pp. 372-387). New York: Simon & Schuster Macmillan.

Gay, Geneva. (1988). Designing relevant curricula for diverse learners. *Education and Urban Society, 20,* 327-340.

Gay, Geneva. (1995). Curriculum theory and multicultural education. In James A. Banks & Cherry A. McGee Banks (Eds.), *Handbook of research on multicultural education* (pp. 25-43). New York: Simon & Schuster Macmillan.

Gay, Geneva. (2000). *Culturally responsive teaching: Theory, research, and practice.* New York: Teachers College Press.

Giroux, Henry. (1981). *Ideology, culture and the process of schooling.* Philadelphia: Temple University.

Giroux, Henry. (1988). *Teachers as intellectuals: Toward a critical pedagogy of learning.* South Hadley, MA: Bergin & Garvey.

Goldstein, Beth L. (1985). *Schooling for cultural transitions: Hmong girls and boys in American high schools.* Unpublished doctoral dissertation, University of Wisconsin-Madison.

Grant, Carl A., & Christine E. Sleeter. (1986). Race, class, gender in education research: An argument for integrative analysis. *Review of Educational Research, 56*(2), 195-211.

Grumet, Madeleine. (1992). Existential and phenomenological foundations of autobiographical method. In William Pinar & William Reynolds, *Understanding curriculum as phenomenological and deconstructed text* (pp. 28-43). New York: Teachers College Press.

Hatch, J. Amos, & Richard Wisniewski. (1995). *Life history and narrative.* London: Falmer.
He, Ming Fang. (1999). A life-long inquiry forever flowing between China and Canada: Crafting a composite auto-biographical narrative method to represent three Chinese women teachers' cultural experiences. *Journal of Critical Inquiry Into Curriculum and Instruction, 1*(2), 5-29.
He, Ming Fang. (2002a). A narrative inquiry of cross-cultural lives: Lives in China. *Journal of Curriculum Studies, 34*(3), 301-321.
He, Ming Fang. (2002b). A narrative inquiry of cross-cultural lives: Lives in Canada. *Journal of Curriculum Studies, 34*(3), 323-342.
He, Ming Fang. (2002c). A narrative inquiry of cross-cultural lives: Lives in North American Academe. *Journal of Curriculum Studies, 34*(5), 513-533.
He, Ming Fang. (2003). *A river forever flowing: Cross-cultural lives and identities in the multicultural landscape.* Greenwich, CT: Information Age.
He, Ming Fang, JoAnn Phillion, & Brigitte Roberge. (1999). Narrative understanding of bilingualism: A review of language, culture and power: Bilingual families and the struggle for quality education. *Curriculum Inquiry, 29,* 447-457.
Heath, Shirley Brice. (1983). *Ways with words: Language, life and work in communities and classrooms.* New York: Cambridge University Press.
Hemmings, Annette (1996). Conflicting images? Being Black and a model high school student. *Anthropology & Education Quarterly, 27*(1), 20-50.
Hermes, Mary. (2005). Complicating discontinuity: What about poverty? *Curriculum Inquiry, 35*(1), 9-26.
Hertzberg, Martha. (1998). Having arrived: Dimensions of educational success in a transitional newcomer school. *Anthropology & Education Quarterly, 29*(4), 391-418.
Herskovits, Melville J. (1958). *Acculturation: The study of culture contact.* Gloucester, MA: Peter Smith.
Hoffman, Eva. (1989). *Lost in translation: A life in a new language.* New York: Penguin Books.
Hollingsworth, Sandra. (1994). *Teacher research and urban literacy education: Lessons and conversations in a feminist key.* New York: Teachers College Press.
hooks, bell. (1991). Narratives of struggle. In P. Mariani (Ed.), *Critical fictions: The politics of imaginative writing* (pp. 53-61). Seattle, WA: Bay.
Hornberger, Nancy H., & Ellen Skilton-Sylvester. (2000). Revisiting the continuum of biliteracy: International and critical perspectives. *Language and Education, 14*(2), 96-122.
Igoa, Cristina. (1995). *The inner world of the immigrant child.* Mahwah, NJ: Erlbaum.
Irvine, Jacqueline Jordan, & Darlene Eleanor York. (1995). Learning styles and culturally diverse students: A literature review. In James A. Banks & Cherry A. McGee Banks (Eds.), *Handbook of research on multicultural education* (pp. 484-497). New York: Simon & Schuster Macmillan.
Isajiw, Wsevolod W. (1999). *Understanding diversity: Ethnicity and race in the Canadian context.* Toronto: Thompson Educational.

Kanno, Yasuko, & Sheila D. Applebaum. (1995). ESL students speak up: Their stories of how we are doing. *TESL Canada Journal/REVUE TESL DU CANADA, 12*(2), 33-48.

Kao, Grace (1995). Asian Americans as model minorities? A look at their academic performance. *American Journal of Education, 103*, 121-159.

Kaplan, Alice. (1993). *French lessons: A memoir.* Chicago: University of Chicago Press.

Kim, U., & Maria J. B. Chun. (1994). The educational *success* of Asian Americans: An indigenous perspective. *Journal of Applied Developmental Psychology, 15*, 329-339.

Kingston, Maxine Hong. (1975). *The woman warrior: Memoirs of girlhood among ghosts.* New York: Random House.

Kozol, Jonathan. (1991). *Savage inequalities: Children in America's schools.* New York: Crown.

Kouritzin, Sandra G. (1999). *Face(t)s of first language loss.* Mahwah, NJ: Erlbaum.

Ladson-Billings, Gloria. (1994). *The dream keepers: Successful teachers of African American children.* San Francisco: Jossey-Bass.

Ladson-Billings, Gloria. (1998). Just what is critical race theory and what's it doing in a nice field like education? *International Journal of Qualitative Studies in Education, 11*(1), 7-24.

Lawrence-Lightfoot, Sara, & Jessica Hoffmann H. Davis. (1997). *The art of and science of portraiture.* San Francisco: Jossey-Bass.

Lee, Jennifer, & Min Zhou. (Eds.). (2004). *Asian American youth: Culture, identity and ethnicity.* New York: Routledge.

Lee, Stacey J. (1994). Behind the model-minority stereotype: Voices of high and low-achieving Asian American students. *Anthropology & Education Quarterly, 25*(4), 413-429.

Lee, Stacey J. (1996). *Unraveling the* model minority *stereotype: Listening to Asian American youth.* New York: Teachers College Press.

Lee, Stacey J. (2001). More than "model minority" or "delinquents": A look at Hmong American high school students. *Harvard Educational Review, 71*, 505-528.

Lee, Stacey J. (2005). Learning about race, learning about *America*: Hmong American high school students. In L. Weis & M. Fine (Eds.), *Beyond silenced voices: Class, race, and gender in United States schools* (pp. 133-146). Albany: State University of New York Press.

Lei, Joy L. (2003). (Un)necessary toughness? Those *loud Black girls* and those *quiet Asian boys. Anthropology & Education Quarterly, 34*(2), 158-181.

Lew, J. (2004). The *other* story of model minorities: Korean American high school dropouts in an urban context. *Anthropology & Education Quarterly, 35*(3), 303-323.

Li, Guofang. (2002). "East is East, West is West"? Home literacy, culture, and schooling. In Joe L. Kincheloe & J. Arthur. Jipson (Series Eds.), *Rethinking Childhood* (Vol. 28). New York: Peter Lang.

Li, Xin. (2002). *The Tao of life stories: Chinese language, poetry, and culture in education.* New York: Peter Lang.

Lomawaima, K. Tsianina. (1995). Educating Native Americans. In James A. Banks & Cherry A. McGee Banks (Eds.), *Handbook of research on multicultural education* (pp. 331-342). New York: Simon & Schuster Macmillan.

Lowe, Lisa. (1991, Spring). Heterogeneity, hybridity, multiplicity: Making Asian American differences. *Diaspora*, 24-44.

McCathy, Cameron. (1990). *Race and curriculum*. London: Falmer.

McCarty, Teresa L. (2002). *A place to be Navajo: Rough Rock and the struggle for self-determination in indigenous schooling*. Mahwah, NJ: Erlbaum.

McLaren, Peter. (1989). *Life in schools: An introduction to critical pedagogy in the foundations of education*. New York: Longman.

Michie, Gregory. (1999). *Holler if you hear me: The education of a teacher and his students*. New York: Teachers College Press.

Minister of Industry. (2003). *Canada's ethnocultural portrait: The changing mosaic* (2001 Census: Analysis series). Ottawa, Canada: Statistics Canada.

Minister of State Multiculturalism. (1988). *Canadian multicultural act*. Retrieved August 4, 2005, from https://www.pch.gc.ca/progs/multi/policy/act_e.cfm

Moodley, Kogila A. (1995). Multicultural education in Canada: Historical development and current status. In James A. Banks & Cherry A. McGee Banks (Eds.), *Handbook of research on multicultural education* (pp. 801-820). New York: Simon & Schuster Macmillan.

Nakanishi, Don T. (1995). Growth and diversity: The education of Asian-Pacific Americans. In Don T. Nakanishi & Tina Yamano Nishida (Eds.), *The Asian American educational experience: A source book for teachers and students*. New York: Routledge.

National Center for Educational Statistics. (2006). Retrieved August 8, 2007, http://nces.ed.gov/pubs2006/dropout/tables/table_6A.asp?referrer= report*Dropout rates in the United States*. Washington, D. C.: Author.

Neumann, Anna, & Penelope L. Peterson (Eds.). (1997). *Learning from our lives: Women, research, and autobiography in education*. New York: Teachers College Press.

Nieto, Sonia. (2000). *Affirming diversity: The sociopolitical context of multicultural education* (3rd ed.). New York: Longman.

Noguera, Pedro. (2003). *City schools and the American dream: Reclaiming the promise of public education* (Multicultural Education Series). New York: Teachers College Press.

Oakes, Jeannie, Tor Ormseth, Robert Bell, & Patricia Camp. (1990). *Multiplying inequalities: The effects of race, social class, and tracking on opportunities to learn mathematics and science*. Santa Monica, CA: Rand.

Organization for Economic Co-Operation and Development. (2006). *Trends in international migration: Annual report 2006 edition*. Paris: Author.

Ogbu, John U. (1978). *Minority education and caste: The American system in cross-cultural perspective*. New York: Academic Press.

Ogbu, John U. (1995). Understanding cultural diversity and learning. In James A. Banks & Cherry A. McGee Banks (Eds.), *Handbook of research on multicultural education* (pp. 582-593). New York: Simon & Schuster Macmillan.

Olsen, Laurie. (1997). *Made in America: Immigrant students in our public schools*. New York: The New Press.

Ovando, Carlos J., & Peter McLaren. (2000). *The politics of multiculturalism and bilingual education: Students and teachers caught in the crossfire*. Boston: McGraw-Hill.
Pang, Valerie Ooka. (1995). Asian Pacific American students: A diverse and complex population. In James A. Banks & Cherry A. McGee Banks (Eds.), *Handbook of research on multicultural education* (pp. 412-426). New York: Simon & Schuster Macmillan.
Park, Clara. C, A. Lin Goodwin, & Stacey J. Lee. (Eds.). (2001). *Research on the education of Asian and Pacific Americans*. Greenwich, CT: Information Age.
Park, Clara. C, A. Lin Goodwin, & Stacey J. Lee. (Eds.). (2003). *Asian American identities, families, and schooling*. Greenwich, CT: Information Age.
Phillion, JoAnn. (1999). Narrative and formalistic approaches to the study of multiculturalism. *Curriculum Inquiry*, 29(1), 129-141.
Phillion, JoAnn. (2002a). *Narrative inquiry in a multicultural landscape: Multicultural teaching and learning*. Westport, CT: Ablex.
Phillion, JoAnn. (2002b). Narrative multiculturalism. *Journal of Curriculum Studies*, 34(3), 265-279.
Phillion, JoAnn. (2002c). Classroom stories of multicultural teaching and learning. *Journal of Curriculum Studies*, 34(3), 281-300.
Phillion, JoAnn. (2002d). Becoming a narrative inquirer in a multicultural landscape. *Journal of Curriculum Studies*, 34(5), 535-556.
Phillion, JoAnn, & Ming Fang He. (2007). Narrative inquiry in English language teaching: Contributions and future directions. In Chris Davison & Jim Cummins (Eds.), *Kluwer handbook of English language teaching* (pp. 919-932). Norwell, MA: Springer.
Phillion, JoAnn, Ming Fang He, & F. Michael Connelly (Eds.). (2005). *Narrative and experience in multicultural education*. Thousand Oaks, CA: SAGE.
Phillion, JoAnn, & Ming Fang He. (2001). Narrative inquiry in educational research. *Journal of Critical Inquiry Into Curriculum and Instruction*, 3(2), 14-20.
Phillion, JoAnn, & Ming Fang He. (2004). Using life-based literary narratives in multicultural teacher education. *Multicultural Perspectives*, 6(3), 3-9.
Phillion, JoAnn, & Ming Fang He. (2007). Narrative inquiry in English language teaching: Contributions and future directions. In Chris Davison & Jim Cummins (Eds.), *International handbook of English language teaching* (Vol. 2, pp. 919-932). Norwell, MA: Springer.
Phuntsog, Nawang. (2000). Immigrant Tibetan children in US schools: An invisible minority group. *Multicultural Perspectives*, 2(4), 17-21.
Pinar, William. (1988). Autobiography and the architecture of self. *Journal of Curriculum Theorizing*, 8(1), 7-36.
Rodriguez, Richard. (1982). *Hunger of memory: The education of Richard Rodriguez: An autobiography*. New York: Bantam Books.
Rolon-Dow, Rosalie. (2004). Seduced by images: Identity and schooling in the lives of Puerto Rican girls. *Anthropology & Education Quarterly*, 35(1), 8-29.
Ruiz-de-Velasco, Jorge, Michael Fix, & Beatriz Chu Clewell. (2000). *Overlooked & underserved: Immigrant students in U. S. secondary schools*. Washington, DC: The Urban Institute Press.
Santiago, Esmeralda. (1993). *When I was Puerto Rican*. New York: Vintage Books.

Schlein, Candace. (in press). The temporal experience of curriculum. *Curriculum and Teaching Dialogue*.

Schubert, William H., & Ana L. Lopez. (1994). Students' curriculum experiences. In Torsten Husen & Neville T. Postlethwaite (Eds.), *International encyclopedia of education* (2nd ed., pp. 5813-5818). Oxford, United Kingdom: Pergamon.

Schumann, John H. (1978). Social and psychological factors in second language acquisition. In J. C. Richards (Ed.), *Understanding second and foreign language learning* (pp. 163-178). Rowley, MA: Newbury House.

Sleeter, Christine E., & Peter L. McLaren. (Eds.). (1995). *Multicultural education, critical pedagogy, and the politics of difference*. Albany: State University of New York Press.

Smith, David. (1991). Hermeneutic inquiry: The hermeneutic imagination and the pedagogic text. In Edmund Short (Ed.), *Forms of curriculum inquiry* (pp. 187-209). Albany: State University of New York Press.

Smith, Louis M. (1994). Biographical method. In Norman K. Denzin & Yvonna S. Lincoln (Eds.), *Handbook of qualitative research* (pp. 286-305). Thousand Oaks, CA: SAGE.

Smith-Hefner, Nancy (1990). Language and identity in the education of Boston-area Khmer. *Anthropology and Education Quarterly, 21*(3), 250-268.

Smith-Hefner, Nancy. (1993). Education, gender, and generational conflict among Khmer refugees. *Anthropology & Education Quarterly, 35*(1), 8-29.

Soto, Lourdes Diaz. (1997). *Language, culture, and power: Bilingual families and the struggle for quality education*. Albany: State University of New York Press.

Statistics Canada. (2002a). *2001 Census analysis series: A profile of the Canadian population: Where we live*. Ottawa, Canada: Author.

Statistics Canada. (2002b). *2001 Census: Immigration and citizenship* (Table IM4: Country of last permanent residence by age group and gender). Toronto, Canada: Author.

Stevenson, Harold W. & James W. Stigler. (1992). *The learning gap: Why our schools are failing and what we can learn from Japanese and Chinese education*. New York: Simon & Schuster.

Swisher, Karen Gayton. (1996). Why Indian people should be the ones to write about Indian education. *American Indian Quarterly, 20*(1), 83-90.

Tan, Amy. (1989). *The joy luck club*. New York: Ballantyne Books.

Tapia, Johnny. (1998). The schooling of Puerto Ricans: Philadelphia's most impoverished community. *Anthropology & Education Quarterly, 29*(3), 250-268.

Tedlock, Barbara. (2003). Ethnography and ethnographic representation. In Norman K. Denzin & Yvonna S. Lincoln (Eds.), *Strategies of qualitative inquiry* (2nd ed., pp. 165-213). Thousand Oaks, CA: SAGE.

Thompson, Gail L. (2002). *African American teens discuss their schooling experiences*. Westport, CT: Bergin & Garvey.

Toohey, Kelleen. (2000). *Learning English at school: Identity, social relations and classroom practice*. Clevedon, England: Multilingual Matters.

Toronto District School Board. (1999) *Equity Foundation Statement*. Retrieved November 17, 2005, from http://www.tdsb.on.ca/_site/ViewItem.asp?siteid=15&menuid=684&pageid=548

Trueba, Henry T., Grace Pung Guthrie, & Kathry Hu-Pei Au. (1981). *Culture and the bilingual classroom: Studies in classroom ethnography*. Rowley, MA: Newbury House.
UNESCO. (2003). *Education in a multilingual world*. France: Author.
United States Census Bureau. (2002). *United States Census 2000*. Washington, DC: U. S. Government Printing Office.
United States Census Bureau. (2004). *Ancestry: 2000. Census 2000 Brief*. Washington, DC: U.S. Government Printing Office.
Valdés, Guadalupe. (1996). *Con respeto: Bridging the distances between culturally diverse families and schools*. New York: Teachers College Press.
Valdés, Guadalupe. (2001). *Learning and not learning English: Latino students in American schools*. New York: Teachers College Press.
Valenzuela, Angela. (1999). *Subtractive schooling: U.S.-Mexican youth and the politics of caring*. New York: State University of New York Press.
Van Manen, Max. (1990). *Researching lived experience: Human science for an action sensitive pedagogy*. Albany: State University of New York Press.
Vasquez, Olga A., Lucinda Pease-Alvarez, Sheila M. Shannon, & Luis Moll. (1994). *Pushing boundaries: Language and culture in a Mexicano community*. New York: The Press Syndicate of the University of Cambridge.
Well, Danny K. (1998). *Toward a critical multicultural literacy: Theory and practice for education for liberation*. New York: Peter Lang.
West, Cornel. (2001). *Race matters* (3rd ed.). New York: Vintage Books.
Westbury, Ian, & Neil J. Wilkof. (Eds.). (1978). *Science, curriculum, and liberal education: selected essays: Joseph J. Schwab*. Chicago: University of Chicago Press.
Willis, Arlette I., Georgia E. García, Rosalinda Barrera, & Violet J. Harris. (Eds.). (2003). *Multicultural issues in literacy research and practice*. Mahwah, NJ: Erlbaum.
Wong-Fillmore, Lily. (1991a). When learning a second language means losing the first. *Early Childhood Research Quarterly, 6*, 323-346.
Wong-Fillmore, Lily. (1991b). Language and cultural issues in the early education of language minority children. In Sharon. L. Kagan (Ed.), *The care and education of America's young children: Obstacles and opportunities. The 90th yearbook of the National Society for the Study of Education* (pp. 30-50). Chicago: The University of Chicago Press.
Wong-Fillmore, Lily, & Lois M. Meyer. (1992). The curriculum and linguistic minorities. In Philip W. Jackson (Ed.), *Handbook of research on curriculum: A project of American Educational Research Association* (pp. 626-658). New York: Simon & Schuster Macmillan.
Xu, Shijing, F. Michael Connelly, Ming Fang He, & JoAnn Phillion. (2007). Immigrant students' experience of schooling: A narrative inquiry theoretical framework. *Journal of Curriculum Studies, 30*(4), 399-422.
Yeh, T. L. (2002). Asian American college students who are educationally at risk. *New Directions for Student Services, 97*, 61-71.
Yow, Valerie R. (1994). *Recording oral history: A practical guide for social scientists*. Thousand Oakes, CA: SAGE.
Zanger, Virginia V. (1994). Not joined in: Intergroup relations and access to English literacy for Hispanic youth. In Bernardo M. Ferdman, Rose-Marie

Weber, & Arnulfo Ramirez (Eds.), *Literacy across languages and cultures* (pp. 171-198). Albany: State University of New York Press.

Zhou, Min, & Carl L. Bankston III. (1998). *Growing up American: How Vietnamese children adapt to life in the United States.* New York: The Russell Sage Foundation.

Zhou, Min, & James V. Gatewood. (Ed.). (2000). *Contemporary Asian America: A multidisciplinary reader.* New York: New York University Press.

CHAPTER 8

THE RELATIONSHIP BETWEEN READING AND ENGLISH COMPOSITION WRITING

Implications for Community Junior Secondary School Teachers in Botswana

Deborah Adeninhun Adeyemi

This chapter reviews the connection between reading and composition writing in English language teaching in the context of teaching English as a second language (ESL) in Botswana. It discusses ways of helping students relate reading and writing skills in order to enhance their ability to compose effectively and with greater ease. Finally, it discusses some of the implications of relating reading to composition writing for teachers of English at the community junior secondary school (CJSS) level in Botswana.

INTRODUCTION

As teachers of English as a second language grapple with the problem of students' inability to do continuous writing, especially English composition writing at the junior secondary school level in Botswana, it becomes necessary that educators explore other options to improve students' performance in this aspect of English language teaching and learning. A recent phenomenon is the idea of teaching reading and writing as processes. The processes involved in learning both skills are similar (Heller, 1995; Ross & Roe, 1990). This chapter supports the premise of relating reading as a prelude to the act of composition writing. This is because of the peculiar problem of learning English as a second language (L2) situation that confronts many Anglophone African countries, of which Botswana is one. Apart from teaching composition writing using the process approach, the problems of vocabulary development, structure and organization continues to persist in students' writing.

Much has been said about the reading and writing connection, with Heller (1995), Ross and Roe (1990) contending that the processes involved in learning both skills are similar. Also, Dionisio (1983) argues that the possession of the basic skill of reading can enhance the skill to compose and write. Questions on the reading/writing connection and the best way to integrate this connection in composition writing instruction needs to be explored further in order to enhance students' skill and ability in composing. Could the reading/writing strategy in conjunction with the process approach to composition writing lead to improvement in students' composition writing ability? Existing research will be cited to justify the idea and its implications for pedagogy in Botswana. Reading, in the context of this write-up, will relate to reading passages, materials, and models that are related to the composition topic. It is believed that the reading, discussion and examination of models in texts, reading passages or materials, as a part of and/or preceding activities in the composition writing process, would be beneficial at the middle level of secondary education. Finally, it is hoped that particular problems of composing such as paragraph organization, identification of main ideas or themes, language use and so on, can be addressed to a large extent through the use of the integration of reading to writing, with some implications for teachers of English at the junior secondary level in Botswana.

Objectives of This Study

The objectives of this work stem from the points previously raised and include to (a) review literature on the relationship between reading in English and English composition writing; (b) discuss efficient ways of helping students to take interest in and be able to transpose reading strategies/skills, to writing in order to enable them to compose effectively and with greater ease; and (c) provide implications of this relationship in enhancing the teaching and learning of English composition writing at the community junior secondary school level in Botswana.

Background to Botswana

The importance of English as an official language as well as the language of instruction in Botswana and the Commonwealth of Nations of which Botswana is a member cannot be overemphasized. Furthermore, it is a major language of intercultural communications and commerce, not only internally in Botswana, but regionally, within the continent of Africa and in the wider global context. Moreover, for a multilingual society, a reality in which many African countries take part, proficiency in English provides an enabling environment for communications.

English is of particular importance in the field of education; it permeates the entire curriculum and is closely linked to the achievement of all the 15 aims of the Basic Education Programme in Botswana (Republic of Botswana, 1994). Furthermore, except for Setswana, the language of the majority group and national language, English is used across the curriculum to teach concepts in other subjects to bring a deeper understanding into the teaching and learning of content materials (Republic of Botswana, 1996). Again, while the English language is a core subject in Botswana's education system, composition or extended writing is seen as one of the problematic aspects of the teaching and learning of English, especially at the junior secondary level.

The junior secondary education in Botswana runs for 3 years (Forms 1 through 3), and comes after 7 years of study at primary school. Junior secondary students are predominantly bilingual, studying English as a second language. A public or government junior secondary classroom in Botswana is mixed ability in nature, as the government's education policy does not allow for streaming of students. Thus, an average classroom consists of high, average, and below average ability groups. In this sense, the students are mostly visual learners, with problems of learning to read and write in ESL context.

Against this background, the importance of the ability to read and write effectively in English is imperative. This chapter, therefore, seeks to review descriptive and research literature on issues pertaining to the relationship between reading and writing and composition writing at the junior secondary level. Areas of emphasis will focus on the similarities in reading and writing as processes and the theories and practices that enhance effective reading and composing. Finally, this chapter will discuss ways of helping students lessen the difficulties they encounter in reading and composition writing in English by applying reading skills to greatly enhance their ability to compose effectively.

Problem Statement

It is observed that there are a series of challenges facing the teachers of English in Botswana in their continuing efforts to improve the writing skill of students in English composition or extended writing. It is also noted that the quality of students' performance in composition writing in the Junior Secondary Final Examinations is not encouraging (Republic of Botswana, 2001, 2005).

Again, a survey project report of the learning achievement of Standard Four pupils produced by the Botswana Ministry of Education (2001) indicates that even at the primary school level, only 21.9% of the pupils tested reached the competency level in literacy in English domains. For composition writing, the percentage competence was 7.2%. It is important to note that, it is the product of this level that will go on to junior secondary level after their primary level education in Standard 7.

From the experience of this author as a junior secondary language teacher for over a decade, there is constant discussion of frustration on the part of teachers at the students' lack of progress in the area of English composition/extended writing.

Writing in Botswana

In Botswana, most children learn to write both in their mother tongue and in English in the first 3 years of primary education and begin literacy in English from Standard (primary) 4 to Standard 7 and beyond (Republic of Botswana, 1994). The background is that learners would have been taught English as a subject from Standard 1 to 3. Thereafter it becomes the medium of instruction from Standard 4 to 7. From Standard 4 and above, learning to write in English becomes a new experience which is acquired laboriously (Honey, 2000).

In spite of these measures, Mooko (1996) notes that the quality of students' writing in Botswana schools is poor. In her study, Adeyemi (2004) concurs with Mooko that the writing competencies of Standard 7 students on entry to junior secondary school are very inadequate.

Certain types of writing, particularly those which involve projection into adult-type roles, tend to cause students difficulty. Arthur (1993), in one ethnographic study which pertains to the writing practice that Standard six pupils received in two primary schools in Botswana, found writing was confined to copying notes from the board, guided writing in which students did cloze exercises and sentence completion. Arthur argues that students' writing tended to vary only with respect to surface level accuracy. Also, Rowell (1991) points out that teachers and administrators in Botswana have made frequent references to inadequacies of students' written English by the time they enter form one of junior secondary school in Botswana.

Furthermore, the Botswana Ministry of Education Report of the Junior Certificate for English Paper 2 (2005), which consisted of composition and letter writing, notes that some centers attained a pass rate of just below 50%. It also notes that there were persistent errors arising from the problem of limited vocabulary and presumably lack of exposure to wider reading. As a result of these situations, writing is said to be more dependent on the use of the linguistic resources of a language and it is not difficult to figure out why writing is a commonly difficult activity for most students and especially for the learners of English as a second language (L2).

The Reading and Writing Connection

On writing effectively in English, it has been argued that reading has an important role to play. In other words, possession of the basic skills of reading can enhance the skills to compose and write (Dionisio, 1989; Graves & Murray, 1980; Ross & Roe, 1990). Further, Heller (1995) reiterates that the acquisition of reading and writing skills enables us to develop into the unique individuals we are capable of becoming and therefore develop into lifelong readers and writers. Simply put, it seems evident that there is a connection between reading and writing as some theorists believe that these two aspects of language, support, complement and contribute to each other's development (Hansen, Newkirk, & Graves, 1985; Sovik, 2003).

Modern Views on the Reading and Writing Connection

Cox (2002) quoting Tierney (1984) rationalizes why reading and writing should be taught together as follows:

- To help students get closer to their own thinking and to allow others to get closer as well.
- To provide a means for students to have a voice, to jot down their ideas for themselves and others and to share, compare and rethink.

- To give students the opportunity to be authors, helping them to realize that texts are written by people like themselves.
- To ensure that students take advantage of texts and resources that can fuel and enhance the meanings they develop and to help them see their own experiences in this light, too.
- To facilitate student-centered and meaning-oriented literacy activities and learning experiences that places a premium on the students' ideas and engagement.
- To motivate students to think and learn, as they read and write their own texts and those of others.
- To increase the amount of meaningful reading material available to students (pp. 353-354).

From the previous statements, it can be deduced that there are some connecting links between reading and writing, yet for at least the last 30 years, reading and writing have not been connected (Hansen et al., 1989). Recently, researchers and teachers are beginning to realize that reading and writing are closely linked. Reading provides the writer with the rich potential of language; writing deepens the reader's understanding of the importance of paying attention to imagery and genre conventions. This is especially true of situations where English is taught as L2. It is equally important that L2 learners have maximum exposure to reading to enrich their repertoire of language and its uses as noted by Judy (1980) and O'Dell (2006) that writers need content and that form grows from content. This seems to be a better way for L2 learners of English to develop content and form by reading from other writers and thereby learn to develop their own ideas and to express them in writing. It is desirable in an L2 classroom for junior secondary teachers in Botswana to emphasize reading as an important resource material that enhances writing.

Modeling and Reading in Composition Writing

The practice of reading model essays to learn writing skills can be traced back through history. Corbett (1965) traces the influence of these texts all the way to sixteenth century Europe. While other strategies have competed for primacy over time, the imitation of model essays has endured as an instructional approach. McCann and Smagorinsky (1988) found that although many texts are now starting to present writing as a process, they do so in a discrete section while retaining an emphasis on the study of model essays. Again, the field of composition writing is not unique in its assumption about the pedagogical soundness of studying models. Strupp and Bloxom (1973) studied the effects of modeling psychotherapy sessions and found that certain type of clients could benefit from watching a model of a therapy session before participating in one themselves. The primary assumption behind using models in writing instruction is that learners will see how good writers organize, develop, and express their ideas. Models are also supposed to be studied, questions asked, and answers debated before students come up with their own writing ideas and forms.

Escholz (1980) is one of the few authorities to defend the use of models in composition courses when he surmises:

> Certainly few people will take exception to the general rule that one good way to learn to write is to follow the example of those who can write well ... professional writers have long acknowledged the value of reading; they know that what they read is important to how they eventually write. In reading, writers see the printed word; they develop an eye—and an ear—for language, the shape and order of sentences, and the texture of paragraphs. (p. 63)

Irwin and Doyle (1992), quoting Escholz (1980) describe a three-stage teaching method for one type of writing as follows: (a) read a *classic*; (b) analyze the features of the model, focusing on organization, thesis, paragraph structure (depending on the need of your learners) and so forth; and (c) write a similar type of essay (pp. 162-163).

Escholz (1980) also concludes that by using models as *theme starters* students can eventually improve their own writing. However, critics of the approach such as Murray (1968) charge that models are irrelevant to writers' real needs and that a model only vaguely illuminates a particular kind of writing problem relevant to the student's own growth in composition. Other critics have also focused on the relationship between form and content. Judy (1980) argues that form grows from content and is inseparable from it, and that one does not simply pick a form and match ideas to it. Also, Gorrel (1977), in his criticism, cautions that if the reading is not related to writing, the course ceases to be a composition course. In support of Gorrel's view in this regard, it is important that teachers ensure that they link relevant reading materials to composition writing tasks or topics (see Liang & Dole, 2006; Nagin & National Writing Project, 2003; Swafford & Bryan, 2000).

On the other hand, Andreach (1976) and Stefi (1981) conclude that studies in which models were brief and stressed a few specific features improved students' writing to a notable extent. It is on this premise that the argument for this analysis is based, on the understanding that this approach will be favorable to learners of ESL. In fact, numerous research findings have attested to the linkage or connection between reading and writing as a more viable strategy in the teaching of writing in L2 situations.

Similarities in the Reading and Writing Process

In a related development, the Wisconsin State Reading Association (1993) reports that research continues to emphasize the link and similarities between the reading and writing processes and notes that:

- K-12 instruction has been conducted in ways that overlook the interrelatedness of reading and writing processes.
- Reading and writing are personal and social activities and are driven by a need to communicate.
- Reading and writing are reciprocal processes. Writers can learn much about writing by reading. Likewise, readers can learn much about reading by writing (p. 27).

This view is equally supported by Escholz (1980) who opines that vocabulary that students see in their readings usually manages to crop up in their writing. The relationship between reading and writing is a complex one and there is no one set of answers or a rigid set of rules. However, for pedagogical reasons alone it seems that reading and writing skills can be developed in an integrated way for students to see the connection and make measurable progress through the performance of realistic and relevant tasks. Moxley (1989) shows the interrelatedness of reading and writing development when he says that there are classroom methods that should be utilized to help writers understand the need for, critical avid reading; a variety of prewriting, revising and editing strategies which are equally the same processes used in the teaching and learning of reading and writing in general.

The Process Approach to Reading and Writing

Current theories of reading and writing go beyond the skills and product perspectives to take the interactive nature of language acquisition into consideration. For example, according to the schema theory in reading as noted by (Rumelhart, 1981), reading comprehension is an interactive process whereby the reader relates already existing knowledge to the meanings in the text. During the process, readers reconstruct the author's message, using prior experience present in the memory to create meaning or comprehend. As a result, comprehension becomes much more than a product or an outcome, but a process that enables the reader to learn from a written text.

Composition writing is also an interactive process as the writer seeks to construct meaning for an intended audience. While composing, the writer joins together, coordinates, and structures information for the purpose of communicating ideas. The schemata theory also applies here as students engage in focused discussion before reading or writing which enables them to use their previous knowledge or experience during comprehending and composing. Knowledge and understanding of text structure referred to by Hedge (2005) as crafting are also important to comprehension and composition because they deal with features of layout and discourse organization, paragraph organization and cohesive devices in writing. Text structure refers to those aspects of language that show how content is organized and related such as at the sentence level, paragraph level, and the whole text. Attention is drawn to these three levels throughout the composing process.

The Role of Reading in Writing

For over 2 decades, it has been known that reading ability, as measured by reading comprehension, is highly correlated with school performance in diverse subjects (Perfetti, 1976). Also, the disadvantage of failing to read early and fluently is clear. Some research findings indicate that those children who do not appear to make sound progress in early reading in their school careers quickly fall behind (Ferreiro & Teberosky, 1982; Stanovich, 1986). Thus the effects of poor reading ability are far reaching, as low academic achievement is linked to low reading ability. The implications of this are that, teaching composition writing to a student without the required reading skill and ability, without the ability to identify basic structure or knowledge of text organization can be frustrating not only for the teacher, but for the learner as well. Teachers of English in Botswana junior secondary schools should take note of this gap in their approach to the teaching of extended writing.

It is also important for teachers in Botswana to note the role of language comprehension in relation to reading and writing. It is suggested that comprehension be attached to reading and writing texts, as it involves meaning associated with printed information that is used for a particular purpose. Again, there are different levels of comprehension. At a basic level, readers access a word's meaning as a consequence of decoding. At a higher level, readers move beyond the words and engage in such activities as drawing inferences, finding main ideas, identifying facts and opinions and so on. Compared with poor readers, skilled readers approach texts with knowledge about how they are organized and with a strategy for acquiring information from them to compose texts, such as paragraph features, introduction, and conclusion. Without the acquisition of these skills by students, composition writing for both students and teachers would be a frustrating exercise. This writer's experience as a junior secondary teacher for over a decade attests to this fact.

Process and Product Approach to Writing Controversy

Nunan (1999) clearly states how very different the process approach is from the traditional product-oriented approach. Whereas the product approach focuses on writing tasks in which the learner imitates, copies and transforms teacher supplied models, the process approach focuses on the steps involved in creating a piece of text. He continues that the primary goal of product writing is an error-free, coherent text, while process writing allows for the fact that no text can be perfect, but that a writer will get closer to perfection by producing, reflecting on, discussing, and reworking successive drafts of a text. Nunan also, affirms that there is no reason why a writing program should not contain elements of both approaches. Jordan (1997) acknowledges that process writing evolved as a reaction to the product approach, in that it met the need to match the writing process inherent in writing in the mother tongue, and consequently allow learners to express themselves better as individuals. He, too, is quick to add that it will be wrong to assume that the product approach no longer exists, nor that it has no practical applications (which the use of modeling entails). Indeed, he says the process approach can still contain elements of product-based writing.

In junior secondary schools, the suggestion is that instructional methodology should aim towards recreating the conditions under which actual writing is performed, including: real academic time constraints; students working on their own disciplines or subjects; students focusing on the needs of a respective readership; and presentation of a text in an acceptable form as students would be expected to extend their writing skills across the curriculum (Norton, 1985).

The communicative approach to language teaching favored by the Botswana government demands that the process approach to composition writing be emphasized to focus on fluency and meaning rather than structure or accuracy in writing and that accuracy be emphasized where it interferes with meaning. The official acceptance of this methodology is reflected in the Junior Secondary English Syllabus (1996) which states:

The emphasis throughout this syllabus is on a communicative approach where the students learn the language by using it in meaningful interactions, communicative activities and problem solving tasks, thereby encouraging more spontaneous and natural discourse. (p. i)

The previously mentioned points, if examined carefully, suggest a sort of balance in the teaching of meaning in language use as well as structure. In order to address this situation, a teacher may attempt to strike a balance, by utilizing a combination of approaches to sensitize her or his students to the importance of form and process.

The discussion stages, so important in helping students to decide what they want to say (a feature of the process-driven approach), and the organization of ideas in note form, brainstorming or mind-mapping can be introduced using a model text at this stage. The use of a model text (a feature of a product-driven approach), at this stage, is not to subjugate students' ideas to their organization, but to make them aware that there is a particular way to express their ideas. In this way, students are given the form in order to enable them to adapt it to carry their own meaning.

According to Kilfoil and van der Walt (1997), extended writing is concerned with the development of discourse competence. In the same way that students have to be able to infer meaning from a text they read, they have to produce a meaningful and coherent text. The cohesive devices that link sentences and paragraphs have to be taught. By teaching students to focus on elements that link ideas (paragraphs), the teacher helps students to produce a coherent text. This aspect to writing can be taught through activities linked to modeling in the process of writing.

Furthermore, research proves that exposure to reading matter seems to be a determining factor in students' success in general, and in writing tasks in particular. As a result of the low socioeconomic position of most students and their parents, many students come from homes in which the printed word is a luxury. Malefo (1986) states that in most homes the only literature available is the child's school books, if there are any. Pretorius (1995) suggests a strategy whereby students are *flooded* with books in an effort to improve their writing abilities. It is evident that the availability and use of reading materials has a beneficial influence not only on writing competence, but on academic performance in general.

Finally, in language teaching and learning, no one approach is deemed ultimate especially in the context of second language learning. Also, this is not an attempt to roll the clock backward on the teaching of extended writing skills or smuggle product writing through the back door. It is just an attempt to evaluate the approaches to writing and explore the possibilities of having the best of two worlds. After all, James (1993) implies a combination of both process and product may reward teacher and students with the best of both approaches and eliminate the "perceived weaknesses" of the process and product approaches.

ESL Writing

Writing in English for ESL learners has been problematic over the years. Even among native learners of English it was problematic. As far back as the 1980s many teachers were realizing that all was not well in the teaching of writing. One of the key problems was that many children were turned off by writing. This was supported by some evidence from the Assessment of Performance Unit (1982). The Assessment of Performance Unit found that as many as 4 in 10 pupils had an active dislike of writing and endeavored to write as little as possible. Nearer home in the African continent in Anglophone Botswana, Mooko (1996), in his investigation notes that the current teaching approaches to composition writing have relegated writing to a solitary, lonely, and boring activity. Adeyemi (2004) notes that for most students writing is still a fearful and uninteresting activity which they would try to avoid as much as possible. Casterton (1986) infers that writing is an arduous, manual, emotional, and intellectual labor. All of this lends credence to the fact that writing is a most difficult activity for most learners, especially, learners of English as L2.

Furthermore, there is the cognitive aspect of writing that has to be dealt with. We grow up learning to speak without much conscious effort or thought and without systematic instruction. Writing on the other hand, is learned through a process of instruction. The written form of language, with its structure, and form which are sometimes less used in speech, but which are equally effective in communication in writing, has to be learned. The organization of ideas in a way that they can be understood by a reader who is not present and who may not be known to us also has to be learned. All these are challenging aspects of learning to write especially for learners whose mother tongue is not English. Finally, writing is a task which is usually imposed on us by circumstances. The psychological effect of what to say, which can be enhanced by vocabulary acquired from reading, may become a hindrance to students who lack the basic skill to do this when they are obliged to write.

All these problems and more, it is believed can be minimized if students are exposed to a model of a particular topic in their textbooks or models selected to fit their writing needs. The content, organization and form can be used as a theme starter for the students own writing. Moreover, the communicative approach to the teaching of language in Botswana schools (Republic of Botswana, 1996) favors the process approach, which many teachers have unquestioningly adopted.

In the modeling or reading strategy, students can be made to, and as part of the writing process, identify the paragraph organization, study content and language use through free discussion that elicit responses of alternative expression of similar ideas, forms and content. Questions on a theme or topic such as, *My Home* that would guide students to write their own composition on the same topic can include, for example:

1. What does Tshepo say about her or his home in paragraphs 1, 2, 3?
2. List what you would say about your own home in your composition in similar paragraphs.
3. Identify the concluding paragraph in Tshepo's writing. What are her or his feelings about her or his home?
4. Do you feel the same way about your home? If not, how do you feel about your home?
5. Unlike Tshepo, which particular information about your home would you share with readers?
6. Use the information you have given about your home to write a composition of three paragraphs.

From this example, students can proceed with activities related to the process approach to plan their own composition about their hometown using Tshepo's story as a theme starter. In this way, particular areas where students encounter difficulties can be highlighted and taught whether it be organization, language use or vocabulary, thereby connecting reading skills to writing skills.

Pedagogical Implications of Relating Reading to Composition Writing

In Botswana, literacy is important as a government policy as well as for economic, social, and educational purposes. For the individual, the ability to read and write is a status symbol; a form of meal ticket or a requirement for the procurement of a job or to offer certain services. In pedagogical terms, the introduction and practice of applying reading and writing skills to writing enables teachers to provide for the following:

1. Different learning styles and needs. Some learners feel more confident if they are allowed to read and write in the foreign language (English).

2. Written work serves to provide learners with some tangible evidence that they are making progress in the new language.
3. Exposure to the foreign language through more than one medium is likely to be more effective than relying on a single medium alone.
4. Most importantly, writing is needed for formal and informal testing (Byrne, 1988, p. 7).

Writing on the whole can be used as part of an integrated skills approach to language learning. It is important to note that writing activities will be largely a reinforcement of language learned by reading. The link between reading and writing can therefore be established. This means that reading can be taught in such a way that it prepares the learners for more realistic forms of writing at a later stage. As learners progress in the learning of language from primary to secondary schools, they need to be provided with written work on a more extensive scale and in particular integrate it more effectively with other skills.

Writing activities at this level can provide a basis for integrated learning through reading and writing. This is so because, students will have to write for examination purposes, as well as for social and economic purposes and on to academic writing of the type they are going to encounter in postsecondary and in later life. All these factors will increase students' motivation for writing and apart from concentrating on forms of writing that have a practical value, specific needs of students will be satisfied in areas of creative writing as well.

Readers and writers can also be compared during the acts of comprehending or composing. For example, while reading, the reader is actively involved both intellectually and emotionally in reconstructing the author's meaning. The reader actively plans, regulates, checks, and rechecks her or his thinking while reading (Palinscar & Brown, 1984).

Writers are also actively engaged intellectually and emotionally in constructing meaning. The writer consciously monitors her or his word choice, sentence structure, or paragraph organization in order to achieve a purpose for writing. The writer also constantly reads, and rereads what she or he has written during the act of composing, which supports the pedagogical implications of the interrelatedness of reading and writing skills. These pedagogical implications should be incorporated into the teacher education program, at the teacher training institutions in Botswana. The teaching and learning of the relationship between reading and English composition writing will enhance the teachers' ability to handle both reading and writing of English at the junior secondary level on graduation.

CONCLUSIONS

The teaching and learning of English as L2 poses a lot of challenges, especially in composition writing in schools in Botswana. The need to explore various options and strategies to overcome the difficulty is imperative. A combination of the reading/modeling and writing processes is an option that is worthy of consideration, not only in Botswana, but also in other Anglophone African countries having similar problems.

Even though relating reading to composition writing is not a new phenomenon, its use in developing countries of which Botswana is one, seems to be controversial as well as confusing. Where to draw the line, so as not to be seen as going against the established practice becomes blurred. Some theorists, especially those of the process school, would bluntly reject modeling/reading in extended writing practice as a feature of the traditional product orientation. On the other hand, the reality of its effect on students' performance suggests there is still much to account for, probably because of the peculiar L2 language situation and other factors that are not very obvious in the Botswana setting. It is hoped that the exposition in this chapter will set the ball rolling for further consideration of effective approaches or strategies that would be most beneficial to the teaching of extended writing in Botswana junior secondary classrooms.

REFERENCES

Adeyemi, Deborah Adeninhun. (2004). *Relative effectiveness of the individualized and the cooperative learning approaches in teaching composition writing at the junior secondary level: A case study.* Unpublished master of education research project, University of Botswana.

Andreach, James R. (1976). The use of models to improve organizational techniques in writing. *Dissertation Abstracts International, 36,* 4980-A.

Arthur, Jo. (1993). English in primary Botswana classrooms: Functions and constraints. In Casmir M. Rubagumya (Ed.), *Researching language in African classrooms* (pp. 66-78). Clevedon, Avon, England: Multilingual Matters.

Assessment Performance Unit. (1982). *Language performance in schools. Primary survey report.* United Kingdom: Department of Education.

Byrne, Donn. (1988). *Teaching writing skills.* London: Longman.

Casterton, Julia. (1986). *Creative writing: A practical guide.* London: Macmillan.

Corbett, Edward P. J. (1965). *Classical rhetoric for the modern student.* New York: Oxford University Press.

Cox, Carole. (2002). *Teaching language arts.* Boston: Allyn & Bacon.

Dionisio, Marie. (1983). Write? Isn't this reading class? *The Reading Teacher, 36,* 746-750.

Escholz, Paul. A. (1980). The prose models approach: Using products in the process. In Timothy R. Donovan & Ben W. McClelland (Eds.), *Eight approaches to teaching composition* (pp. 210-215). Urbana, IL: National Council of Teachers of English.

Ferreiro, Emilia, & Ana Teberosky. (1982). *Literacy before schooling*. London: Heinemann.

Gorrel, R. M. (1977). Question 11, 7. In Shuman R. Baird (Ed.), *Questions English teachers ask* (pp. 59-61). Rochelle Park, NJ: Hayden.

Graves, D., & Murray, Donald (1980). Revision in the writer's workshop and in the classroom. *Journal of Education, 162*, 38-56.

Hansen, Jane, Thomas Newkirk, & Donald H. Graves (Eds.). (1989) *Breaking ground: Teachers relate reading and writing in the elementary school*. Portsmouth, NH: Heinemann.

Hedge, Tricia. (2005). *Writing*. London: Oxford University Press.

Heller, Mary. F. (1995). *Reading-writing connections, from theory to practice*. White Plains, NY: Longman.

Honey, John. (2000). Language and social studies teaching. In Michael B. Adeyemi (Ed.), *Social studies in African education* (pp. 25-33). Gaborone, Botswana: Pyramid.

Irwin, Judith W., & Mary Anne Doyle. (1992). *Reading/writing connections: Learning from research*. Newark, DE: International Reading Association.

James, K. (1993). Helping students to achieve success in the information structuring of their academic essays. In George M. Blue (Ed.), *Language learning and success: Studying through English developments in English language teachers* (pp. 41-52). Hemel Hempstead: Phoenix ELT.

Jordan, Robert. R. (1997). *English for academic purposes: A guide and resource book for teachers*. Oxford, England: Oxford University Press.

Judy, Stephen. (1980). The experiential approach: Inner words to outer words. In Timothy R. Donovan & Ben W. McClelland (Eds.), *Eight approaches to teaching composition* (pp. 195-209). Urbana, IL: National Council of Teachers of English.

Kilfoil, W. R., & C. van der Walt. (1997). *Learn 2 teach: English language teaching in a multicultural context*. Pretoria, South Africa: J. L. van Schaik.

Liang, Lauren Aimonette, & Janice Dole. (2006). Help with teaching reading comprehension instructional frameworks. *The Reading Teacher, 59*(8), 742-753.

Malefo, B. M. (1986). Language in Black education: The environment outside the school. *Papers presented on the role of language in Black education*. Pretoria: Human Sciences Research Council.

McCann, Thomas, & Peter Smagorinsky. (1988). *Prospectus for composition textbook*. Unpublished manuscript, Department of Instructional Leadership and Academic Curriculum, University of Oklahoma, Oklahoma City.

Mooko, Theophilus. (1996). *An investigation into the impact of guided peer feedback and guided self-assessment on the quality of compositions written by secondary school students in Botswana*. Unpublished doctoral dissertation, University of Essex, England.

Moxley, Joseph M. (Ed.). (1989). *Creative writing in America: Theory and pedagogy*. Urbana, IL: National Council of Teachers of English.

Murray, Donald. M. (1968). *A writer teaches writing*. Boston: Houghton Mifflin.

Nagin, Carl, & National Writing Project. (2003). *Because writing matters: Improving student writing in our schools*. San Francisco: Jossey-Bass.

Norton, Donna. E. (1985). *The effective teaching of language arts*. Columbus, OH: Charles Merrill.

Nunan, David. (1999). *Second language teaching and learning*. London: Heinle & Heinle.

O'Dell, Felicity. (2006). Extensive reading activities for teaching language. *Modern English Teacher, 15*(3), 81-83.

Palinscar, Annemarie Sullivan, & Ann L. Brown. (1984). Reciprocal teaching of comprehension-fostering and comprehension-monitoring activities. *Cognition and Instruction, 1*(1), 117-175.

Perfetti, Charles A. (1976). Language comprehension and the de-verbalization of intelligence. In Lauren B. Resnick (Ed.), *The nature of intelligence* (pp. 283-292). Hillsdale, NJ: Erlbaum.

Pretorius, Elizabeth J. (1995). Reading as an interactive process: Implications for studying through the medium of a second language. *Communication, 21*(2), 29-31.

Republic of Botswana. (1994). *Revised national policy on education*. Gaborone, Botswana: Government Printer.

Republic of Botswana. (1996). *The three-year junior secondary syllabus (English)*. Gaborone, Botswana: Department of Curriculum and Evaluation.

Republic of Botswana. (2001). *Report on the monitoring of learning achievement*. Gaborone, Botswana: Ministry of Education, Examinations and Testing Division.

Republic of Botswana. (2005). *JC English paper 2 report*. Gaborone, Botswana: Department of Curriculum and Evaluation.

Ross, Elinor P., & Betty D. Roe. (1990). *An introduction to teaching language arts*. Chicago: Holt, Rinehart and Winston.

Rowell, Patricia M. (1991). *Communicating in the classroom: An interpretative study of two junior secondary schools*. Unpublished report submitted to IEES Research Foundation, University of Albany, New York.

Rumelhart, David E. (1981). Schemata: The building blocks of cognition. In John T. Guthrie (Ed.), *Comprehension and teaching: Research reviews* (pp. 3-26). Newark, DE: International Reading Association.

Sovik, Nils. (2003). *Writing: On developmental trends in children's manual and composition writing*. Hauppauge, NY: Nova Science.

Stanovich, Keith. E. (1986). Matthew effects in reading: some consequences of individual differences in the acquisition of literacy. *Reading Research Quarterly, 21*(4), 360-407.

Stefi, Locoque D. (1981). The effect of a guided discovery approach on the descriptive paragraph writing skills of third-grade pupils. *Dissertation Abstracts International, 42*, 2493-A.

Strupp, Hans H., & Anne L. Bloxom. (1973). Preparing lower-class patients for group psychotherapy: Development and evaluation of a role induction film. *Journal of Consulting and Clinical Psychology, 41*, 373-384.

Swafford, Jeanne, & Jan K. Bryan. (2000). Instructional strategies for promoting change: Supporting middle school students. *Reading and Writing Quarterly, 16,* 139-161.
Tierney, Robert J., & Margie Leys. (1984). What is the value of connecting reading and writing? In Bruce T. Peterson (Ed.), *Convergences: Transactions in reading and writing* (pp. 38-45). Urbana, IL: National Council of Teachers of English.
Wisconsin State Reading Association. (1993). *Position statement*: Madison: Wisconsin State Reading Association.

CHAPTER 9

DEVELOPING MULTICULTURAL SENSITIVITY THROUGH INTERNATIONAL STUDENT TEACHING

The Challenges Faced by a Southern University

Judy C. Davison and Terrence K. McCain

This chapter discusses the experiences of the faculty and students from a medium-sized university in the southern region of the United States in implementing an international student teaching experience. Most of the students from the teacher education program at this university are from rural communities with little exposure to diversity. Through a series of interviews with student teachers conducted before their experience and upon their return, we hoped to gain a better understanding of the successes and the challenges with our international student teaching project. Although research methodology was used, this chapter should be considered more as a fact-finding discussion than a major research endeavor.

PURPOSE

Education majors nationwide are increasingly facing classrooms of diverse students. The southeast region of the United States in particular, has witnessed a huge increase in the number of new arrivals to this country. The area our university serves has seen an increase in over 300% in the last 5 years of children representing 22 countries and speaking 26 languages (Mohl, 2003).

The population of teacher education students here follows the national trend with most being White, middle-class females. Most come from rural and small agriculture communities. They have little experience with global issues and even less with cultural and linguistic diversity. The experiences that they do have are usually in the form of church related mission trips for short periods of time to areas in Latin America or the Caribbean. According to Karen Cockrell, Peggy Placier, Dan Cockrell, and Julie Middleton (1999) those experiences only marginally contribute to cultural sensitivities. Cockrell et al. further state that the *culture gap* that results in part by teachers who lack an understanding of cultural diversity and their students continues to widen. It is our intent to assist in closing that gap for these students.

Education can be viewed as either domesticating or liberating (Sleeter et al., 2005). A domesticating education prepares students to follow authority figures with little or no resistance and accept their place in the system without questioning. Defining what counts as valued knowledge, skills, and traditions, as well as who gets to ask, maintains the power structure found in many institutions of public education. The students who participated in our Belize student teaching program are mostly first generation college students who have received the *knowledge transmission* factory model of teacher education. They acquire their knowledge and training for teacher education from those who are knowledge transmitters as opposed to producers as discussed by Sleeter et al.

Because we saw the need to raise cultural awareness among our students and also as a result of our university's membership in the Consortium for Belize Educational Cooperation (COBEC), we began a program to send our student teachers to Belize for a portion of their student teaching experience. By offering our students the opportunity to live and teach in an international setting we hope that they will become more culturally aware and more effective educators for the diverse population of students they will encounter in their classroom.

COBEC was established in the late 1980s to link postsecondary educational institutions in Belize and other countries for the purpose of strengthening and expanding their capabilities in higher education. At the present time 29 universities and colleges in the United States and Belize are members of COBEC. For over 20 years COBEC has maintained the following goals:

- Design, develop, and implement collaborative programs and activities that address higher education needs in Belize.
- Contribute to the internationalization of member institutions.
- Strengthen the organizational capacity of COBEC as a mechanism for meeting higher education needs in Belize and internationalizing member institutions.

Western Kentucky University (WKU) has been a member of COBEC since its initiation. One of the former vice presidents of the university was a founding member of COBEC and still maintains an active role in the organization's activities and projects. With his support we were able to integrate our student teaching program within the framework of the COBEC goal of contributing to the internationalization of member institutions. Our project was to organize service learning opportunities and internship (student teaching) experiences for students from both Belizean and non-Belizean member institutions.

Student teachers from the WKU International Student Teaching Program would be provided the opportunity to fulfill the following goals:

- Have the opportunity to apply teaching strategies in a cross-cultural setting.
- Learn to live in another culture, be flexible in new situations, and become better problem solvers and listeners.
- Experience firsthand the uniqueness the setting has to offer and share that experience with future students.
- Develop a global education perspective.

GETTING STARTED

In order to develop our program it was necessary for faculty from WKU to travel to Belize to make contacts, arrangements, site visits, and interviews with prospective administrators, teachers, and host family members. In February of 2004, two WKU faculty members attended the annual COBEC conference in Orange Walk Town, Belize. During that conference contacts were made and the feasibility of beginning a student teaching program there was discussed. Based on discussions with our contacts in Belize and the needs of our students, two areas of the country were chosen as potential placements sites. Our contacts at Galen University located in

San Ignacio agreed to collaborate with us to initiate this program. They have hosted our students since inception in November 2005.

San Ignacio is located about 18 miles from the Guatemalan border in western Belize. It is a small (15,000) community, and as is the case with much of the country, has a very diverse population. It is also the home of Galen University, a new and private university of less than 100 students and a member of COBEC. The university offers our students access to technology and contact with Belize college students, two areas lacking in other sites we considered. Our contacts in Galen were interested in our project for several reasons. They believed that it would open up dialogue between the two universities and offer opportunities for further faculty and student exchange as well as sharing teaching methods and strategies with our student teachers.

It was imperative that we consider certification requirements for our state as we developed the experience. Our student teachers placed in Belize follow the same curriculum and criteria as preservice student teachers placed in Kentucky schools. These include the following:

- Fulfill all WKU requirements for admissions to Teacher Education and student teaching.
- Ten semester hours credit for the student teaching.
- Supervised teaching by an on-site university supervisor or WKU coordinator.
- Participation in 16 weeks (12 in state and 4 in Belize) of student teaching.
- Reflective journals and writings used for self and university assessment purposes.
- Completed Teacher Work Sample, documentation of classroom teaching impact on learning.
- Participation in university seminars for student teaching.

Students who are interested in participating in our international student teaching program must satisfy these additional procedures prior to departure:

- Involve significant others in the early planning and discussions of this experience.
- Apply to the student teaching and/or international program by filing a request form indicating their choice of placement with a brief rationale.
- Submit letters of recommendation.

- Provide strong disposition evaluations including being flexible, friendly, self-reliant, and optimistic in new situations.
- Attend a screening interview with the program committee to discuss personal strengths and reasons for wanting to participate in an international student teaching assignment.
- Prepare a predeparture portfolio to learn about and prepare for the student teaching experience and the community.
- Provide for health insurance and any required immunizations.
- Sign an acceptance contract to student teach in an international school if an invitation to teach in Belize has been offered.

Ana Maria Villegas and Tamara Lucas (2002) write that in order for future teachers to understand their students, they must have an understanding of who they are culturally and socially. They need to know who they are through autobiographical reflection and critical self-analysis in order to understand the groups to which they belong. These groups include, gender, race, ethnicity, social class, and language. By understanding their attachments to these groups they can understand how belonging to these groups has shaped their personal and family attitudes toward others. By having an experience away from their own culture and being emerged into another culture, we anticipate a deeper understanding of their own and another culture to be achieved. We found the process of establishing international student teaching opportunities more difficult than anticipated. It is certainly more complex than just finding a site and students sign up to go.

CHALLENGES IN PROGRAM DEVELOPMENT

Recruitment

Initially few students responded to the opportunity for international student teaching. Faculty announcements were largely unproductive due to a number of reasons. Some reasons proposed are that faculty: (a) have time restraints, (b) have had some disappointing past experiences with international projects, and (c) not involved directly, lacked commitment to the program. Recruitment numbers for the first group were less than 20. Numbers of interested students have steadily increased to the present number of over forty. This increase is due in large part to the ongoing successes of returning groups and faculty members who are involved on a day-to-day basis with the project actively visiting classrooms and speaking to potential participants.

Financial

Our students typically come from low to middle social economic status. Therefore, when recruiting students, there is a common initial concern, often entirely discounting the opportunity, about the amount of finances required. Other international experiences offered on campus cost substantially more because of extensive travel components, housing accommodations, and often additional registration and/or admission fees which contributes to the perception that costs will be prohibitive in our program. However, we have been very conscious of this and strive to keep our cost at a minimum for students. Since we do not have significant funding for the international student teaching programming we cannot assure students of a set amount of money to assist them. However, we have been able to obtain minimal amounts from our college which sends a message of support from us. In addition, they have been able to receive varied scholarship amounts from the university international programs.

Faculty

Since we do not have funding for personnel to coordinate international programs through our college of education, any efforts for international collaborations are accomplished through faculty member's personal interest and willingness to contribute time and energy to develop such opportunities for students. This is also dependent on connections that faculty have made through personal and professional associations here and abroad. Furthermore, no financial compensation or teaching release has been available so, despite beliefs of individual faculty that international experiences are of significant benefit to our students, the time commitment can become burdensome and result in feelings of burnout of faculty who are heavily involved. For an international program to be successful there needs to be consistency to build and maintain trust from our partners. In addition, the student teaching director must also be committed and willing to contribute time and resources. We have been fortunate that our director has been not only supportive, but highly involved dedicating substantial time to the program's success despite the same time restraints as regular faculty. For those who may be considering implementation of international student teaching experiences, it should be noted that without the support of their student teaching director, it is unlikely that a program would be initiated.

Safety Issues

It is critical that we consider the personal safety risks involved in sending students to any area with limited supervision. We had originally requested funding to send a faculty member with groups of students to closely monitor the students teaching and travel and also collaborate with the local schools. However, our lack of funding made this prohibitive so we have relied on an onsite colleague to be available to students and monitor their experiences to a lesser degree. Despite preparations with students ahead of time, there is always an uncertainty to how they will respond to being in a totally different situation and, for some, the first time they have experienced the adventure of a foreign country and different culture.

Considering the background of our students, we were concerned that they would respond to the extremes of being too cautious and not taking any risk to really integrate into the local culture or being too adventurous and not recognize risky or dangerous situations. We have found it critical to clearly discuss safety issues with students in orientation sessions.

METHOD

Although this is primarily a descriptive account about initiating an international program, we did choose to use a qualitative approach to determine strengths, weaknesses, and impact of this new international student teaching experience for our teacher education students. Qualitative inquiry is the avenue through which interactions between individuals can be best examined (Rorty, 1989; Smith, 1993). Therefore, an examination of this international student teaching program through the use of interpretivist principles provides a better understanding of the perceptions of the participants in their decision to apply for international student teaching abroad and their interpretations of the benefit/impact to them after 4 weeks in Belize.

It is not the goal of this descriptive inquiry to include a random sample, but rather as a method to select individuals who have a genuine desire to learn from the Belize teaching experience and have dispositions that would be favorable for a successful learning experiences in that environment. In addition, we anticipated insight from the interviews would assist us in determining the success of the program and need for change in program implementation.

Participants

Student teachers participating in this international experience are in their final year of their preservice teacher education at this medium sized southern university. They come mostly from rural, agricultural communities. They have little or no exposure to cultural, racial, or language diversity. They are also overwhelmingly White and female. In the three groups that have participated there has been a total of 18 students, including only one male and one student of color. Those two participants were also the only participants who were secondary education majors. The others were elementary education majors or kindergarten through high school (K-12) certification.

Procedures

Prior to their international experience, students were interviewed about their perceptions on their personal life experiences and attachments and impact on their dispositions and choices. In addition, they shared their expectations about living and becoming a part of the community in which they would live in Belize. Semi-structured interviews were conducted with a question protocol that focused on background experiences, perceptions of Belize teaching experience and dispositions/attitudes that would be conducive to a successful international teaching experience. Personal interviews were taped, transcribed and analyzed for emerging themes.

RESULTS

Preexperience Interviews

Students often shared with us that if they have had any exposures to other foreign cultures, it has been from mission trips for short periods of time. Many of the students expressed a view of their international student teaching participation as a form of mission trip. The attitude that can come from this type of experience is one that can best be described as *helping those less fortunate*.

> I expect to see a lot of poverty, not a fast paced society. I expect to see low education standards. I am interested in mission work—it is a personal thing with me. (John)

> I originally wanted to go to Spain, but the timing was right for me this time. I have done mission work so I feel like I am ready. (Lou Ann)

> I have never been out of the country before; never been on a plane either. I don't know much about any other cultures other than White and Christian, but I am anxious to go on this trip. (Sherry)

White, middle class values are still the most valued in our society. Culturally aware and sensitive educators understand that this sense of dominance is derived from the power of the White, middle class groups not from sociocultural superiority (Villegas & Lucas, 2002).

Of the student teachers who had international experience, their view of student teaching in Belize was seen as an extension of that experience. It is somewhat as if they had their convictions reaffirmed as to the superiority of White, middle class America.

> I traveled in Asia and I saw things that are probably much worse than in Belize. I know how to react and what to say and I think the others might need me if things get difficult. I am very outspoken and not afraid to say what is on my mind. I know that we come with all this cultural baggage from the U.S. and expect them to think and behave as we do. I really want to show them that all Americans are not the same. (Shelley)

> I ultimately wanted to engage in this experience to make a difference in the children's life. Yeah, we have to adapt to another culture but it is worth it to teach the Belize children about our culture. (Heather)

Some of the students used the terms, *third world, backward, and primitive* to describe the people and culture of Belize. This is no doubt a result of lack of experience, misinformation and cultural bias perpetuated by popular culture and the widely held practice of comparing lifestyles and economic status with that of the United States. Ironically, their narrow view of Belizeans was in contrast to their expectations to find and take advantage of the rich natural resources of the country.

> I hope to see as many Mayan ruins, beaches, reefs, caves, and forests as possible and to get to know the other student teachers that are going on this trip. I hope that we are all able to travel and do lots of other exciting things together. (Lisa)

> The real reason I decided to go is to take a chance. I want to live my life to the fullest. I want to see all there is to see. More than anything I don't want my fears to hold me back from great things. (Theresa)

Postexperience Interviews

As with Kenneth Cushner and Jennifer Mahon (2002), our students reported an impact on their beliefs about self and others through increased cultural awareness and improved self-efficacy, as well as professional development in terms of global-mindedness. Intercultural consciousness is a more appropriate educational goal than multicultural competence (King & Baxter Magolda, 2005). Although we would like to have our students return multiculturally aware, if they return with at least a raised consciousness that reflects personal and professional growth, that is a step in the right direction. Our current groups are only immersed for four weeks so we acknowledge the limitations for such an abbreviated time.

Professional Growth

Through their successful teaching experiences in teaching in a culturally different setting, students are likely to acquire a greater sense of self-assurance in their personal and professional lives. Having a first hand experience of being an *outsider* develops sensitivity to their own future students who are displaced physically or through societal limitations. This change impacts on the way in which they teach. Although more longitudinal studies need to be done on the long-term effects, our students state they will be more multicultural in their teaching. One student interviewed 2 years after her experience reported that she not only is more multicultural in her teaching, she added the English as a second language (ESL) certification to work primarily with immigrant students.

> After my experience in Belize I realized what was always in the back of my mind, I really wanted to work with immigrant students. I left behind my thoughts of business education at a high school and am now an English as a second language teacher in a grade school and I love it. (Debbie)

In addition, students report that their international experience and broader knowledge of educational systems has made them more employable. Sandra L. Bryan and Marsha M. Sprague (1997) state that 9 of 10 returning students reported their beliefs that their international experience was a very positive factor in their teaching interviews, often resulting in more discussion of that experience than any other teaching qualities. Amy indicated this as well when she said, "Just about all the principal wanted to talk about was my experience in Belize."

Personal Growth

Those who are becoming teachers should have a chance to cross over through their studies and their personal experiences to a culture different from the one in which they have been born and raised. By working within a culture different from their own, they are provided a significant experience on which to compare. Through facing their personal anxieties and testing their own limitations, students create a space for opportunity and empowerment. In the words of Mahon and Cushner (2002), "Through the combination of different settings, the opportunity to form new relationships, and an expanded exposure to different pedagogical philosophies, student teachers can achieve self-assurance and a sense of accomplishment" (p. 5). This was likewise expressed in voices of our students:

> I really gained a sense of purpose from this experience. I now have more confidence and know that I will be great teacher. (John)
>
> I feel that I can get along with people now much better than before this trip. I know that I am more patient and flexible now. People were not concerned about the time like we are ... slower paced and less stressed. (Shelley)
>
> The people of Belize had a lot more to offer me than I had to offer them. People there are more patient than we are. We tend to be demanding and frustrated when things don't go our way. (Lou Ann)

Students also indicated they gained an appreciation for and understanding of their own culture, the similarities and differences to the Belizean culture. Shelley stated, "In many ways they are better off than we are. They aren't so materialistic and worried about things." A student interviewee in a Sleeter et al. (2005) study expressed this appreciation best, "As I'm looking back in time, I now understand that I had to travel abroad, beyond the borders of my country to understand and appreciate both my country's culture and history as well as the whole world's" (p. 292).

Mary C. Cross (1998) states that students, and international workers in general, develop a sense of self-confidence and self worth due to their global experience. Furthermore, she found that returned Peace Corps teachers had higher self-efficacy and an increased sense of confidence due to their experiences abroad than did a comparison group of teachers. This was reflected in comments made by our student teachers as well.

> I returned with more self-confidence and now I know I am able to do things I never thought I'd be able to do. (Debbie)

RECOMMENDATIONS

International experiences, while not for every student, can be a meaningful and powerful growth experience. The experience should make them more culturally aware while *honing* instructional skills. We have previously discussed many challenges in establishing international student teaching programs. As we continue to develop our program we recommend the following:

- Maintain relationships and extend to other areas.
- Pursue additional opportunities: Mexico, Bureau of Indian Affairs schools, Europe.
- Collaborate with other institutions sending students to Belize.
- Collaborate with other WKU colleges & departments seeking international experiences.
- Interview or survey first groups for lasting impact and transfer of knowledge into their teaching.
- Expand preparatory requirements to encourage deeper cultural understanding.

Laura L. Stachowski and James M. Mahan (1998) state that extensive preparatory requirements not only develop more cultural awareness in the students, but also is a vehicle to screen out those applicants who only want to play "tourist" as they tend to not be willing to do the amount of preparation work. Unfortunately, we have found that a few of our students who participate in international student teaching tended to have a "tourist attitude" about the experience. We witnessed that with one group in particular. They collectively decided to spend the minimum of time student teaching and took advantage of their host families and schools by traveling and site seeing in the name of cultural enhancement. Some other students became disillusioned, got homesick, or had unrealistic expectations and attempted to leave the program early.

> The food wasn't good and our family didn't feed us very well. It was the same thing everyday. Our rooms were small and uncomfortable so we moved out into a hotel. (Lou Ann)

> I just really wanted to go home, there wasn't anything new to do and I was spending too much money. (Sherry)

> I spent as much time in Guatemala as I could, I wanted to see as much there as possible in the time that we had. (Lisa)

PREPARATION OF STUDENTS

Cultural identity plays an important part in how people view and react to their world, how they view themselves, and how they learn. Mahan (1982) notes that it is essential that teachers serving a different cultural group than their own become highly knowledgeable concerning the culture, conditions, and aspirations of the people they teach (p. 164). Furthermore, Stachowski and Mahan (1998) recommend that participants in cultural immersion projects undergo extensive preparation (including seminars, reading, workshops, and sessions with consultants from the host cultural groups (p. 156). While we did not have necessary support to conduct the suggested extensive recommended activities, we did what we could on a more informal basis. This is an area that will be improved, especially now that the program has been successful and drawing larger numbers of students each year. The following are suggested possibilities as part of a student selection process and also in preparing students for the international experiences:

- Academic criteria—grade point averages of 3.00 and above.
- Cultural—cultural sensitivity as reflected in interviews with the committee.
- Readings—assigning specific readings related to cultural awareness in general and also specific to the area in which they are teaching.
- Seminars—sessions planned that related to adjustments and cultural awareness.
- Research paper on the country—may be required as a way to build background knowledge but to also eliminate those students who do not take the opportunity seriously.
- Two-and-a-half day intensive workshop (24 instructional hours)—led by those who are a part of the committee or from other related colleges such as anthropology or sociology.
- Twelve weeks of in-state student teaching first for evidence of effective classroom teaching.
- Completion of two interviews over required books dealing with education and culture of host nation and also interviews with selection committee for gaining perceptions of student's attitudes and interpersonal skills.

CONCLUSIONS

If preparation to work with diverse populations is valued, and especially in international teaching experiences, then we need to be more purposeful in designing those experiences. To visit another country is to be informed, educated, and entertained but to immerse oneself is to be transformed. In addition, we learn how our country and U.S. citizens appear from the outside. Significant international experiences are ways these new teachers can examine their own sociocultural identity. Having an opportunity to be distanced from the groups to which they belong may force them to introspect on the nature of those attachments and how it has shaped their lives.

In preservice teacher programs, we discuss issues related to cultural differences and attempt to build empathy for those coming into our system. However, the component that is really missing is the interaction with others *different* than they. The student teaching abroad is intended to be a vehicle for those willing to achieve a deeper level of understanding.

REFERENCES

Bryan, Sandra L., & Marsha M. Sprague. (1997). The effect of overseas internships on early teaching experiences [Electronic version]. *The Clearing House, 70*(4), 199-201.

Cockrell, Karen, Peggy Placier, Dan Cockrell, & Julie Middleton. (1999). Coming to terms with *diversity* and *multiculturalism* in teacher education: Learning about our students, changing our practice. *Teaching and Teacher Education, 15*, 351-366.

Cross, Mary C. (1998, April). *Self efficacy and cultural awareness: A study of returned Peace Corps teachers.* Paper presented at the annual meeting of the American Educational Research Association (AERA), San Diego, CA. (ERIC Document Reproduction Service No. ED429976)

Consortium for Belize Educational Cooperation (COBEC). Retrieved January 15, 2007, from http://www.cobec.org/cobec_site/home.html

Cushner, Kenneth, & Jennifer Mahon. (2002). Overseas student teaching: Affecting personal, professional, and global competencies in an age of globalization. *Journal of Studies in International Education, 6*, 44-58.

King, Patricia M., & Marcia B. Baxter Magolda. (2005). A developmental model of intercultural maturity. *Journal of College Student Development, 46*, 571-592.

Mahan, James M. (1982). Community involvement components in culturally oriented teacher preparation. *Education, 103*, 163-172.

Mahon, Jennifer M., & Kenneth Cushner. (2002). The overseas student teaching experience: Creating optimal culture learning. *Multicultural Perspectives, 4*(3), 3-8.

Mohl, R. (2003). Globalization, Latinization and the *nuevo*/new South. *Journal of Ethnic History, 22*, 31-66.

Rorty, Richard. (1989). *Contingency, irony, and solidarity.* Cambridge: Cambridge University Press.

Sleeter, Christine, Bob Hughes, Elizabeth Meador, Patricia Whang, Linda Rogers, Kani Blackwell, Peggy Laughlin, & Claudia Peralta-Nash, (2005). Working an academically rigorous, multicultural program. *Equity & Excellence in Education, 38*, 290-298.

Smith, John K. (1993). Hermeneutics and qualitative inquiry. In D. J. Flinders & G. E. Mills (Eds.), *Theory and concepts in qualitative research: Perspectives in the field* (pp. 183-200). New York: Teachers College Press.

Stachowski, Laura L., & James M. Mahan, (1998). Cross-cultural field placements: Student teachers learning from schools and communities. *Theory into Practice, 37*, 155-162.

Villegas, Ana Maria & Lucas, Tamara. (2002). Preparing culturally responsive teachers: Rethinking the curriculum. *Journal of Teacher Education, 53*(1), 20-32.

PART III

SOCIOCULTURAL IDENTITIES AND CONTEXTS OF HUMAN GROWTH AND DEVELOPMENT

CHAPTER 10

AN INTRODUCTORY REFLECTION ...

SCIENCE AND SPIRITUALITY

A Synergy Made in Heaven

Clay M. Starlin

We are not human beings having a spiritual experience. We are spiritual beings having a human experience.

—Pierre Teilhard de Chardin

Some suggest that scientific and spiritual[1] processes are different ways of knowing and thus incompatible (Gould, 1997; Wells, 1962). However, such a perspective promotes dichotomous thinking. I believe we are better served by viewing these ways of knowing as complementary and synergistic. Spirituality relates to the nonmaterial or supernatural realm existing outside normal human experience or knowledge, while science involves deriving knowledge from systematic observation and experimentation in order to determine the nature or principles of the object of study.

Psychiatrist Scott Peck (1987) in his book *The Different Drum* suggests the following four stages of spiritual development. It is interesting to note in Peck's stages that a scientific perspective is a stage along the way to full spiritual development, but not the final stage.

- Stage 1: Chaotic, antisocial (often demonstrated by young children);
- Stage 2: Formal, institutional (often represented by those who follow religious dogma without questioning);
- Stage 3: Skeptic, individual (often represented by a scientific perspective); and
- Stage 4: Mystic, communal (often represented by those who accept a certain mystery and see the connection of all things).

Since Copernicus (sixteenth century), scientific methods have been used to confirm or refute various hypotheses or theories many of which were founded in spiritual traditions. It is instructive to note that the blending of spirituality and science is not uncommon. Table 10.1 summarizes five prominent scientists and their beliefs.

Table 10.1. Some Prominent Scientists and their Beliefs

Scientist	Nationality	Field	Contributions	Era	Belief System
Copernicus	Polish	Astronomer; priest	• Heliocentricity theory of universe	1473-1543	Christian (Catholic)
Galileo	Italian	Astronomer; mathematician; physicist	• Supported Copernican theory • Improved telescope • Scientific method	1564-1642	Christian (Catholic)
Kepler	German	Astronomer; mathematician	• Planetary motions	1571-1630	Christian (Lutheran)
Newton	English	Mathematician; physicist	• Laws of gravity, motion • Calculus • Set course of modern science	1642-1727	Christian (Anglican; rejected concept of Trinity, belief in Arianism)

Einstein	German/Swiss/American	Physicist	• Relativity
			  • Special-space-time
			  • General-gravity
			• Quantum mechanics
				1879-1955	Impersonal God, Spinozian

Table 10.1 is not intended to imply that all or most scientists are spiritual. Numerous scientists in the past (e.g., Charles Darwin, Bertrand Russell) and in the present (e.g., Francis Crick, Stephen Hawking) are agnostic or atheist. And, it is important to note, that with the exception of Einstein, the four other scientists in Table 10.1 lived during eras that to question or renounce the prevalent faith was to court imprisonment or execution.

However, those scientists who probe the deep mysteries of the physical universe (e.g., physicists and astronomers) often develop an awe and reverence of its majesty and a belief that the creation and functioning of the universe is not random but by design (Davies, 1993; Jammer, 1999). [An interesting anecdote underscores this point. J. P. Moreland, a prominent theologian (see Moreland, 2004; Moreland & Nielsen, 1993), commented in a debate on the PAX network's *Faith Under Fire* program that when looking for an atheist to argue the side against God we inquire in the university's philosophy department not the physics department.]

Natural/Supernatural

I would argue that everything that happens in the universe is naturalistic. The events we label as *supernatural* are either due to ignorance or superstition (untrue), not accessible through our human sensory systems, or outside our current understanding.

Scientifically, we define *natural* in terms of what our human sensory systems can directly observe or detect through instrumentation. Yet we know that human sensory systems are limited. For example, human hearing senses sounds between 20-20,000 Hz while other animals sense information humans cannot (e.g., elephants hear below 20 Hz, dogs hear above 20,000 Hz).

Extrasensory perception suggests a person has tapped into sensory information not *normally* experienced through human perception. Persons with *near death experiences* often comment about encountering *energy beings* vibrating at frequencies outside normal perception (see Blackmore, 1993, 2004; Randie, 1994). Since most persons do not experience such extrasensory information it is viewed with skepticism within the scientific community that requires external verification. However, it is unscientific to deny, a priori, that events outside our current detection systems do not exist or do not behave in lawful ways.

The discussion in the psychology literature regarding inner behavior/private events is parallel to the suggestion that we explore the supernatural/spiritual world scientifically. Because thoughts, feelings, and urges are not observable to anyone other than the person experiencing them, they do not meet the scientific dictums of external observability and replication. Fortunately, we have begun to probe this inner world using the tools of science (see Anderson, Hawkins, Freeman, & Scotti, 2000; Calkin, 2002).

When we consider the first law of thermodynamics (i.e., the law of conservation of energy—nothing is created or destroyed; it only changes form) which is described in Einstein's famous formula—$E=mc^2$, it is not unreasonable to consider that when we are no longer in human *matter* form we are in an *energy* (a.k.a. *spirit*) form. Joseph Campbell (1988) suggested, "consciousness and energy are the same thing" (p. 14). Is it possible we maintain our consciousness in an energy form after our matter form ceases to exist?

Science has historically, although not always smoothly, pushed back the vale of ignorance by replacing beliefs based on superstition or faulty science. Sometimes science postulates what seems *impossible, irrational* and *counterintuitive*. What an elegant irony it would be if the tools of science were to verify the existence of God. This paper is focused on the possibility of this elegant irony.

There are two fundamental questions that need to be addressed in this exploration. First, what does our current evidence and reason tell us about the how the material universe came into existence? Second, if the evidence points to a Creator (God), what does our current evidence and reason tell us about what religious/spiritual traditions, if any, are true? The remainder of the chapter hinges on these two questions.

HOW DID THE MATERIAL UNIVERSE COME INTO EXISTENCE?

The eternal mystery of the world is its comprehensibility.
—Albert Einstein

In recent years, two broad explanations have been prominent regarding the origins of the universe:

1. The origin of the universe is "a glorious accident" (Gould, 1989, p. 347) and will be explainable through the laws of science without the need to postulate a Creator (God) (see Hawking, 2001). (This position is often supported by agnostic or atheist scientists.)
2. A Creator (God) designed the universe and brought it into existence. (This position is often supported by believers of various religious faiths.)

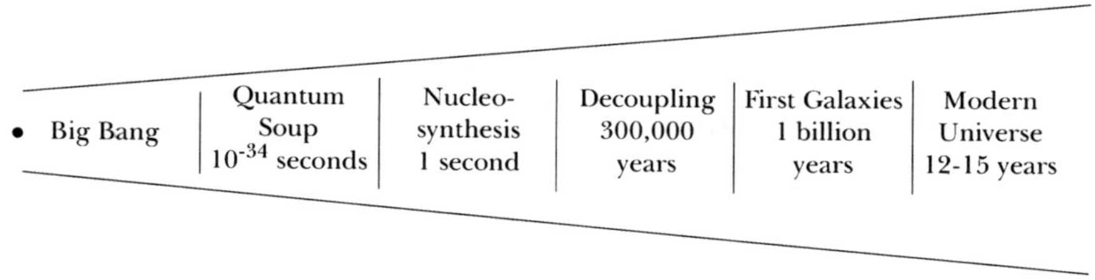

| Big Bang | Quantum Soup 10^{-34} seconds | Nucleo-synthesis 1 second | Decoupling 300,000 years | First Galaxies 1 billion years | Modern Universe 12-15 years |

Source: Adapted from Thorne (2005).

Figure 10.1. The evolution of the universe.

In relationship to the first explanation there have been a variety of theories offered to explain the origins of the universe. These have ranged from: the universe is eternal and had no origin *to* the universe evolved from nothing *to* various theories that gained support but then fell into disrepute (e.g., steady state theory, chaotic inflation theory) *to* some of our current theories.

It is generally agreed that our universe started from an infinitesimally small amount of matter that rapidly expanded filling the universe with all matter that exists today (see Figure 10.1). This rapid expansion was sarcastically labeled "The Big Bang" by British physicist Fred Hoyle[2] who discounted the theory. But the name stuck. The Big Bang was the beginning of our material universe, as we know it.

As I consider the proposition that the universe evolved from nothing, I am reminded of the 1974 Billy Preston song: "Nothin' from nothin' leaves nothin'." We know that in the early universe, the expansion was occurring exponentially—by multiplying. Basic mathematics teaches us that we cannot multiply out of zero (nothing).

A current theory that has a good deal of support in the scientific community is called The "theory of everything" which is designed to combine *relativity* and *quantum mechanics* to unify all physical laws and thereby provide greater insight into the beginning and functioning of the universe (see Gribbin, 1999; Hawking, 2001). However, as Jim Brau (2005), director of the University of Oregon's Center on High Energy Physics, recently commented "the bulk of the universe is still a mystery." Thus, the current theories await further investigation and data collection.

Those who support the second explanation point to the 50 constants of the universe as markers of a conscious, intelligent Creator behind the universal design (see Strobel, 2004).

> If *any* of the constants varied by a minute degree, life would not have appeared. For example: (a) if gravity were fractionally stronger or weaker, if

the expansion had proceeded just a little more slowly or swiftly—then there might never have been stable elements to make you and me and the ground we stand on; (b) if the conversion of hydrogen to helium varied by a thousandth of a percent the universe as we know it would not exist. (Bryson, 2004, p. 15)

Please think of some *person-created-entity* (Pause: for the reader to consider before continuing to read). Whether the thought was of a bell, book, candle, some prized possession, a musical score, or a work of art—some human conscious thought preceded the creation of the item thought about. Theoretical physicist Amit Goswami (1995) emphasizes this reality in his book *The Self-Aware Universe: How Consciousness Creates the Material World*. As we look around at our material world, it is evident that consciousness creates material reality.

I cannot fathom something as complex as the space shuttle evolving through random probabilities. Then I consider the complexity of the universe and have even more trouble considering that it is a random occurrence. Maybe it is not so preposterous to postulate that some intelligent consciousness created the finely tuned universe.

The resolution of the God/No God question is arguably the preeminent question of all time. My reading of the current evidence/reason/logic leans toward a Creator (God). I will operate under this assumption in the remainder of the chapter. Of course, if this assumption proves to be false then the following discussion is moot.

THE MULTITUDE OF SPIRITUAL PATHS

In Figure 10.2 I depict the choices we might make in considering a spiritual path. As we look across the world we see persons following these various paths. It may be politically correct to embrace all spiritual paths as equally valid but it is not scientifically correct. There are inherent contradictions in these paths thus they cannot all be true.

If we postulate a monotheistic God, then those belief systems in Figure 10.2 that are not monotheistic are untrue on the God dimension. In Table 10.2, I summarize the three major spiritual/religious traditions that adhere to a monotheistic God—Christianity, Islam, and Judaism. The question now becomes, of the religions noted in Table 10.2, what evidence/reason exists to support or refute the tenets of the spiritual/religious tradition?

If a Supreme Being created the universe, then any *miraculous* claims made by any of the religions in Table 10.2 would not seem impossible compared with creating the universe. I find the most prominent *truth ques-*

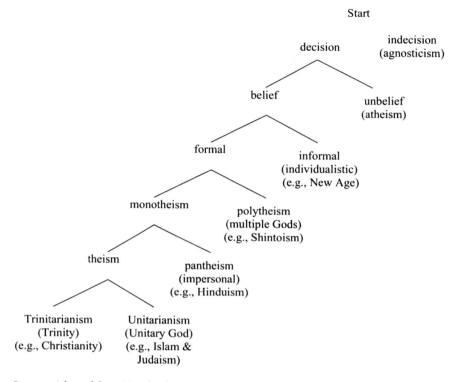

Source: Adapted from Moreland & Nielsen (1993, p. 15).

Figure 10.2. Spiritual path decision tree.

tion that evolves from these comparisons is: Was Jesus who he said he was (i.e., God in human form)? If the preponderance of evidence supports Jesus as God in human form, then more of Christian theology would be true and less of the other monotheistic religions.

WAS JESUS GOD INCARNATE?

Lee Strobel (1998), in his book, *A Case for Christ,* presents the historical evidence regarding Jesus. Below is a summary of this evidence.[3]

1. Accuracy of the Bible biographies of Jesus (see Blomberg, 1987): (a) biographies reflect accuracy of eyewitness testimony; (b) testi-

Table 10.2. A Comparison of the Major Monotheistic Religions

Comparators	Christianity	Islam	Judaism
Brief description	Follows the teachings of the Bible and believes Jesus was the Son of God.	Follows the teachings of the Quran and views Muhammad as divinely inspired Prophet.	Follows the teachings of the Torah and believes a variety of prophets provided divine guidance.
Conception of God	• Personal God • Belief in Trinity—God, Christ, Holy Spirit	• Personal God • Unitary God (not Trinity)	• Personal God • Unitary God (not Trinity)
Exclusivity	The only right path to God. (Note: This is more of a historic view. Increasingly, some Christian theologians are considering that Jesus may not be the only right path to God.)	The only right path to God.	The chosen people.
Major figure(s)	Jesus (4 BC-30 A.D.) St. Paul (4-64 A.D.)	Muhammad (570-632 A.D.)	Abraham, Moses, Elijah, Amos, Hosea, Isaiah, Jeremiah (1200-200 BC)

monies recorded within the first 2 years of Jesus's death reducing likelihood of legendary invention; (c) harmony among gospels on essential facts; (d) early church took root and flourished in Jerusalem where numerous eye-witness contemporaries could have challenged false gospel; (e) gospels pass the eight evidential tests of historically accurate records.

2. Evidence outside biblical biographies: In his work *The Historical Jesus*, Gary Habermas documents "thirty-nine ancient sources that corroborate more than one hundred facts concerning Jesus' life, teachings, crucifixion, and resurrection" (in Strobel, 2004, p. 294).

3. Archaeological evidence: *Archaeology and the New Testament* (McRay, 1991) indicates that no archaeological discovery "has ever disproved a biblical reference" (in Strobel, 2004, p. 294).

4. Evidence for Jesus as the Messiah: dozens of Old Testament prophecies foretell of the coming of a Messiah and his attributes; throughout history, only Jesus matches these prophecies; eyewitness testimony to "miraculous feats of healing, power over nature," and his resurrection.

The majority of scholars agree that the preponderance of evidence supports that Jesus did exist (see White, 2004). However, considerable debate continues regarding whether Jesus was God incarnate (see Borg, 2001; Crossan, 1995). Where the major monotheistic religions diverge is regarding the question of Jesus' divinity. Consequently, from a scientific point of view, the divinity question is an important follow-up question to the existence of God question.

If the evidence at some point in the future were to support Jesus as God in human form this is not an endorsement of the dogma of Christianity. Archaeologist Michael White in his book *From Jesus to Christianity* (2004) documents "how four generations of visionaries and storytellers created the New Testament and Christian faith" (the subtitle of the book). John Shelby Spong (2005), a retired Episcopal bishop, in his book *The Sins of the Scriptures* highlights how Biblical scripture has been used throughout history to justify practices that are, in fact, contrary to the teaching of Jesus.

In looking at a concordance of the Bible (Strong, 2001), if we focus on the words of Jesus, as opposed to the elaborations that have been contributed by storytellers and visionaries, the following is the fundamental message—LOVE.

- Love God (Luke 10:27)
- Love your neighbor as yourself (Luke 10:27)
- Love your enemies (Matthew 5:44)

The message of love is a common thread throughout major religions and other spiritual practices. As humans we desire to love and be loved. In a previous monograph, I defined love as "the gift of behaving to enhance life" (Starlin, 1985, p. 7). Regardless of our current belief system, presumably something we can all agree on is to be loving in our thoughts, words and actions, and as a result enhance our life and the lives of others.

FOR FURTHER CONSIDERATION

The intuitive mind is a sacred gift, the rational mind a faithful servant. It is paradoxical that in the context of modern life we have begun to worship the servant and defile the divine.

—Albert Einstein

I am not a great fan of the *culture of science* or the *culture of religion*. I find too often both cultures promote a *regression toward the mean* rather than encouraging adherents to break the mold and soar into unexplored territory. Those *believers* and *nonbelievers* that I respond to most favorably are those who have questioned the *belief* or *nonbelief* passed down to them from their family and culture. These persons demonstrate the best in the scientific tradition. Having doubts and pushing back the unknown until becoming satisfied with a preponderance of evidence (empirical, intuitive, logical) rather than *blind religious faith* or *the faith of the closed scientific mind*. The conclusions they come to may prove to be incorrect, as continued scientific exploration frequently makes corrections, but they have demonstrated the courage to search for the truth.

The Crucial Questions

I believe the two crucial questions for the scientific and spiritual communities to work together to build *evidence consensus* around follow:

1. What is the evidence for or against a Creator (God) who designed and brought the material universe into existence?
2. If the answer to #1 affirms a Creator (God): What is the evidence for or against Jesus being God in human form?

The foundational question is question number one. If the preponderance of evidence points to no Creator, then atheism describes reality and we adjust our beliefs and behavior accordingly. If the preponderance of evidence points to a Creator, then we move on to the evidence for the divinity of Jesus. We can either confirm His divine nature or disconfirm it. Confirming His divine nature resolves some inherent contradictions in the teachings of the different monotheistic religions. Disconfirming the divinity of Jesus leaves the interpretation open to build evidence for other beliefs.

A significant portion of our difficulty in merging science and spirituality is that persons steeped in the different traditions have *committed* to a belief territory. The spiritual adherent often insists that we believe based on faith without proof. The scientific adherent often insists that the claims of faith are supernatural and cannot be verified.

In the scientific world, we are warned to protect ourselves from *experimental bias* (i.e., finding what you are looking for regardless of the evidence). Being too strongly committed to a belief system can blind us to important information. We need to care more about the *truth* than we care about the outcome.

I find the debate over evolution often demonstrates experimental bias on both sides of the debate. As I read the evidence I am persuaded by the data for *within* species evolution but not for across species evolution (see Simmons, 2004; Strobel, 2004). However, the question of the creation of the universe trumps the evolution debate. If an intelligent consciousness brought the material universe into existence, then other miraculous events are certainly feasible. Let us take a more inductive, evidence-building approach, versus the theory-driven, deductive approach, to answering these two questions and develop consensus around the evidence that we currently have and continue to collect data and see where it leads us.

IN CONCLUSION

The laws of science have been developed and refined over the centuries shifting what seemed to be supernatural into the natural realm. If we can come to an agreement regarding the truth or falsehood of various spiritual beliefs we can look forward to a time when we have a unitary and unifying system of belief. At that point, we would truly have a theory of everything. The supernatural would yet again give way to the natural and we would have the synergy of science and spirituality.

Whether the reader is a committed atheist, agnostic, or a person confident in her or his spiritual faith, I hope this introductory analysis will encourage the reader to continue to explore and stay open to new knowledge. Remember: the pursuit of truth through science has often strengthened faith versus extinguished it. Significant questions remain to be answered as do those we have not yet thought to ask. Let us support each other in our spiritual and scientific endeavors and synergize our efforts in pursuit of the truth.

Imagination is more important than knowledge.

—Albert Einstein

POSTSCRIPT:
RECOMMENDATIONS REGARDING EDUCATIONAL PRACTICE

People's religious and spiritual practices are fundamental to how they view and interact with the world. However, too often in the past and currently, the perceived differences in these practices are a source of personal and governmental conflicts. A major tenet of enlightened education is to teach students to be critical thinkers. To examine their beliefs, to understand how their beliefs compare with other belief systems and to make informed choices about what they wish to believe. A first recommendation is that schools provide a comparative religion/spirituality class that helps students understand the commonalities and differences between different religious/spiritual traditions. (e.g., an elaboration of Figure 10.2 and Table 10.2). A second recommendation is to use the tools of science to (a) explore the claims of various religious/spiritual traditions (e.g., the existence of a monotheistic God) and (b) as an arbitrator in resolving conflicting claims between various traditions (e.g., the evidence for Jesus as God incarnate). The commitment in this process needs to be to the truth rather than selecting information that supports a current belief system.

Reading this chapter could be a point of departure for individual and class explorations and discussions. A culminating accomplishment for all educational systems would be to contribute more loving citizens to the world. This would be in keeping with all ethical religious and spiritual traditions.

ACKNOWLEDGMENTS

This chapter is based on a paper presented at the 31st annual Association for Behavior Analysis Conference, May 28, 2005, Chicago, IL. Carrie Robinson was my support system in the preparation of this paper. She typed the manuscript, formatted the tables and figures, and searched for information, while adding her sensitivity and professional touch to the finished product. Thank you. Steve Overman, senior pastor of the Eugene, Oregon, Faith Center, generously reviewed the manuscript for factual accuracy and contributed a number of helpful comments. Thank you.

NOTES

1. I tend to use *religious* and *spiritual* as synonyms when referring to more established religious traditions. My focus is on the basic tenets of a spiritual/religious tradition not on the religious dogma that too often obscures the basic spiritual tenets of a faith.
2. The theory was the only serious alternative to the Big Bang that agreed with key observations of the day, namely Hubble's red shift observations. Fred Hoyle was a strong critic of the Big Bang. Ironically, he is responsible for coining the term Big Bang on a BBC radio program, *The Nature of Things*, while criticizing the theory; the text was published in 1950. For more information, see http://en.wikipedia.org/wiki/History_of_the_Big_Bang_theory
3. This summary is a synthesis of an appendix in Lee Strobel's (2004) book *A Case for a Creator* where he summarizes his book *A Case for Christ*.

REFERENCES

Anderson, C. M., Hawkins, R. P., Freeman, K.A., & Scotti. J.R. (2000). Private events: Do they belong in a science of human behavior? *The Behavior Analyst, 23*(1), 1-10.

Blackmore, Susan J. (1993). *Dying to live: Near-death experiences.* Buffalo, NY: Prometheus Books.

Blackmore, Susan J. (2004). *Consciousness.* Oxford: Oxford University Press.

Blomberg, Craig L. (1987). *The historical reliability of the Gospels.* Downers Grove, IL: InterVarsity Press.

Brau, Jim. (2005, May 19). *Realizing Einstein's dream.* Lecture presented at the University of Oregon, Eugene, OR.

Borg, Marcus J. (2001). *Reading the Bible again for the first time: Taking the Bible seriously but not literally.* San Francisco: Harper.

Bryson, Bill. (2004). *A short history of nearly everything.* New York: Broadway Books.

Calkin, A. (2002). Inner behavior: Empirical investigations of private events. *The Behavior Analyst, 25*(2), 255-259.

Campbell, Joseph. (1988). *The power of myth.* New York: Doubleday.

Crick, Francis. (1994). *The astonishing hypothesis: The scientific search for the soul.* New York: Charles Scribner's Sons.

Crossan, John Dominic. (1995) *Jesus: A revolutionary biography.* Harper: San Francisco.

Darwin, Charles. (1871/1981). *The descent of man, and selection in relation to sex.* Princeton, NJ: Princeton University Press. (Original work published 1871)

Darwin, Charles. (1859/1964). *On the origin of species.* Cambridge, MA: Harvard University Press. (Original work published 1859)

Davies, Paul. (1993). *The mind of God: The scientific basis for a rationale world.* New York: Simon & Schuster.

Einstein, Albert. (n.d.). *Collected quotes.* Retrieved November 26, 2007, from http://rescomp.stanford.edu/~cheshire/EinsteinQuotes.html

Goswami, Amit. (1995). *The self-aware universe: How consciousness creates the material world.* New York: G. P. Putnam's Sons.

Gould, Stephen Jay. (1989). *Wonderful life: The burgess shale and the nature of history.* New York: W. W. Norton.

Gould, Stephen Jay. (1997). Nonoverlapping magisteria. *Natural History, 106,* 16-22.

Gribbin, John R. (1999). *The search for superstrings, symmetry and the theory of everything.* New York: Little Brown.

Habermas, Gary R. (1996). *The historical Jesus.* Joplin, MO: College Press.

Hawking, Stephen. (1988). *A brief history of time: From the big bang to black holes.* New York: Bantam Books.

Hawking, Stephen. (2001). *The universe in a nutshell.* New York: Bantam Books.

Hawking, Stephen. (Ed.). (2002). *On the shoulders of giants: The great works of physics and astronomy.* Philadelphia: Running Press.

Jammer, Max. (1999). *Einstein and religion.* Princeton, NJ: Princeton University Press.

McRay, John. (1991). *Archaeology and the New Testament.* Grand Rapids, MI: Baker.

Moreland, James Porter. (2004). The end of faith [Television talk show episode]. In Jim Berger & Joni Holder (Co-Executive Producers), *Faith under fire*. (Available from Pax TV Network)

Moreland, James Porter, & Kai Nielsen. (1993). *Does God exist? The debate between theists and atheists*. New York: Prometheus Books.

Peck, Morgan Scott. (1987). *The different drum: Community making and peace*. New York: Simon & Schuster.

Quotiki. (n.d.). Retrieved November 26, 2007, from http://www.quotiki.com/quote.aspx?id=11143

Randie, K. D. (1994). *To touch the light*. New York: Pinnacle Books.

Russell, Bertrand. (1957). *Why I am not a Christian*. New York: Touchstone.

Simmons, Geoffrey. (2004). *What Darwin didn't know*. Eugene, OR: Harvest House.

Spong, John Shelby. (2005). *The sins of the scriptures*. New York: Harper Collins.

Starlin, Clay. (1985). *Love and fear: A look at describing, monitoring and teaching affective behavior* (Iowa Monograph Series in Education). Des Moines: Iowa Department of Public Instruction.

Strobel, Lee. (1998). *A case for Christ*. Grand Rapids, MI: Zondervan.

Strobel, Lee. (2000). *A case for faith*. Grand Rapids, MI: Zondervan.

Strobel, Lee. (2004). *A case for a creator*. Grand Rapids, MI: Zondervan.

Strong, James H. (2001). *The new Strong's expanded exhaustive concordance of the Bible: Red-letter edition*. Nashville, TN: Thomas Nelson.

Thorne, Kip S. (2005, March 29). *Einstein's legacy in the modern world: Black holes to quantum cryptography*. Lecture presented at the University of Oregon, Eugene, OR.

Teilhard de Chardin, Pierre. (n.d.). *Quotes*. Retrieved November 26, 2007, from http://thinkexist.com/quotation/we_are_not_human_beings_having_a_spiritual/346797.html

Wells, Donald A. (1962). *God, man and the thinker: Philosophies of religion*. New York: Random House.

White, L. Michael. (2004). *From Jesus to Christianity: How four generations of visionaries and storytellers created the New Testament and Christian faith*. New York: Harper Collins.

CHAPTER 11

EXPERIENCING TRIBES

Perceptions of Teacher Education Students

Richard G. Berlach and Annette Sanders

Tribes[1] is a process rather than a program per se in that it aims to facilitate interactive learning via the engendering of a positive classroom climate. Devised in the United States and imported into a number of contexts internationally, uptake in Australia has been considerable. Thirty second and third year bachelor of education students undertook the training hosted by Cooloongup Primary School, Western Australia, prior to participating in a 10-week practicum. Data sets pertaining to Tribes as a resource were collected prior to the training phase, posttraining, and at the conclusion of the practicum. This paper reports the perceptions of students regarding the nature of Tribes as a resource, their participation in the training, and the value of Tribes training for practicum purposes.

INTRODUCTION

By identifying itself as a "Tribes school," Cooloongup Government Primary School in Western Australia has chosen to embrace the precepts of a learning system pioneered by Jeanne Gibbs (1995, 1998) in the United States. In this venture, Cooloongup has joined a growing number of schools—especially primary schools—which have trialed and subsequently integrated the program into their overall conceptualization of education. Take-up in secondary schools has been far more limited, possibly because the strategies and concomitant activities have greater appeal to younger children. This trend finds some support in studies undertaken in the United States (Kiger, 2000).

Gibbs (2001) offers an approach that provides sequenced instructions on how to build a Tribes Learning Community to support children's development and hopefully, obviate major problems in the movement toward adolescence. Her perspective on human development is a systems approach that encourages schools, families, and communities to create an integrated, cooperative environment conducive to children's development and learning. The teacher's role is one of facilitator of process. As such, teachers help to shape attitude; inculcate the strategies necessary for community participation; and encourage personal and interpersonal reflection regarding the value and effectiveness of the process.

According to CenterSource Systems (Helping America's Youth, n.d.), more than 4,500 schools are currently implementing the Tribes process throughout the United States, Canada, Australia, and other countries. Available studies evaluating the approach have generally reported favorable results (Cheswass, 2003, 2004; Holt, 2000; Kiger, 2000). Conclusions typically align with those of Beloit School District (Wisconsin) which undertook a comprehensive longitudinal study on the Tribes process. A final report (Nightingale, 2004) indicated that,

> A three [sic] year intensive evaluation was done in the Beloit school and showed that when Tribes was fully implemented in classrooms ... they were more collaborative, safer, more caring, and there were fewer behavioral problems ... there was a very positive impact on classroom and school environment ... and on student achievement.

Teachers who were interviewed from both Beloit and Burdge Elementary School, where Tribes had been operating for a number of years on a whole-school basis, were equally affirming, with one commenting that, "Children learn to feel included in the classroom and as one student put it 'the class is like a big family.'" And, as another stated, "Children learn through the Tribes process to work well in groups, they learn to be responsible for their own learning and can offer ideas and different ways to solve problems with their classmates." It was also reported that as a result of the successes encountered, all teachers and intending teachers at Beloit are now required to undertake Tribes training and organize their classrooms in a Tribes-friendly fashion.

Similar findings have been reported by teachers and administrators throughout the Central Oahu School District of Honolulu, Hawaii. A review of the Tribes process undertaken by Brown and Ushijima (1998), indicated that in this school district,

> Teachers reported the climate of the classrooms and school as more comfortable, settled, and respectful. A second important change was the use of the common Tribes language by students and teachers. The common language used throughout schools fostered a sense of community where all adults felt responsible for all students. School-wide changes were consistent with the classroom changes–positive climate and common language were repeatedly mentioned. Staff members repeatedly stated that their school had changed to a safe and positive learning environment. (para. 35-36)

The system is based on four main agreements to which all students, teachers, and administrators are expected to subscribe. The four agreements are attentive listening (honoring what the person is saying by giving her or him full attention in communication); mutual respect (treating others as you yourself would like to be treated); right to participate or pass (action on the basis of voluntary participation rather than external coercion); and appreciations/no put-downs (looking for gratitude-expressing opportunities rather than relating to others in a negative fashion). Tribes aims to create an environment that is safe and caring. It also offers strategies for building a culture of learning which is active rather than passive in nature. Further, it insists that the consequences of misbehavior must be made known in advance, thus offering the student a choice regarding whether or not to behave in a certain fashion. The four agreements, when operating properly, are intended to provide an environment where innovative and creative teaching and learning can flourish.

Tribes offers a framework, or interpretive lens, through which to view the activity of a classroom in a holistic fashion. The approach is premised on a set of democratic principles utilized to facilitate key classroom activities such as knowledge transmission, personal development, and socialization. Tribes promotes itself not as an intruder into existing classroom process, but as a facilitator of process, as a "new way of learning and being together ... a new pattern of interaction" (Gibbs, 1995, p. 15). In fact, the ideas are not all that new but rather, represent an eclectic compilation of work on *classroom climate* dating back to the 1960s. What is new, however, is the way in which this existing body of knowledge has been synthesized and *packaged* for contemporary pedagogical practice.

Gibbs appears to draw on past research in areas such as humanistic psychology (Maslow, 1968; Rogers, 1961/1974); classroom ethnography (Dunkin & Biddle, 1974; Good & Brophy, 1973); cooperative learning (Bennett & Smilanich, 1994; Slavin, 1983); classroom ecology (Bronfenbrenner, 1979; Vygotsky, 1978); assertive discipline (Canter & Canter, 1976); choice theory (Glasser, 1969; Kohn, 1993); contemporary approaches to intelligence (Gardner, 1983; Goleman, 1995); motivation (Pintrich & Schunk, 1996; Weiner, 1980); lateral thinking (De Bono, 1967, 1972) and resilience training (Benard, 1993). In this, Gibbs' approach appears to have a sound research pedigree, and together with current studies (e.g., brain research), ideas are bundled to form what purports to be a coherent and sequentially presented system of community-based learning.

In an attempt to keep Tribes from being misunderstood or misused, Gibbs recommends that those interested in implementing Tribes undertake an introductory course with an accredited trainer. An accredited trainer is one who has, at a minimum, participated in the basic Tribes course; implemented the Tribes process in her or his teaching milieu for at least 12 months; and engaged in five full days of advanced training at the Tribes Summer Institute. Specific training experiences may vary, but typically, each day's training is centered around the following broad topics:

- creating a resilient learning community;
- the artistry for learning;
- the impact and implementation of Tribes;
- showcasing best practice; and
- participating in Tribes-related workshops and talks.

The second author is an accredited trainer, who after experiencing considerable success with Tribes at Cooloongup Government Primary School, offered to train the 2006 group of bachelor of education (4-year course) student teachers (primary and early childhood) at Notre Dame University.

Sample and Pretraining Data Collection

For logistical reasons revolving around general practicum requirements, volunteers were called for from the second- and third-year cohorts. Of the 36 students who volunteered, 30 were randomly selected for course participation. All students were female. This is hardly surprising given that the Early Childhood Education (ECE) course enrollment is 100% female and the Primary 85% female, a trend reflected throughout the country. As such, it may be that a Tribes approach is more likely to appeal to female than male teachers, however, this hypothesis was not able to be tested given the design of the present study. Two students withdrew on the day the training was to commence, thus leaving a training group of 28 (Table 11.1). Training was to be completed during the scheduled 10-week practicum program. The first week was dedicated to Tribes training at Cooloongup Government Primary School with the other 9 weeks being completed at one of eight designated practice schools, where newly acquired skills could then be implemented.

Broadly, training consisted of providing the students with a background to the Tribes process; examining the research that underpins its conceptualization; and detailing typical outcomes that can be expected upon successful implementation of the process. Specific outcomes identified included a decrease in the need for behavior management and an increase in student learning and retention. Participants also learned strategies for introducing Tribes into their normal teaching processes. Further, they were introduced to, via the use of collaborative activity, skills such as inclusivity, group processes, community building, problem solving, and conflict resolution. Finally, with regard to the training process itself, participants were encouraged to reflect on what was learned, how the group interacted, and how the individual felt about the learning that took place.

Data were collected at three points of the study. Initial data collection consisted of obtaining demographic and precourse information. The greater majority of students were training as primary teachers. The sample distribution as presented in Table 11.2 fairly accurately mirrors the general distribution between the two courses. Age range was between 18 (school leavers) and 55 (mature age) with almost two thirds of the sample comprised of school-leavers (Table 11.3). A typical training day commenced at 9 A.M. and concluded at 4 P.M., providing some 30 hours of contact time (inclusive of breaks) over the course of the 5 days.

The sample was also asked to respond to six questions which would later be used for comparison with both posttraining and postpracticum data. The major objective of the study was to obtain insight into the perceptions of students regarding the nature of Tribes as a resource, their

Table 11.1. Sample Distribution by Year Group (n = 28)

Year of Course	Frequency	Percent	Cumulative Percent
2	17	60.7	60.7
3	10	35.7	96.4
4	*1	3.6	100.0

*Although technically a fourth year, this student was repeating a failed third-year practicum.

Table 11.2. Distribution of Sample by Course (n = 28)

Course	Frequency	Percent	Cumulative Percent
BEd (ECE)	10	35.7	35.7
BEd (Prim)	18	64.3	100.0

Table 11.3. Distribution of Sample by Age (n = 28)

Age	Frequency	Percent	Cumulative Percent
< 20	18	64.3	64.3
21-25	4	14.3	78.6
26-35	2	7.1	85.7
36-45	3	10.7	96.4
46-55	1	3.6	100.0

Table 11.4. Responses to the Question "Why Did You Choose to Undertake This Training Course?" (n = 28)

Response	Frequency	Percent	Cumulative Percent
Generally valuable	8	28.6	28.6
Inexpensive	2	7.1	35.7
Friends doing it	1	3.6	39.3
Be a better teacher	11	39.3	78.6
Uncertain	6	21.4	100.0

Table 11.5. Responses to the Question "How Much Do You Know About Tribes at This Point?" (n = 28)

Response	Frequency	Percent	Cumulative Percent
Fair amount	5	17.9	17.9
Very little	12	42.9	60.7
Nothing	11	39.3	100.0

participation in the training, and the value of Tribes training for practicum purposes. The six questions, together with responses ($n = 28$), are detailed in Tables 11.4-11.8.

The picture painted by Tables 11.4-11.8 suggests that most students knew very little about what they were getting themselves into, although

Table 11.6. Responses to the Question "Do You Think You Will be Able to Utilize Your Tribes Training During the Forthcoming Practicum?" (n = 28)

Response	Frequency	Percent	Cumulative Percent
Yes	15	53.6	53.6
Uncertain	13	46.4	100.0

Table 11.7. Responses to the Question "Have You Investigated Whether Tribes is Being Implemented in Your Practice School?" (n = 28)

Response	Frequency	Percent	Cumulative Percent
Yes	9	32.1	32.1
A little	14	50.0	82.1
No	5	17.9	100.0

Table 11.8. Responses to the Question "What Do You Hope to Achieve as a Result of the Tribes Training?" (n = 28)

Response	Frequency	Percent	Cumulative Percent
Professional value	23	82.1	82.1
Personal value	2	7.1	89.3
Curious	3	10.7	100.0

the majority perceived that the training had professional value, even though only about a quarter of the group did it for that reason. Over half thought it would be useful for the upcoming practicum, probably as a result of having investigated the existence of Tribes in their assigned schools.

Posttraining Data Collection

Posttraining, students were encouraged to apply their newly acquired skills as opportunities presented themselves. Posttraining data were collected to determine students' perceptions regarding the value of the course. Participants were asked to complete a brief questionnaire using the semantic differential descriptors strongly agree (SA), agree (A), dis-

Table 11.9. Responses to Posttraining Statements (n = 28)

Semantic Statement	%SA	%A	%D	%SD
1. The course met my expectations.	53.6	42.9	0	3.6
2. The Tribes Text by Jeanne Gibbs is a valuable resource.	82.1	14.3	0	3.6
3. The training material is structured in a logical and sequential fashion.	60.7	35.7	0	3.6
4. Much of what I learned was new to me.	35.7	42.9	21.4	0
5. Tribes provides valuable strategies for helping to maximize student learning.	67.9	28.6	0	3.6
6. Knowing something about Tribes makes me better equipped to foster a positive classroom environment.	78.6	17.9	0	3.6
7. Tribes is not a "gimmick" but helps to promote learning and enrich a classroom environment in an *authentic* way.	53.6	42.9	0	3.6
8. The Tribes approach can easily be integrated into the Curriculum Framework and Progress Maps.	42.9	53.6	0	3.6
9. I intend using the Tribes principles in my teaching.	50.0	46.4	0	3.6
10. It was worth giving up a week of teaching practice to undertake this course.	71.4	25.0	0	3.6
11. I would recommend this course to other students.	71.4	25.0	0	3.6
Σ x	60.7	34.1	1.9	3.3

agree (D), and strongly disagree (SD). All 28 students participated and responded to all eleven statements presented. The statements, together with a brief analysis of responses, are presented in Table 11.9.

Table 11.9, together with anecdotal comments which were provided, indicates that the overwhelming majority of students found the course to be of considerable value. A closer examination of raw data indicated that a score of 3.6% for the SD category for virtually all statements was made by the same student. This indicates that the student was either genuinely disgruntled with the course, or misread the direction of the semantic categories. In the absence of written clarification being volunteered, a total average of 3.3% for the SD category represents an outlier which may best be dealt with by being categorized as an anomaly.

Overall, some 95% of students responded positively (SA or A) to the statements as presented. Students seemed to perceive that Tribes was not merely an ephemeral market-driven *gimmick* but an authentic resource which possessed real potential for improving *classroom climate* and with it the quality of student learning (statements 5, 7). They found the textbook by Gibbs (2001) to be of value in terms of furthering their professional development (statements 1, 2). They also rated presentation highly, being complimentary regarding the skills and passion displayed by the trainer (statements 10, 11). Although 18% initially indicated they knew a fair amount about Tribes (Table 11.5), the vast majority indicated that they had learned new information as a result of having participated in the training (statement 4). Statement 6 indicates that 96% (SA+A) thought that Tribes was a very desirable vehicle for fostering a positive classroom environment. The same percentage felt that Tribes could be easily operationalized in the outcomes-based environment which is currently the raison d'être of education in Western Australia (statement 8). Finally, 95% (SA+A) gave the course the highest affirmation–being prepared to recommend it to their peers.

Postpracticum Data Collection

Seven weeks into the 10-week practicum, participants were sent a questionnaire containing 11 semantic statements which called for responses along similar lines to those used in Table 11.9. The statements, generated by the authors, were designed to provide information on the extent and receptivity of Tribes in primary schools; the value of Tribes from a trainee teacher's perspective; and whether the training course succeeded in providing an entry-level Tribes induction. Fifteen students responded to the questionnaire. A follow-up letter at the conclusion of the practicum yielded a further six responses, so providing a data set of 21 respondents. The questions, together with results are provided in Table 11.10.

With reference to question one, students had no control over the school where they completed their practicum. Tribes capacity, for logistical reasons, is not a criterion when school placements are negotiated. Although Tribes-trained students only attended a limited number of practice schools, over one-quarter of these had a whole-school Tribes approach in place. Assuming randomization, the take-up rate of Tribes in primary schools is impressive. Even in those schools where Tribes had not been systemically adopted, the vast majority of teachers were aware of its existence (Question 2).

Responses to Question 3, relating to the use of Tribes as a resource, are clearly related to the first two questions regarding the availability of Tribes. Even though only 33.4% are self-designated Tribes-schools, 71% (SA+A, Question 5) are very supportive of the Tribes approach. What is

Table 11.10. Responses to Post-Practicum Statements (*n* = 21)

Semantic Statement	%SA	%A	%D	%SD
1. My practice school was a "Tribes school" (i.e. whole-school Tribes approach is used).	28.6	4.8	33.3	33.3
2. My class teacher was aware of Tribes as a resource.	33.3	38.1	28.6	0
3. My class teacher utilized Tribes as a resource.	9.5	23.8	47.6	19.0
4. (Whether in a "Tribes environment" or not) I utilized Tribes principles and found them to be useful.	38.1	57.1	4.8	0
5. My class teacher encouraged me to utilize Tribes.	19.0	52.4	23.8	4.8
6. Tribes provided valuable strategies for helping to maximize student learning.	38.1	57.1	4.8	0
7. Knowing something about Tribes was generally useful for fostering a positive classroom environment.	66.7	33.3	0	0
8. During the practice I consulted the Tribes text by Jeanne Gibbs.	23.8	57.1	14.3	4.8
9. I intend using the Tribes principles in my future teaching.	42.9	47.6	9.5	0
10. Whether or not I specifically utilized a Tribes approach during this practice, the course was worth doing.	76.2	19.0	4.8	0
11. I would recommend the Tribes course to other students.	81.0	14.3	4.8	0

even more pleasing from a course provider's point of view, is that some 95% (SA+A, Questions 4, 6) of the Tribes-trained students found the Tribes approach to be beneficial for pedagogical practice, and all of them (SA+A, Question 7) indicated that Tribes helped foster a positive classroom environment. Doubtless, this is a reflection of the Tribes-friendly attitude expressed by their cooperating teachers.

Gibbs' (2001) key text proved to be a valuable repository of ideas and strategies for classroom practice (Question 8). Unlike many textbooks assigned in university work, this one was directly consulted during the practicum by 81% of students. In fact, the greater majority of students found the text to be so valuable that they had every intention of utilizing it during future teaching experiences (Question 9). Even those students who may not have consciously implemented Tribes imperatives, 95% (SA+A, Question 10) indicated that the training course was very worthwhile. The same percentage was sufficiently impressed to recommend the course to other students.

Written Protocols

Written postpractice comments provided further insight into student experiences with Tribes. The following selected vignettes from students provide an overview of how the Tribes was generally viewed:

> The Tribes training was incredibly useful and really helped my teaching.
>
> Tribes gave me strategies for student instruction and in a values environment.... I thought it was extremely beneficial.... I think Tribes really helped me in completing my practicum.... The course was full of invaluable teaching and behaviour management strategies.

Another respondent clearly saw the value of Tribes training although questioned the need for the extended times of reflection:

> I enjoyed the Tribes training week, although I can't believe how drained out I was! I believe there were too many *getting to know you* activities. It was nice to learn the strategies and put a few into practice however there was way too much reflection. By cutting out even half of the reflection the Tribes course [would] not have been so long, boring, and tedious. But it was still nice to have had the opportunity to complete the course.

Several respondents provided insight into the value-added benefits of Tribes. One saw Tribes as having a far broader application than merely within the one classroom to which she had been assigned; and the other even more broadly, in terms of integrating some of the principles into her understanding of teaching per se:

> I found the Tribes agreements most useful for my class and being able to respond to students from other classes and in the playground. I found the program a valuable experience. I used it in my prac and have since used the program as a resource in my studies. Although I may not fully use the program in my classroom, I will use some strategies and the overall philosophy.

One insightful student questioned the value of Tribes for older children, wondering whether the lack of receptivity in the higher grades had to do with age or more with the fact that the children may not have been inculcated in a Tribes approach from their early years of schooling:

I was in a year 7 class and I found it was more the younger students who responded to the Tribes approach, especially *active listening* and *mutual respect*. I think it needs to be taught from a young age to still have benefits in the older classes.

The gap between theory and practice requires comment. Such a disparity became evident when the comments received from two students were compared. One wrote: "The course helped people from uni who don't usually spend time together to work as a team and to develop a friendship." This was counterbalanced by the experience of another who wrote:

On the last day of Tribes training we wrote sayings to our Tribe members on a postcard that would be sent back to us during the term (weeks 6/7). I have not received a postcard back and I feel it would have been beneficial to have received this to motivate us through the rest of the prac.

Such reflections suggest that the positive experiences created during the training course might be difficult to sustain away from the supportive environment which created them. For those who have a more sensitive disposition or lack a little confidence, this paucity of continued connectivity may prove very disappointing, even distressing. It may simply be a fact of life that such an intense level of relationship is impossible to maintain, or it may be that separation and closure could be better managed. Tribe members being separated by practicum commitment immediately after the training may have compounded any feelings of alienation. In the future, it may be better to assign students to schools by Tribe, if at all logistically possible. There is a lesson here for school staff. A whole-school setting may be of value in terms of harnessing an existing structure for fostering ongoing postcourse relational support. Principals considering arranging such training for their staff would be well advised to keep this aspect in mind.

In the main, it would appear that students found the training to be very useful for pedagogical practice. It seemed that Tribes provided them with a structure around which to conceptualize classroom dialogue in a relationally and pedagogically efficacious manner.

International Relevance

Care must be exercised when considering programs for a culture other than the one for which they were created. As a program that originated in the United States, Tribes is quite transportable into similar Western cultures such as that found in Australia. Were one to consider program relevance for say, Asian, Middle Eastern, or African cultures, portability might be more problematic. A detailed analysis of the Tribes-related challenges posed for non-Western cultures is beyond the purview of this chapter. Nevertheless, broad considerations as these may relate to a cross-cultural environment are now briefly addressed.

Tribes revolves around such principles as mutual cooperation, child-centered learning and personal reflection. Children reflect not just on what they have learned but also on how they worked as a group, felt about the task, and reacted to responses and discoveries, while they were participating. In other words, the process is metacognitive in orientation. As such, it may not be perceived as being relevant in cultures where educational philosophies emphasize compliance rather than mutual learning; where pedagogies revolve around expository teaching rather than discovery learning; where differentiated instruction is not the norm; and where critical reflection is not particularly valued. This is not to say that educational paradigms which are premised on a more formal and directive philosophy of education are inferior to the more Dewey-influenced informal, experiential and reflective practices currently found in the education systems of most Western countries. What it does mean is that any difference needs to be respected in terms of what programs are and are not likely to deliver within any given system.

A strange paradox also exists within the Tribes framework. Even though the system seems to be successful within a child-centered pedagogy, it is nevertheless quite structured in terms of how strategies are interpreted and applied. Such rigor may be mistakenly perceived as being a technical and formulaic requirement, instead of an organic and creative process. Such a misunderstanding would likely lead to a perception of artificiality on the part of students, possibly resulting in a stifling of creativity and interpersonal relationships. This may be a real danger in environments where process is misinterpreted as a product-manual application of strategies. Such misinterpretation is more likely to occur where individuals versed in a more didactic approach are attempting to move into more child-centered pedagogies. Further, as with all instructional *packages*, since ECE and Primary teachers tend to be rather concrete sequential in their orientation, the additional challenge of contextualization and relevance must be considered.

One of the major strategies of Tribes is the use of *energizers* to lift the mood of students and so reactivate them. Energizers are a short physical activity which "engage many of the multiple intelligences primarily: body/kinaesthetic, musical/rhythmic, interpersonal and visual/spatial" (Gibbs, 1995, p. 212). Again, some education philosophies may consider such energizers as an intrusion into thinking and disruption to concentration rather than as a strategy that enhances the process of learning.

A further consideration is that Tribes strategies may be misinterpreted, with the activities being used primarily as *time fillers* or worse still, as a substitute for curriculum content. Gibbs insists that the key to effectiveness is understanding. Unless appropriate high quality training accompanies the package, Tribes may in fact be counter-productive in terms of providing an adequate learning experience. The process underpins but does not replace classroom curriculum or proven pedagogy for delivering that curriculum. Such a misunderstanding is a real danger even in Western countries where the package has a greater chance of success—a danger compounded in countries that may not provide adequate training prior to implementation.

CONCLUSIONS

Tribes claims to be an approach which promotes inclusion via establishing new patterns of interaction. It does this by the creation of bonded groups (as a result of process) that work better together (product). The experience of the Notre Dame cohort, as facilitated by Cooloongup Primary School, appears to attest to the value of Tribes as a way of providing what may best be described as *supportive education*.

Most students who engaged in the training had very little idea of what Tribes offered, although most had heard of it as a resource and knew that it had something to do with community-building. Postcourse, most were convinced that the theory had benefits for pedagogy. Although it might be argued that such a response could be explained in terms of the Hawthorne Effect, or be related to the charisma of the presenter rather than the course content, this is mitigated by postpracticum data which indicted that students were convinced that the theory clearly worked in practice. Such developmental discovery underscores the importance of thorough training prior to implementation. Absence of such training may well result in misunderstanding the philosophy and lead to consequent implementation difficulties, resulting in a negative experience.

The value of Tribes reported by this inaugural group of students was so compelling that it has been decided to offer a further round of training to a new cohort in 2007. Within 48 hours of the availability of the course being advertised to students, all 30 places had been filled, with a waiting list being created. The student grapevine, it seems, is alive and well with regard to announcing the value Tribes as a resource for pedagogical practice.

NOTE

1. Tribes is also known as Tribes Learning Communities, or Tribes TLC. For ease of reference, the term *Tribes* will be used consistently throughout this chapter.

REFERENCES

Benard, Bonnie. (1993). *Resiliency requires changing hearts and minds.* Portland, OR: Western Center News, Northwest Regional Educational Laboratory.

Bennett, Barry, & Peter Smilanich. (1994). *Classroom management: A thinking and caring approach.* West Ajax, Ontario, Canada: VISU*TronX* Bookation.

Brown, Laura, & Teri Ushijima. (1998). *Building school communities: A district success story.* Retrieved August 1, 2007, from http://www.Tribes.com/article_building_communities.htm

Bronfenbrenner, Uri. (1979). *The ecology of human development: Experiments by nature and design.* Cambridge, MA: Harvard University Press.

Canter, Lee, & Marlene Canter. (1976). *Assertive discipline: A take-charge approach for today's educator.* Santa Monica, CA: Canter & Associates.

Cheswass, Roger. (2003). *Evaluation of the implementation and impact of Tribes TLC®.* Preliminary Evaluation Report. San Francisco: WestEd Regional Educational Laboratory.

Cheswass, Roger. (2004). *Evaluation of the implementation of Tribes TLC®: Second year study.* Final Evaluation Report. San Francisco: WestEd Regional Educational Laboratory.

De Bono, Edward. (1967). *New think.* New York: Avon Books.

De Bono, Edward. (1972). *Children solve problems.* New York: Penguin.

Dunkin, Michael, & Bruce Biddle. (1974). *The study of teaching.* New York: Holt, Rinehart & Winston.

Gardner, Howard. (1983). *Frames of mind: The theory of multiple intelligences.* New York: Basic Books.

Gibbs, Jeanne. (1995). *Tribes: A new way of learning and being together.* Sausalito, CA: CenterSource Systems.

Gibbs, Jeanne. (2001). *Tribes: A new way of learning and being together* (7th ed.). Windsor, CA: CenterSource Systems.

Gibbs, Jeanne. (1998). *Guiding your school community to live a culture of caring and learning: The process is called* Tribes. Sausalito, CA: CenterSource Systems.

Gibbs, Jeanne. (2001). *Discovering gifts in middle school.* Sausalito, CA: CenterSource Systems.

Glasser, William. (1969). *Schools without failure.* New York: Harper & Row.

Goleman, Daniel. (1995). *Emotional intelligence.* New York: Bantam Books.

Good, Tom, & Jere Brophy. (1973). *Looking in classrooms.* New York: Harper & Row.

Helping America's Youth. (n.d.). Retrieved February 23, 2007, from http://guide.helpingamericasyouth.gov/programdetail.cfm?id=684

Holt, Judith. (2000). *Tribes training and experiences lower the incidence of referral actions for teachers and students.* Research Summary. Tulsa, OK: Tulsa Public Schools.

Kiger, Derick. (2000). *The Tribes process: Phase 3 evaluation–Executive summary.* Beloit, WI: Research and Accountability Department, School District of Beloit.

Kohn, Alfie. (1993). Choices for children–Why and how to let students decide. *Phi Delta Kapan, 75*(1), 8-20.

Maslow, Abraham. (1968). *Toward a psychology of being* (2nd ed.). New York: Van Norstrand.

Nightingale, Kay. (2004). Video of the *Tribes* process produced in conjunction with the Beloit School District. Retrieved February 22, 2007, from http://www.sdb.k12.wi.us/Tribes/TRIBES-WebVideo/index.html

Pintrich, Paul, & Dale Schunk. (1996). *Motivation in education: Theory, research, and applications*. Englewood Cliffs, NJ: Merrill/Prentice Hall.

Rogers, Carl. (1974/1961). *On becoming a person: A therapist's view of psychotherapy*. London: Constable.

Slavin, Robert. (1983). *Cooperative learning*. New York: Longman.

Vygotsky, Lev. (1978). *Mind in society: The development of higher psychological processes*. Cambridge, MA: Harvard University Press.

Weiner, Bernard. (1980). *Human motivations*. New York: Holt, Rinehart & Winston.

CHAPTER 12

A SENSE OF PURPOSE AND MISSION

Graduate Students' Perceptions of Writing Their Ethical Beliefs Statement

Ilene L. Ingram and Kevin H. Brockberg

Established policies and formal procedures cannot begin to account for every situation arising in today's classrooms and school campuses. Dilemmas abound in schools, pitting individuals or ideals against one another, demanding swift decisions and significant results. Upon what foundation can individuals depend for probing perplexing problems and arriving at just actions? As an assignment in a 2-year program leading to an education specialist degree, students write a personal *ethical beliefs statement*. This statement, we surmise, grounds student knowledge within a clear, succinct framework for the dispositions and performances demanded of current and prospective educational leaders. To test this conjecture, mixed-methods research captured graduate students' perspectives on the merit of this assignment as a foundation for moral and virtuous decision making in educational settings.

Sound ethical decision-making starts with being in touch with your own core ethical values.

—Rushworth Kidder (1995)

Woefully, in our world, the moral lapses of leadership move our culture to the edge of an ethical morass. Media reports abound with shifty shortcuts to profit and selfish personal schemes (Callahan, 2004; Johnson, 2005). The field of education is not immune; school leaders are susceptible to the same gaffe, poor judgment, and criminal conviction of corporate executives and government officials (Lipman-Blumen, 2005). Valid criticisms claim that the study of ethics and moral education is not treated comprehensively in educational administration training, nor in its knowledge base, at a time when "the moral challenges that schools confront are enormous" (Starratt, 2004, p. 4). As Sergiovanni (2007) observes, an emphasis on certain proxies, such as norms, commitment, or professional standards substitutes for true leadership of "competence plus virtue" (p. 91). Is it even possible, if ventured, to gain an ethical foothold through the many traditions of epistemology taught in our administrative preparation programs in higher education?

Education has a moral purpose and "educators who wish to be responsible for the practice of education must be prepared to take individual responsibility for thinking through defensible positions on difficult ethical questions" (Strike, Haller, & Soltis, 1988, p. ix). There is no single blueprint, no fixed, one-size-fits-all protocol, for the challenges and dilemmas school leaders encounter. Educational leaders, therefore, must have an intimate knowledge of the values and beliefs that guide their actions and the "ethical consequences associated with exercising influence over others" (Johnson, 2005, p. 4). This cultivating is of human and social value, not scientific prescription. Simply stated, ethics is an essential part of the leader's job (Strike et al.), and the ethical dimension of leadership is no longer an area of education administration preparation that can be taken for granted or reduced to simple, standardized, empiricist, logical prescription (Beckner, 2004). Nor should it be overlooked!

Exploring the ethical and moral dimensions of educational leadership is complicated by fundamental disagreements within the knowledge base of educational administration. Four decades ago Saunders, Phillips, and Johnson (1966) argued that, "defining theory, and identifying and understanding its role in educational leadership and school administration, constitutes one of the significant problems confronting educators" (p. 4). In these ensuing years, this scientific penchant for theory, roles, protocol, and standardization has dominated educational theory and practice. Donmoyer, Imber, and Scheurich (1995) in their text, *The Knowledge Base in Educational Administration: Multiple Perspectives,* side with this scientific approach, whereby "various groups within the field of education have attempted to articulate knowledge bases for their particular subfield.... These efforts sought to catalog the knowledge that the practitioners of a particular field ought to possess" (p. 1). Scientific designs for school administration prevail today (Glass, 2004).

The work of Culbertson (1988), Griffiths (1988), and Nicolaides and Gaynor (1989) led Scheurich (1995) to conclude that the "extensive body of knowledge available for use in educational administration is predominantly positivist or functionalist" (pp. 19-20). Greenfield (1986) traces the educational and administrative embrace of positivist inclinations to Herbert Simon (1957). Eaton (2004) reviewed textbooks in university training for educational administration during an even earlier era, 1914-1933, assessing them as *cookbookish* recipes for intervention (p. 41). Glass (2004) in his review concluded that even "the specialization of the professoriate fits classical scientific management theory" (p. 6). Positivism relies upon verifiable routines and resolute factual propositions for scientific administrative knowledge and decision making (Heath, 1996). Acton (1996) suggested positivism leaves no room for speculative attempts to gain knowledge by reason or through personal beliefs. Fueled by the "mere matter of logic" (p. 255), positivistic school administration would cruise along a predictable course like a fine-tuned machine. Yet the journey of schools is hardly predictable, neither is it wholly prescriptive, nor is it completely positivistic. There are ethical detours and moral obstacles along the way to an educational destination. Issues of student attendance, cheating, insolence, bullying, and legal threats shackle opportunities for learning. A recent survey by Common Good (2004) revealed 70% of teachers encountered serious problems with students disrupting the learning process in classrooms. The presence of the achievement gap, the allocation of increasingly scarce resources, and the ever-present reality of teacher attrition are other difficulties encountered in the day-to-day life of schooling.

In contrast to the positivistic inclinations of educational leadership, Greenfield (1986) notes that "administrators know administration; scientists don't" (p. 75). Strawson (1996) posits there are indeed those situations and dilemmas which confound logic, pit resolute facts against other resolute facts, and "offer for contemplation a shift in our ideas, a revision in our concepts, a new way of looking at the world" (p. 203). Take for instance, the recent incident in the Katy Independent School District (Radcliffe & Eriksen, 2007), in which a middle school student scrawled graffiti on a gym wall. Katy school officials felt their hands were tied by the law, necessarily pressing charges for a felony conviction (with consequences equivalent to making terrorist threats or assault with bodily injury), yet in other school districts the matter could have resulted in lesser charges of criminal misconduct and a fine, or resolved with a phone call to parents. Sergiovanni (2007) advocates transformational leadership invoking moral involvement, duty, and obligation for the good of schooling to be done, and done with virtue. Administrative decision making becomes humane in metaphysical transcendence, rather than by adhering to a fixed science of positivism or the letter of the law.

In *Reculturing the Profession of Educational Leadership: New Blueprints* (2002), Joseph Murphy, the coauthor of the Interstate School Leaders Licensure Consortium standards, advances the central problem in administration. He stated:

> This default to positivism and our fascination with building the academic infrastructure of school administration [which] has produced some serious distortions in what is primarily an applied field ... keeping the spotlight focused on academic knowledge also leads to or, at least, reinforces, the belief that better theories will be the savior of administrative practice. That is, if we can just develop better theories, the educational world would be stronger, and graduates would be more effective leaders. (p. 69)

Starratt (2004) concurs, noting that "issues that school leaders face tend to be presented and interpreted primarily as technical, rationalizable problems resolvable by technical, rational solutions" (p. 4). Strike et al. (1988) further posit that long-held beliefs view administration as a science of decisions, actions, results, policies, and goals that others deem to be desirable.

Greenfield (1986) suggests "we must consider more fully such philosophical issues as the nature of *value* and the question of *right* value. What constitutes *good* or *right* in administrative affairs and how can administrators gain knowledge of it?" (p. 76). Rebore (2001) argues that ethics is concerned with human conduct and one's conduct is rational because it is intentional. Little attention has been given to philosophy and ethical studies in administration preparation programs; ethics often seem far removed from the everyday challenges of the school administrator. This is essentially the question raised at the outset of this article, namely, is it possible to incorporate an ethical foothold through advanced studies of leadership and management in our administrative preparation programs in higher education in our university classrooms?

To explore the breadth and depth of ethical and moral development in its connection with leadership in university coursework, this research team recruited graduate students in an on-campus cohort to participate in the study. Seeking to uncover students' perceptions about writing their personal ethical beliefs statements, we forged two research questions: "To what degree and in what ways has the education specialist program contributed to your ethical beliefs?" and "To what degree, and in what ways, has the assignment to write an ethical beliefs statement helped to frame your understanding of educational leadership?"

METHODOLOGY

Population

Twelve of the 16 students enrolled in the education specialist (EdS) program at a Midwestern university participated in the study ($n = 75\%$), and all 12 of these students consented to participate in the follow-up focus group session. These graduate students worked in elementary and secondary public schools in urban, suburban, and rural districts. Of these 12, four already worked as administrators and eight were teachers preparing for administrative certification. Six females and six males participated in the research.

Mixed Methods

The cohort students would initially respond to a questionnaire comprised of six items for quantitative ratings and two open-ended questions. The data collection would close with a qualitative focus group session for the entire cohort. This mixed method design employed Eisner's (1997) conception of "binocular vision" where "one mode of conception [quantitative] and one form of disclosure [qualitative] is simply inadequate to exhaust the richness of educational life" (p. 72) and, we would contend, the bedrock of the ethical beliefs captured by both scientific means and personal expression.

To study the multidimensionality of meaning as a relational concept, we employed a questionnaire (Appendix A) to survey the value of the assignment of the ethical beliefs statement by means of a semantic differential format. Somewhat similar to the continuum of a Likert scale, semantic differentials explore the spectrum of beliefs, attitudes, and opinions through a range of possible responses anchored by opposing pairs of adjectives or phrases. According to Heise (1970),

> Semantic differentials delve deeply into personal convictions with three basic dimensions of response ... which have been labeled evaluation, potency, and activity (EPA), [and] have been verified and replicated in an impressive variety of studies...using a few pure scales of this sort, one can obtain, with considerable economy, reliable measures of a person's overall response to something. (p. 235)

The research team considered both utility and reliability in selecting the semantic differential format for the questionnaire. These quantitative measures would provide a succinct, initial snapshot of the students' perceptions of the ethical beliefs assignment.

The questionnaire also included two open-ended questions "to build upon and explore participants' responses" (Seidman, 1991, p. 9). These two questions served the dual purpose of gathering feedback free from researcher assumptions and restraints inherent in a closed-item questionnaire, as well as identifying potential starting points for the focus group questions. "The intent of using the [focus] group for the discussion was to encourage the participants in the session to interact with each other so that the quality of the output is enhanced" (Greenbaum, 2000, p. 3), getting to "self-disclosure among participants" (Kreuger & Casey, 2000, p. 7). The focus group process is outlined in Appendix B. Combined with the semantic differentials questionnaire, these mixed methods fully explored the reaches of the ethical beliefs assignment.

Data Collection

Two doctoral students assisted the research team, administering the questionnaire to the participants and then tabulating the descriptive statistics from the semantic differentials. These two students also extracted themes from the open-ended responses in the questionnaire, adeptly drawing out shared meanings and noting divergent reflections, and presented these combined results to the research team.

While Krueger and Casey (2000) advise three to four focus group members, the research team opted to conduct the focus group process with the entire group of 12 students. Capitalizing on the close-knit nature of the cohort developed over the course of two years would enhance the interaction, catalyze self-disclosure, and probe deeply into the value of the ethical beliefs assignment. The relatively small size of the group and the permissive and non-judgmental climate within the cohort facilitated the single focus group session.

For 33 minutes, the two doctoral students moderated the focus group process outlined by Krueger and Casey (2000) and presented in Appendix B, leading the cohort through *opening* and *introductory* questions, and warming up the participants to the topic with *transition* questions. Responses to the two key questions ("Ideally, what would your administrative preparation look like if it were optimally supporting the development of ethical leaders?" and "What are some practical steps the Department of Educational Leadership at this university can take to make this EdS program more effective at fostering the development of ethical leadership?")

commanded a majority of the session. Debriefing the process closed with *ending* questions. Throughout the session, the first moderator kept field notes about the discussion, while the second moderator guided the process to its conclusion. The session was digitally recorded with the permission of the focus group.

The doctoral students reviewed the recording, examined the field notes and then prepared a written summary of the focus group session. To verify the reliability of the focus group summary, two participants from the cohort were randomly selected to read the summary to determine the accuracy of this digest, suggesting any changes that would better capture what was shared in the focus group session. This technique of member checking (Lincoln & Guba, 1985; Stringer, 2004) safeguards the reliability of the results leading to fitting conclusions.

RESULTS

Three waves of results capture the value of the ethical beliefs assignment. The first two waves emanate from the questionnaire and the third is derived from the focus group session.

Questionnaire

First, Table 12.1 presents the mean scores and the standard deviations for the six semantic differentials. Pairs of questions in Table 12.1 organize and indicate the perceived importance (semantic differential prompts 1 and 2) of, the felt personal impact (prompts 3 and 4) from, and the relationship (prompts 5 and 6) of the ethical beliefs assignment to the EdS program. The mean is the average value selected by the 12 participants; a mean of 4.00 represents the middle value on the 7-point continuum, while a value of 7.00 represents a perfectly positive response and a value of 1.00 a purely negative response. The standard deviation is also a very significant indicator, representing the spread of the responses. A large standard deviation (*SD*) means outlying values from responses shift and distort the mean away from a true average. Hence, both the means and the standard deviations are necessary for understanding the perceived value of the ethical beliefs statement assignment.

Both the importance of and the personal impact of the ethical beliefs assignment not only rank very high (all four means > 6.00 on a seven-point scale), the small standard deviations ranging from 0.453 to 1.165) further indicate a high level of agreement on these four items among the participants regarding importance and personal impact of the

Table 12.1. Mean Scores and Standard Deviations for Semantic Differential Prompts

Prompt	Mean[a]	SD
1. Ethical beliefs are important/unimportant in differing facets of school administration	6.42	1.165
2. I place great/little importance on ethical beliefs in my current role	6.75	0.452
3. Critically examining my own ethical beliefs has proved to be applicable/unconnected to my current role	6.08	0.996
4. Critically examining my own ethical beliefs has proved to be valuable/unimportant	6.50	0.674
5. Coursework throughout the EdS program emphasized the centrality of ethical beliefs in an administrator's role and performance	4.36	1.629
6. As I progressed through the EdS program, my ethical beliefs changed significantly/remained unchanged	2.67	1.371

[a]On a 7-point continuum, a mean of 4.00 would be the middle value, with a value of 7.00 anchoring the positive pole and 1.00 anchoring the negative pole.

assignment. The mean of 4.36 for prompt 5 concerning the prevalence of connections made to the ethical beliefs statement in course content and its corresponding larger standard deviation ($SD = 1.629$) indicates a greater difference of opinion for this item. The low mean (mean = 2.67, $SD = 1.371$) for the final prompt indicates that students entered the EdS program already with a set of core ethical beliefs; this low mean indicates these beliefs did not change significantly because of the EdS program.

Second, written responses to the open-ended questions closely coincided with the results from the semantic differentials. Only four respondents listed specific examples (particular courses, memorable dilemmas, and mentorship experience) of how the ethical beliefs statement surfaced in the program. One participant wondered if the written ethical beliefs statement might be more effective when assigned in the middle or even the end of the program; another student noted, "It needed to be much more connected throughout the program and not a mere glimpse provided in the first class [course] and never touched again." All students wrote about the value of the assignment, expressing personal and professional understanding, grounded and solidified values, its appropriateness as a tool for reflection, and suggesting the worth of revisiting or revising the ethical beliefs statement throughout the 2-year program.

Focus Group Session

Third, the moderators collaborated and composed a summary of the information gathered in the focus group session from their notes, the recording, and the verification from member checking. The focus group procedures outlined by Kreuger and Casey (2000) serve as the progression (see Appendix B) for the summary which follows.

Comments to the introductory question (What is the first thing that comes to mind when you hear the phrase *ethical beliefs statement?*) included "soul-searching," "integrity," "high level of engagement," "values," "morals," "ethical standards," "deep, personal reflection," and "professional introspection." These responses correspond to the personal impact (semantic differential prompts 3 and 4) and the open-ended responses in the questionnaire.

To make the transition to the two key questions (Ideally, what would your administrative preparation look like if it were optimally supporting the development of ethical leaders? and What are some practical steps the Department of Educational Leadership at this university can take to make this EdS program more effective at fostering the development of ethical leadership?), the moderators interjected clarifying prompts (see Table 12.1) as necessary to help participants expand on their remarks made to the introductory question. These revealed that their ethical values were already well-known to each of the individuals, so the assignment was initially viewed as "easy" (corresponding to the 2.67 mean on standard deviation prompt 6 about changing beliefs). As the discussion ensued, participants shared that actually expressing ethical beliefs was "hard," indeed "narrowing it down" in writing and "putting in on paper" proved perplexing and most challenging. Condensing deeply held beliefs into written statements led one participant to explain there were "not enough words to express my beliefs." One student expressed that the ethical beliefs statement "represents and supports how I make decisions about what to do in those cases where the answers aren't easy."

Regarding key question 1 (Ideally, what would your administrative preparation look like if it were optimally supporting the development of ethical leaders?), there was consensus in the group that throughout the sequence of courses in the EdS program, connections between the course content and the ethical beliefs statement from the first course should be made, supporting the assertions made in prompt 5 and the open-ended questions. "Going back" to the ethical beliefs statement for "reviewing" and "modifying" received much support, and several topics and assignments from classes and mentorship experiences were offered as examples in which the connection with the ethical beliefs statement could embellish the understandings and meanings of coursework and thereby enlighten administrative practice. In sum, participants expressed all classes did not "push" the importance and application of the ethical beliefs statement. One individual expressed that optimal administrative preparation would "qualify me as a resource for others." Another noted that the ethical beliefs statement became a key resource to review in preparing for an interview.

Further, for key question 2 (What are some practical steps the Department of Educational Leadership at this university can take to make the EdS program more effective at fostering the development of ethical leadership?), the group wondered whether or not instructors in the sequence of courses knew about this "cornerstone" of the EdS program. It was strongly suggested that the ethical beliefs statement should not be an exercise for one course, but must interweave throughout the entire program. Practically speaking, ethical beliefs would "benefit me as a leader, not a lawyer" in the school law class, should be "brought in" to the school finance course, and would have much background for "aspects of diversity" considered in some other courses. Several of these themes echoed in the results from the questionnaire.

Leading to closure, ending question 1 (When all things are considered, how valuable is the ethical beliefs statement to the EdS program?) yielded reflections expressed as "foundational," "integral," and "must be revisited frequently." The belief that "leadership cannot happen without it [ethics]" seemed to capture the intrinsic value of the ethical beliefs assignment in the EdS program.

Finally, ending question 2 (Is there anything else we should have discussed that we didn't?) led to discourse about the format of the ethical beliefs statement. It was expressed again that the assignment was "hard." Responses cited that a sample ethical beliefs statement was "helpful" and there was a need for more examples; however, caution was also expressed that the beliefs statements do not become "cookie cutter assignments." The group desired flexibility in the format and wondered about the "grading" of beliefs, preferring a rubric for elements within the ethical beliefs statement.

The three waves of data, namely; the semantic differentials, the open-ended responses, and the focus group process generated significant insights into the value of the ethical beliefs assignment for practicing and aspiring school administrators. To fathom the experience of these students in writing their assignments through the focus group session moved this beyond a positivist research design, for leadership cannot be confined solely to positivist orientations.

CONCLUSIONS

The results and revelations from both the questionnaire and the focus group session converge and lead to important conclusions. From this research study we realize the immense value students attribute to this course assignment. Clearly, these graduate students recognized the imperative foundation, and even rehearsed the application of their ethical beliefs leading to moral action. We surmise that the intense process of critical, ethical reflection promotes the value ascribed to the process, and that the perceived gain in maturity in ethical reflection in turn lends symbiotic credence to the assignment. This maturity in ethical thinking and decision making and the greater consideration for the moral and ethical roles of leaders moves one beyond the mere state of moral maturity to an even more fundamental awareness of life purpose. What matters from a leadership context is the way leaders respond to social issues such as racism, poverty, world hunger, world peace, and issues of social justice as well as preventing harm. At its best, ethical leadership engenders praxis that contributes to a better society. Thus, writing one's personal ethical beliefs statement evokes ethical consciousness, whereby students look honestly and deeply within themselves to determine "who" they are as people, as world citizens, and as educational leaders shouldering ethical obligations to schools and society.

As an extension, with such personal and professional impetus, at the university we must begin to make the ethical beliefs statement, initiated in the first course, integral to all classes in the program. Instructors must first become aware of this research, recognizing the value students place on the ethical beliefs statement. Then, as a department, the faculty must discuss how this statement can thread its way into the fabric and sequence of courses leading to the education specialist degree. We believe the assignment to require aspiring and practicing educational leaders to formulate and write individual personal ethical platform statements leads to a better understanding of "self" and places students not only at the center of their own ethical decision making but also as a foundation for their praxis. Today's educational leaders should expect to encounter many ethical dilemmas in their school settings, and the ethical beliefs statement can serve to affirm, inspire, and guide our students to be leaders of virtuous character with a sense of ethical purpose and moral mission.

APPENDIX A: ETHICAL BELIEFS STATEMENT QUESTIONNAIRE

Directions: To indicate your response, make heavy marks in the circles as the prompts direct you. Please mark only one circle per item. Your completion of this questionnaire conveys your consent to voluntarily participate in the survey. As the survey is voluntary, you may quit at any time.

I am ____.		
○ a practicing administrator	○ a nonadministrator/ teacher	○ a former administrator

Coursework throughout the EdS program emphasized the centrality of ethical beliefs in an administrator's role and performance.		
neglected	○ ○ ○ ○ ○ ○ ○	incorporated

Ethical beliefs are ____ in differing facets of school administration.		
important	○ ○ ○ ○ ○ ○ ○	unimportant

As I progressed through the EdS program, my ethical beliefs.		
remained unchanged	○ ○ ○ ○ ○ ○ ○	changed significantly

Critically examining my own ethical beliefs has proved to be.		
valuable	○ ○ ○ ○ ○ ○ ○	unimportant

Critically examining my own ethical beliefs have proved to be ____ in my current role.		
unconnected	○ ○ ○ ○ ○ ○ ○	applicable

I place ____ importance on my ethical beliefs in my current role.		
great	○ ○ ○ ○ ○ ○ ○	little

Please write your narrative responses in the spaces that are provided. Use the back of the paper, if necessary.

1. What are some examples of ways in which the ethical beliefs statement is supported in your administrative preparation in the Education Specialist Program?
2. Is the assignment to develop the Professional/ethical beliefs statement valuable in terms of framing your understanding about the role of the educational leader (principal)? Explain why or why not.

APPENDIX B: FOCUS GROUP PROCESS

Overview—Moderators present alternately:

1. Thank you for your voluntary participation.
2. We are teaming this for the EdS program director.
3. Purpose is to formally gather feedback about the ethical beliefs statement.
4. No right or wrong answers to our questions, we are sounding out differing points of view.
5. Tape recording for our benefit as analysts. Your comments are confidential, your names will not be included in any reports.
6. We are interested in hearing from each of you.

A. *Opening Question*—Moderator 1

"How much time are you willing to spend on this topic tonight?"

B. *Introductory Question*—Moderator 2

"What is the first thing that comes to mind when you hear the phrase *ethical beliefs statement?*"

C. *Transition Question*—both moderators ask clarifying questions as needed to process and clarify responses to the introductory question.

D. *Key Questions*—Moderator 1

1. "Ideally, what would your administrative preparation look like if it were optimally supporting the development of ethical leaders?"
2. "What are some practical steps the Department of Educational Leadership at this university can take to make this EdS program more effective at fostering the development of ethical leadership?"

E. *Ending Questions*—alternating

1. Moderator 1 "When all things are considered, how valuable is the ethical beliefs statement in the EdS program?"
2. Moderator 2 gives an oral summary of what happened this evening in two or three minutes maximum.
3. Moderator 1 asks how well moderator 2's summary captures what was discovered this evening.

4. Moderator 2 gives a closing statement (which is a restatement of the *Overview*)
5. Moderator 1 "Is there anything else that we should have discussed that we didn't?"

REFERENCES

Acton, H. B. (1996). Positivism. In J. O. Urmson & Jonathan Ree (Eds.), *The concise encyclopedia of Western philosophy and philosophers* (2nd ed., pp. 252-256). New York: Routledge.

Beckner, Weldon. (2004). *Ethics for educational leaders*. New York: Pearson.

Callahan, David. (2004). *The cheating culture: Why more Americans are doing wrong to get ahead*. Orlando, FL: Harcourt.

Common Good. (2004, 1 May). *Teaching interrupted: Do discipline policies in today's public schools foster the common good?* Retrieved August 13, 2007, from http://cgood.org/society-reading-cgpubs-polls-3.html

Donmoyer, Robert, Michael Imber, & James Joseph Scheurich. (Eds.). (1995). Framing the debate: Philosophical, historical and practical issues. In *The knowledge base in educational administration: Multiple perspectives* (pp. 1-13). Albany: State University of New York Press.

Eaton, William. (2004). From ideology to conventional wisdom: School-administration texts, 1915-1933. In Thomas E. Glass (Ed.), *The history of educational administration viewed through it textbooks* (pp. 31-44). Lanham, MD: Scarecrow Education.

Eisner, Elliot W. (1997). Critique. *Anthropology & Education Quarterly, 8*(2), 71-72.

Glass, Thomas E. (2004). *The history of educational administration viewed through it textbooks*. Lanham, MD: Scarecrow Education.

Greenbaum, Thomas L. (2000). *Moderating focus groups: A practical guide for group facilitation*. Thousand Oaks, CA: SAGE.

Greenfield, Thomas B. (1986). The decline and fall of science in educational administration. *Interchange, 17*(2), 57-80.

Heath, P. L. (1996). Logical positivism. In J. O. Urmson & Jonathan Ree (Eds.), *The concise encyclopedia of Western philosophy and philosophers* (2nd ed., pp. 182-187). New York: Routledge.

Heise, David R. (1970). The semantic differential and attitude research. In Gene F. Summers (Ed.), *Attitude measurement* (pp. 235-253). Chicago: Rand McNally.

Johnson, Craig E. (2005). *Meeting the ethical challenges of leadership: Casting light or shadow*. Thousand Oaks, CA: SAGE.

Kidder, Rushworth M. (1995). *How good people make tough choices*. New York: William Morrow.

Kreuger, Richard A., & Mary Anne Casey. (2000). *Focus groups: A practical guide for applied research* (3rd ed.). Thousand Oaks, CA: SAGE.

Lipman-Blumen, Jean. (2005). *The allure of toxic leaders: Why we follow destructive bosses and corrupt politicians and how we can survive them*. New York: Oxford University Press.

Lincoln, Yolanda S., & Egon G. Guba. (1985). *Naturalistic inquiry*. Newbury Park, CA: SAGE.

Murphy, Joseph. (Ed.). (2002). Reculturing the profession of educational leadership: New blueprints. In *The educational leadership challenge: Redefining leadership for the 21st century* (pp. 65-78). Chicago: University of Chicago Press.

Radcliffe, Jennifer, & Helen Eriksen. (2007, July 30). Katy graffiti case boosts need for code flexibility. *Houston Chronicle*. Retrieved August 12, 2007, from http://www.chron.com/disp/story.mpl/front/5009923.html

Rebore, Ronald W. (2001). *The ethics of educational leadership*. Upper Saddle River, NJ: Prentice-Hall.

Saunders, Robert L., Ray C. Phillips, & Harold T. Johnson. (1966). *A theory of educational leadership*. Columbus, OH: Charles E. Merrill Books.

Scheurich, James J. (1995). The knowledge base in educational administration: Postpositivist reflections. In Robert Donmoyer, Michael Imber, & James Joseph Scheurich (Eds.), *The knowledge base in educational administration: Multiple perspectives* (pp. 17-31). Albany: State University of New York Press.

Seidman, Irving. (1991). *Interviewing as qualitative research: A guide for researchers in education and the social sciences*. New York: Teachers College Press.

Sergiovanni, Thomas J. (2007). *Rethinking leadership* (2nd ed.). Thousand Oaks, CA: Corwin.

Simon, Herbert. (1957). *Administrative behavior: A study of decision-making processes in administrative organization* (2nd ed.). New York: The Free Press.

Strawson, P. F. (1996). Metaphysics. In J. O. Urmson & Jonathan Ree (Eds.), *The concise encyclopedia of Western philosophy and philosophers* (2nd ed., pp. 202-208). New York: Routledge.

Starratt, Robert J. (2004). *Ethical leadership*. San Francisco: Wiley & Sons.

Strike, Kenneth A., Emil J. Haller, & Jonas F. Soltis. (1988). *The ethics of school administration*. New York: Teachers College Press. Retrieved March 18, 2007, from http://www.refresher.com/!moralleadership.html

Stringer, Ernie. (2004). *Action research in education*. Upper Saddle River, NJ: Pearson.

CHAPTER 13

IDENTITY DEVELOPMENT FOR HOLISTIC GLOBAL INTERCONNECTEDNESS

Douglas F. Warring

Culturally responsible pedagogists need to transfer the knowledge bases about social justice and equity into actions, behaviors, and practices to work for peace and social justice. One of the ways to work for equity and social justice is to expand the knowledge of our college and university students about themselves and their identity and the process of identity development. In our classes we can work toward the continuing identity development of our students by helping them to first learn about themselves. This chapter describes research focused on the use of reflective self-reporting, cultural self-awareness, and identity development assessment to determine the impact of a human relations and multicultural education course on university student's growth and development for social justice, global awareness, global acceptance, and peace.

THE COMPLEXITIES OF IDENTITY DEVELOPMENT FOR SOCIAL JUSTICE AND PEACE

People are involved in complex interactions of variables operating multidimensionally to understand self and others. One of these dimensions is a global one. Merryfield (1997) emphasizes the following perspectives in describing elements of a global education; to achieve cross-cultural understanding, "one must develop, in part, an understanding of one's own culture and heritage" and "the role of one's own culture in the world system, while seeking to understand the "multiple identities" and "worldviews" of others" (p. 9). Educators, then, are encouraged to design practices that promote the development of consciousness of perspectives. When a person understands the cultural, social, spiritual, and historical contexts in which a behavior is occurring, or the application of an individual's reality, the individual is better equipped to engage in appropriate activities for peace and social justice. Multiple factors continuously interact at a conscious and subconscious level to impact identity and identity development. Gollnick and Chinn (2004) state that teaching for social justice and peace requires a disposition of caring and social responsibility for all students. Since teaching and working for social justice and peace is a difficult journey that begins with self-awareness, it is important to understand how to assist people in this journey. (For further consideration of teaching for social justice, see Huber-Warring & Warring, 2006, 2007; Warring, 2007; Warring & Huber-Warring, 2006.)

Identity construction is a phrase used by many researchers who discuss development as a process of potential progression throughout life where identity is a personal belief about self (Noel, 2000). This progression is not a consistent process contingent upon one's age nor a function of age but rather of life experience and an awakening of awareness of those experiences and reflection upon them. A healthy personal identity will assist learners in doing well educationally because it is rooted in a positive feeling of self. Since personal identity is a dynamic interaction between self-image, attitudes, beliefs, and feelings, when a person feels positive about him or herself the person is more likely to entertain ideas previously ignored (D'Andrea & Daniels, 1990). This entertainment of ideas represents a complex interaction of psychosocial context, physical characteristics, personality attribute, unique experiences, and personal choices according to Babad, Birnbaum, and Benne (1983).

Researchers have begun to develop models to examine peoples' worldview or relationship to global connections as part of their attitudes toward themselves. A key element of Western individualistic models is the need for choice and autonomy (Katz, 1985). Self-theorists in both psychology and sociology believe that self and self-concepts have meaning based on interaction and relationships with other people and groups (Niedenthal & Beike, 1997).

Culture refers to the customs, practices, languages, values, and worldviews that define groups such as those based on ethnicity, region, or common interests. Daniel (1996) contends that cultural identity is important for people's sense of self and how they relate to others. Cultural reference group, language spoken, cultural or other factors in development, involvement with culture of origin, involvement with host culture, cultural explanations of behavior, cultural norms, psychosocial environment, sociocultural, sociohistorical, spiritual, and interrelated issues all impact identity development. These items create a mosaic, which is constantly changing and is valuable in understanding contextual issues related to identity development.

Identity development, a significant element in belief formation, grows, or has the potential to grow, from a self-focused or narrow identity to a more expansive and inclusive one challenging beliefs and ideas and thereby allowing an individual to examine peace, social justice, race, gender, socioeconomic status, exceptionality, and other significant identities and combinations. The personal view and orientation of one's belief about others will influence which aspects are selected and how they are configured (Myers et al., 1991). Identity development then, is not a one-dimensional concept but a process with the potential for continual ongoing growth.

This work is focused on the need to understand the potential impact of a human relations and multicultural education course on university student's growth and development for social justice, global awareness, global acceptance, and peace. The next sections of this chapter will review factors involved in identity development; describe research focused on the use of reflective self-reporting, cultural self-awareness, and identity development assessment; and discuss the optimal theory applied to identity development-revised analysis based on the levels of identity development (Haggins et al., 1996) to assess beliefs, dispositions, and actions that would indicate levels of identity development and working for social justice and peace.

SELF AND IDENTITY DEVELOPMENT

An individual's culture, background, training, history, social interactions, community, and other factors and experiences, as well as the ability to reflect on these, have an impact on identity and identity development, and views of the self. The views of self differ depending upon the type of culture in which a person is socialized. Triandis (1989) contends that the focus and belief of self differs in collectivistic and individualistic cultures. In an individualistic culture, a belief exists that self is located within the individual (I). In a collectivistic culture, the sense of self is based on affiliation with the group (We). Can an integration and synthesis, which fosters a positive identity of self, be nurtured in both types of cultures?

Huitt (2004) defines *self-concept* as a knowledge of one's self and *self-esteem* as one's subjective evaluation of one's value or worth. It remains fluid and is subjective. The two terms *self-esteem* and *self-concept* are often used interchangeably, but they differ in how they refer to the way a person feels about him or herself in the formation of identity (Huitt, 2004). For the purposes of this discussion, *self-esteem* is our view of ourselves as others see us and *self-concept* is our own interpretation of how we see ourselves.

In the early stages of formation, people are impacted by the perceptions of others that affect our self-esteem and, to a lesser extent, our self-concept. Because of this fluidity, identity is unstable and susceptible to change. Thus, you can have a highly developed stable self-concept and be in a new situation where you are unsure of the rules and be more susceptible to influences by others (self-esteem). Self-concept is more stable and consists of our view of ourselves interpreted by us; thus, it is much more concrete and less susceptible to change. As people mature, they have the potential capacity to be impacted more by their own self-concept. Mature, self-assured adults also develop the ability to compartmentalize issues identifying and enhancing areas of strength or success while minimizing the importance of areas that lack strength. Thus an accomplished math teacher may be untroubled by admitting a lack of ability for athletics.

Erik Erikson (1968) believed in having an identity consistent with one's society and focused on psychosocial development, which was culturally relative. Individuals who are members of more than one group or subculture can often identify with each group. When this identification occurs in fairly equal amounts, a synthesized identity can result. This is often the case for those expressing a pluralistic identity. Daniel (1996) contended these individuals often recognize the commonalities among reference groups and at the same time appreciate the differences, which is an integrative, yet, pluralistic identity (Cross, 1991).

The spiritual dimension is often seen as a key component regardless of the personal religious beliefs of the individual. Fukuyama and Sevig (1997) have explored this dimension and state that, "the spiritual journey often appears as a dynamic, highly personal experience. Each person's spiritual journey was unique and reflective of a diversity of faith development models" (p. 235). Whether one believes in Erikson's model of psychosocial development or other models, all possess similarities in the potential movement toward growth.

RACIAL/ETHNIC IDENTITY DEVELOPMENT

Most racial identity theorists describe psychological development from the perspective of racial, rather then ethnic identity. Racial identity theories describe multidimensional and multifaceted aspects of identification.

Racial identity is comprised of attitudes, thoughts, feelings, and behaviors toward oneself and as a member of a racial group, toward members of other groups. Family, community, and society all impact racial identity. Because one's personality is formed in the context of racial group membership, the relationships between racial identity and personality are quite complex and interrelated, particularly as one considers the psychosocial environment in which they evolve.

Social scientists identified the relationship between racial identity and personality and the individuals rather than just the movements and some developed dynamic stage models. Helms and Carter (1990) suggested a shift from earlier models of invariant types or stage theories to one of attitudes or levels and discussed the importance of the most predominant level or attitude (Cross, 1991; Helms, 1990; Helms & Carter, 1990; Sue & Sue, 1990; Thomason, 1994). These theories are all stage-based and sequential. Thus, personality includes race and racial identity in extremely dynamic and complex ways and, taken together helps to explain elements of individual identity development.

Phinney (1990) contends, "ethnic identity is central to the psychological functioning of members of ethnic and racial minority groups" (p. 499). Ethnic identity also assists white ethnics in better understanding their development. A problem according to Yeh and Huang (1996) is that many theories of ethnic identity are over simplistic due to their failure to account for issues such as social context and the malleability of identity within these and other frameworks. In reality, all of these are impacting the interrelationship of race, gender, class, affectional orientation, religion, ethnicity, etc., and combinations within and between. They are not easily separated although most theorists dealing with self-image and identity development attempt to separate them. Helms (1995) also contends that context is especially important in examining racial identity.

Identity is a dynamic ongoing process involving historical, social, cultural, and differential group identification processes. Identity formation depends on a process of exploration within these contexts. This will vary dramatically based on numerous factors. If a child is bicultural and raised in a family system which values one above the other or in fact ignores both, the developmental process will be much different than that of a child raised in a family system that truly values both cultures. Ignoring a part of ones development means it remains unchanged. An African proverb says that not everything that is faced can be changed, however nothing can be changed until it is faced.

Similarly impacted, according to Hollingsworth (1997), are the developmental processes including racial identity and self-image, which is highly impacted by self-esteem in transracially/transethnically adopted children. Age has also been noted to be a significant factor in these studies. The fields of psychology and psychiatry have shown more interest in identity formation and demonstrated increased cultural sensitivity by incorporating cultural considerations in their diagnostic and statistic manual (Takeuchi, 2000).

Interestingly most groups, including models of white, multiracial, and gender awareness and identity development, parallel developmental stage models. Another model by Myers et al. (1991) has seven phases and includes global dimensions, which are often ignored. Arnett (2002) maintains that due to globalization, youth are developing a culture that creates a bicultural identity or a hybrid identity that is quite complex and may even be transcultural (Suárez-Orozco & Suárez-Orozco, 2001).

The identity development models are often examining psychosocial development from the perspective of racial identity and describe multidimensional and multifaceted aspects of identification. The culture of the group itself impacts activities, language, family structure, values, and other factors seen as significant within a specific subgroup which often include beliefs about social justice and peace. The specific emphasis on social justice and peace may be a byproduct of global transcultural identity (Myers et al., 1991).

Most of the previous identity development models are stage-based theories, which are sequentially developmental much like climbing a staircase. For movement to the next stage or step, a significant change has to occur. Parham (1989) proposed a different process than typical stage theory, that of going through cycles in the process of identity construction. The theory of passing around a circle is an interesting way to conceptualize this model of stages of progression. Some cultures believe physical life to be one stage in a cycle while others view it differently. Another theorist, Helms (1990) suggests that racial theories may be additive, successive, or representative of a unique restructuring of experiences.

Noel (2000) builds a strong case for examination of the identity (development) construction process with respect to a person's ability to understand multicultural education and, similarly social justice. Noel (2001) examines the connection between a people's understanding of multicultural education and their identity construction. In her work, Noel uses the identity construction of her students to understand whether or how well they have internalized the importance of the field of multicultural education. In order to more effectively assess this, she begins with a 6-stage model of identity development: unexamined identity, search for identity, construction of identity based on devaluation of others, clarified identity, expanded sense of identity, and use of clarified identity to achieve societal change.

According to Noel (2001), people will need to reach the final stage in order to more fully recognize, understand, and address societal change.

Tatum (1997) contended that people at this stage will be actively antiracist within their areas of influence and become aware of other forms of oppression, not just racism. In their dispositions one could expect to see more action oriented statements describing positive actions for change where they confront negative statements made by others and become more actively involved in seeking positive change.

OPTIMAL THEORY APPLIED TO IDENTITY DEVELOPMENT MODEL

Most racial and other group development models, including models of White, multiracial, gender awareness, and identity development, parallel the previously discussed models. The optimal theory applied to identity development (OTAID; Myers et al., 1991) is a model that examines one's personal identity and can provide unification for people at the global level, which will assist in understanding the entire process of working for peace and social justice. The initial purpose is to gain self-knowledge, which is a process of coming to know who and what we are. All components can then be integrated into a holistic sense of self. This model is neither linear nor categorical and is conceptualized as an expanding spiral according to Myers et al. This model is based on a spiritual dimension and, according to Haggins et al. (1996), "incorporates the assumption of a world-view that does not segment the spiritual dimensions of life and compartmentalize them to be experienced apart from other aspects of daily functioning" (pp. 175-176).

A unique feature of the OTAID model compared to others is that it examines peoples' worldview and not just their attitudes, where the concept of *self* grows from a narrow definition to a broader, more inclusive one, including global acceptance and peace. It also follows a predictable sequence to a broader worldview, a spirituality that according to Shafranske and Gorsuch (1984) "is the courage to look within and to trust. What is seen and what is trusted appears to be a deep sense of belonging, of wholeness, of connectedness, and of openness to the infinite" (p. 233). *Spirituality* refers to a unique, personally meaningful experience and is not related to a specific form or appearance (Shafranske & Gorsuch, 1984). Zinnbauer and Pargament (2005) make the link between spirituality and peace indicating a significant connection is an important part of one's worldview.

A worldview of global peace and acceptance is consistent with the OTAID and suggests there is a transcendent dimension that can be achieved within the human existence. According to Haggins et al. (1996), the OTAID instrument was developed to assess identity development incorporating the assumptions of a non-fragmented world-view that does not segment the spiritual dimensions of life and compartmentalizes them to be experienced apart from other aspects of daily functioning. (p. 175)

This supports other contentions that a person's worldview does not have to be shaped by a religion per se, and can be a unifying system when viewed through the lens of spirituality on a universal level.

Cahill and Adams (1998) discuss identity and the seven phases of the OTAID model (see Figure 13.1). The OTAID model uses the term *phases* while other identity research uses the term *stages* to identify critical points in development. Both the original OTAID (designated OTAID-O) and the revised OTAID (designated OTAID-R) utilize the same seven phases; however, the OTAID-R was revised by Haggins et al. (1996), who "deleted, added, and changed some questions from the original OTAID-O [with permission from Sevig (1993)] in an attempt to strengthen the instrument in terms of its relationship to theory" (p. 180). Two additional changes made in the study being reported are that while the OTAID uses 0-6 for its phases, the author used 1-7 for the class and also used both terms *stage* and *phase* believing it easier for the students to comprehend and thus be able to respond in a more accurate manner.

In the OTAID model (both the original and revised versions), phase 1 is labeled "Absence of Awareness" and described as no awareness other than to view one's own experience. This is based on the view that all a child knows is its own sense of self. Phase 2 is labeled "Individuation" and is described as a phase where individuals lack awareness of the dominant culture's view of the self and rarely assign particular meaning or value to any aspect of their identity. Phase 3 is labeled "Dissonance" and is described as a phase where individuals effectively experience those aspects of self that are devalued by others. The experience triggers conflict between the familiar self-image and the newly experienced feelings of anger, guilt, confusion, insecurity, or sadness, which may accompany the encounter with the devalued aspects of self.

Phase 4 is labeled "Immersion" and described as a phase where individuals fully embrace others like themselves who are devalued. Phase 5 is labeled "Internalization" and described as a phase where individuals have effectively incorporated feelings of worth associated with the devalued aspects of self, resulting in an increased sense of security. Phase 6 is labeled "Integration" and is defined as a phase where individuals have developed a stronger sense of inner security and their sense of community has expanded due to a connection to more groups of people because differences are accepted (global awareness and social justice). Phase 7 is labeled "Transformation" and is described as a phase where the self is

Please circle the number that best describes where you see yourself based on the 7-phase OTAID identity development model.

PHASES OF OTAID (Optimal Theory Applied to Identity Development)

1. **Absence of Awareness:** "Life is inherently good."
   Individuals have no awareness other than to view one's own experience. This is based on the view that all a child knows is his or her own sense of self.
2. **Individuation:** "The world is just fine the way it is."
   Individuals lack awareness of the dominant culture's view of the self and rarely assign particular meaning or value to any aspect of their identity. Individuals may lack awareness of the part of self that is devalued by others. They may move from a *family* view to a broader *community* view.
3. **Dissonance:** "The world is not the way I thought it was."
   Individuals effectively experience those aspects of self, that are devalued by others. The experience triggers conflict between the familiar self-image and the newly experienced feelings of anger, guilt, confusion, insecurity, or sadness, which may accompany the encounter with the devalued aspects of self. This may be triggered by an act of discrimination.
4. **Immersion:** "The world is so unfair to people like me."
   Individuals fully embrace others like themselves who are devalued. This acceptance enables people to appreciate the devalued aspects of themselves. Individuals may *immerse* themselves, directly and/or vicariously, in the culture of the devalued group. *This is often toughest for teachers and other school personnel to understand. *
5. **Internalization:** "The world does not define who I am; I feel good about myself and more accepting of others."
   Individuals effectively incorporate feelings of worth associated with the devalued aspects of self-resulting in an increased sense of security. The devalued part of self is recognized as just one of many components of self-identity.
6. **Integration:** "With my deeper understanding of the world, I want to overcome oppression for everyone." *Global Awareness [Social Justice]*
   Individuals' sense of self has developed to a stronger place of inner security so that relationships and perceptions of others reflect this degree of inner peace. Individuals' sense of community has expanded due to a connection to more groups of people because differences are accepted.
7. **Transformation:** "We are one." *Global Acceptance [Peace]*
   Individual self is redefined toward a sense of personhood that is multidimensional, focusing on internal control and self-mastery. Individuals experience a shift in worldview based on the realization of the interrelatedness and interdependency of all things. All forms of life are accepted and valued for their contribution to the greater good of the whole; all are unique manifestations of the spirit as the individuals define it.

Prequestions:

At this point in my life I believe I am at stage or phase	1	2	3	4	5	6	7
The first day of this class I believe I was at stage or phase	1	2	3	4	5	6	7

Postquestions:

The first day of this class I believe I was at stage or phase	1	2	3	4	5	6	7
At this point in my life I believe I am at stage or phase	1	2	3	4	5	6	7

Source: Adapted from Cahill and Adams (1998).

Figure 13.1.   OTAID instrument.

redefined toward a sense of personhood that is multidimensional, focusing on internal control and self-mastery. Individuals in this phase experience a shift in worldview based on the realization of the interrelatedness and interdependency of all things (global acceptance and peace).

RESEARCHING IDENTITY DEVELOPMENT FOR SOCIAL JUSTICE AND PEACE

The current study examined the responses on the OTAID identity development instrument from candidates enrolled in an introductory teacher education course. The course is required for licensure. The scores from the third week of classes and the last week of classes in each course were compared and analyses were run to see if changes had occurred. Dispositions that were self-reported were also examined to check for consistency of comments related to each level.

Participants and Course Format

All participants were candidates for licensure enrolled in courses required in their respective programs of study. The courses include three sections of a graduate course in human relations/multicultural education (one of which was combined with undergraduates), and one section of a course in undergraduate human relations/multicultural education that met concurrently with a graduate class. All participants were students enrolled in a private, predominantly White, university located in a metropolitan area in the Midwest.

The participants were asked to voluntarily list their sex, age, race, and ethnic/cultural background as well as some other descriptors each time they filled out the survey. They were asked for self-identification of race and also of ethnic/cultural background rather than being asked to identify pre-established categories or boxes to be checked. The results were then transcribed and compiled.

The participants included 38 students, 29 with paired samples (see Table 13.1) consisting of 8 males and 21 females. The 29 paired pre-/post-respondents identified the following racial categories (see Table 13.2): African American 1, Asian American 3, European American 20, Hispanic American 2, Biracial American 2, and other 1.

Participants were enrolled in courses required as core courses and devoted to human relations and multicultural issues. At this institution, core programs are defined as those that require all students who plan to graduate to successfully complete those courses that are specified as requirements. All sections of the courses in human relations/multicultural education had the same instructor, the author, a predominantly European

Table 13.1. Participants

Participants	Frequency	Percent
Females	21	27.59
Males	8	72.41

Table 13.2. Participants by Self-Defined Race

Participants	Number	Percent of Participants
African American	1	3.4
American Indian	0	0
Asian American	3	10.3
Biracial American	2	6.9
European American	20	68.9
Hispanic American	2	6.9
Missing	1	3.4
Total	29	100*

*Percent may not total 100 due to rounding of numbers.

American heritage male professor with a doctorate in educational psychology and 33 years of experience teaching in this field. Although there were minor differences in length of requirements between the graduate courses and the undergraduate course, they all required the same content and had similar expectations. All sections of the courses met once a week for 150 minutes for 15 weeks.

All of the sections were assigned the same readings by authors from a variety of cultural backgrounds and given assignments to analyze their own culture and at least one other culture and make specific applications to the classroom. They were also given specific criteria and assigned the task of conducting a community-based analysis and interview with a person who self-defines as a member of a specific cultural group (different than their own). All assignments were designed to increase and assess awareness, knowledge, skills, and make applications of multicultural concepts.

Procedures

The intent of this research was to determine if a 15-week course on multicultural education would have any impact on students' beliefs about their growth according to the OTAID phases of identity development model. A research packet on identity development based on the OTAID instrument and a personal data sheet were distributed to all students. Participation was anonymous and voluntary; the students who volunteered to participate signed an informed consent form that informed them that there was no reward or penalty for participation.

The instrument used the term stage instead of phase, since most theories on identity development use this term and it was commonly discussed during the semester. The preinstrument was completed during the third week of classes and the postinstrument was completed during the last, or 15th week of classes. The third week of class was selected to provide some familiarity with the instrument for the participants and to allow for time to settle into the semester and consider the instrument's overall meaning. All forms were completed and placed in manila envelopes by the students, collected by a student volunteer, and returned to the instructor in each course. The courses were completed and all grades were assigned prior to opening the envelopes and beginning to tabulate the results.

On the preinstrument, the participants were asked to read over the seven stages and circle a response that most closely indicated where they thought they were according to the OTAID. Prequestions were #1, *At this point in my life I believe I am at stage or phase* (circle 1-7); and prequestion #2, *The first day of this class I believe I was at stage or phase* (circle 1-7). On the postinstrument, the participants were asked to read over the seven stages and circle a response that most closely indicated where they thought they were according to the OTAID. The post questions were reversed. Postquestion #1, *The first day of this class I believe I was at stage or phase* (circle 1-7); Postquestion #2, *At this point in my life I believe I am at stage or phase* (circle 1-7).

Because this derivation resulted in a new instrument, a factor analysis and a Cronbach's alpha were run. The factor analysis examined the type of relationship that might exist between the two questions on a pretest and on a posttest. The factor analysis confirmed that a difference should exist in pre and posttests since the class was conducted between administrations of the instrument. The Cronbach's alpha was 0.75 showing interitem correlation meaning the same construct was being measured. When reliability was run using a Cronbach's alpha, it was 0.042 showing a significant change in the self reported beliefs of the participants as to their level of identity.

Analysis and Results

OTAID scoring was based on a 7-point Likert-type scale, where participants were asked to circle the number from 1 through 7 most closely corresponding to the level of identity development where they felt they

Identity Development for Holistic Global Interconnectedness 237

Table 13.3. Pre- and Postscores

OTAID Phase	Third Week of Classes				Fifteenth Week of Classes			
	Pre Item #1 Now	Pre Item #1 Now	Pre Item #2 Beg	Pre Item #2 Beg	Post Item #1 Beg	Post Item #1 Beg	Post Item #2 Now	Post Item #2 Now
	Freq	%	Freq	%	Freq	%	Freq/	%
1	0	0	0	0	1	3	1	3
2	0	0	0	0	2	7	1	3
3	1	3	0	0	7	24	4	14
4	0	0	0	0	3	10	2	7
5	15	52	4	14	9	31	13	45
6	13	45	19	66	7	24	9	31
7	0	0	6	21	0	0	0	0
Total	29	100	29	101	29	99	29	103

Note: Due to rounding of percentages totals may not equal 100 for the columns.

personally were. Twenty-nine paired samples were selected for analysis. See Table 13.3 for beginning of the semester (pre-) and for end of the semester (post-) results. However, when the postscores comparing item #2 (At this point in my life ...) with postscores on item #1 (The first day of class I believe I was at ...) were analyzed, data showed significance at the 0.012 level indicating participants believed that at the end of the course their identity levels had, in fact, declined over where they believed themselves to be at the beginning of the course. This indicates that students often lack sufficient knowledge of topics and issues and based on their lack of knowledge overinflate their beliefs about their knowledge or in this case, level of development.

The greatest levels of variance were between item #2 of the preassessment, "The first day of this class I believe I was at stage or phase ..." and item #2 of the postassessment, "At this point in my life I believe I am at stage or phase ..." Eighty-seven percent indicated they believed they were at stage or phase 6 or 7 week three, while only 31% indicated being at phase or stage 6 or 7 at the end of the class. This variance indicates how unrealistic students can be without really understanding themselves or their development. This shows a strong belief in their growth over the 12 weeks of class between the administrations of the questionnaire assessments in their understanding of themselves and the understanding of what it actually takes to be at a higher level of development.

When items #1 "The first day of this class I believe I was at stage or phase ...," and #2 "At this point in my life I believe I am at stage or phase..." of the postassessment were compared, there was also a significant increase in scores on item #2 (31% choosing stage or phase 6 or 7) over #1 (24% choosing stage or phase 6 or 7), indicating growth (significance at the 0.01 level). Thirty-one percent of the students indicated they were now at phase 6 at the end of the course compared with 24% at the beginning and from the preassessment 66% believed they were at phase 6 with none reporting phase 7 on the postassessment; 21% believed they were at phase 7 at the beginning of the class. On both of the preassessments only 3% indicated being at a level of 4 or lower while on the postassessment 27% indicated the belief they were actually at a level 4 or lower.

Comparison of items also indicated that participants were not consistent in the ratings of themselves at the beginning of the class compared to the end of the class in reflecting back on where they thought they were at the beginning of the class (see Table 13.3 & 13.4). Table 13.4 also shows that based on Wilcoxon signed ranks test there was a significant difference in ratings of prior to class on preassessment or postassessment ($p < 0.11$).

Comparison of preassessment and postassessment items clearly indicated a more realistic self-analysis, as scores were significantly lower. An instructor evaluation of participants is also occurring and written comments are being analyzed to compare with self-ratings as next steps in the process. Data reported in Table 13.5 show that the greatest levels of variance is between the rating now (pre-) and rating now (post-). This is a delineation of a more conscious awareness of each of the levels and where participants actually see themselves. Analysis reported in Table 13.6 shows a high level of significance, $p < 0.05$, or at a 95% confidence interval that the changes in the participants did not happen by accident or luck, but by treatment. In this case, since the treatment effect was the class itself, more research needs to be conducted to determine which aspect or aspects of the course were responsible for the change.

Due to the limited number of questions and small sample size (not all students enrolled in the course chose to participate in the voluntary research), additional research needs to be conducted in this area using a variety of instruments to assess beliefs, dispositions, and actions that

Table 13.4. Wilcoxon Signed Ranks Test

	OTAID Rating Before (Post) - OTAID Rating Before (Pre)	*OTAID Rating Now (Post) - OTAID Rating Now (Pre)*
Z	−1.589[a]	−3.661[a]
Asymp. Sig. (2-tailed)	0.112	0.000

[a]Based on negative ranks.

Table 13.5. Total Variance Explained

Component	Initial Eigen Values			Extraction[a] Sums of Squared Loadings		
	Total	% of Variance	Cumulative %	Total	% of Variance	Cumulative %
1	1.882	47.038	47.038	1.882	47.038	47.038
2	1.069	26.729	73.767	1.069	26.729	73.767
3	0.757	18.936	92.703			
4	0.292	7.297	100.000			

[a]Extraction method: principal component analysis.

Table 13.6. Wilcoxon Signed Ranks Test

	OTAID Rating Before (Post) − OTAID Rating Now (Pre)	OTAID Rating Now (Post) − OTAID Rating Now (Pre)	OTAID Rating Before (Post) − OTAID Rating Now (Post)
Z	−2.514[a]	−3.661[b]	−4.077[a]
Asymp. Sig. (2-tailed)	0.012	0.000	0.000
Exact Sig. (2-tailed)	0.012	0.000	0.000
Exact Sig. (1-tailed)	0.006	0.000	0.000
Point probability	.002	0.000	0.000

[a]Based on positive ranks.
[b]Based on negative ranks.

would indicate levels of identity development and working for social justice and peace. As demonstrated in this study, a possible instrument is the OTAID-R, which consists of a 60-item analysis based on the levels of identity development by Haggins et al. (1996).

TEACHING AND WORKING FOR SOCIAL JUSTICE AND PEACE

Learning to teach and work for social justice and peace is a difficult journey that begins with self-awareness. Without self-awareness, one cannot begin to move along on the journey of developmental progress. Instruments such as the OTAID-O (original), later renamed the Self-Identity Inventory (SII) (Sevig, 1993), and the OTAID-R (revised) can aid in understanding what experiences assist the development and synthesis of a positive self-identity. The combination of optimal theory with identity development theory can provide a system of unified understanding of our own and others growth and development.

The third week of the class the students were given the OTAID and asked to rate themselves on where they thought they were at the beginning of the semester and where they thought they were at this point in time. The third week of class was chosen to give the students the opportunity to begin the semester and start to deal with some of the course concepts. No assignments other than readings were completed during this time. In the last or 15th week of class students were again given the OTAID and asked to rate themselves on where they thought they were at the beginning of the semester and where they thought they were at this point in time. During the course of the semester the students had studied their own individual racial/ethnic identity, given short presentations on their own self-identity, and written a paper on their own culture. They also were given assignments to go into the community and learn about other cultures and give a group report to the class on the other cultures they had studied. They also were required to submit a paper making applications of culture and learning style to schools and classrooms. All of these assignments were self and instructor evaluated and the presentations were also peer evaluated. The following sections will explore the importance of these types of assignments.

Understanding Self

In order to engage in self-awareness one must first examine one's own culture and view of identity. The courses these students were enrolled in stressed identity development and reflection through assignments and discussions. The assignments consisted of self-analysis and experiential learning activities, which engaged the students outside of the classroom in the community. It also consisted of written and verbal feedback from others. The self-analysis and questioning by peers and the instructor from a cultural point of view is a form of critical culturally conscious reflection.

It is essential to provide experiential learning and critical reflection activities for students to be able to understand and begin to apply concepts of social justice to life situations. A first step in this process is the identification of the self, their group, and the initial assumptions tied into each. This can assist the individual in the identification of stumbling blocks to the learning process. Next, experiences must be examined in the light of their assumptions with an understanding of the role of social justice to work for peace. Lastly, the guided reflection should occur in writing and/or in discussion in a trusted community, that brings diverse perspectives and is critically culturally conscious.

In order to meet the goal of starting where the learner is operating and aiding the learner in understanding his or her own individual culture and self-awareness, an assignment should allow for or cause individual examination of one's culture. Some of the strategies that have been found successful in the process (Cahill & Adams, 1998; Ndura, 2003: Noel 2001; Salet & Koslow, 1994; Tatum, 1997) include dialogue, collaboration, exploration of specific heuristics, culture rubrics, cultural analysis processes, identity development, discussion of elements of social justice and peace, active engagement, community involvement, personal self-evaluation, and reflection. Activities or assignments that involve these strategies and cultural identification processes can be employed in teaching, self-monitoring explorations, reflection, peer coaching, supervision of curriculum development, P-12 or college classrooms, and community environments. These activities assist the students in becoming the authors of their lives and take the responsibility for their own beliefs, identity, relationships, and worldview (Magolda, 2004).

Understanding Others

Teaching for social justice and peace requires a disposition of caring and social responsibility for all students (Gollnick & Chinn, 2004). This is predicated upon an understanding of others. A shared power with others and an equitable distribution of resources including education, housing, health care, and adequate nutrition are part of this disposition. Society is constantly being critically analyzed for oppression and democratic classrooms engage the learners and teachers together. The disposition of one who is committed to social justice and peace should be articulated to students who could then be actively engaged in approximating/accomplishing/strengthening a social justice and a peace disposition. The dispositions and actions can be examined at each phase of the identity development model.

Students, and others, can learn to think critically about their experiences and their education, and not be passive consumers in the process. This is encouraged through active participation, critical analysis, critical reflection, community-based work, evaluation of self and by others, and action. The students in this study shared cultural identity through presentations and papers focusing on understanding and sharing their own culture and cultural identity; and learned about others' cultures through engagement in the community with cultures different than their own and conducting interviews and writing focused papers They were also involved in discussions and presentations on culture and identity. The students in this study were challenged to self evaluate all assignments using rubrics, and to evaluate their peers and the instructor whenever issues arose, which served as a useful form of critically conscious feedback (Warring & Huber, 2004).

Quezada and Romo (2004) contend that it is necessary to intentionally challenge students and their beliefs to assist them to think critically. People must be able to view issues and events from multiple perspectives or the reflective processes become extremely limited. Freire (1985) insisted that people must have the ability or permission to take risks and question so they can develop their own answers in the process of liberation. Without the ability to develop perspective-taking skills, reflection is severely limited to a repetition of a monocultural perspective. Reflection on self and the world and the ability to see issues and ideas from others' points of view is critical to developing the knowledge and understanding requisite to practicing equity in education according to Ndura (2003).

In so doing, educators move to a resource-based curriculum with the resources coming from a variety of global sources rather than more traditional conceptualizations of monoperspective thinking. The focus then shifts from a local to national and then to a global one where issues are considered in light of international events. This creates a deepening of knowledge and facilitates the inter relationship of knowledge sharing and integration. According to Townsend and Otero (1999), this progression is not a linear progression, but a revelation. Evidence of this shift is the collective nature of interactions and integrated reflective processes and was exemplified in the ways the students discussed issues and interacted with each other, which is important as noted by Townsend and Otero (1999).

CREATING CRITICALLY CONSCIOUS CURRICULUM

For instructors to facilitate social identity awareness and development in students it is essential for educators to understand their own cultural frameworks and consciously reflect on their personal and professional impact as global interactions and applications (Noel, 2000). Readings and discussions on racism, prejudice, poverty, privilege, and other related topics is an attempt to uncover the presence and impact of these individual practices institutional systems on people in society (Helms, 1990; Noel, 2000). Even though cultural differences and other similarities are important, the OTAID-R places the greatest value on interconnectedness and on the interrelatedness of all people (Haggins et al., 1996). A significant part of the interconnectedness occurs through spirituality.

Globalization presents challenges that differ depending upon one's status, whether native-born or immigrant. According to Suárez-Orozco (2004), the children of immigrants must make a flexible sense of self within the parent culture and the new culture and those in the host culture must broaden their perspectives and incorporate cultural elements from the new immigrants for accommodation of cultures to occur.

Reflection upon these variables, which must be embedded within the curriculum and teaching strategies, should enable teachers to better understand not only themselves but also their students and colleagues (Ndura, 2003). This should enable their students to understand themselves and others regardless of their status. This in turn will lead to the understanding and support for social justice and peace across cultures as multiple identities are developed and supported. However, given the small number of participants in this study, more data needs to be collected and analyzed with a larger sample size and in a mixed-methods analysis incorporating instructor evaluation of candidates also being analyzed.

The process demands what Warring and Huber (2004) have identified as *critical culturally conscious reflection*. As they explain,

> *Critical culturally conscious reflection* involves questioning that which is otherwise taken for granted and involves looking for unarticulated assumptions and seeing from new perspectives. With these new perspectives comes the empowerment to understand our identities and actions with the context of complex global issues. The new perspectives assist in the development of global understandings and relevant and necessary applications in the teaching~learning process.

Culturally conscious and responsible critical reflection facilitates an understanding of the process necessary for teachers to understand and engage students. Through this process all parties are better able to develop the along the desired identity development stages or phases and develop dispositions for social justice and peace. This new understanding applies to all facets of learning both inside and outside of the classroom and helps in understanding contextual factors involved in the interaction and learning processes. With the proper agents of change, movement toward higher levels of identity development can occur. Movement toward higher levels or stages or phases of identity development has the potential to foster global awareness, global understanding, interconnectedness, and to facilitate peace and social justice. A possible instrument to assess beliefs, dispositions, and actions that would indicate levels of identity development and working for social justice and peace this development is the OTAID-R (Haggins et al., 1996). Due to the limited number of questions and small sample size reported in this study, additional research needs to be conducted in this area. Though a difficult journey, our engagement in teaching~learning about identity development moves us forward in learning to teach and work for social justice and peace.

REFERENCES

Arnett, Jeffrey Jensen. (2002). The psychology of globalization. *American Psychologist, 57*(10), 774-783.
Babad, Elisha Y., Max Birnbaum, & Kenneth D. Benne, (1983). *The social self: Group influences on personal identity.* Beverly Hills, CA: SAGE.
Cahill, B., & Eve Adams. (1998). Identity and engagement in multicultural education. In Rudolfo Chávez Chávez & James O'Donnell (Eds.), *Speaking the unpleasant: The politics of (non) engagement in the multicultural education terrain* (pp. 29-46). Albany: State University of New York Press.
Cross, William E. (1991). *Shades of Black: Diversity in African-American identity.* Philadelphia: Temple University.
D'Andrea, Michael D., & Judy Daniels. (1990). Exploring the different levels of multicultural counseling training in counselor education. *Journal of Counseling and Development, 69*, 78-85.
Daniel, G. Reginald. (1996). Black and white identity in the new millennium: Unsevering the ties that bind. In M. P. P. Root (Ed.), *The multiracial experience: Racial borders as the new frontier* (pp. 121-139). Thousand Oaks, CA: SAGE.
Erikson, Erik H. (1968). *Identity: Youth and crisis.* New York: Norton.
Freire, Paulo. (1985). *The politics of education: Culture power and liberation.* New York: Bergin & Garvey.
Fukuyama, Mary A., & Todd D. Sevig. (1997). Spiritual issues in counseling: A new course. *Counselor Education & Supervision, 36*(3), 233-244.
Gollnick, Donna M., & Philip C. Chinn. (2004). *Multicultural education in a pluralistic society* (6th ed.). Upper Saddle River, NJ: Merrill.
Haggins, Kristee L., Linda James Myers, Suzette L. Speight, Pam S. Highlen, Chikako I. Cox, & Amy L. Reynolds. (1996). Assessing optimal theory applied to identity development: The OTAID-R instrument. In R. L Jones (Ed.), *Handbook of tests and measurements for Black populations* (pp. 175-190). Hampton, VA: Cobb & Henry.
Helms, Janet E. (Ed.). (1990). *Black and white racial identity: Theory, research, and practice.* Westport, CT: Greenwood Press.
Helms, Janet E., & Robert T. Carter. (1990). Development of the White racial identity attitude inventory. In J. E. Helms (Ed.), *Black and White racial identity: Theory, research and practice* (pp. 67-80). Westport, CT: Greenwood Press.
Hollingsworth, Leslie Doty. (1997). Effect of transracial/transethnic adoption on children's racial and ethnic identity and self-esteem: A meta-analytic review. *Marriage and Family Review, 25*(1-2), 99-121.
Huber-Warring, Tonya, & Warring, Douglas F. (2006) Are you teaching for democracy? Developing dispositions, promoting democratic practice, and embracing social justice and diversity. *Action in Teacher Education, 28*(2), 38-52.
Huber-Warring, Tonya, & Warring, Douglas F. (2007). Assessing culturally responsible pedagogy in student work reflections, rubrics, and writing: A global worldview in the teaching/learning process. In Larry Hufford & Teresita Pedrajas (Eds.), *Educating for worldview: Focus on globalizing curriculum and instruction* (pp. 41-71). New York: University Press of America.

Huitt, William. (2004). *Educational psychology interactive: Self-concept and self-esteem.* Valdosta, GA: Valdosta State University. Retrieved August 1, 2007, from http://chiron.valdosta.edu/whuitt/col/regsys/self.html

Katz, Judith H. (1985). The sociopolitical nature of counseling. *The Counseling Psychologist, 13*(4), 615-624.

Magolda, Marcia B. Baxter. (2004). Evolution of a constructivist conceptualization of epistemological reflection. *Educational Psychologist, 39*(1), 31-42.

Merryfield, Mary M. (1997). A framework for teacher education in global perspectives. In Mary M. Merryfield, Elaine Jarchow, & Sarah Pickert (Eds.), *Preparing teachers to teach global perspectives: A handbook for teacher educators* (pp. 1- 24). Thousand Oaks, CA: Corwin.

Myers, Linda J., Suzette L. Speight, Pam S. Highlen, Chikako I. Cox, Amy L. Reynolds, Eve M. Adams, et al. (1991). Identity development and worldview: Toward an optimal conceptualization. *Journal of Counseling and Development, 69*(2), 54-63.

Ndura, Elavie. (2003). A multicultural instructor's reflective self-analysis: Facing the challenge of teaching and learning. *Multicultural Education, 11*(2), 42-45.

Niedenthal, Paula, M., & Denise R. Beike. (1997). Interrelated and isolated self-concepts. *Personality and Social Psychology Review, 1*(2), 106-128.

Noel, Jana. (2000). *Developing multicultural educators.* New York: Longman.

Parham, Thomas A. (1989). Cycles of psychological Nigrescence. *The Counseling Psychologist, 17*(2), 187-226.

Phinney, Jean S. (1990). Ethnic identity in adolescents and adults: Review of research. *Psychological Bulletin, 108*(3), 499-514.

Quezada, Reyes, & Jaime J. Romo. (2004). Multiculturalism, peace education & social justice in teacher education. *Multicultural Education, 11*(3), 2-11.

Salet, E., & K. Koslow (Eds.), (1994). *Race, ethnicity, and self: Identity in multicultural perspective.* Washington DC: National Multicultural Institute.

Shafranske, Edward P., & R. L. Gorsuch. (1984). Factors associated with the perception of sprirituality in psychotherapy. *Journal of Transpersonal Psychology, 16*(2), 231-234.

Sevig, Todd D. (1993). *The development and validation of the self identity instrument.* Unpublished doctoral dissertation, The Ohio State University.

Suárez-Orozco Carola. (2004). Formulating identity in a globalized world. In Marcelo M. Suárez-Orozco & Desirée Baolian Qin-Hilliard (Eds.), *Globalization: Culture and education in the new millennium* (pp. 173-202). London: University of California Press.

Suárez-Orozco, Carola, & Marcelo M. Suárez-Orozco. (2001). *Children of immigration.* Cambridge, MA: Harvard University Press.

Sue, Derald Wing, & David Sue. (1990). *Counseling the culturally different: Theory and practice* (2nd ed.). New York: Wiley.

Takeuchi, Jason. (2000). Treatment of a biracial child with schizophreniform disorder: Cultural formulation. *Cultural Diversity & Ethnic Minority Psychology, 6*(1) 93-101.

Tatum, Beverly Daniel. (1997). *Why are all the Black kids sitting together in the cafeteria? And other conversations about race.* New York: Basic Books.

Thomason, T. C. (1994). Counseling Native Americans: An introduction for non-Native American counselors. *Journal of Counseling and Development*, *69*(4), 484-491.

Townsend, Tony, & George G. Otero. (1999). *The global classroom. Activities to engage students in the third millennium schools.* Melbourne, Australia: Hawker Brownlow Education.

Triandis, Harry C. (1989). Cross-cultural studies of individualism and collectivism. *Nebraska Symposium on Motivation*, *37*, 43-133.

Warring, Douglas F. (2007). *Understanding and applying human relations and multicultural education: Teaching~learning in a global society* (6th ed., Rev.). Scottsdale, AZ: Leadership.

Warring, Douglas F., & Tonya Huber. (2004, July). *The use of culturally conscious critical reflection in intercultural understanding.* Paper presented at the 11th Triennial World Conference of the World Council for Curriculum and Instruction, Wollongong, Australia.

Warring, Douglas F., & Tonya Huber-Warring. (2006, April 27). *Developing dispositions, promoting democratic practice, and embracing social justice and diversity.* Paper presented at the 26th annual seminar of the International Society for Teacher Education, Stellenbosch, Western Cape, South Africa.

Yeh, Christine J., & Karen Huang. (1996). The collectivist nature of ethnic identity development among Asian-American college students. *Adolescence*, *31*, 645-662.

Zinnbauer, Brian J., & Kenneth I. Pargament. (2005). Religiousness and spirituality. In R. Paloutzian & Crystal, Park (Eds.), *Handbook of the psychology of religion and spirituality* (pp. 21-62). New York: Guilford Press.

CHAPTER 14

EMOTIONAL INTELLIGENCE IN THE CLASSROOM

A Behavioral Profile of an Effective Teacher

Melinde Coetzee and Cecelia A. Jansen

The purpose of this study was to explore how the concept of emotional intelligence relates to behaviors that effective teachers display in the classroom and whether a specific behavioral profile can be developed. A purposive sampling method was used to identify African Grade 12 learners ($n = 35$) from a South African socially deprived school environment. Qualitative methods were used to collect and analyze learners' views on the behavior of the ideal teacher. Based on the findings a behavioral profile of an ideal teacher was developed which indicates specific learner-centered behaviors related to emotional intelligence. The research contributed new knowledge to the field of education by presenting a framework of specific behaviors that contribute to a more humanistic and nurturing educational environment as perceived by learners from a historically disadvantaged school environment.

Growing a Soul for Social Change: Building the Knowledge Base for Social Justice
pp. 247–268
Copyright © 2008 by Information Age Publishing
All rights of reproduction in any form reserved.

INTRODUCTION

The concept of emotional intelligence has grown in popularity over the last two decades, generating interest both at social and professional level (Freshwater & Stickley, 2004). Concurrent developments in teacher education relate to the recognition of emotional literacy training for educators to improve the quality of teacher-learner interaction in the classroom (Goldsworthy, 2000; Morris, 2002). Many curricula now make reference in some way to the notion of emotionally intelligent teachers who need to be in intimate contact with their emotions and are able to facilitate learning in learners from a position of self-knowledge. Integrating emotional intelligence into the curriculum provides teachers with a greater opportunity to understand themselves and the way in which they create relationships with learners (Freshwater & Stickley, 2004; Zembylas, 2003).

Another prominent trend in education is the focus on how teachers' mindsets and behavior toward learners creates a general classroom atmosphere that has a profound impact on learners' performance (Bredemeier, 2001; Gerson, 2000; Mather & Goldstein, 2001). According to the Nelson Mandela Foundation's report on education in South African rural communities (2005), teachers are vital role models who can make a difference as to whether learners feel safe, respected, and valued. Teachers' relationships with parents and learners, and the school community at large, influence the overall ethos and climate of teaching and learning (Nelson Mandela Foundation, 2005; Tichenor & Tichenor, 2004). Teachers who are able to demonstrate emotionally intelligent behavior in the classroom have been known to be more effective in achieving the academic goals they have set for themselves and their learners (De Klerk & Le Roux, 2004; Morris, 2002). Demonstrating emotionally intelligent behavior helps create an emotional climate which enhances the learning environment, reduces peer conflicts, and creates a more desirable teaching situation (Barth, Dunlap, Dane, Lochman, & Wells, 2004; Cobb & Mayer, 2000).

The focus on the role of the teacher in directing learner success in the classroom has spawned a renewed interest in determining the profile of a so-called *ideal* teacher (Bredemeier, 2001; Coetzee & Jansen, 2007; Mather & Goldstein, 2001; Morris, 2002; Tichenor & Tichenor, 2004; Zembylas, 2003). In the context of this research the concept of an *ideal* teacher is defined as teachers who have a firm grasp of the subjects they teach and are true to the intellectual demands of their disciplines. They are able to analyze the intellectual, emotional, and social development needs of the learners for whom they are responsible and know that they are responsible for meeting these needs (Tichenor & Tichenor, 2004; Zembylas, 2003). They are regarded as effective or professional teachers who are respected for their attitude, behavior, communication and working relationships with parents, colleagues and learners (Tichenor & Tichenor, 2004).

However, the problem is that limited research exists on how the behavioral characteristics of an effective teacher relate to emotionally intelligent behavior in the classroom context, particularly in the socially deprived school environment of historically disadvantaged South African learners. The socially deprived school environment is generally characterized by poverty and poor educational conditions due to limited resources for enhancing the quality of education. This may have a more pronounced influence on learners' intellectual, emotional and social development needs (Nelson Mandela Foundation, 2005).

Generally, this study sets out to determine how the concept of emotional intelligence relates to behaviors that ideal or effective teachers display in the classroom and whether a specific behavioral profile can be drawn up. The construction of a behavioral profile of an ideal teacher in the context of this research is therefore based on subjective accounts of learners in the South African school environment. The idea developed in this study is that an investigation of the behavioral characteristics of teachers as demonstrated in the classroom and therefore experienced by the learners, could yield a rich understanding of how a teacher's general demeanor and behavioral style influence learners' motivation to learn and perform (Coetzee & Jansen, 2007; Gerson, 2000; Mather & Goldstein, 2001). Such a behavioral profile could also be used to inform the curriculum design for the education and development of teachers in the general South African context.

Emotional Intelligence

The term emotional intelligence was originally coined by Salovey and Mayer (1990) to complement the traditional view of general intelligence by emphasizing behavior that requires emotional and behavioral control in social situations (Mayer, Salovey & Caruso, 2004). Although the construct is still in a stage of active development, four findings are emerging that provide an early picture of emotional intelligence: (1) emotional intelligence is distinct from, but positively related to, other intelligences, more specifically, it is the intelligence (the ability to grasp abstractions) applied to the life domain of emotions; (2) emotional intelligence is an individual difference, in the sense that some people are more endowed and others are less so; (3) emotional intelligence develops over a person's life span and can be enhanced through training; and (4) emotional intelligence involves particular abilities to reason intelligently about emotions including identifying and perceiving emotion (in oneself and others), as well as the skills to understand and to manage those emotions successfully (Ashkanasy & Daus, 2005; Locke, 2005).

The concept of emotional intelligence implies that people are both rational and emotional beings (Thingujam, 2004). Adaptation and coping abilities in a social context depend on the integrative functioning of rational (cognitive) and emotional (affective) capacities (Fineman, 2000). It is through reason that individuals identify what emotions they are experiencing, discover the beliefs and values that gave rise to it, and decide what action, if any, to take on the face of it (Locke, 2005).

Two general models of the construct emotional intelligence are (1) the *ability model* that defines emotional intelligence as a set of abilities that involves perceiving and reasoning abstractly with information that emerges from feelings, accessing and generating emotions so as to assist thought, understanding emotions, and reflectively regulating emotions so as to promote emotional and intellectual growth (Mayer, Caruso & Salovey, 1999), and (2) the *mixed model* which incorporates the underlying abilities postulated by the ability model and emphasizes emotional competence, that is, the skills that are necessary for navigating the demands of the immediate social context. These responses are adaptive and help the individual reach goals, cope with challenges, manage emotional arousal such that effective problem solving can be undertaken, discern what others feel and respond sympathetically as the case may be, and recognize how emotion communication, and self-presentation affect relationships (Buckley, Storino & Saarni, 2003).

The definitions of the construct emotional intelligence provided by the ability and mixed model approaches appear to emphasize the cognitive, affective and social aspects of emotionally intelligent behavior (Coetzee, 2005). The *cognitive* aspect of emotionally intelligent behavior relates to the intelligent reasoning about the emotions one is experiencing and includes skills such as emotional awareness, self-control, and assertiveness (Cooper & Sawaf, 2000; Eisenberg, Cumberland, & Spinrad, 1998; Gardner, 1983; George, 2000; Mayer & Salovey, 1997). It includes individuals' self-regard which is associated with feelings of security, inner strength, self-adequacy, and self-confidence (Bar-On, 1997). Self-regard is dependent upon self-respect and self-esteem, which are based on a fairly well-developed sense of identity (Bar-On, 1997). According to Fineman (2000) and Locke (2005) individuals' self-esteem creates emotions on a subconscious level that impel them to act or behave in a particular manner, that is, they are not always aware of why they are doing something, or what they are doing. From this perspective many of people's emotions defy conscious control and regulation.

The term emotion refers to individuals' affective state which includes emotions and mood (George, 2000). Emotions are generally regarded as the primary forces that arouse, direct, and sustain activity (Stuart & Pauquet, 2001). The affective aspect of emotionally intelligent behavior therefore refers to the ability to harness one's emotions and mood as a source of energy to positively influence one's well-being, goals, plans, survival, and social role performance. It also includes personality aspects such as general mood, optimism, and happiness (Bar-On, 1997; Cooper & Sawaf, 2000; George, 2000; Martinez-Pons, 2000).

The *social* aspect of emotionally intelligent behavior relates to individuals' personal effectiveness in interpersonal interactions. It includes the ability to notice and make distinctions between other individuals, in particular between their moods, temperaments, motivations and intentions and to use this information to regulate and guide one's thinking and actions in achieving one's goals in a socially acceptable manner. It includes skills such as empathy, demonstrating respect, unconditional acceptance of others and flexibility (Bar-On, 1997; Cooper & Sawaf, 2000; Fox & Spector, 2000; Gardner, 1983).

Based on these cognitive, affective, and social aspects of emotionally intelligent behavior, the term *emotional intelligence* is for the purpose of this study defined as a particular set of learned abilities and knowledge-building attitudes that enable people to tap into their feelings and emotions as a source of energy to foster self-understanding, personal effectiveness in interpersonal relations and the ability to achieve personal goals in a socially and culturally appropriate manner (Coetzee, 2005). These abilities and knowledge-building attitudes can be developed and thus form part of teacher education and development curricula (Saarni, 1997, 1999).

Classroom Climate and Effective Teacher Behavior

The classroom climate is the shared perception of learners about the classroom environment which includes the conditions, circumstances, and influences surrounding and affecting the development and performance of learners (Coetzee & Jansen, 2007; Landy & Conte, 2004). These include, for example, the physical conditions of the school and classroom, and the teacher's physical appearance, body language, behavior, and attitudes toward learners (Bredemeier, 2001; Coetzee & Jansen, 2007; Mather & Goldstein, 2001). The personal values of teachers influence to a large extent how they treat and interact with their learners (Bredemeier, 2001). The values that teachers model through their behavior create a particular emotional climate or classroom atmosphere that can be sensed by learners (Landy & Conte, 2004). Values such as self-respect, personal growth, responsibility, social rights, purposeful living, self-discipline, personal integrity, fairness/justice, self-acceptance, and forgiveness facilitate healthy relations with the self and others and are generally regarded as being pertinent to helping professions such as teaching (Branden, 1994; Rothwell, Sullivan, & McLean, 1995).

The classroom climate can range from a warm, welcoming, and nurturing atmosphere in which learners feel honored and accepted for their uniqueness to one that is characterized by coldness and indifference (Bredemeier, 2001; Coetzee & Jansen, 2007; Mather & Goldstein, 2001). Marilyn Osborn (1996) regards effective teaching and learning as affective in that it involves human interaction. As the quality of teacher-learner relationships is vitally important to the learning process, the teacher plays a major role in creating a safe and supportive learning environment.

The behavior that effective teachers display in the classroom are generally associated with five learner-centered practices that engender an emotionally warm classroom climate: (1) creating psychological safety; (2) creating positive self-images in learners; (3) establishing feelings of belonging in the classroom; (4) engaging learners in purposeful behavior and, (5) developing a sense of competence in learners (Elias, 2001; Mather & Goldstein, 2001; Morris, 2002; Reasoner, 1992).

A sense of psychological safety is typically created through the establishment of clearly identified classroom procedures, policies, and practices that reduce anxiety and enable the teacher and learners to perform comfortably in the classroom (Reasoner, 1992). Learners develop positive self-images when they experience an emotional connection with their teacher. This connection makes them feel accepted and respected as unique individuals. Receiving constructive feedback on strengths and weaknesses also facilitates more positive images of the self and the motivation to learn (De Klerk & Le Roux, 2004; Reasoner, 1992). A sense of belonging includes feelings of connectedness gained from engendering an emotionally warm classroom atmosphere in which teachers and learners feel they are a part of something larger than themselves. As contributing members of a winning team they feel valued by others (Mather & Goldstein, 2001; Reasoner, 1992). A sense of purpose is gained as a result of teachers and learners taking responsibility for and initiative in the learning process. This is achieved for example by setting realistic expectations and supporting and encouraging learners to gain the confidence to strive for achievable personal goals. Recognizing the accomplishment of these goals typically helps learners to gain a sense of competence (Elias, 2001; Reasoner, 1992).

Educators with an emotionally warm style appear to be able to create an emotionally warm classroom atmosphere characterized by feelings of being a close-knit unit, mutual goodwill, empathy, and cooperation among the teacher and learners. The relationship with learners is embraced and cherished (Bredemeier, 2001). An effective educator appears to have an awareness of the learners' cognitive and emotional needs, unconditionally accepts and respects learners for their uniqueness and shows an authentic interest in learners' well-being through open and honest communication. Discipline is handled in a fair, reasonable, and consistent manner (Mather & Goldstein, 2001).

Against the foregoing, it stands to reason that the emotionally warm behavioral style engendered by learner-centered classroom practices could be related to the ability of the teacher to demonstrate emotionally intelligent behavior in the classroom. Studies conducted by Paulo Lopes et al. (2004) and Lopes, Salovey, Côté, and Beers (2005) have demonstrated that the ability to manage emotions contributes positively to the quality of social interactions. Individuals who are socially well adapted tend to display emotionally intelligent behavior. That is, they tend to be aware of their own emotions and how they impact others with their overt behavior. They also tend to express their emotions more appropriately to others and are better able to read and respond to the emotions of others in social interactions (Cooper & Sawaf, 2000; Goleman, 2001). Emotionally intelligent individuals are able to use their emotional and cognitive presence to monitor the socioemotional climate and are able to engage in behavior that facilitates emotional security in themselves and others (Cobb & Mayer, 2000; Worline, Wrzesniewski, & Rafaeli, 2002).

In view of the foregoing, the purpose of this study was to determine how the concept of emotional intelligence relates to behaviors that effective teachers display in the classroom environment. More specifically, the goal was to investigate whether (1) a general behavioral profile of an ideal teacher as perceived by learners in the South African socially deprived school environment could be established, and (2) whether the identified behaviors relate to emotionally intelligent behavior in the classroom context. Due to the unique circumstances and conditions of the socially deprived school environment it was assumed that the learners' intellectual, emotional, and social needs would have been more pronounced and therefore yield a rich understanding of the behavioral characteristics of an effective teacher.

METHOD

The Research Setting

The school that was approached for the purpose of this study was a historically disadvantaged Black secondary school situated in a township in South Africa's North-West Province. The economic circumstances in the feeding area of the school range from desperately poor to relatively affluent people. According to Nelson Mandela (Nelson Mandela Foundation, 2005), the socially deprived school environments present the most profound challenges in terms of improving the quality of education. Teacher education initiatives should therefore acknowledge the *voices* (or unique perspectives and needs) of members of these school communities (Nelson Mandela Foundation, 2005).

Research Approach

Merriam (2002) recommends that a qualitative approach be used when the research objectives are exploratory and descriptive. Qualitative researchers assert that the social world can only be understood if its social context is taken into consideration (Bogdan & Biklen, 1998). The main objective of qualitative research is therefore to understand the dynamics of human meaning in its natural setting, with minimal interference from the researcher. Since the study objectives pertain to understanding and describing a particular phenomenon about which very little is known, the qualitative approach appeared to be the most suitable for gaining insight about participants' subjective experiences of the effective (or ideal) teacher's behavior in the classroom context. Qualitative research enables a researcher to understand the participants' experience when trying to understand situations from a particular perspective (Creswell, 1998).

The methodology and its analytical process in this study were guided by certain assumptions of phenomenology. The phenomenological tradition in social science holds that social reality is a perceptual construct, in other words a generally agreed-upon consensus among ordinary people in particular situations as to what events and interactions mean. Qualitative researchers using phenomenology as a research framework attend to unravelling and understanding the meaning of events and interactions of ordinary people in specific everyday situations (van Aswegen & Schurink, 2003).

Participants

Thirty-five African grade 12 learners ($n = 35$) from a historically disadvantaged Black secondary school situated in a township in South Africa's North-West Province were approached for the present study. Their selection was based on the following two criteria: (1) the learners were academic performers and regarded as leaders by their teachers and (2) their level of knowledge and experience of teacher behavior in the classroom was assumed to be rich in the information needed by the researchers due to the years they have been exposed to teacher behavior in the classroom. Furthermore, as the focus of the study was on exploring the behaviors that effective teachers demonstrate in the classroom, it was assumed that the high-performing students would have been able to describe teacher behaviors which motivated them to perform to the best of their ability. Since qualitative methodologies are employed to access a richness of diverse information from a few participants, participant numbers of 10 and even below are often regarded to be sufficient (Schurink, 2003).

Method of Data Gathering

In line with the aim and objectives of this study, qualitative methods were used to collect and analyze data on the ideal teacher's behavior in the classroom context. Participants were requested to write a brief essay on how they envisioned the behavior of the ideal teacher. The essays that the respective participants were requested to compile are known as narratives (Denzin & Lincoln, 2000). Every narrative or essay describes the characteristics of the ideal teacher as subjectively experienced by each participant.

Procedure

First, permission was obtained from the participants' parents and from the principal of the school where the study was conducted. Thereafter the researcher contacted the teachers of the participating learners. Both the teachers and learners were briefed on the reason and format of the study by means of a short introduction. Learners were given the opportunity to decline participation in the study. They were then requested to write a brief essay on how they perceived the behavior of an ideal teacher.

Data Analysis

The solicited essays generated extensive soft data. The detailed descriptions of the experiences, beliefs, and thoughts of the learners were broken down into manageable units and classified according to the concepts and interpretations they used. Based on the suggestions of Strauss and Corbin (1990) and Creswell (1998), data analysis was systematically conducted whereby the researcher kept track of emerging themes during the data gathering process, and developed concepts and propositions to make sense of the data. The most salient categories that emerged from the data were identified, and then the concepts and categories were developed. This was followed by further analysis to discover, develop and provisionally verify patterns and concepts that related to literature perspectives on emotionally intelligent and effective teacher behaviors. Finally, the themes were interpreted in the light of existing literature on the topic, allowing for meaningful interpretation of the results. For the purpose of confidentiality, all recognizable data were carefully disguised or omitted.

Results

Generally, the responses of learners indicated that an ideal teacher helps participants feel motivated, emotionally secure, and accepted. They valued feeling part of a team which motivates a sense of responsibility for giving their best to the teacher, the team, and the subject. The participants appeared to develop positive self-images and confidence in their ability to succeed when feeling honored for their uniqueness. These feelings are engendered when they experience themselves being accepted unconditionally and cared about by the teacher. The general demeanor of the teacher, such as kindness, friendliness, patience, passion, and enthusiasm for the subject seems to encourage the participants to perform to the best of their abilities, thus creating a sense of purpose and competence.

In what follows, the data are mainly presented in terms of the indigenous or concrete constructions of the participants. Excerpts from the essays or narratives are used as illustrative material. Only the clearest and most representative excerpts are presented. In certain cases, however, the excerpts were edited or paraphrased for the sake of brevity.

EMOTIONALLY INTELLIGENT BEHAVIORS

The solicited essays give a clear account of particular emotionally intelligent behaviors displayed by the ideal or effective teacher. The following excerpts capture the views reasonably well. The behavioral characteristics indicated in parentheses show the linkage to teacher behaviors identified in the literature review.

Cognitive Behavior

- *Talks to us smartly and doesn't shout at us—is not loud and crazy* (emotional awareness/self-control—Mayer & Salovey, 1997; Saarni, 1999);

- *Keeps his/her smile every time he/she talks to you* (self-control—Mayer & Salovey, 1997; Saarni, 1999);
- *Leaves his/her problem where he/she started it, and treats us friendly* (self-control—Mayer & Salovey, 1997; Saarni, 1999);
- *Has discipline in the class* (assertiveness—Mather & Goldstein, 2001); and
- *Is firm and strict* (assertiveness—Mather & Goldstein, 2001).

Affective Behavior

- *Happily greets you* (happiness—Bar-On, 1997; Bredemeier, 2001);
- *Speaks gently and kindly with a happy face* (happiness/kindness/friendliness—Bar-On, 1997; Bredemeier, 2001);
- *A teacher who is always happy* (happiness—Bar-On, 1997; Bredemeier, 2001);
- *Guides me toward a better future* (optimism—Bar-On, 1997; Mather & Goldstein, 2001);
- *Always looks forward to teaching his students* (enthusiasm—Bar-On, 1997; Mather & Goldstein, 2001);
- *Lifts my spirit* (enthusiasm—Bar-On, 1997; Mather & Goldstein, 2001);
- *Has passion and devotion to teaching learners* (passion—Mather & Goldstein, 2001; Morris, 2002);
- *Has lots of energy* (aliveness/energy—Bar-On, 1997; Mather & Goldstein, 2001);
- *Is active and has energy for his/her work* (aliveness/energy—Bar-On, 1997; Mather & Goldstein, 2001);
- *Has a positive attitude toward others* (positive attitude—Bar-On, 1997; Mather & Goldstein, 2001); and
- *Has time to hear our problems and explain so we can understand* (patience—Mather & Goldstein, 2001).

Social Behavior

- *Can communicate with learners and hear their problems* (communication/listening/empathy—Bar-On, 1997; Bredemeier, 2001; Morris, 2002; Saarni, 1999);
- *Talks softly and sweetly (politely) so learners feel treated with respect* (tone of voice/respect—Mather & Goldstein, 2001);

- *Greets with a smile and talks well to us—doesn't call us names* (body language/tone of voice/respect—Mather & Goldstein, 2001);
- *Using the word "pass" is very motivating* (social responsibility—Bar-On, 1997);
- *Smiles at us and sometimes makes a good joke* (body language/humor—Mather & Goldstein, 2001);
- *Uses words such as "good luck," "we can do it"* (language patterns—Mather & Goldstein, 2001);
- *Use of "we" is very important* (language patterns—Mather & Goldstein, 2001);
- *Respects learners and does not judge us* (respect/unconditional acceptance—Branden, 1994);
- *Has a heart for whatever question one asks* (empathy/openness—Morris, 2002; Saarni, 1999);
- *Teaches with understanding* (empathy—Morris, 2002; Saarni, 1999);
- *Willing to help one find solutions* (openness/social responsibility—Bar-On, 1997); and
- *Helps me with my school work and my personal problems* (social responsibility—Bar-On, 1997)

Values

- *Must have self-respect* (self-respect—Branden, 1994; Rothwell et al., 1995);
- *Is always willing to learn something new from students* (personal growth—Branden, 1994; Rothwell et al., 1995; Tichenor & Tichenor, 2004);
- *Has responsibility* (responsibility—Bar-On, 1997; Branden, 1994; Tichenor & Tichenor, 2004);
- *Respects the right of all* (social rights—Branden, 1994; Rothwell et al., 1995);
- *Guides me toward a better future* (purposeful living—Branden, 1994);
- *Is punctual and on time for his class* (self-discipline—Branden, 1994);
- *Has morals and good qualities* (personal integrity—Branden, 1994);
- *Leads by example, is a good role model* (personal integrity—Branden, 1994);
- *Treats children equally and with respect* (fairness/justice—Branden, 1994; Rothwell et al., 1995); and
- *Accepts correction for mistakes* (forgiveness—Branden, 1994).

LEARNER-CENTERED BEHAVIORS

The following excerpts demonstrate the views on the importance of learner-centered behaviors.

Creating Psychological Safety

- *Gives learners information and explains so we can understand* (clear boundaries);
- *Tells me how to behave and pass my matric* (clear boundaries/learner responsibility—Branden, 1994; Reasoner, 1992);
- *Follows the protocol of teaching, is on time, respects time of teaching* (rule enforcement—Branden, 1994; Reasoner, 1992);
- *Is firm and strict—we must have discipline in the class* (rule enforcement/consistency— Branden, 1994; Reasoner, 1992);
- *Creates a good classroom atmosphere, keeps the classroom clean and neat* (physical conditions—Reasoner, 1992); and
- *We need to feel safe and be in a clean classroom and have the resources we need* (physical conditions—Reasoner, 1992).

Creating Positive Self-Image

- *Does not put me down or try to undermine me because I am slower to understand* (learner uniqueness—Branden, 1994; Reasoner, 1992);
- *Understands we don't think alike, there are learners who are slow* (learner uniqueness—Branden, 1994; Reasoner, 1992);
- *He is my friend, my teacher and a father to us; she is not only a teacher but also a mother so that she could connect with us to help with school and personal problems* (rapport/mentor/parent—Branden, 1994);
- *Motivates me to see myself as the most significant person in my life* (motivation/self-awareness—Branden, 1994);
- *Gives me a learning spirit* (motivation—Branden, 1994; Reasoner, 1992);
- *Asks and finds out about my weaknesses* (self-awareness—Branden, 1994; Saarni, 1999); and
- *Proud of the teacher—she makes you believe in yourself* (rapport/motivation—Branden, 1994).

Establishing Feelings of Belonging

- *The environment should be filled with warmth and love from students and teachers* (harmony—Morris, 2002);

- *We must be a family, saying "we must pass together"/"we must work together so we harvest good results"* (cohesiveness/group pride/peer support—Reasoner, 1992);
- *Treats children equally and respects us* (equal treatment—Branden, 1994; Reasoner, 1992); and
- *Willing to build strong relationships between learners* (peer support—Reasoner, 1992).

Engaging in Purposeful Behavior

- *Supportive and caring* (support/guidance—Branden, 1994; Reasoner, 1992);
- *Motivates us to study hard so we can achieve* (encouragement—Branden, 1994; Reasoner, 1992);
- *Helps you where he/she can* (support/guidance—Branden, 1994; Reasoner, 1992);
- *Likes to motivate me and advise me about my education and my future* (goal-setting/guidance/encouragement—Branden, 1994; Reasoner, 1992);
- *Guides and encourages me toward a better future/helps me to achieve my dream* (support/guidance/encouragement—Branden, 1994; Reasoner, 1992);
- *Believes in his/her students and encourages them all the time* (faith/confidence in abilities—Branden, 1994); and
- *We must be able to learn from him/her so that we can achieve more than what they have achieved* (challenges—Reasoner, 1992).

Developing a Sense of Competence

- *Gives me some life skills so I am able to do things on my own* (problem solving/decision making—Branden, 1994; Reasoner, 1992);
- *Willing to help me find solutions* (problem solving/decision making/feedback/support— Branden, 1994; Reasoner, 1992);
- *We want to pass matric— if a learner passes, it shows that the teacher is good* (recognition—Branden, 1994; Reasoner, 1992); and
- *We must be able to learn from him/her so that we can achieve more than what they have achieved* (feedback/support—Branden, 1994; Reasoner, 1992).

Discussion

The goal of this study was to investigate whether (1) a general behavioral profile of an effective (or ideal) teacher as perceived by learners in the South African socially deprived school environment could be established, and whether (2) the identified behaviors relate to emotionally intelligent behavior in the classroom context. To facilitate illumination, the participants' views will also be related to existing empirical findings and relevant abstract theoretical concepts.

EMOTIONAL INTELLIGENCE PROFILE OF AN EFFECTIVE TEACHER

The responses of the participants were analyzed and interpreted with reference to the cognitive, affective, and social aspects of emotional intelligence. The relevant behaviors will be discussed in turn.

Cognitive behavior: The cognitive aspect of emotionally intelligent behavior relates to the intelligent reasoning about the emotions one is experiencing (Mayer & Salovey, 1997; Salovey & Mayer, 1990). An ideal or effective teacher seems to have the ability to preserve his or her composure when engaging in some form of class discipline. This entails the perceived ability to control aggression, hostility, and irresponsible behavior toward the participants.

Affective behavior: The affective aspect of emotionally intelligent behavior refers to the ability to harness one's emotions and mood as a source of energy to positively influence one's well-being, goals, plans, and social role performance. It also entails individuals' ability to honestly assess how their self-regard influenced their affective state (Bar-On, 1997). An adult's behavior can be seen as a reflection of personal feelings (Gerson, 2000). According to Bar-On (1997), individuals with a high self-regard tend to have a great self-respect and generally have a greater self-awareness of their emotions and feelings.

The responses suggest that an ideal teacher is perceived to have an emotionally warm style by showing empathy and a positive attitude toward learners. The results further suggest that a happy disposition (evident in the passion and enthusiasm demonstrated by an ideal teacher for the subject he or she teaches, the energy radiated by the teacher), generally motivate learners to perform well. These findings confirm observations from various authors in the literature (Gerson, 2000; Mather & Goldstein, 2001; Morris, 2002).

Social behavior: The social aspect of emotionally intelligent behavior relates to individuals' personal effectiveness in interpersonal relations. It also includes the ability to notice and make distinctions between individuals' moods, temperaments, motivations, and intentions and to use this information to regulate and guide one's thinking and actions in a socially acceptable manner (Worline et al., 2002).

The results suggest that an emotionally warm style helps to establish and maintain mutually satisfying relationships. An effective teacher also appears to act in a socially responsible manner toward the learners as demonstrated by their willingness to provide guidance and support until learners were able to master their assignments and classroom tasks. According to Lopes et al. (2004), individuals with positive self-esteem tend to show caring and compassion for people by having a concern for their well-being, growth and development. Individuals with positive self-esteem experience feelings of self-worth that they derive from being authentic and they therefore tend to act in a socially responsible manner toward their learners (Bar-On, 1997; Reasoner, 1992).

The results indicate the importance of teachers' communication style which includes their body language (such as greeting learners with a smile) and tone of voice (talking gently and politely) as a means to establish rapport with learners and gain their respect. Language patterns such as the use of *we* and the avoidance of language that humiliates learners were also regarded as important. As noted by Mather and Goldstein (2001), the findings also indicate humor as an important aspect of teacher communication.

It appears from the findings that a set of core values may support teachers' ability to demonstrate emotionally intelligent behavior (Bredemeier, 2001; Mather & Goldstein, 2001; Rothwell et al., 1995). These include values such as self-respect, developing oneself, taking responsibility for one's actions, honoring the social rights of others by treating them equally and with respect, living purposefully by being dedicated to creating a better future for oneself, demonstrating self-discipline and personal integrity by setting an example to learners. Teachers who demonstrate these values seem to be able to create a sense of harmony and overall positive classroom atmosphere.

Teacher Behavior and the Classroom Climate

Overall, the results suggest that learner-centered behaviors support the demonstration of emotionally intelligent behavior and help to create an emotionally warm classroom climate in which learners feel safe, respected, and valued. According to the Nelson Mandela Foundation's report on education in South African rural communities (2005), a relationship of mutual respect between teachers and learners is essential. A lack of respect between them increases an unfavorable climate that actually stifles effective learning. At the heart of learners' vision for change in the quality of education they receive, is a school and classroom that respects them as human beings and recognizes their right to learn in an environment that makes them feel safe and valued (Nelson Mandela Foundation, 2005).

In addition, as the teacher is regarded as a role model, and even as a parent, the general mood, tone of voice and body language of the teacher appear to have a profound impact on learners and consequently the classroom atmosphere. Enforcing discipline in ways that preserve self-respect seems to contribute to the experience of emotional security. In line with observations from various authors in the literature, the findings suggest that honoring the uniqueness of learners and creating a climate of acceptance and caring facilitate positive images in learners of what they are capable of (Mather & Goldstein, 2001; Morris, 2002; Reasoner, 1992). Feelings of belonging and emotional security also appear to reduce learners' feelings of isolation and generally facilitate feelings of pride in their own and the group's achievements (Reasoner, 1992). Apart from positive teacher behaviors, the physical conditions of the classroom and the school also appear to have a profound impact on learners' general motivation to learn and perform.

Furthermore, the sense of belonging created by the general classroom climate appears to contribute to learners having a sense of purpose and wanting to perform at their best in a particular subject. In addition, the guidance and support provided by the ideal or effective teacher seem to build the participants' confidence and faith in their abilities and motivates them to perform at their best. As noted by various authors in the literature, this in turn helps to facilitate a sense of competence in learners. Learners seem to feel they are able to demonstrate the required knowledge, skills, behaviors, and attitudes (Branden, 1994; Gerson, 2000; Reasoner, 1992).

Based on these findings, a behavioral profile of an ideal or effective teacher was developed. Figure 14.1 provides an overview of the key behaviors of an effective teacher as deducted from the literature review and suggested by the empirical findings.

CONCLUSIONS AND RECOMMENDATIONS

The research process was transparent as the subjects were not only willing participants but saw their participation as an opportunity to share their experiences and emotional needs regarding teachers' behavior in the classroom context. The qualitative methodology utilized provided contextual insight and some initial understanding of a number of aspects related

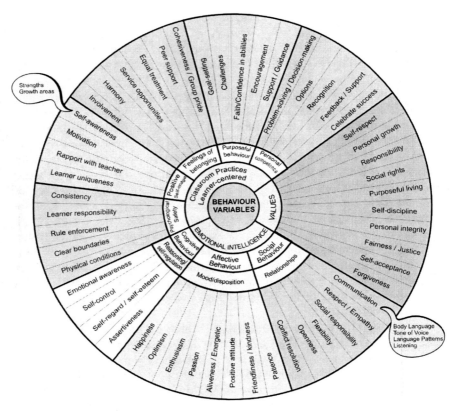

Figure 14.1. Proposed behavioral profile of an effective teacher.

to the impact and importance of emotionally intelligent behavior in the classroom context.

This exploratory study points to the importance of achieving a balanced perspective on the development of teachers. The research is groundbreaking as it provides new knowledge regarding the subjective experiences of learners from a socially deprived and historically disadvantaged school environment. The findings indicated that the characteristics of ideal teachers as envisioned by learners from a socially deprived historically disadvantaged South African school environment are related to general behaviors of effective teachers observed by South African and international authors. The behavioral profile that has been derived from the literature review and the empirical findings suggest that learner-centered classroom behaviors, teachers' values and emotionally intelligent behaviors are essential to effective teaching practices. Teachers' emotional competence and hidden resources such as their feelings, beliefs, perceptive abilities, values, and attitudes are regarded as major assets in the classroom environment.

As with all research, this study has limitations. It must be noted that the findings cannot be generalized to all teachers and classroom situations because of the qualitative nature of the study and the demographic limitations of the sample. There is still a great deal of research to be done to establish the validity of the findings by using more rigorous measures. Ongoing qualitative and quantitative research with a broader representation of all gender and race groups across a broad spectrum of schools is suggested to enhance the existing body of knowledge on the behavioral profile of effective teachers and the role of emotional intelligence in the classroom.

It is recommended that rather than forming an addendum to educator curricula, emotional intelligence needs to be firmly placed at the core. Whilst it is realized that emotional intelligence is not a panacea for all the ills of teaching and teacher education, it is recognized to be at the heart of learning to care, both for oneself and others, and as such deserves to be examined in more depth (Freshwater & Stickley, 2004). The findings imply further research possibilities in the area of emotional intelligence in relation to education science. The importance of developing emotional intelligence skills at all levels in the school environment should be further clarified by empirical research in the field, particularly in the South African context. The preliminary insights provided in this chapter contributed new knowledge to the field of education by presenting a framework of effective teacher behaviors in the form of a behavioral profile. The suggested profile of effective behaviors attempts to show how emotional intelligence integrates important personal and interpersonal skills with learner-centered behaviors and values which can lead to better quality of teaching, creating a more humanistic, compassionate and nurturing environment in education.

REFERENCES

Ashkanasy, Neal M., & Catherine S. Daus. (2005). Rumors of the death of emotional intelligence in organizational behavior are vastly exaggerated. Journal of *Organizational Behavior, 26,* 441-452.

Bar-On, Reuven. (1997). *Bar-On emotional quotient inventory: Facilitator's resource manual.* Toronto, Ontario, Canada: Multi-Health Systems.

Barth, Joan M., Sarah T. Dunlap, Heather Dane, John E. Lochman, & Karen C. Wells. (2004). Classroom environment influences on aggression, peer relations, and academic focus. *Journal of School Psychology, 42,* 115-133.

Bogdan, Robert C., & Sari Knopp Biklen. (1998). *Qualitative research for education: An introduction to theory and methods.* Boston: Allyn & Bacon.

Branden, Nathaniel. (1994). *Six pillars of self-esteem.* New York: Bantam.

Bredemeier, Mary E. (2001). Happy classrooms or joylessness? *Education, 97*(2), 192-198.

Buckley, Maureen, Meri Storino, & Carolyn Saarni. (2003). Promoting emotional competence in children and adolescents: Implications for school psychologists. *School Psychology Psychologist, 18*(2), 177-191.

Cobb, Casey D., & John D. Mayer. (2000). Emotional intelligence: What the research says. *Educational Leadership, 58*(3), 14-18.

Coetzee, Melinde. (2005). *The relationship between personality preferences, self-esteem and emotional competence.* DLitt et Phil (Industrial and Organisational Psychology) unpublished thesis, University of South Africa.

Coetzee, Melinde, & Cecelia A. Jansen. (2007). *Emotional intelligence in the classroom: The secret of happy teachers.* Cape Town, South Africa: Juta.

Cooper, Robert K., & Ayman Sawaf. (2000). *Executive EQ: Emotional intelligence in business.* New York: Texere.

Creswell, John W. (1998). *Qualitative inquiry and research design: Choosing among five traditions.* Thousand Oaks, CA: SAGE.

De Klerk, Rina, & Ronel Le Roux. (2004). *Emosionele intelligensie.* Pretoria, South Africa: Human & Rousseau.

Denzin, Norman K., & Yvonna S. Lincoln (Eds.). (2000). *Handbook of qualitative research.* Thousand Oaks, CA: SAGE.

Eisenberg, Nancy, Amanda Cumberland, & Tracy L. Spinrad. (1998). Parental socialization of emotion. *Psychological Inquiry, 9*, 241-273.

Elias, J. Maurice. (2001). Easing transitions with social-emotional learning. *Principal Leadership, 1*(7), 20-25.

Fineman, Stephen. (2000). *Emotions in organizations.* London: Sage.

Fox, Suzy, & Paul E. Spector. (2000). Relations of emotional intelligence, practical intelligence, general intelligence, and trait affectivity with interview outcomes: It's not just G. *Journal of Organizational Behavior, 21*, 203-220.

Freshwater, Dawn, & Theodore Stickley. (2004). The heart of the art: Emotional intelligence in nurse education. *Nursing Inquiry, 11*(2), 91-98.

Gardner, Howard. (1983). *Frames of mind: The theory of multiple intelligence.* New York: Basic Books.

George, Jennifer M. (2000). Emotions and leadership: The role of emotional intelligence. *Human Relations, 53*, 1027-1041.

Gerson, Richard F. (2000). The emotional side of performance improvement. *Performance Improvement, 39*(8), 18-23.

Goldsworthy, Richard. (2000). Designing instruction for emotional intelligence. *Educational Technology, 40*(5), 43-48.

Goleman, Daniel. (2001). *An EI-based theory of performance.* In Cary Cherniss & Daniel Goleman (Eds.), *The emotionally intelligent workplace.* San Francisco: Jossey-Bass.

Landy, J. Frank, & Jeffrey M. Conte. (2004). *Work in the 21st century.* New York: McGraw-Hill.

Locke, Edwin A. (2005). Why emotional intelligence is an invalid concept. *Journal of Organizational Behavior, 26,* 425-431.

Lopes, Paulo N., Marc A. Brackett, John B. Nezlek, Astrid Schütz, Ina Sellin, & Peter Salovey. (2004). Emotional intelligence and social interaction. *Personality and Social Psychology Bulletin, 30*(8),1018-1034.

Lopes, Paulo N., Peter Salovey, Stéphane Côté & Michael Beers. (2005). Emotion regulation ability and the quality of social interaction. *Emotion, 5*(1), 113-118.

Martinez-Pons, Manuel. (2000). Emotional intelligence as a self-regulatory process: A social-cognitive view. *Imagination, Cognition, and Personality, 19,* 331-350.

Mather, Nancy, & Sam Goldstein. (2001). *Learning disabilities and challenging behaviors.* Baltimore: Brookes.

Mayer, John D., David R. Caruso, & Peter Salovey. (1999). Emotional intelligence meets standards for traditional intelligence. *Intelligence, 27,* 267-298.

Mayer, John D., & Peter Salovey. (1997). What is emotional intelligence: Implications for educators. In Peter Salovey & David J. Sluyter (Eds.), *Emotional development, emotional literacy, and emotional intelligence: Educational implications.* New York: Basic Books.

Mayer, John D., Peter Salovey, & David R. Caruso. (2004). Emotional intelligence: Theory, findings and implications. *Psychological Inquiry, 15*(3), 197-215.

Merriam, Sharan B. (2002). *Qualitative research in practice: Examples for discussion and analysis.* San Francisco: Jossey-Bass.

Morris, Elizabeth. (2002). Emotional literacy training for educators: Developing the whole person—Linking hearts and minds in all learners. *Gifted Education International, 16,* 133-137.

Nelson Mandela Foundation. (2005). *Emerging voices* (Research Report on Education in South African Rural Communities). Cape Town, South Africa: HSRC Press.

Osborn, Marilyn. (1996). Book reviews—The highs and lows of teaching, sixty years of research revisited. *Cambridge Journal of Education, 26,* 455-461.

Reasoner, Robert W. (1992). *Building self-esteem in elementary schools.* Palo Alto, CA: Consulting Psychologists Press.

Rothwell, William, Roland Sullivan, & Gary N. McLean. (1995). *Practising organisational development: A guide for consultants.* Johannesburg, South Africa: Pfeiffer.

Saarni, Carolyn. (1997). Emotional competence and self-regulation in childhood. In Peter Salovey & David J. Sluyter (Eds.), *Emotional development and emotional intelligence: Educational implications* (pp. 35-66). New York: BasicBooks.

Saarni, Carolyn. (1999). *The development of emotional competence.* New York: Guilford.

Salovey, Peter, & John D. Mayer. (1990). Emotional intelligence. *Imagination, cognition, and personality, 9,* 185-211.

Schurink, J. Willem. (2003). Qualitative research in management and organisational studies with reference to recent South African research. *SA Journal of Human Resource Management, 1*(3), 2-14.

Strauss, Anselm, & Juliet Corbin. (1990). *Basics of qualitative research: Grounded theory procedures and techniques.* Newbury Park, CA: SAGE.

Stuart, Anita D., & Andrea Pauquet. (2001). Emotional intelligence as a determinant of leadership potential. *SA Journal of Industrial Psychology, 27*(3), 30-34.

Thingujam, Nutankumar S. (2004). Current trend and future perspective on emotional intelligence. *National Academy of Psychology, 49*(2/3), 155-166.

Tichenor, S. Mercedes, & John M. Tichenor. (2004). Understanding teachers' perspectives on professionalism. *Professional Educator, 27*, 89-95.

van Aswegen, Berendien, & Willem Schurink. (2003). From the worst to the best: An exploratory qualitative study of the process of social change at a South African secondary school. *SA Journal of Human Resource Management, 1*(3), 54-61.

CHAPTER 15

WOMEN AND DEVELOPMENT

The Case of Women in Military and Police Barracks in Nigeria

Eno Edem

The quality of gender relationship is dependent on the norms and values of the environment. This relationship is an important determinant for different situations, constraints, and potentials of males and females in that environment, the surrounding in which an individual lives and learns. An environment with quality liaison of gender provides an enabling platform for development. *Development* on the other hand, involves the participation of people in the determination of their environment. This chapter discusses the contributions of wives in military and police barracks in Nigeria in the development of their environment and its implications for gender relations, women advancement, and girl child education in Nigeria.

INTRODUCTION

From childhood, the traditional African woman is trained to fit into the cultural mores that dictate what she can do or cannot do. Extreme pressures are on her to behave according to the dictates of the society. She is expected to keep the home, manage the kitchen, care for children and participate in farm work. In some families and societies, she is denied education because educated women may not be considered to make good wives or resources are lean hence her brother's education takes precedence. Gender stereotyping encourages girls to behave in *feminine ways* and to develop gendered career aspirations (Sharpe, 1976). In school, certain subjects are regarded as traditional female subjects. These include home economics, biology, food and nutrition, home management, history, etc., while physics, chemistry, mathematics, and technical subjects are supposedly male subjects. In the primary school curriculum, gender stereotyping and biases are displayed through lesson schemes and curricular content that emphasize the different positions of men and women in the society (Whyte, 1983). Women are underrepresented in textbooks, the curriculum, and lesson plans. The generalized *he* is used to represent males and females in the curriculum, subject textbooks and the classroom (Petty, 2001). When this term is used, it communicates to female learners that males are of higher status (Wood, 2005).

As Joseph Emekalam (2000), in his paper "Common Misconceptions About Women," noted, "It has been said time and again that women are weaker vessels. They are created to be perpetually under men. They are ordinary. In some ancient societies they were not even counted as human beings" (p. 2). Thus, in African societies, behavioral patterns emerge which reinforce attitudes, beliefs, and value systems with obvious negative gender influences.

However, education and economic progress brought about by urbanization have greatly accelerated the disintegration of traditional social relations. The modern African culture now upholds that men and women can be equal even though men may still feel superior. Many African countries are signatories to many international conventions and bills of charter such as Convention on the Elimination of all Forms of Discrimination Against Women, the Beijing Platform, and the Rio+10. Women now have education and have acquired defined skills to contribute to the development of their communities. Takyiwaa Manuh (1998) reports that African women's contributions in their households, food production systems, and national economies are increasingly being acknowledged within and outside Africa. Women are now organized at grassroots and national levels for self-enhancement and community development purposes.

The present report aims at creating awareness of the multidisciplinary role of women in an enabling environment, using military and police environments in Nigeria as the reference point. Information for the report was obtained from records, documents, publications, newsletters, and memos about the activities of the associations obtained from the various secretariats of the associations in Abuja. Also, the book *DEPOWA Legacy: A Decade of Service* edited by Fatimah Ogohi and Zuwaira Gambo (2003), a former president and secretary general of Defense and Police Officers' Wives Association (DEPOWA) respectively, enables national presidents of the wives associations to chronicle activities and programs of their associations. The present author is also a training consultant to these associations and was involved in some of the activities (e.g., DEPOWA Green Corps project, Sanitation Workshops, etc.) mentioned in this report. Discussion will include strategies for fostering girl child education and women's advancement. It will also include suggestions for changing certain practices that are detrimental to women's advancement and welfare in the barracks and Nigeria.

The major wives' associations in Nigerian Armed Forces and the Police include Nigerian Army Officers' Wives Association (NAOWA), Naval Officers' Wives Association (NOWA), Nigeria Air Force Officers' Wives Association (NAFOWA), and Nigeria Police Officers' Wives Association (POWA). Wives of service chiefs and the inspector general of police lead the associations respectively.

Over the years, these associations have metamorphosed from mere social associations to community-based organizations (CBOs) and have positively influenced lives of families in the barracks through their welfare and capacity building programs, investments and assets (Ogomudia, 2003). The associations have also contributed significantly to women's emancipation in Nigeria. Faith Nwachuku (1997) maintains that these associations have contributed a lot to the development of Nigerian society. POWA, for example, is involved in literacy education. Literacy education programs are critical to the empowerment of women (Tuedor, 2005).

MILITARY AND POLICE ENVIRONMENT IN NIGERIA

The regimental nature of the military and police profession demands an environment that is conducive for the job, the personnel and his or her family. Hence barracks the living place of military and police personnel, are created to cater for these needs. Numerous environmental problems—overpopulation, poor sanitation, erosion, poor waste disposal, pollution, poverty, unemployment, youth and adolescent problems face Nigerian society of today. The barracks share these problems. Ben Aigbomian (2000) reports that there is no family in the barracks that does not have an unemployed child or dependent. According to the author, what ones sees in a typical working day in barracks are hordes of able-bodied men and women milling around doing nothing and warns that these youths are veritable recruitment sources for criminal labor employment, being used to guns all their lives. He therefore advised women in the barracks to rescue the situation through effective leadership and sustainable income generating ventures.

Other problems in the barracks include poor sanitation, overpopulation, teenage pregnancies, and health related problems. The need to tackle these problems in Nigerian barracks cannot be overemphasized considering the spate of militancy and HIV/AIDS pandemic in the country.

Women in Nigerian Barracks

A typical barrack in Nigeria—be it military or police, is a close-knit community where various Nigerian cultures, traditions and religions of ethnic groups melt to produce a peculiar and distinct habitat of oneness, cooperation, tolerance, mutual understanding, and neighborly love. The development of this unique environment in the barracks has been a collective responsibility of women bound by a common destiny—marriage to military and police personnel (Ogohi & Gambo, 2003).

These women play very important roles in the success or failure of their husbands. They are expected to imbibe the culture, norms and ethos of the profession as well as give their whole-hearted attention to the good of their husbands and the nation (Jalo, 1981). Leadership, discipline, subordination to higher authority, hard work, selflessness, loyalty, and teamwork are among the culture and ethos of the armed forces and the police (Aigbomian, 2000). A military wife cares for her family under difficult conditions and has a lot of responsibilities by virtue of the fact that her husband is prone to incessant postings, courses, and exercises that takes him away from home (Aigbomian). This makes it near impossible for his wife to pursue any career as the responsibility of running the family rests on her shoulders (Ogohi, 2001). Apart from that the labor market generally does not favor wives of military and police personnel, as locations for their husbands' duties do not always provide employment opportunities, frequent postings of husbands makes it impossible for them to stay in jobs. Thus many women in the barracks have sacrificed their careers for the good of their husbands and the nation.

Wives in the barracks are women who are constantly living with the threat of widowhood and have the responsibility of counseling as well as providing emotional support to each other (Edem, 2007). Specifically, the role of a wife in the barracks includes (a) motherhood and wifely duties; (b) fostering the bond of friendship among themselves; (c) self-development to enable her to contribute to her family, the force, and the nation;

(d) charity work; (e) involvement in social and sporting activities and in self-help projects (Nigerian Officers' Wives Association, 1987).

To be able to carry out these roles as well as provide succor for themselves and their children while their husbands are on their regimental duties, wives' associations are created. These associations are supported by the military and police establishments who, are noted for their gender friendly system in Nigeria. This phenomenon is due to the fact that the career of a military and police personnel and his family go hand in hand according to Fatimah Ogohi and Zuwaira Gambo (2003, p. 51). What affects one, affects the other. Major General Jalo, a one time chief of army staff, in his address to officers' wives in 1987 said that the meeting was "to emphasize the importance we attach to the Army Wives' Association" and appealed that the women dedicate themselves "to the success of the association for the benefit of the Nigerian Army and the country in general." While assuring the women their "cooperation and support both physically and morally in any field you will require our assistance."

Family Health

The wives' associations carry out periodic immunization exercises in the barracks against child deadly diseases. Wives' associations in the barracks were very prominent in the launching of the National Program on Immunization.

In 2002, the concern about poor maintenance and sanitation culture in military and police barracks in the country prompted a 3-day workshop for families to sensitize them on the need to keep their environment clean. Defense and Police Officers' Wives Association in collaboration with Defense Headquarters, Abuja, organized the workshop. At the end of the 3-day workshop some resolutions were made, including

- improvement of the existing maintenance culture in the barracks by authorities and residents;
- effective control of human population in the barracks;
- establishment of a modern shopping complex in place of *mammy* (make-shift) markets so as to control waste disposal and moral decadence among residents in the barracks;
- the revival of the traditional roles of *Magajias* (women community leaders) who would serve as sanitary inspectors, among other duties, in the barracks; and
- regular seminars and workshops on contemporary issues such as drug abuse, teenage pregnancies, burglary/stealing, child abuse,

and so on, to address the cause of these problems in the barracks as well as provide strategies for curbing them effectively (Ogohi & Gambo 2003, pp. 49-50).

As an incentive to ensure a clean environment, POWA for example, gives out trophies to the cleanest barracks/blocks (Balogun, 2003). In order to introduce environmental education to families and schools in military and police communities, the DEPOWA Green Corps scheme was developed with the motto "Save Our Environment." The DEPOWA Green Corps scheme is an environmental friendly program designed to help in reducing truancy and moral laxity among youths in the barracks. This author (Edem, 2006) studied the 5-month pilot project which involved 55 participants with severe emotional and personality problems and found that all the participants were rehabilitated and gainfully integrated into their communities. The result led to the suggestion that concerns in curriculum development should not only be for the formal system of education. Curriculum experts should also address issues in the informal system.

Agriculture

Some of the associations (e.g., NAOWA and NOWA) have ventured into agriculture in order to make food available and affordable (Afolayan, 2003). Presently there are farms established by these associations in Minna, Kaduna, and Ikorodu-Lagos to mention a few. These farms have contributed to food production thus contributing to the fight against poverty and hunger in Nigeria.

Recreational/Social Activities

In order to create and strengthen the bond of friendship and unity among themselves, other organizations, their children, and between wives and husbands, social activities are organized for these groups. Variety shows, *tom bola*, husbands' nights, tea parties, send off parties, children's parties, cultural shows, dramas, songs and dances, are some of such social activities organized by these women.

The women undertake sporting activities for fitness and health. In 2002, the DEPOWA Youths' Sports Development was launched to enable talent hunts in sports among children and youths in the barracks.

Philanthropy

The wives' associations have positively touched the lives of the less privileged members of the Nigerian society in many ways. As women committed to the service of their communities and humanity, they have over the years engaged in philanthropic activities such as visits and donations to motherless babies' homes, Save Our Souls Villages, institutions for the disabled, hospitals, and other such needy organizations like the Nikky Cancer Trust Fund.

Education

Education is perhaps an area where the women have made the most remarkable impact. The women themselves are very educated. They are professionals in various fields: nurses, teachers, accountants, lawyers, and so forth, even though many of them are not pursuing their careers. Secondary education is the minimum education level of the women.

At least one NAOWA or POWA or NOWA or NAFOWA school exists in major towns in Nigeria. NAFOWA has one of the best computer training schools in the country. The school is affiliated to the University of Lagos. Admission into these vocational centers is open to the various sectors of the Nigerian society (Wuyep, 2003). Low fees are charged in schools established by the women to ensure equal access to education of children in the barracks.

As a means of encouragement, scholarship schemes are established for children of low ranking personnel and those of personnel who lost their lives in the course of their duties. Prominent among such is the Police Officers' Wives scholarship scheme for children of police officers. The association also has the Widows' Trust Fund, for police wives who lost their husbands in the cause of duty.

Discussion

The indispensable role of women in the development of their environment cannot be overemphasized. The efforts of wives in Nigerian barracks confirm Crowley, Levitin, and Quainin's (1972) findings that women are concerned about opportunity for self-actualization, opportunity to excel, and to improve. Women can positively influence communities for better performance. They are builders of economies, political and social agents of enormous potency and organizers of the forces of labor. The present report confirms Mary Anagbogu's (2005) assertion that the basic needs of women are developmental. These include food production and processing, education, healthcare, sanitation. Therefore, the way forward as shown by the present report is to challenge the status quo of women through gender relations, integration, and role sharing.

GENDER RELATIONS AND DEVELOPMENT

Gender is the relationship between men and women that is socially constructed (Oakley, 1975). The relationship is determined by the norms, values and ethos of a given environment or society. Thus gender relation differs from society to society or culture to culture and manifests in specific roles and behaviors of men and women. From our present report, it is safe to say that gender relation is related to development—the more positive and constructive the relationship (as obtained between military and police authorities and their wives) the more the achievement of both sexes. Sadly, this relationship is yet to be achieved in Africa despite the dynamism that African women display in the economic, cultural, and social lives of their communities through their various associations (Manuh, 1998). This in turn is a barrier to development.

In the words of Moreno (2007), the director of United Nations International Research Institute for Advancement of Women at an international gathering in Belgium, "Persistent gender discrimination only brings development efforts down and generates more poverty for both men and women." This summarizes the problem in Africa and Third World countries where women are marginalized and cannot play significant roles in development. Men and women must play complementary roles for any meaningful development to occur. Men and women cannot achieve without each other. Hence, the need to relate on a level playing field considering their roles in the family and the larger society (Busari, 2005).

Gender and Access to Resources

To mainstream gender into development planning, it is important that women have access to resources (Manuh, 1998: Moreno, 2007; Msuega, 2005; Ogohi, 2001). The achievement of women in Nigerian barracks is due to the support from the military and the police institutions, their husbands, donations, and resources generated through their various investments. Manuh (1998) notes that the contributions of African women though highly acclaimed, is yet to translate into improved access to resources by women in Africa. Though the efforts of wives in the barracks have sparked off several wives' associations in Nigeria, none has created any appreciable impact as these associations cannot sustain themselves.

Generally, women in Africa are faced with many sociocultural obstacles that create barriers to their advancement and emancipation. Many Nigerian women for example, are subjected to widowhood practices, domestic violence, and early marriage. Also, some cultural and traditional beliefs deprive women access to information, education, wealth-creating assets like land and credit facilities, thus contributing to their low participation in politics, commerce, and decision-making. The common saying in Nigeria that poverty wears a female face readily gives the picture of gender gaps and access to resources in the country. Though men control the resources it does not usually translate into improved family or household welfare. This results in household pressures on women enabling them little or no input in politics, decision making and national development. Development involves the opportunity for people to choose and use their resources to the maximum capacity.

Implications for Women and Girl Child Education

Enweani (2005) argues that there is a definite interplay between education, economics, culture, and women's freedom. Lack of access to formal education and training has been identified as a key barrier to women's employment and advancement in Africa (Kassim-Oghiator, 2005; Msuega 2005). Education is an essential factor in human life and virtually all aspects of human endeavor. It is synonymous to development and also one of the most important instruments of change. Education brings about desirable changes in the behavior of individuals through the acquisition of new attitudes, skills, knowledge, and appreciations. Education awakens the numerous potentials that lie within individuals enabling them to develop to their fullest potentials.

Edewor (2001) identifies education as a tool that liberates women from the shackles of ignorance, backwardness, suppression, and dehumanization. Women education is therefore that education which enables women to become aware of themselves and their capacity to exploit their environment. Once educated, women are empowered. It brings them liberty and awareness and enables them to have a stronger voice in decision-making and to be involved in policies that drive the development agenda of their various communities (Manuh, 1998). Education enables women to understand their constitutional rights, and helps to eradicate legal, cultural, social and religious constraints, which are barriers to the attainment of social justice and equality in the society (Emarievbe, 2005). The overemphasis on the social roles of women as wives and the absence of cultural expectations of women's contribution to development among other things are detrimental to women education. Educated women are generally considered not suitable for marriage.

However, investment in girls' education is the key to efforts to curb societal problems. It translates directly and quickly into better nutrition for the family, better healthcare and population control, etc. Substantial evidence shows that educated girls who have completed secondary educa-

Table 15.1. Estimated Illiteracy Rates by Gender in Developed and Third World Countries (2000-2004)

Country	Men	Women
Albania	0.6	0.5
Angola	17.9	46.2
Argentina	3	3
Bulgaria	0.9	1.9
China	4.9	13.5
Israel	2.7	6.6
Niger	69.6	89.4
Nigeria	25.6	40.6
Palestine	46.6	71.5
Philippines	7.5	7.3

Source: United Nations Educational, Scientific and Cultural Organization (2005).

tion were less likely to marry young, to have unwanted pregnancies, and to engage in high-risk behaviors (Enweani, 2005). Sadly, girls account for 60% of the estimated 113 million out of school children (Akintunde, 2001). To be able to participate in a modern society certain skills are very important. Most notably is the ability to read, write, and perform some basic arithmetic tasks. Everett (1990) observed that women constitute the largest illiteracy rate, lowest enrollment rate in primary and secondary schools, and the highest attrition rate. Table 15.1 shows the estimated illiteracy rates in some developed and developing nations.

The illiteracy rates clearly show gender disparities in education globally, even though this is more pronounced in Asian and African countries. In Nigeria, gender imbalance in education is caused by a number of factors, which include, poverty, social beliefs against girl child education, and early marriage. The Federal Ministry of Education (2002) gives the median age at first marriage in rural Nigeria as 15 for girls and 22 for boys. In the urban areas this increases to 20 for girls and 26 for boys. Benefits of having more educated women in Nigeria should be considered.

1. Women are generally good resource managers, hence are likely to help Nigeria develop significantly if given the opportunity to manage the country's resources thereby curbing corruption in the country.

2. Social problems such as infant mortality, poverty, family health, human trafficking, female genital mutilation, prostitution, and illiteracy would be eradicated.
3. More women in positions of authority mean better policies and sincere ways of doing things in the country. The few women that have held such positions have significantly influenced the society positively. For example, under the leadership of Professor Dora Akunyili, director general, National Agency for Food and Drugs Administration and Control (NAFDAC), NAFDAC has brought sanity to the drug industry in Nigeria. To check against this, drugs imported or manufactured in Nigeria must display their NAFDAC registration number. This has created a lot of public awareness and has saved many lives in the country.
4. Living standards of households would improve.

STRATEGIES FOR WOMEN EDUCATION AND ADVANCEMENT IN NIGERIA

Responsive Curriculum Practice

A pragmatic approach is needed toward women and girl child education in Nigeria. This is through responsive curriculum practice, which is driven by the needs of particular learners, situation, and environment. This is in contrast to unresponsive curriculum, which is fixed, rigid, unyielding and not flexible in principle and practice (Edem, 2006). Unfortunately, curricular practice in Nigeria is generally unresponsive with fixed time/periods of study, examination dominated and no relevance to the world of work. The relevance of responsive curriculum practice is in terms of the requirements of the world of work which tend to place strong premium on life skills required to survive in the knowledge based economy as Nigeria. If women and the girl child are to benefit from education, the curriculum, teaching and assessment methods should be gender responsive. Individualized instruction and home tuition enhance the participation the girl child. Home tuition is particularly relevant in areas where women are secluded due to cultural and religious practices.

There must be friendly social context of learning that helps the girl child have a positive self-concept. Government should be involved in less formal methods such as adult education and on-the-job-training. The curriculum should include (a) literacy education, (b) entrepreneurship, (c) health education, (d) information communication technology, and (e) skills training.

The curriculum at the formal level should emphasize, among other things, (a) science and technology education, (b) information communication technology, (c) language education, and (d) entrepreneurship education. In addition, education should be linked with the world of work and entrepreneurship to enable women to see the relevance of education to their needs, and prospects.

Distance Learning

Many women and young girls have constraints of time as they are involved in domestic chores and some income generating ventures, thus distance learning helps to overcome barriers to their participation in education. Women can learn in their homes and at their own space and can take up vocations and skills for their economic advancement. This is particularly relevant to wives in the barracks. These women can develop themselves through distance learning regardless of their circumstances. Another advantage of distance learning is the cost factor—one of the barriers to women and the girl child education. Distance education is generally affordable.

Enlightenment Programs

Effective communication through enlightenment programs is critical. It helps to eliminate ignorance. The girl child for example, must first of all appreciate the challenges of her circumstance and the appropriate measures to overcome them. She needs information about her peers in developed countries (Esiobu, 2005). There is a need to reach out to people as much as possible to help change their mindset about women education and other societal issues.

Through enlightenment programs, the girl child in particular would understand the consequences of prostitution, drug trafficking and addiction, human trafficking and contracting HIV/AIDS. The media, government and nongovernmental organizations, and other stakeholders have a role to play.

Leadership Training for Women

According to Ms. Soukeyena Ba (1998), president of Women Development Enterprise in Africa, "Africa is overflowing with women leaders. They lack only training and the means to bloom." Though leadership is not an easy task, every officer's wife is a potential leader. A leader needs intellectual, attitudinal, emotional, and psychological capabilities to be able to lead successfully. Oftentimes, women in the barracks find themselves ill equipped mentally, attitudinally, and emotionally for the leadership role they are expected to play (Edem, 2000). Training develops women's capabilities and leadership skills and enables them to take up challenges. They should be ready for leadership roles by developing themselves.

Some of the ways include (a) learning a vocation if not in employment, (b) engaging in some economic activities, (c) participating in outreach programs, and (d) building computer literacy and information communication technology skills.

Legislation to Protect Women

Laws should protect women's rights, freedoms and opportunities. Development can only be achieved through changes in social, economic, and cultural life with the active participation of all. There is a dire need to amend or abolish customary laws that are detrimental to the development and well-being of women and children. Practices such as widowhood, female genital mutilation, inheritance, early marriage, and so forth should be abolished.

Military authorities should address issues associated with widowhood. Widows of personnel are known to undergo dehumanizing treatments in the hands of in-laws who dispose them of their late husbands' properties. The authorities can alleviate the suffering of widows by mandating military and police personnel to make their spouses or children their next of kin rather than members of their extended families.

Also, wives should be protected from husbands who are HIV positive by making safe sex mandatory for such couples by military authorities. The fear of contacting the deadly disease from their husbands is one of the nightmares of wives in the barracks and, in fact, wives in Nigeria.

RECOMMENDATIONS

In order to mainstream women in Nigeria, the following should be considered:

- Nigerian government should give priority to girl child education by giving scholarships and making enrollment compulsory.

- Gender studies should be introduced into the curriculum of schools from primary to tertiary levels of education and policy makers should be trained on gender issues.
- Relevant agencies should ensure that women are adequately represented in all activities designed to improve the environment.
- Ministries of Women Affairs at federal and state levels should be staffed with people who are knowledgeable in gender issues and are gender sensitive so that they can initiate programs to support and uplift women.
- More women should be appointed into decision-making positions in the country.

Implications for Curriculum and Instruction

The women's approach to solving environmental problems, rehabilitating and empowering emotionally disturbed youths in the barracks has implications for formal education and curriculum development. As earlier reported, all the participants ($n = 55$) have been gainfully integrated into the society. There is need to evaluate the project in terms of its efficacy and methodology and its relevance to the formal system.

The content of the DEPOWA Green Corps Project included (a) physical education and drill, (b) security/safety, (c) health education, (d) moral and religious instruction, (e) environmental education, (f) horticulture, (g) leadership and team work, (h) road safety and traffic control, (i) English language/report writing, (j) basic accounting, (k) time management, (l) general knowledge, and (m) counseling. Should skills training, and physical and moral education, for example, be included in formal programs for counseling and rehabilitation? Are projects of this nature the answer to militancy in Nigeria? This needs to be studied by curriculum planners in Nigeria.

Environmental literacy creates awareness, appreciation, enhances knowledge of natural systems, and ecological concepts and helps in understanding environmental issues (Mbina, 2006). Unfortunately, environmental education is not important in the curricula of primary and secondary schools in Nigeria. This is also a challenge from women in Nigerian barracks to educators in Nigeria.

CONCLUSIONS

The issues raised in the present report are of inevitable importance to the quality of life and development of the African society, in general, and Nigerian society, in particular. Women are catalysts in development, and

African societies would experience more development if African women were empowered and mainstreamed in their various societies. To achieve this, the author has called for such major efforts as women and girl child education through responsive curriculum practice and governments' efforts in respect to women education and mainstreaming of women.

There is no doubt that Nigerians have been sensitized on gender equality, women and development, and girl child education. What is needed are conscious efforts to actualize these. Nigerian women should develop themselves so as to contribute to the development of their societies as well as curb gender stereotyping prevalent in traditional societies especially in Africa and third World countries. It would also enable them to meet the challenges that their careers and situations may demand of them. The aim is not that women and men become the same, but that their opportunities and life chances become and remain equal.

REFERENCES

Afolayan, Treasure. (2003). The Naval Officers' Wives Association. In Fatimah Ogohi & Zuwaira Gambo (Eds.), *DEPOWA legacy: A decade of service* (pp. 105-110). Lagos, Nigeria: Workstation.

Aigbomian, Ben. (2000, June) *The changing roles of military and police wives in the barracks.* Paper presented at a workshop for Defence and Police Officers' Wives Association, Lagos, Nigeria.

Akintunde, Dorcas Olu. (2001). *African culture and the quest for women's rights.* Ibadan, Oyo State, Nigeria: Sefer.

Anagbogu, Mary. (2005). *Mainstreaming gender in community development.* Paper presented at UNICEF Project for the Mainstreaming of Women, Ekwusigo, Anambra, Nigeria.

Balogun, Funke. (2003). The police officers' wives association. In Fatimah Ogohi & Zuwaira Gambo (Eds.), *DEPOWA legacy: A decade of service* (pp. 118-123). Lagos, Nigeria: Workstation.

Busari, Ola. (2005). Women in science and technology education in Nigeria. In Uduogie Ivowi (Ed.), *Science and technology education for development* (pp. 109-121). Lagos, Nigeria: Adcross.

Crowley, Joan E., T. Levitin, & R. P. Quainin. (1972). Facts and fictions about American working women. In Ola Sheyin (1997), The role of family support programme in promoting education for national development (A case study of Oyo State FSP). *Journal of Education for National Development and International Co-operation, 2*(1), 42-50.

Edem, Eno. (2000, June). *Leadership skills and basic survival strategies for new leaders.* Paper presented at a workshop for Defence and Police Officers' Wives Association, NNS Quorra, Naval Base, Apapa, Lagos, Nigeria.

Edem, Eno. (2006, August). *The DEPOWA Green Corps Project: A rehabilitation program for youths in military barracks in Nigeria.* Paper presented at the 12th

World Council for Curriculum and Instruction conference, Manila, Philippines.

Edem, Eno. (2007, July). *Etiquette and protocol for wives of police officers.* Paper presented at Police Officers' Wives' Association a workshop on Etiquette and Security, Garki, Abuja, Nigeria.

Edewor, Kate (2001). Cultural attitude of women's educational and economic empowerment. In Stella Emerievbe (Ed.), (2005) Women's right and education in the Nigerian society. *International Journal of Forum for African Educationalists Nigeria, 1*(2), 65-74.

Emarievbe, Stella. (2005). Women's right in the Nigerian society. *International Journal of Forum for African Educationalists Nigeria, 1*(2), 65-74.

Emekalam, Joseph. (2000). *Some common misconceptions about women.* Paper presented at the workshop for Defence and Police Officers' Wives Association, Lagos, Nigeria.

Enweani, Ifeoma. (2005, April). *Challenges and prospects of educating women scientists in Nigeria.* Paper presented at the International Regional Workshop/Conference of Forum for African Women Educationalists, Nnamdi Azikiwe University, Awka, Nigeria.

Esiobu, Gladys Uju. (2005). Gender issues and technology education for development. In Uduogie Ivowi (Ed.), *Science and technology education for development* (pp. 137-156). Lagos, Nigeria: Adecross.

Everett, Jana. (1990). *The global empowerment of women, in Nigeria strategic country gender assessment.* Abuja, Nigeria: Federal Ministry of Women Affairs.

Federal Ministry of Health. (1988). *The national health policy and strategy to achieve health for all Nigerians.* Lagos, Nigeria.

Jalo, General. (1981, March). Address at a meeting with Nigerian Army Officers' Wives Association, Onikcan, Lagos, Nigeria.

Kassim-Oghiator, F. E. (2005). Culture as a constraint in women education: A study of Ukwuani women in Delta state. *International Journal of Forum for African Educationalists Nigeria, 1*(2), 42-47.

Manuh, Takiwaa. (1998, April). Women in Africa's development: Overcoming obstacles, pushing for progress. *Africa Recovery Briefing Paper, No. 11.* United Nations. Retrieved August 2, 2007, from http://www.un.org/ecosocdev/geninfo/afrec/bpaper/maineng.htm

Mbina, Anthony. (2006) Environmental education and sustainable development in developing nations. In Udo Etuk (Ed.), *University education and sustainable development: A forum* (pp. 105-110). Uyo, Nigeria: Minder.

Moreno, Carmen. (2007, July). Director of United Nations International Research Institute for Advancement of Women (UN-INSTRAW) an address at an international gathering in Belgium. In Takyiwaa Manuh (Ed.), (1998) *Women in Africa's development: Overcoming obstacles and pushing for development. Africa Recovery Briefing Paper. No. 11.* United Nations. Retrieved August 2, 2007, from http://www.un.org/ecosocdev/geninfo/afrec/bpaper/maineng.htm

Msuega, Ordean. (2005). Poverty and access to education in Nigeria. *International Journal of Forum for African Women Educationalists Nigeria, 1*(2), 147-154.

Nigerian Officers' Wives Association. (1987, March). Minutes of meeting. Lagos, Nigeria: Onikan.

Nwachukwu, Faith. (1977). The impact of women liberation in national development. *Journal of Education for National Development and International Co-Operation, 2*(1), 107-112.

Oakley, Ann. (1975). Sex, gender and society. In Steve Bartlett, Diana Burton & Nick Peim (Eds.), *Introduction to education studies*. London: Paul Chapman.

Ogohi, Fatimah. (2001, July). *Viewpoint on professionalism in the armed forces and the police*. Paper presented at the Workshop on Reflections and Challenges of Armed Forces and Police Professionalism: The Role of Officer's Wives, Abuja, Nigeria.

Ogohi, Fatimah, & Zuwaira Gambo. (2003). *DEPOWA legacy: A decade of service*. Lagos, Nigeria: Workstation.

Ogomudia, Iwuyemi. (2003). The Nigerian Army Officers' Wives Association. In Fatimah Ogohi & Zuwaira Gambo (Eds.), *DEPOWA legacy: A decade of service* (pp. 95-103). Lagos, Nigeria: Workstation.

Petty, Geoffrey. (1998). *Teaching today*. United Kingdom: Nelson Thormes.

Sharpe, Sue. (1976). Just like a girl: How girls learn to be women. In Steve Bartlett, Diana Burton, & Nick Peim (Eds.). *Introduction to education studies* (p. 205). London: Paul Chapman.

Tuedor, F. M. (2005). Language education: The tool for women enlightenment and national development. *International Journal of Forum for African Educationalists Nigeria, 1*(2) 34-41.

United Nations Educational, Scientific and Culture Organization. (2005). *Indicators on illiteracy*. Retrieved May 2006, from http://www.uis.unesco.org

Wood, Julia T. (2005). *Gendered lives: Communication, gender and culture*. Belmont, CA: Thomas.

Whyte, Judith. (1983). Beyond the Wendy house: Sex-role stereotyping in primary schools. In Steve Bartlett, Diana Burton, & Nick Peim (Eds.), *Introduction to education studies*. London: Paul Chapman.

Wuyep, Makami Lami. (2003). The Nigeria Air Force Officers' Wives Association. In Fatimah Ogohi & Zuwaira Gambo (Eds.), *DEPOWA legacy: A decade of service*. Lagos, Nigeria: Workstation.

PART IV

EXPERIENTIAL KNOWLEDGE

CHAPTER 16

AN INTRODUCTORY REFLECTION ...

MIRACLE IN WHITWELL

Barbara Wind

A paper clip will never be the same again; nor will a butterfly. I've just come back from Whitwell, Tennessee. In what is an ordinary American town, I was privileged to witness the most extraordinary event: the dedication of a Holocaust museum.

When I got into the van that was taking several New Jerseyans to the airport, a member of the MetroWest Holocaust Council, Martha Rich, handed me a ziplock bag filled with dried fruits, candy, and a snack-size pack of chocolate chip cookies. I was surprised, and this must have showed. Martha is quite glamorous and doesn't impress anyone as the typical den mother. Another woman in the van who has traveled with Martha many times said, "Martha always brings goody bags for everyone who travels with her."

I thought of the first time I met Martha. Several years ago she came to a local college to speak about her experience as a Holocaust survivor. She was a young girl in 1944 when she and the rest of the Jews in her Hungarian shtetl were rounded up and sent to Auschwitz. At that time,

Auschwitz had no special meaning for them. All they knew was that they would be going to work camps somewhere in the east. Each passenger could bring no more than a single suitcase. To prepare for the journey, Martha's mother baked cookies. Those would be the last cookies Martha would see until after liberation.

Martha organized this trip to Tennessee. The previous April, a friend had sent her an email about the Paper Clip Project. She immediately decided she had to go to Whitwell.

WHITWELL, TENNESSEE, HOME OF THE PAPER CLIPS PROJECT

Whitwell is a small town, a population of 1,600. It doesn't boast a hotel or cinema. Many of its residents live below the poverty line and have never traveled beyond Chattanooga, about an hour away. There are no Jews in Whitwell nor have there ever been. Martha, who lost most of her family in the Holocaust, felt compelled to express her gratitude to people who chose to honor the memory of 6 million Jews. "I wanted to shake their hands," she said.

In 1998, two teachers and Linda Hooper, the principal of Whitwell Middle School, initiated a project in response to a request from several students. The goal was to collect 6 million paper clips in an effort to impress upon students studying the Holocaust the magnitude of the number of Jews who had been murdered. Why paper clips? The paper clip was invented by a Norwegian, and many Norwegians wore a paper clip in their lapels to show their solidarity against the Nazi invasion and occupation of Norway.

As ubiquitous as paper clips are, Whitwell was far from meeting its goal until news of the children's efforts hit the Internet. After that, paper clips began to flood in. So did the media. Dagmar and Peter Schroeder, German journalists based in Washington D.C., came, saw, and wrote a book in German, *Das Paper Clip Pojekt*. The clips kept coming in. With more than 28 million paper clips, the school is requesting that no more clips be sent.

Whitwell had originally intended to melt those clips down into a memorial. However, the paper clips quickly took on a special symbolism, each representing a life cut short. The school was faced with the problem of what to do with such bounty, and the project inspired others throughout the world to tremendous acts of generosity.

The Schroeders helped the school obtain one of the few remaining boxcars that had been used to ship Jews to concentration and death camps. The German government donated the boxcar as a *manchmal*, a memorial. A shipping company offered its services to transport the boxcar from Baltimore Harbor to Whitwell. A company in Tennessee that manufactures railroad tracks found some tracks they had made in 1943 and donated them to the school. The local Home Depot supplied lumber for the steps and ramp leading up to the boxcar. Whitwell never asked anyone for help, but offers and money came pouring in. Jennifer Shepherd, a high school student in Nashville, pledged to raise $10,000 and did. That money helped pay for the fence that surrounds the boxcar.

This museum signifies democracy at its height. Created without architects and sophisticated fund-raising campaigns, this is a memorial built by and for people. Begun in 1998, it has amassed thousand of letters, articles in newspapers and periodicals, as well as artwork and artifacts. The artifacts are not displayed in galleries but on the walls of Whitwell Middle School. Anyone walking past can stop and peruse the thousands of letters, articles, and artifacts (I know, I have just returned from another bus trip to Whitwell to do just that!). Knowledge of foreign languages is helpful as some of them are in languages other than English.

When Martha Rich came to Whitwell that April and met Linda Hooper, the school's principal, they immediately connected. Both are women of spirit, charm, and steely determination. Martha, was one of the first Jews to set foot in Whitwell. She promised to return for the dedication of the boxcar and bring others along.

Some consider seven a lucky number. I consider myself very lucky to have been one of the seven that comprised Martha's retinue. What we witnessed in Whitwell was America at its very best. The entire community had become involved in making this dedication a glorious occasion.

Because she believes that butterflies symbolize continuous life, Linda Hooper commissioned a local artist to do copper wire sculptures of butterflies in the small garden that fronts the boxcar as well as to create colored butterfly insets in the concrete path that leads to it. When the artist expressed reservations about her ability to complete the insets, Ms. Hooper—a steel butterfly herself—coaxed, cajoled and bullied her into it. Students scrubbed the walk not once but three times, in preparation for the dedication ceremony. Local churchwomen baked up a storm. Parents decorated the cafeteria and hallways with butterflies and flowers. The only concession to commercialism was a table where school mothers were taking orders for tee shirts emblazoned with Linda Hooper's motto, "Changing the world ... one class at a time." They also sold prints and postcards of the boxcar drawn by Whitwell's art teacher.

What an event it was! The school choir sang "I Never Saw Another Butterfly"; the orchestra played a moving piece written by a German composer for the occasion; students from a Jewish day school in Atlanta chanted Kaddish, the Hebrew memorial prayer; a minister gave a very moving invocation; a local judge read a poem.

Source: Photo by Douglas F. Warring (September 2007).

Figure 16.1. Part of the Holocaust Memorial, Whitwell, Tennessee. The monument houses 11 million paper clips—one for each victim of the Holocaust.

Chairs and bleachers were filled. The extraordinarily well-behaved Whitwell students sat on blankets on either side of the memorial. Because there wasn't room on the landing that served as a dais, the speakers were seated inside the boxcar. One of those speakers was Martha. What a long way she had come from her first trip in a boxcar.

Whitwell is set in a valley. Behind us, from the top of the mountain smoke rose and descended. Weeks ago, an arsonist had set a fire in the forest. Despite teams of firefighters from as far away as Arizona, the fire was still raging, sending up smoke eerily reminiscent of both the Holocaust and the latest act of irrational hatred and mass murder, the September 11 attack on our nation. Yet, the sun shone brightly.

Martha hates talking about the Holocaust but does it because she understands the importance of being a witness. Nervous tension had kept her up most of the night and sitting in the boxcar exacerbated it but she managed to appear utterly composed when it was her turn to speak. There were several standing ovations particularly when she spoke of not allowing the Nazis to take her spirit away from her and her faith that Americans who could create what Whitwell created would never be crushed.

If a summery day of sunshine in November were not blessing enough; if the gathering of people of good will, people of diverse backgrounds bound by respect for one another were not enough; if the warm welcome we received from the citizens of Whitwell were not enough; if the bowls of punch and mounds of cookies and cakes were not enough; if the thoughtful words of all the speakers on the program were not enough; if the songs and music and bell ringing were not enough to make us aware that we, were indeed, blessed to be in Whitwell, I saw a butterfly.

In the midst of Martha's speech, a yellow butterfly flew past me. A butterfly in November and here of all places! This was really too much, too Hollywood! I nudged my friend. I wanted to make sure she didn't miss it. Most of all I wanted a witness to what I might otherwise come to believe was only a mirage.

The last words of so many before Hitler's minions killed them was "Remember and Tell." Had someone told them that they were not dying in vain, they might have gone to their deaths with some glimmer of solace. Who, then, could know that such a day would come? Smoke from the mountains descending on us, a butterfly before us, a town filled with people of good will inspiring each other and the rest of the world to remember and to tell—miracles do happen.

CHAPTER 17

SEEKING SOLIDARITY THROUGH GLOBAL AND INDIGENOUS SERVICE-LEARNING

Kelly C. Weiley

As a part of the international community and an ever-shrinking world, postsecondary institutions today face a difficult challenge to not only connect students to others around them, but to connect them to the world community. Putnam (2000), in his book *Bowling Alone*, details the decline of civic participation and lack of connection that Americans experience as a part of their daily routine. Putnam confirms, "most Americans feel vaguely and uncomfortably disconnected" (p. 402). Putnam points to the stress of two-career families, suburbanization, and White flight, the effects of electronic entertainment with an emphasis on TV in addition to generational change as the main culprits for the decline (p. 283). This "disconnect" is illustrated on a global level in that only approximately one quarter of American citizens have a passport (Tevlin, 2007). Tevlin continues to note that with the exception of traveling to Mexico or Canada, which before 2007 did not require passports, "almost 75 percent of our

---

Growing a Soul for Social Change: Building the Knowledge Base for Social Justice
pp. 295–344
Copyright © 2008 by Information Age Publishing
All rights of reproduction in any form reserved.

[U.S.] citizens probably have not been nor plan to be out of the country" (p. G1).

INTRODUCTION

How can universities help facilitate connections for students to feel allied to their international and indigenous brothers and sisters when, in reality, many may never have the opportunity to travel to countries outside of the United States? In today's global village, it is not uncommon for the average American to misconstrue the ways in which global politics and economy affect the world community. In addition to those beliefs, with the limited U.S. history most receive through secondary school, many do not understand the global impact of decisions made within the United States. Negative attitudes, beliefs of inferiority, and misconceptions that many Americans hold toward "others" and indigenous peoples all over the globe are pervasive. Schniedewind and Davidson (2006) noted that in the post 9/11 culture in the United States, "Many adults today fear perceived external threats to our society, are alienated from their work and mourn the loss of community" (p. 1). They went on to describe "people perceived as *other* are easily blamed, just as ideas that challenge a person's coherent worldview are easily feared" (p. 1). Before solidarity is possible, connections must be created and maintained. This study explores the capacity of service-learning to facilitate connections among diverse groups of people from many different personal, cultural, racial, ethnic, socioeconomic and religious backgrounds. Specifically, students from a rural Midwestern state university in an introductory course on human relations and race engaged in service-learning projects with people involved in an HIV/AIDS grassroots organization, a family maintaining an orphanage in South Africa, a family establishing an orphanage and educational program for children in India, members of an intertribal university student organization, programs working with Somali refugees and immigrants in the local community, and those working in areas of strife and conflict to bring safe and environmentally friendly light sources to areas of Africa and the Middle East.

PURPOSE OF THIS STUDY OF SERVICE-LEARNING

I have come to this research because I see and am very concerned about the vast deficit that many Americans hold in regards to global and cultural understanding and, consequently, resulting action. Although the number of students studying internationally has been increasing steadily over the past few decades (Institute for International Education, 2006), a number of students still face many obstacles that prevent them from doing so. Because of the difficulty for many students to travel internationally, this inquiry explores the possibility and impact of connections through a socially responsible, indigenous, international, globally focused service-learning project that does not necessitate students to travel to participate on-site with the international community. The following questions guided this research project:

1. What are the distinctive features for a globally focused service-learning curriculum based on principles of social justice and global reconciliation at a public higher education institution?
2. Realistically, understanding the limitations of many students at public higher education institutions, is it possible to set up and incorporate meaningful global service-learning that does not necessitate participation on-site with the international community?
3. What factors make a difference in the outcome of critical consciousness achieved by the students engaged in a globally focused service-learning curriculum?

MY POSITIONALITY

Because I aim for transparency and trustworthiness in my research, it is imperative I share my positionality. Daniel (2005) explained that, "the researchers positioning can affect the questions being asked, the theoretical paradigms that are adopted, and the interpretation of the research data" (p. 69). To be transparent regarding my passion for meaningful international service-learning and my role as a researcher, I will explore my positionality in regards to service-learning and this study.

Service-Learning Background

My passion for service-learning blossomed during my 2 years working with the Corporation for National and Community Service's AmeriCorps*National Civilian Community Corps (NCCC) program. AmeriCorps*NCCC, loosely modeled after the Civilian Community Corps of the 1930s, is a 10-month direct service program in which teams of 10-12 older youth, ranging in age from 18-24, travel within a region of the United States performing various duties to assist community identified problems with sustainable community created solutions. In addition to completing environmental, unmet human needs, education, public safety, and homeland defense projects, all AmeriCorps*NCCC members are trained in Red Cross Disaster Relief. I dedicated two terms of service to AmeriCorps*NCCC, one 10-month commitment as a Corps Member and a year-long commitment as a team leader.

With AmeriCorps, I spent approximately 2 years in 10 different communities throughout the United States—San Diego, CA; Vaughn, WA; Blythe, CA; Pacific Palisades, CA; Pasadena, CA; Roseburg, OR; Sacramento, CA; Salt Lake City, UT; Hanapepe, HI; Pocatello, ID. I was fortunate to experience a multitude of cultures and understand the links throughout them. It was a gift to see firsthand how each community welcomed us in its own way. I found that each community with which we worked had faced hardship and oppression and the fact that situations in these communities hadn't changed in decades weighed heavy on me. I was constantly impressed with the resiliency of the people and increasingly outraged with the unjustness of each situation.

Teams were afforded only a short amount of time to research the history, people, and cultures before arriving in a community. I found that what I learned from the people I met were things that I could never find on the Web or in a book. I experienced traditions and explored history I was never taught in school. The more I learned, the more frustrated I became. I knew the signers of the Declaration of Independence by heart, but never heard of César Chávez. We reviewed the Louisiana Purchase in many different history classes, but never covered how the United States usurped the Hawaiian Islands. The more I learned, the more it strengthened my desire to explore other cultures and seek opportunities to work to expose and counter injustice.

Once I learned about the beliefs, histories, and traditions of each community we served in AmeriCorps*NCCC, everything began to unfold and make sense to me. Each community that we met seemed to form a different piece of the puzzle. I discovered that differences between cultures, if unexplored, can and do cause miscommunications that have potentially infinite repercussions. Each person sees the world through his or her own lens, an ideology that reflects the culture and knowledge unique to that individual experience. If a person, a community, or a nation is only familiar with one perspective, misunderstanding, misinterpretation of actions, and miscommunications are bound to occur.

Within the context of the structure provided by the Corporation for National and Community Service, service-learning was stressed as an integral and important part of almost every aspect of our work. By working within communities situated all over the Western United States, I became empowered with knowledge to begin making connections. I was able to experience and see the impact of situations in which the solutions came from the community in contrast to situations that had a majority amount of outside influence. Working side by side with people from the various communities, *it* clicked with not only me, but I saw *it* click with my teammates, fellow corps members and team leaders. *It* represents a number of different elements: the actual realities of social services and many government programs, the lack of respect and opportunity for communities of color, and the importance of community-derived solutions, among many others.

Service-Learning "Done Well"

During my second year as a team leader, I had direct influence on how service-learning was carried out within my team and surroundings. I had the fortunate opportunity of seeing the first-hand results of service-learning done well and areas which could benefit from development and implementation. When I refer to service-learning *done well*, I mean to say that the implementation includes the importance of proper preparation, reflection (labeled briefing/debriefing in NCCC), and contextualization. I have experienced service-learning as an effective learning tool. I came to this research with the belief that, when service-learning is done well with the proper groundwork, with the consistent use of preparation, guided reflection, contextualization, and more reflection, the impact is powerful. Once learning is experienced on a level which transcends words to become action, it is very likely to change one at his or her core; service-learning has the potential to provide that opportunity.

Many of my predispositions concerning service-learning come from the experiences and approaches throughout my experience with Ameri-Corps*NCCC. I bring a critical eye to this research as I have witnessed and experienced the power that service-learning can hold. Regrettably, I also have observed situations in which service-learning has produced the opposite of cultural understanding and enlightenment. Service-learning holds the hazardous potential of enabling students to separate themselves from a situation and *other* people and communities with which they work. Framing situations where the community partner is the only position reflected upon "allows us to create *their problem* while we, as white people, avoid looking at our own complicity" (Max, 2005, p. 85). Therefore, service-learning requires attention to implementation and intentional contextualization in framing and processing the experiences of each partner.

Upon completion of my second term in AmeriCorps, my whole being and direction in life changed. I no longer saw the world in the way that I had before and, for that, I am thankful. Five years later, as I write about this study, I still find myself processing experiences from those 2 years and changing my actions and intentions to align myself as an ally for human rights and equality. Service-learning has the possibility to engage others to join the struggle for social justice and reconciliation all over the globe.

Grounded in Theory

Taking my experiential knowledge from AmeriCorps, I felt the need to ground my understanding in theory. In the realm of social responsibility, it is imperative to know the lens through which I see the world and the lens with which I decide to work. Karen Max (2005) observes "my social location, class, skin color, gender, sexuality, race, and level of ability all conspire to form the lens through which I make sense of the world" (p. 81). I was born in United States and am working as a White, female, able-bodied, heterosexual, middle class American woman of Irish-German descent, who was currently a university graduate student working toward a master's degree.

Ontologically, I believe in a worldview of social justice. My social justice perspective serves to explain what I believe I need to do with the privilege bestowed on me. I chose, instead of living blindly with my privilege, to use my privilege to work in solidarity with those who have been denied or stripped of the same privileges from which I benefit. In this study, I use the privilege of my education and my role as a teaching assistant at a university to work in solidarity with our partners in service. Epistemologically, I also come to this research believing it is imperative to follow an anticolonial, antiracist, liberatory agenda incorporating indigenous perspectives. Anticolonial research recognizes the "struggle to asses and claim humanity" that has been taken away from indigenous peoples and that has all humans as having the same potential and ability to create "history, knowledge, and society" (Smith, 2006, p. 26). In synchronicity with anticolonial research, antiracist research also adheres to inclusion and contextualization. Dei (2005) has operationalized "*anti-racist* [sic] research as research on racial domination and social oppression" with the necessity to "proceed with an objective of providing local subjects with an opportunity to speak about their experiences within the broader contexts of structural and institutional forces in society" (p. 11). Dei further explained that, "theorizing and researching anti-racism [sic] issues does not insure anti-racist work. Antiracist research is action oriented in the sense that it is not reactive but proactive in addressing racism and social oppression" (p. 18). Freire's (1970) liberatory theory and pedagogy called for proactive action in addressing all forms of oppression. *Liberatory theory* as defined by Freire encompasses antiracist, anticolonial action in critical consciousness that "asks for mobility or social action, not just an understanding of the world" (Johnson-Hunter & Risku, 2003, p. 103). I am approaching my research from a social justice, social responsibility lens within a liberatory theory, antiracist, anticolonial frame to ground my study.

CONTEXT OF THE STUDY

During the semester I began my thesis work, the origin of this study, I received and eagerly accepted an invitation to work on a grant to collaborate in the creation of a service-learning program for an introductory course on human relations and race. During that same semester, I attended a series of workshops to support design of service-learning programs intended for grant recipients held by the Center for Excellence in Teaching and Learning. As a part of the development process, I also participated in meetings of service-learning team leaders to plan the set-up and implementation of the multiple globally focused service-learning projects that would be offered as part of this service-learning course project, the focus of my study.

In addition to participating in the planning process during the fall, I also served as a teaching assistant for two sections of the human relations and race course, serving under the same professor who led the planning in the fall and the implementation of the service-learning project in the following spring. During the spring, my role in the classroom became even more active as I served as a teaching assistant, a team leader for one of the globally focused service-learning projects, and collected data for my thesis to assess the program.

DEFINING SERVICE-LEARNING

While reviewing the professional literature, it became apparent that the term *service-learning* has served to encompass a wide variety of interpretations. There appears to be hundreds of different definitions that identify as service-learning. The main thread included in all of the found definitions is some sort of service performed by students that meets a community need. The spelling of the term also varies—spelled both with and without a hyphen. The importance for including the hyphen between the two terms is articulated well by Jacoby (1996): "the hyphen in service-learning is critical in that it symbolizes the symbiotic relationship between service and learning" (p. 5). For this reason, I choose to use the hyphen in my spelling of *service-learning*.

When defining my terms, I am being purposeful to be as specific as possible. For the purposes of this study, I use *service-learning* as an integral praxis of experiential education. I will build on the foundation laid by Kendall and Associates (1990) which is a two-part definition for service-learning, the first taken from a definition given from the Southern Regional Education Board in 1969: "Service-learning programs emphasize the accomplishment of tasks which meet human needs in combination with conscious educational growth" (p. 20). The second part Kendall noted is "an overall philosophy of education that reflects a particular epistemology and set of values" (p. 20) in which "one which emphasizes active, engaged learning with the goal of social responsibility" (p. 22).

The type of service-learning operationalized in this study was one within a social justice/social responsibility paradigm. This means that the creation of each project was a joint venture of equal partnership where the community partner(s) defined the need in addition to setting the parameters for the proposed solution and the plan of action which was collaborative, both community partner(s) and school partner(s) working as allies.

International service-learning, when defined, is most often referred and conceptualized as a study-abroad program incorporating some sort of service to the community while in the country (Roberts, 2000, p. 48). However, for the purposes of this study, international service-learning was conceptualized as a reciprocal relationship of service that is not confined to physical shared space. In other words, it was possible to carry out international service-learning without actually leaving the United States. Therefore, *indigenous,* international service-learning has been used to refer to service-learning that engages the university student participants in research, learning, and service with civic engagement targeting social change and human rights.

Critical consciousness, the focus concept of my third research question, is a term which actually represents praxis within itself. Paulo Freire (1970) in his transformative work *Pedagogy of the Oppressed* stated that, "*Conscientização* is the deepening of the attitude of awareness characteristic of all emergence" (p. 109). Huber-Warring (2006, 2007a) elaborates Freire's concept for students in her human relations and race classes in one of the assignments titled *Disposition Analysis Rubric*: "His life-long work challenges us to become fully conscious of our situations and then intervene and come forward—emerge as transformative leaders—an emergence that is necessarily constant, ongoing, lifelong." As mentioned earlier, critical consciousness is praxis that includes the essential components of reflection and action. In fact, "Freire's definition of *praxis* is 'action and reflection upon the world in order to transform it'" (Rosenberger, 2000, p. 31).

The importance of reflection should not be overlooked or underappreciated. Inman (2000) points out that within service-learning practitioners, "many instructors believe that personal reflection is enough, and therefore they also get the opportunity to 'feel good' due to their contribution—via syllabi—to the community" (p. 7). Although it is important to acknowledge the efforts of both partners in service, it is dangerous to only encourage individual reflection. If the instructor or service-learning coordinator's goal is helping students to critical consciousness, personal reflection is not sufficient. For the purposes of my study, I incorporate a definition given by Huber-Warring (2006) that encapsulates reflection as

> substantial rethinking—guided, intended, informed—the kind of thinking that requires time to revisit the deep wells of memory, personal experience, and personal belief in order to extract a clearer picture of the personal meanings intended and the extrapolated meaning that readers can subsequently take and apply to their own lives, circumstances, and work with curriculum and instruction. (p. 41)

Therefore, reflection is seen as a multistep process through which students are guided and assisted to examine the issue or event through multiple lenses.

Putnam (2000) suggests that often in American culture, reciprocity consists of "I'll do this for you if you do that for me" (p. 20). Alternatively, I work to use the concept of reciprocity within the frame of the Bolivian concept of *Ayni*. The *Ayni* framework for reciprocity challenges the Western ideas of value and exchange—requiring the concept of exchange without the conceptualization of a financial amount to be assigned for service and a basic reciprocal understanding that one gives more than one receives (Porter & Monard, 2001, p. 15).

What Service-Learning Is and Is Not

Although service-learning has been in practice for decades, even in the most recent literature there are discrepancies in terms of the structure, goal, and implementation of service-learning. The Corporation for National and Community Service's Learn and Serve narrows the broad definition of service-learning by citing the National Commission on Service Learning who provided examples of what they deem is and is not school based service-learning in their 2001 Report *Service in Deed*.

> School based service-learning *is* a method of teaching that combines community service with curriculum-based learning; linked to academic content and standards; about students helping to determine and meet real, defined community needs; reciprocal in nature, benefiting both the community and the student; an effective way to encourage and foster active citizenship as

part of public education; an approach to teaching and learning that can be used in any curriculum area as long as it is appropriate to learning goals; for all ages, even the youngest children.

Service-learning *is not* a volunteer or community service program with no ties to academics; an *add on* to the existing curriculum; logging a certain number of service hours to graduate; one-sided—benefiting either the students or the community; compensatory service assigned as a form of punishment by the courts or service administrators; only for use in social studies classes, civics, or American government; only for high school or college students. (p. 7)

Although the term is used quite often within scholarly literature (a search of the ERIC database using the descriptor service-learning over a 4-year time limit revealed more than 400 matches), and despite the discrepancies of definitions found within the plethora of literature available, some authors have chosen not specify their conception of service-learning. A common definition of service-learning found within the literature refers to service-learning as "when an internship or volunteer activity linked to study includes providing a service to the community, the term service learning is used" (Albert, 1994, in Marlin-Bennett, 2002, p. 385). Many argue that solely linking community service with a volunteer activity does not comprise service-learning. The above definition can include many aspects of service but fails to specify what the actual learning goal is, how the connections are made, or how learning occurs. The definition that simply links an activity and study leaves out the pedagogical process that is required for the *learning* component of the relationship.

The difference between the aforementioned definition of *service-learning* and the type of service-learning utilized most often in the experiential educational realm is "intentional effort made to utilize the community service experience as a learning resource" (Howard, 1993/2003, p. 101). The intentional effort that is made focuses around the linkage of the community action with the course material of a class, "Thus coursework is informed by student action, and action is informed by, and occurs within the context of, the academic study of relevant topics" (Krain & Nurse, 2004, p. 192).

Does Community-Based Learning = Community-Based Research = Service-Learning?

The terms *community-based learning* and *community-based research* can often be seen together with service-learning. Community-based research, according to Stoecker (2003), "is designed to combine community empowerment with student development, to integrate teaching with research and service, and to combine social change with civic engagement" (p. 35). This definition seemingly fits the definition of service-learning. Alternatively, community-based learning usually involves events such as field trips or outings, but does not generally include the service aspect to the venture (Kraft, 1996, p. 136) and, therefore, would not fit within the service-learning model.

International Service-Learning

Although this study envisions international or global service-learning as a possibility for students who do not leave the United States, the definition as currently employed in the literature consistently includes exiting the United States as part of the definition. As Roberts (2000) stated, international service-learning "implies that students from U.S. colleges and universities go abroad to live, study, and provide some type of needed service to people of another country" (p. 48).

CLARITY IN TERMS: SERVICE, VOLUNTEERING, AND COMMUNITY SERVICE

Charity Versus Solidarity

For clarity of meaning, when using the term service-learning it is imperative to be clear about the meaning. Readers may conceptualize the separate terms that together comprise service-learning differently. For example, "Service-learning, also called community-based learning, is often confused with community service or volunteerism" (Cipolle, 2004, p. 13). Barber and Battistoni (1993) highlighted the fact that "The term service is often segregated from civic responsibility, and is instead associated with altruism or charity" (p. 235). Further, due to that lack of clarity, a charity-based approach has been taken with many service-learning programs (Stoecker, 2003, p. 37).

The association with charity is the one that becomes problematic, as *charity*, in its original conception, carries roots in a hegemonic, colonial and imperialistic ideal and is contrary to the mission and intention of many service-learning programs and projects. "A charity perspective perpetuates the community as needy, whereas critical and social-change perspectives view the community as an equal partner involved in identifying problems and coming up with solutions" (Ward & Wolf-Wendel, 2000, p. 771). Leonard (2007) illustrated the charity approach as "a top-down process" (p. 731). In addition, another problematic issue that lends itself to the importance of connecting service and learning with the hyphen as Kendall and Associates (1990) stated the term *service* "suggests an inequity between the *servers* and those being served" (p. 24).

Alternatively, there are programs, which view partners as equals, allies in solidarity with one another. Leonard (2007) explained solidarity as "based on an idea that social inequalities exist in a context that one needs to take time to understand" (p. 731). As Stoecker (2003) has explained, it isn't until recently that a "social change emphasis has developed into some service-learning programs" (p. 37).

Goals of Service-Learning

A divergence that can be found within the service-learning realm lies in the goal or desired outcome of the service-learning. For example, service-learning has been used within the political science realm to encourage students to be more involved in government, politics, and instill a form of civic responsibility. It is clear that program goals differ because of the way in which those who structure programs theorize the best way or approach to take to obtain a desired affect or outcome. I would argue that the goal of the political science realm isn't contradictory to that of the social justice paradigm, however, the approaches differ and social justice goals add additional levels and goals that are more specific and tailored to the community or issue at hand.

The definition of service-learning supported by Eyler and Giles (1999) gives the goal of service-learning "to prepare students who are lifelong learners and participants in the world" (p. 14). In keeping with service-learning focused on principles of critical consciousness, social justice, and global reconciliation, it is important to ask the question, does service-learning, under the guise of *doing good*, exist to provide a vehicle to maintain social inequalities or to change them?

SCHOOLS OF SERVICE-LEARNING

Categorization of the different schools of thought within service-learning evolves three different categories. The first would define service-learning as Albert (1994, as cited in Marlin-Bennett, 2002) did: "an internship or volunteer activity linked to study includes providing a service to the community, the term service learning is used" (p. 385). The second would be similar to the definition provided by the Corporation for National and Community Service (1990) which delineates more specific components of service-learning, but still leaves some room for interpretation. The third would gravitate more toward the definition given by Kendall and Associates (1990) which includes the integral component of social responsibility.

Service-Learning School #1: Loosely Linked

This first school of service-learning simply takes the rhetoric of service-learning, with goals of increasing critical thinking, cross cultural communication, social growth, and carries out a process that in most cases does not meet the many, if any, of those goals nor does it resemble the other two schools of service-learning. The student participant, who is often privileged, is usually the focus of the project here, and the emphasis of the project is what they can glean from the situation at hand working with *needy people*. This approach fails to place emphasis on the process or include a strong connection to course content. If the main outcome were to reinforce social norms and class positions, this approach would work well. Subconsciously and consciously, many people believe it is important to conform to what considered the norm in society. Durkheim (1922) noted that

> Society can survive only if there exists among its members a sufficient degree of homogeneity; education perpetuates and reinforces this homogeneity by fixing in the mind of a child, from the beginning, the essential similarities that social life demands. (p. 203)

In this mindset, the loose framework of so called service-learning would produce the end result. Haphazard or unstructured service-learning programs such as the types that can be found in the first school are often more hazardous than not attempting to engage students at all.

Because the normative requirement of working with a community that has identified a problem or issue to address, it is difficult to not be exposed to the areas which call for social justice. O'Grady (2000) noted that it is possible for service-learning to "perpetuate racist, sexist, or classist assumptions about others and reinforce a colonialist mentality of superiority" (p. 12). Hollis (2004) studied this phenomenon with two classes. One section she implemented a very loosely unstructured service-learning program in which students had a requirement to perform the service with the service projects only being indirectly related to course content without time spent on specifics of what the communities were facing, and so on. Alternatively, the second section received a more complete preparation and direct connection to the course content. Hollis found that participants in the structured service learning group were much more likely to discuss issues related to class, gender, and racial inequality than their counterparts involved in the earlier unstructured service learning assignment who tended to attribute social problems such as poverty, to the individuals' characteristics and the culture in which they lived. (p. 593)

In addition, those students who participated in the unstructured program throughout the semester "moved from naive optimism to relatively ardent victim blaming" (p. 594). As is evidenced by the study above, service-learning programs that are not structured well reinforce class structure and divisions among young impressionable youth and provide fuel to common misconceptions and stereotypes as to why certain groups maintain specific *lower* positions of society.

Good Intentions ≠ Good Service-Learning

Within the first school of service-learning, the student performs the duty asked and possibly reports back to the classroom about the experience, but is no intentional effort to understand the context of how systems work or why or how one might go about changing them. In essence, students serve a role and maintain their privilege while reinforcing and reproducing their stereotypical thoughts and actions. Often what occurs in these situations is the creation of projects that are one-sided. Ward and Wolf-Wendel (2000) found that "service-learning at predominately White institutions, emphasizes service that is centered on the campus—that is, service that is focused on *doing for* [italics added] the community" (p. 768).

Service-learning projects that work toward *doing for* do not help a community and, often, completely ignore the voices of the people that they are claiming to help.

> The *missionary ideology* that currently underlies the service-learning movement is mostly the result of a series of decisions intended to *do good things* for others and so the movement does not directly acknowledge what those others, particularly communities of color, might have to offer. (Weah, Simmons, & Hall, 2000)

If students are encouraged to participate in programs that are not fully developed, do not provide the adequate support, or are not entered into with the appropriate community collaboration and participation (i.e., identification of issue and resolution for that issue), then, as Maybach (1996) pointed out, these interactions can become detrimental for both students and the community:

Despite the complexity of the issues of service, students are encouraged to engage in service provision without a clear understanding of how their service is affecting the communities around them. Without accountability for or an understanding of the needs of the individuals in the urban community, the effects of service-learning projects may indeed be viewed as malevolent by the very individuals whose lives the service was intended to enhance, despite the best of good intentions. (p. 224)

Thus, the first school of service-learning stands out as unproductive and harmful to all parties involved. Evidence supports that planning, preparation and implementation need to be scrutinized and carefully constructed to meet the actual goals of service-learning.

Service-Learning School #2: Cultural Understanding and Reform

The second definition provided by the Corporation for National and Community Service (CNCS) (1990) would serve to fit well with the next sphere of service-learning, one that is focused on improving life within structures and existing systems. The CNCS, a direct descendant of the federal government, continues to be influential in the area of service-learning. The approach taken by the Corporation is to work within systems to spread knowledge and critical thinking to improve the current system. The focus of this model is to engage in service-learning with the goal of education, engagement and future participation that may lead to reform.

The CNCS Learn and Serve provides parameters for the broad definition of service-learning by citing the National Commission on Service Learning who provided examples of what they deem *is* and *is not* school based service-learning in their 2001 report *Service In Deed*. The definition delineated earlier in this chapter, although giving seven broad examples of what does and does not constitute service-learning, details how and when service-learning should be incorporated.

Dewey's influence. This second school of service-learning has more of a connection to course content and requires praxis based largely on the connection between active learning and experiential education theorized by John Dewey (1859-1952). Dewey drew inspiration for experiential education from more than just the educational realm. In fact, as Cohen (1998) points out, Dewey was most concerned about things that reached "far beyond education" (p. 428). According to Cohen (1998) one of the largest matters that Dewey was concerned about, "was the greater importance of knowledge to economic and social life owing to scientific and technical progress but the rapidly diminishing knowledge required from individual workers owing to increased specialization" (p. 428).

It was Dewey's concerns about societies and how they were rapidly changing which directly affected his theories on education. Within the education realm, Dewey's focus was on the individual student and was concerned about the way in which schooling was a system that was teaching information that was not relevant and enforcing rote memorization as the only means of learning. Dewey (1930), whose desired outcomes went beyond those of Durkheim, noted:

> The bare fact that a child goes to school in order to learn tends to make learning a synonym for taking in and reproducing what other persons have already found out. Ready-made materials in material things have their oppressive counterpart in ready-made intellectual information and ideas, and education is supposed to consist in a transfer of these goods into the mind. (p. 9)

Dewey's approach to trying to prevent reproduction is one that has been widely adapted in the education and multicultural education realm. Cohen (1998) explained, "Dewey was one of the most hopeful of this 19th Century Pathenon, for he believed that reformers could solve basic and economical problems by acting directly on minds, morals, and culture" (p. 429). He also wrote a great deal on education and citizenship had a goal of creating an engaged participatory democracy. He believed in focusing on youth and education as a way to change and reform the capitalist system. His approach to education was an individualistic approach with the goal of making learning relevant and applicable. One of his most emphasized goals was to create critical thinkers. Eyler and Giles (1999) note that as opposed to the traditional ways of showing knowledge through testing, the learning that is honed during service-learning focuses around critical thinking and "the ability to call it up (information) when it is relevant to a new situation and use it in that situation" (p. 15). This ability to "call up" is used repeatedly in processing service-learning experiences, both during and after. Dewey (1930) stated, "The primary requisite of critical ability is courage; its great enemy is cowardice, even tough it take that mitigated form called intellectual laziness" (p. 13).

Advocacy and working-with the community. Dewey's approach to education and social and structural issues were influenced by the theorizing of Durkheim and Weber. Although Durkheim would approve of Dewey's approach to work within systems to create change, Dewey went further to encourage individual critical thinkers to provide the impetuous for their social change. The second school approach asks the community for the problem, which is an important aspect of service-learning, but the solution often comes from those who *work with* the community. Stoecker

(2003) noted that, "social service casework developed as a professional model quite similar to charity service-learning and action research in its structural control by professionals, its lack of focus on political action, and its emphasis on social integration rather than social change" (p. 41). Another way to that the second school of service-learning portrays these values is by working with organizations that work for the benefit of the community, but not necessarily with the community. "Advocacy is a practice of professional work on behalf of or for a group, while community organizing involved the group advocating for itself" (p. 42).

Keith Morton and Sandra Enos (2002) discuss some of the issues that arise by working with government or nonprofit agencies as opposed to working-with the community and encouraging students to actively participate in democratizing the "political and cultural landscape in which the students live" (p. 88). They noted that

> The nonprofit human-service sector focuses on helping individual clients, with a generic goal of upward mobility, thereby acting as a conservator of the values of the dominant culture. It avoids, on the whole, addressing the root causes of social inequality and communal disintegration. (p. 94)

Moving Toward Social Justice

In more recent years the area of service-learning has seen more literature on the contradictions between charity based service-learning and social justice oriented. As Kendall (1990) stated: "A good service-learning program helps participants see their questions in the larger context of issues of social justice and social policy—rather than in the context of charity" (p. 20). Many of the programs that are structured work with the charity model, and some move to create consciousness within that model to move toward the third school of service-learning focused on action and social justice. O'Grady (2000) pointed out that "responding to individual human needs is important, but if the social policies that create these needs is not also understood and addressed, then the cycle of dependence remains" (p. 13).

School of Service-Learning #3: Social Justice Participatory

Service-Learning and the Possibility of Transformation

In the definition of service-learning, supported by Eyler and Giles (1999), they detailed how "Learning is transforming in the sense that as students move along in their service they shift from working with a charity focus to one of social justice" (p. 19). Warren (1998) pointed out that "An examination of social justice by its very nature mist look at issues of power" (p. 136). Much discussion in service-learning focuses energy toward the "common good" or the "benefit to the community." In the third school of service-learning, solutions come from the oppressed groups and not from experts. This type of method is anti-hegemonic and inclusive. Marlin-Bennett (2002) noted, "Service learning works against goals of increased understanding and community engagement when programs are focused around paternalistic, doing for the community exercises" (p. 386).

Facilitating Social Change

Within the social justice and social responsibility paradigm, an intrinsic belief is to not work solely towards an quick solve in the immediate, often referred to as a band-aid solution, but to work toward eliminating the root of the problem so as to eradicate the problem itself. As Warren (1998) suggested, "The goal of social service is to provide immediate help to those in need, while social change work focuses additionally on changing the societal, political, and cultural barriers that hold the need for social services in place" (p. 137). Shifting the focus of service-learning projects to social justice models is therefore needed and necessary. Understanding this paradigm, one must incorporate this structure to every aspect of the project: approach, structure, development, implementation, collaboration, and continuation.

Of late, there is more literature available that critique traditional service-learning practices with different sets of outcomes. The majority of service-learning programs found in the first and second schools leave out an integral component to the social justice/social responsibility realm: *action*.

Liberatory Service-Learning

In professional literature, an extension to the goals of a solely Dewey-based service-learning model is one with a Freirean liberatory frame. Both theorists believed that the purpose of education should create critical thinkers. The ways in which theorists frame their solutions are directly affected on how they theorize the way in which systems work. As Stoecker (2003) pointed out, "Dewey did not see structural barriers to the increasing democratization of society under capitalism. For Freire, capitalism and the unequal structural power it creates builds barriers to democracy" (p. 38).

The manifestation of the Dewey systems puts students learning and working with governmental agencies or social service organizations whose main purpose can be used to control and maintain the current power structure. Holst (2006) pointed out that while in Chile,

Freire began to realize that his earlier humanistic analysis insufficiently explained movements that were clearly of a class nature. His further ideological development, then, increasingly incorporated Marxist categories and analysis. While never dropping his humanism, it became a Marxist humanism. (p. 260)

A Freirean model of service-learning, then, takes this goal of critical thinking to the next level. Therefore, the goals of the third school of service-learning are directed towards emancipatory, participatory, service-learning with goals of critical consciousness that extend to *action* or *action with*.

COMPONENTS OF SERVICE-LEARNING

Partners

To be successful in service-learning, one must have partners with whom to work. Throughout most of the literature, those who are involved in service-learning projects are usually named service-providers (usually students or institutions of higher education) and service-recipient (the community which is benefiting from the service). These terms illustrate a relationship where one entity is active and one who is passive. Maybach (1996) called attention to the fact that "the terms *service provider* and *service recipient* are problematic in that they perpetuate the hegemonic, one sided view of a service provision" (p. 231). She offered the term or phrase *partners in service* to emphasize the reciprocity of the relationship. Kraft (1996) also commented on partnership recommending to use "a vision that moves peoples away from the margins of society through partnerships based on equal concern, equal voice, equal opportunity to serve and explore new perspectives, a vision that allows each partner to lean from the other" (pp. 139-140).

Reciprocity

Equal partnership, or *reciprocity*, is a cornerstone that many service-learning practitioners believe is vital to the creation and implementation of a service-learning program. In fact, Kendall (1990) pointed out reciprocity as one of the two components that separate service-learning from community service (p. 21). On an international service-learning study, Porter and Monard (2001) explained a concept they had learned from the indigenous peoples with whom they worked in the Andes Mountains of

Bolivia—"*Ayni*, the exchange of comparable work or goods as part of an ongoing cycle of reciprocity" (p. 6). However, *Ayni* is significantly more complex—Porter and Monard provided the eight principles of *Ayni:*

1. Service programs must be built upon a foundation of genuine need as expressed by the recipients.
2. Ownership and responsibility for the project must be clear and shared.
3. Real people must perform hands-on services; participants cannot buy their way out of personal obligations.
4. Communal labor means strenuous physical engagement.
5. Workers must come with an open heart and a generous spirit, as *Ayni* exchanges cannot be performed begrudgingly or with a sour disposition.
6. *Ayni* cycles involve a different conception of time and place participants in an ongoing relationship that extends both generation and geography.
7. The *Ayni* exchange is equitable, with each side feeling that they received at least as much work as they gave.
8. The *value* of reciprocal work cannot and should not be calculated in simple monetary terms (p. 8).

Ayni expands the traditional Western conceptualization and understanding of reciprocity. It challenges the Western ideology of individualism and represents "a promise that all parties will benefit as they, working together for the common good, serve a greater purpose than individual self-interest" (p. 6).

Reflection

Eyler and Giles (1999) pointed to the "Five C's" for effective service-learning reflection: connection, continuity, context, challenge, and coaching (p. 183). The first C represents *connection*. Connection within service-learning is the understanding that learning is not isolated, but rather, connected from the people in the community to the classroom learning. Because service-learning incorporates action and interaction that often creates connections that had not existed previously, it is important to connect what is learned in the classroom and what is learned/applied on site. A fundamental principle "at its heart, service-learning rests on the assumption that learning cannot be compartmentalized between the classroom and the use of what is learned later, in the community, or between affective and cognitive learning" (p. 183).

Continuity is the second C of reflection. It incorporates the idea that reflection must be continuous. Reflection should not end when the class period is over, or the course, but must be continued throughout one's life. Reflection is not just to be utilized after a session, but before, during, and after. The third C integral to service-learning: *context*. Eyler and Giles (1999) noted "reflection is not just about thinking, but about thinking about something" (p. 184). Learning within context and within communities helps students obtain a true picture of the circumstances and issues facing a community. When working within communities, it is often imperative to help guide students who could otherwise use the surface information to reinforce stereotypes. The next C is *challenge*. Growth often occurs when students are taken out of their comfort zone and are given a new perspective with which to see the world or a problem. "Growth rests on puzzlement, on challenge to current perspectives, and of the challenge to resolve conflict" (p. 184). The final C represents *coaching*. When faced with new surroundings and situations outside the comfort zone, students experience strong emotions and are in need of coaching to be able to process those emotions and situations.

MAKING THE CONNECTION

Thus far, I have noted the definitions of service-learning, the history of service-learning, the three different schools of service-learning and the components of service-learning. Service-learning facilitates change—but how? I have discussed how students work as partners with a community or group of people with whom they probably wouldn't have contact in the first place. So, what it is it about the process of service-learning that precipitates change?

Personal Connections

Eyler and Giles (1999) pointed out that learning begins with personal connections. Learning is useful in terms of the ways in which students become skilled at making connections, learning is developmental in terms of often providing cognitive dissonance with which students have to work through, and learning is transforming in the sense that as students move along in their service they shift from working with a charity focus to one of social justice.

Brown (2004) explained that students who have a small amount of experience with other cultures will come to a multicultural course with either interest or apathy and those with negative experiences with other groups will bring a "contentious or emotional state" (p. 327). She noted that "Allport (1979) proposed that many prejudices are established in early childhood and that prejudiced students use selective perception, avoidance, and group support strategies to resist confronting and modifying or changing their beliefs about self and others" (p. 326). This resistance poses a challenge in a class that incorporates a service-learning component. Service-learning takes student out of their comfort zones and places them in surroundings and with people whom they might normally avoid, whether consciously or unconsciously. Moely, McFarland, Miron, Mercer, and Ilustre (2002) noted that service-learning gives students opportunities to "interact with people different in age, social class, and race from those they see every day, providing opportunities for development of social and problem solving skills including communication, role-making, and conflict resolution" (p. 23).

Brown (2004) cited teacher education experts that identify "training designed to examine self-concept, perception, and motivation will generate a more receptive attitude toward multicultural tenets" (p. 326). Brown explained that she has found that approach that has found to be successful: "those who reach the desired exit level have explored their personal histories and value systems; developed an understanding, respect, and value for other cultures; and expanded their reference group membership to include others" (p. 327). Therefore, by having students explore their own cultures, histories, and selves they work toward understanding others. Rosenberger (2000) explained that "a critical service-learning approach means becoming conscious and reflecting critically on our own positional power and on the dissonance that critical consciousness creates for us personally" (p. 36). In addition, this reflection of one's self which facilitates the ability to connect better with others only makes room for more connections. Putnam (2000) discusses the phenomenon that when people feel more comfortable, they are more apt to join in social groups and civic organizations. He noted that "joiners become more tolerant, less cynical, and more empathetic to the misfortunes of others. When people lack connections to others, they are unable to test the veracity of their own views" (p. 288).

The Power of Choice

In addition, it has been noted that students benefit from having an option of service-learning activities. When students are given an option of projects to work on, they have the opportunity to see how best they might be able to contribute. Rosenberger (2000) stated

Students benefit from choosing the service learning experience. By grappling with the decision about the type of service learning activity, students have the opportunity to think about the connections to course content, the implications of different projects, how needs and action might be defined, and the inherent dynamics of power and privilege. In the act of choosing, they develop a sense of ownership. (p. 40)

By providing opportunities for students to choose projects it engages them on a variety of levels. Monard-Weissman (2003) found that through service-learning, once students are engaged and focusing on social justice issues, "students could not turn away after coming across poverty, abandonment, illness, and ignorance. They examined ways they ought to act in order to strive for social change" (p. 167). Monard-Weissman also went on to stress that "service-learning helped them reiterate their commitment to be agents of change, not only locally but globally" (p. 168).

GLOBALLY FOCUSED SERVICE-LEARNING RESEARCH METHODOLOGY AND DESIGN

All three guiding questions looked at the affects of globally focused service-learning on students who attended a Midwestern public institution of higher education nestled in a town of approximately 65,000 within an 80-mile radius of a metropolitan center. The research involving students took place in a 15-week time frame within a single semester. Participants were purposively selected as all students enrolled in the required, 100-level human relations course for which I, as the researcher, was serving as a teaching assistant, were included in the study. IRB approval was received prior to the first class meeting and consent forms were received from each participant before any data was collected.

An entire semester was spent on preparation and planning to incorporate a variety of projects into service-learning options for students of this human relations class. The professor invited past students who already had existing relationships and had been currently working with communities to come to the table to create these possible options for students. As someone who was invited to the planning process, I took an active role on the student committee as a student leader and teaching assistant for the class with which the projects would be implemented.

Because service-learning is experiential, students may be affected on multiple levels. Considering that students process service-learning in many different ways and on individual timetables, I used information from 3 surveys, class assignments, and service-learning team focus group inquiry interviews to gather a broad range of information across the course of the academic semester of 15-weeks. The first survey, Semester

Table 17.1. Semester Survey

1. Are you taking this class to satisfy the racial issues requirement?
    Yes   No

1a. If yes, have you taken more than one racial issues class?
    Yes   No   Don't Know

2. Are you minoring in human relations?
    Yes   No   Don't Know

3. What semester and year did you start at SCSU?
    Fall   Spring   Summer   Year

4. Are you a transfer student?
    Yes   No

4a. If so, when did you transfer here (semester and year)?
    Fall   Spring   Summer   Year

Survey (see Table 17.1), was an existing survey administered by the department of human relations and multicultural education that offered this course.

The department asked questions which aim to retrieve information such as reasons students enrolled in the course, what year they are in school, and so on. Because this course qualified as a required race issues course, it was helpful to know whether students were there by choice, or whether they were only present because of the university's racial issues class requirement.

The second survey, Service-Learning Background Survey (see Table 17.2), contained more specific questions regarding background in terms of self-defining race, ethnicity, gender, spiritual connection, and national identity. This tool was compiled by myself and the instructor for the course specifically for use in this study with the intent of gaining a greater amount of information about the previous experiences of the student participants and to provide a possible glimpse as to what influences or preconceived notions students brought with them to the beginning of this process.

The third survey, titled Service-Learning Dispositions (see Table 17.3), included questions that focused on dispositions toward personal responsibility, social responsibility, personal and social awareness, and knowledge gained after the course. This survey was created with questions adapted from the Minnesota Campus Compact's (2001) America Reads Tutor

Table 17.2. Service-Learning Background Survey

Eight Digit SCSU Student ID #   Today's Date:
(Also place on bubble sheet under id #)   (Place on bubble sheet under "Birthdate")

Please respond as completely as possible to the following:

1. Please mark the number of semesters you have attended SCSU:

    A. First semester
    B. 1-2
    C. 3-4
    D. 5-6
    E. 7 or more

2. Number of completed college credits earned at SCSU:

    A. 0
    B. 6-12
    C. 13-19
    D. 20-25
    E. 26 or more

3. Please list the ethnic/racial group with which you most closely identify:

    A. Latin Diaspora
    B. African Diaspora
    C. Asian Heritage
    D. European Heritage
    E. Native American Heritage

    Specific Ethnic/Tribal Identity:
    Gender:
    Spiritual Connection:
    National Identity:

4. Have you ever taken a K-12 course with a service-learning, community-based component?

    A. Yes
    B. No
    C. I'm not sure
    If Yes, what was the service-learning, community-based component?

5. Have you ever traveled outside of the United States?

    A. Yes
    B. No

6. If your answer to question 5 was Yes, how many times have you traveled outside the United States? (If your answer was No, please skip to question 7)

    A. 1
    B. 2-3
    C. 4-6
    D. 7-9
    E. 10 or more

(Table continues on next page)

Table 17.2. (Continued)

7. Have you ever studied outside the United States? If so, where and how long?

   A. Yes
   B. No

8. Are you interested in studying outside the United States?

   A. Yes
   B. No

9. Have you ever lived outside the United States? If so, where and how long?

   A. Yes
   B. No

10. Do you journal?

    A. Daily
    B. Weekly
    C. At least once or twice a month
    D. Occasionally
    E. Never

11. What has been your most meaningful learning experience(s) from grades pre-K to 12? Why? (Not a specific person or teacher, but experience)

12. What has been your most meaningful learning experience(s) from college? Why? (Not a specific person or teacher, but experience)

In your own words, please give a short definition or example for each word listed below:

13. Volunteer
14. Service
15. Charity
16. Community Service
17. Learning
18. Service-Learning

Evaluation II, Kapi'olani Community College Survey for Students—Spring 2001, and two additional questions written by me.

In regards to class assignments, all students' work that was submitted was reviewed. Students were required to complete two STEPS to Critical Consciousness assignments. The STEPS assignment was created and designed by Huber-Warring (2007b) (see Table 17.4 for STEPS assignment and Table 17.5 for STEPS evaluation rubric). Students were required to attend at least three speakers or events with speakers that had been approved by the professor either on or off campus that addressed human relations and race issues. The STEPS worksheet contained three

Table 17.3. Service-Learning Disposition Pre-/Postassessment

Service-Learning Dispositions Pre/Post	Strongly Disagree	Disagree	Uncertain	Agree	Strongly Agree
1. I feel that social problems are not my concern.	SD	D	U	A	SA
2. Having an impact on community problems is within reach of most individuals.	SD	D	U	A	SA
3. Adults should give some time for the good of their community.	SD	D	U	A	SA
4. I feel that social problems directly affect the quality of life in my community.	SD	D	U	A	SA
5. Problems in education are complicated and therefore more difficult to solve than I used to think.	SD	D	U	A	SA
6. The problems that cause people to need social services are frequently the result of circumstances beyond their control.	SD	D	U	A	SA
7. I feel uncomfortable working with people who are different from me in such things as race, wealth, and life experiences.	SD	D	U	A	SA
8. For the most part, each individual determines whether or not he or she is well-educated.	SD	D	U	A	SA
9. It is important to me personally to influence the political structure.	SD	D	U	A	SA
10. We should reach out to specific people in need rather than creating programs to address social issues.	SD	D	U	A	SA
11. It is important to me to have a career that directly or indirectly involves helping people.	SD	D	U	A	SA
12. If someone is illiterate, it is most likely because he or she is not intelligent.	SD	D	U	A	SA
13. My own problems are too large to spend time helping others.	SD	D	U	A	SA
14. It is important to work for equal opportunity for all persons, regardless of their race, nationality, or disability.	SD	D	U	A	SA
15. My involvement in the world community improves the lives of others.	SD	D	U	A	SA
16. People are poor because they don't try hard enough.	SD	D	U	A	SA
17. Poverty, crime, and other problems affect the whole community.	SD	D	U	A	SA
18. Reflecting/debriefing on my experiences make them more meaningful to me.	SD	D	U	A	SA

(Table continues on next page)

Table 17.3. (Continued)

Service-Learning Dispositions Pre/Post	Strongly Disagree	Disagree	Uncertain	Agree	Strongly Agree
19. I help people see that things can change.	SD	D	U	A	SA
20. This course helped me to see how the subject matter I learned in class can be used in everyday life.	SD	D	U	A	SA
21. This course was ok, but I doubt it will affect my future behavior.	SD	D	U	A	SA
22. I intend to be more involved in my local community due to this course.	SD	D	U	A	SA
23. I intend to be more involved in the global community due to this course.	SD	D	U	A	SA
24. This course will/ has helped me learn more about decision making and/or problem solving.	SD	D	U	A	SA
25. This course will/ has helped me learn more about people in my community.	SD	D	U	A	SA
26. This course will/ has helped me learn more about people in the world community.	SD	D	U	A	SA
27. This course will/ has helped me learn more about how to communicate with others.	SD	D	U	A	SA

Sources: Questions 1-13 adapted from the Minnesota Campus Compact evaluation for America Reads Tutor Evaluation II: Outcome Evaluation. Questions 14-27 adapted from Kapi'olani Community College Survey for Students, Spring 2001.

columns. The first column of the worksheet asked students to list specific awarenesses that they have identified from the speaker or presentation they attended. The second column in the STEPS assignment asked for students to connect the awarenesses from the first column to course content (usually in the form of assigned reading material, speakers in class, or class discussions). In the third column students were asked to detail meaningful actions to take as a result of the awareness. Of the three columns of information requested from the students on these worksheets, the third column was the column utilized in the inquiry as that location was where students noted what steps they plan to take or were currently taking in response to the new awareness. To analyze the third column actions from STEPS assignments, the constant comparative method of analysis was utilized (Maykut & Morehouse, 1994).

In following with antiracist and anticolonial research, focus groups were utilized because they allow for students to choose what they want to say and how they want to say it. Two specific class periods were dedicated

Seeking Solidarity Through Global and Indigenous Service-Learning   323

Table 17.4. Steps to Critical Consciousness Regarding Human Relations and Race Rubric

Awareness	*Connection*	*Action Steps*	*Citation & Usage*
Identify at least 5 important issues/topics significant to the study of human relations and social justice (part A) *and* the specific awareness, information, or quotation about the issues/topics (part B). This is a two-part response. [Column 1 on Steps grid]	*Explain* at least 2 course connections for each topic in a deep and meaningful way *without* major interpretive flaws. A quotation from course content is meaningful, but the connection/interpretation must be explained for full credit. [Column 2 on Steps grid]	Identification of personal *action steps* already taken *and/or* steps taken in your service-learning project [Column 3 on Steps grid; be sure to include these action steps in your Disposition analysis, as well]. Use of culturally responsible and unbiased language evidencing commitment to social justice. Note: Use of language identified as *problematic* or *biased* may result in no points for this component. [Addressed throughout the entire analysis]	Citation: Complete references should be attached on a separate sheet with each of the following categories labeled: required readings, films, reserve readings, additional references. Connections should represent a wide range of course material—guest speakers, films, and *at minimum* 5 different required readings, at least one film/documentary, and at least reserve reading. Each course connection must be supported by an author and page citation. Usage: Meaningful, effective communication (spelling, grammar, usage based on APA guidelines)
Steps 1 ___/10 Steps 2 ___/15 Steps 3 ___/20	Steps 1 ___/20 Steps 2 ___/25 Steps 3 ___/30	Steps 1 ___/10 Steps 2 ___/15 Steps 3 ___/20	Steps 1 ___/20 Steps 2 ___/25 Steps 3 ___/30
Bonus Steps 1 ___/2 Bonus Steps 2 ___/2 Bonus Steps 3 ___/2	Bonus Steps 1 ___/8 Bonus Steps 2 ___/8 Bonus Steps 3 ___/8	Bonus Steps 1 ___/2 Bonus Steps 2 ___/2 Bonus Steps 3 ___/2	Bonus Steps 1 ___/8 Bonus Steps 2 ___/8 Bonus Steps 3 ___/8

Student _____ Instructor _____

Steps 1 Total ___/60
Steps 2 Total ___/80
Steps 3 Total ___/100

Bonus Steps 1 ___/20
Bonus Steps 2 ___/20
Bonus Steps 3 ___/20

Source: Huber-Warring (2007b, p. 286). Reprinted with permission and the author's update.

Table 17.5. Steps to Critical Consciousness Regarding Human Relations and Social Justice

Speaker/Event: Location:	Date: Student:	Total Time:
Specific Topic and Awareness from Speaker/Film /Presentation	Specific Connection to Course Readings/Films/Discussions Two for Each Awareness	Detailed Action Steps to Be Taken or Affirmation of Actions Already Taken
1A. 1B.	1A1. 1B1.	1.
2A. 2B.	2A1. 2B1.	2.
3A. 3B.	3A1. 3B1.	3.
4A. 4B.	4A1. 4B1.	4.
5A. 5B.	5A1. 5B1.	5.

Source: Huber-Warring (2007b, p. 287). Reprinted with permission.

to focus group sessions in which students answered questions formulated by myself (see Table 17.6 for focus group questions). Groups met with the researcher who also served as the focus group facilitator. Students received three-four main questions to answer on paper and then when each person was finished a discussion ensued. Students were asked to respond on paper first to ensure each student had an opportunity to give their voice and opinion.

Seeking Solidarity Through Global and Indigenous Service-Learning

Table 17.6. Focus Group Questions

Focus Group 1-3 Questions

QUESTION # 1: Out of the service-learning project options given as a part of this class, why did you choose the specific project that you are currently working on?

QUESTION # 2: Describe briefly (by listing nouns and verbs) how you see yourself in this service-learning project.

QUESTION # 3: We've asked you to focus on indigenous/international projects for your service-learning options—do you think this is a meaningful way to understand people/issues?

Focus Group 4-6 Questions

QUESTION #1: Is it important to be involved/active in the international and Indigenous communities? Why or why not?

QUESTION #2: What factors made/make a difference in your involvement with your service-learning projects?

QUESTION #3: Given what you know now, would you have done anything differently? Why or why not?

The following codes were employed for each data source: Service-Learning Background pre- and post- marked by the code SLBP for pre- and SLBPP for post- followed by the question number; Service-Learning Dispositions pre- and post- respectively SLDP, SLDPP also followed by the question number. The code for the Researcher's Journal follows: RJ represents researcher's journal; the C with a number directly following represents what class the data was taken from, and the following number represents the location of the data within the specific class notes chart. The data from STEPS #1 and STEPS #2 classroom assignments were initially unitized and analyzed separately and then compared. Coding for the teaching-learning artifacts STEPS follows: S represents STEPS; the following number represents the STEPS number (1 or 2) and the column (1-3). The final number represents the row location (1-5) of the unit. For instance, S1-3 4 would represent the information from STEPS #1, column 3, row 4. The focus groups were transcribed and segregated into units each on a separate note card to enable constant comparative analysis (Maykut & Morehouse, 1994). The data was divided into two forms, students' responses and focus group notes as taken by the facilitator. The written answers from each of the students was transcribed verbatim and charted. Both the facilitator notes and the student written answers were coded by the source and the focus group number (I-III). In the case of focus groups 2 and 3, which each contained two teams; the units were coded and subdivided into the respective service-learning team. Focus

Table 17.7. Units of Data

Data Origin	Number of Units[1]
STEPS #1	89
STEPS #2	112
Focus group 1-3 Facilitator notes	74
Focus group 1-3 Student notes	62
Focus group 4-6 Facilitator notes	98
Focus group 4-6 group notes	98
Total number of units	533

[1] As defined by constant comparative analysis, a unit may appear in more than one category of a finding (or not at all). Therefore, the total number of units supporting a finding may exceed the total number of units.

groups were coded as F with the second letter to represent the facilitator (F) notes or to represent the student (S) notes; the number relates to the specific focus group. In two instances in the first set of focus groups, two teams were combined because of numbers and time. In those cases, directly following the focus group number, an A or a B represents the different teams within that focus group. The numbers following those represent where one can find the data, either in a line number or chart number. For example, FF2-B 21 would represent data from the facilitator notes from the second focus group, Team B, in line 21. The unitization of STEP #1, STEPS #2, Focus Groups 1-3, and Focus Groups 4-6 yielded a total of 533 units for analyzation (see Table 17.7 for total of units per data set). As part of the social responsibility discipline within an anticolonial, antiracist framework, the research approach I took for this project was one of an emergent paradigm that employed triangulation of this mixed-methods design.

METHOD OF ANALYSIS

My primary method of data analysis that was used was the constant comparative method created by Glaser and Strauss, in 1967, with additions by Lincoln and Guba, in 1985, as described by Maykut and Morehouse (1994). This type of analyzation is emergent and inductive, and the relevant variables for data collection are not predetermined (pp. 126-127).

The constant comparative method of analysis (CCM) allows for themes to emerge from the data by a "process of inductive reasoning" (p. 127). In application in this study, after each type of data was analyzed within its category, it was then compared, or triangulated, with the other forms and types of data sources. In supporting nonpositivist, antiracist, anticolonial research, Denzin and Lincoln (1998) noted that "Objective reality can never be captured. Triangulation is not a tool or a strategy of validation, but an alternative to validation" (pp. 3-4).

SERVICE-LEARNING INTRODUCTION

Students were greeted on the first day of class by the instructor and myself with a welcome, a brief explanation of the course by the instructor, surveys, followed by a brief introduction to service-learning prepared and delivered by the researcher/service-learning team leader and teaching assistant, myself. The students were introduced to the concept of service-learning after completing the surveys. The concept of service-learning was introduced with a PowerPoint presentation which illustrated multiple examples of service-learning through an explanation of a project that I completed in AmeriCorps*NCCC. In attempts to give a basic introduction to service-learning, a basic definition to describe it was provided. Service-learning was defined to the students as "an experiential education process in which engaging partners in service work while learning together" (RJC1, 11). In keeping with an anticolonial and antiracist grounding, it was important to introduce this concept with the framework of *doing with* instead of *doing for*. The power point presentation also explained service-learning projects as being "reciprocal relationships built on mutual respect, ownership, responsibility, and earned trust" (RJC1, 12).

Service-Learning Implementation

Of the 30 students in the selected section on the first day of class, 26 identified as European descent, three identified as Asian heritage, and one student identified as Latin Diaspora. Given the opportunity to self-identify gender, recognizing that there are more possibilities than "traditional" male/female options, out of 30 students enrolled in the section, 12 of the students identified as female, 8 students identified as male, and 10 students did not complete that line on the survey. Two of the 30 students were first semester freshman; 18 of the students had completed one-two semesters of college; 6 students had completed three-four semesters; 3

students had completed five-six semesters; and 1 student had completed seven or more semesters. Twenty-three students in the class noted that they were taking the course as a racial issues required course and the remaining seven were taking it for other reasons.

To provide more information and contextualization for service-learning, as part of their first group of assigned readings, students were asked to read an article by Leonard (2007) titled *Rethinking Volunteerism in America*. Leonard's article addressed, among other topics, the issues of solidarity vs. charity, privilege, and equal partnership.

Service-Learning Project Selection

During the first week of the semester, students were presented with six projects options to complete their service-learning hours. The options presented were (a) working with Native American Indigenous populations on an alternative spring break program; (b) working with Native American Indigenous students in the All Tribes Council student organization to create a presentation for the university on a specific Native American issue; (c) working with the Organization for the Prevention of AIDS in Africa, a grass roots student organization, on HIV/AIDS education and fundraising for an orphanage in South Africa/Africa; (d) expanding the HIV/AIDS education initiative to include working on fundraising for an orphanage in India; (e) working with Fifty Lanterns International, a local nonprofit, to provide safe, reliable and environmentally friendly light to those who live in areas of strife, natural disaster and conflict, particularly in the Middle East and in Africa; and/or (f) tutoring recent Somali Refugee children in the local community.

Students were given 2 weeks to explore each topic before having to commit to one group. Opportunities to contact student team leaders in addition to the instructor and teaching assistant to provide them information for each project was also available to allow each student to make an informed decision. In total, five teams working with different focus areas emerged. Students chose to work on four of the six proposed projects with the fifth comprising a small group of two students who came to the instructor, teaching assistant, and Native American Issues service-learning team leader with a proposal which was accepted for an additional project option.

Aligning in Solidarity

Because equal partnership was a paramount priority for both the instructor and team leaders, as was ensuring the community defined the need, the actual implementation of the service-learning projects ended up differing from the original plans for the project work. The subject areas and organizations had been in the planning stages for months; however, the ultimate requests from the organizations changed the original project plans. The originally designed projects included students working with members of the Somali community recording folk tales in attempts to assist preservation of oral tradition, awareness campaigns for HIV/AIDS in Africa and India, and volunteering on site with an alternative spring break program. Throughout working with our partners on the orphanages in Africa and India as well as the Fifty Lanterns International organization, the two main requests were to spread awareness and to fundraise. Fundraising was not a part of the original inception for the projects. In addition, the request from the Somali community was to help students and adults with learning English instead of recording oral tradition. In solidarity and in the spirit of *Ayni*, the instructor and service-learning team leaders shifted efforts to focus on the requests of the partners-in-service.

Service-Learning in Action

Multiple opportunities appeared throughout the semester for students to work in solidarity throughout their service-learning initiatives. Projects included an event entitled *Coffee for a Cause* which consisted of collaboration by the 50 Lanterns student team in with a social responsibility graduate program documentary and speaker series on campus to spread awareness and sell fair-trade coffee while promoting the documentary film *Black Gold* (Francis, 2006). The Bear Butte team created and displayed a presentation at a 2-day, university-wide event, titled the *Real* Real World, which was supported by multiple university departments and student organizations. The goal of the event was to present interactive presentations or displays on oppression issues from multiple perspectives. Three of the students worked with an afterschool, drop-in center and assisted students from K-12 with homework in various subjects. Two of the students worked with pre-school age youth to work on early childhood skills while the children's parents were taking English classes. The students in the tutoring project carried out their tutoring on a weekly basis with individual regular schedules.

Three teams (HIV/AIDS Africa, HIV/AIDS India, 50 Lanterns International) prepared and displayed poster presentations at the university research colloquium to educate and spread awareness of their project areas. All five teams participated and displayed information at multiple university events. In addition, all teams contributed in soliciting donations, promoting, and working a 1-day silent auction event at the university student center to raise awareness and funds for the organizations with which the students were working and a separate 3-day kiosk at the university student center to display information and sell awareness bracelets. More than $3,200 was raised through the silent auction, kiosks, and Coffee for a Cause that was donated to the organizations with which the students were partnering.

FINDINGS

The constant comparative method of analysis (Maykut & Morehouse, 1994) used to traiangualte data from multiple surveys, focus groups, teaching-learning artifacts, and researcher's journal revealed many propositions and rules of inclusion for this study. Although each were considered important, out of that group, some shone more brightly than others. Many of these propositions fit together to form five discoveries which follow one another in the pattern of emersion in which each discovery from the data builds and contributes upon the previous. These discoveries include (a) students care, (b) their intentions lead to action, (c) to make contributions and impacts, (d) connections, (e) and work in solidarity. The discoveries discussed below include students' statements from data which support the findings.

Students Care

Active Learning Strengthens Meaning

When asked for examples of meaningful learning experiences in both pre- and post- service-learning assessments, learning which was active and involved people was described as most meaningful by the majority of the class. In the preassessment 15 of the 19 responses illustrated active learning by noting examples of volunteering, meeting and living with others, or figuring out how to balance life and school after coming to college.

> Experiences that come with maturity, meeting new people has taught me the most. (Connecticut, S-LBP 12)

The importance of socially interacting integrated with active learning was increased in the service-learning post-assessment which showed 19 students pointing to that semester's service-learning experience another active learning experience as most meaningful.

Volunteering at Hands Across the World because I connected and interacted with people from a different culture. (Idaho, S-LBPP 12)

Finding Time—Willing to Try

Students demonstrated that they cared about global issues though a variety of propositions that emerged from multiple data points. Students were not aware of the service-learning component upon registration, but were informed on the first day of class of the additional service-learning requirement in this 1 of the 13 offered sections of the course. Confirmation of participation limitations were revealed during the second set of focus groups when some students noted, with 12 supporting units, that their jobs and lack of available time hindered their involvement in their service-learning projects. Because of this and multiple other limitations, many students do not report having a lot of free time: "My participation was hindered by my job" (Kentucky, FF5 10).

However, despite the lack of reported free time, after students were informed that they were enrolled in the section which would carry a service-learning requirement of a minimum of 10 out-of-class hours, the instructor reported only one student dropped or transferred citing the time component as a reason (RJC26, 2-3). Nine units from the second set of focus groups support that students wanted to, in fact, spend more time on their projects than was required: "You have to leave but you wish you could stay. I wish there was more time for me to do this" (Jersey, FF4 55-56).

Although students noted a lack of time, as a class, students exceeded their service-learning hours by more than twice the required number for the course. Twenty-four students who completed the semester successfully were asked to have dedicated approximately 240 hours for their service-learning projects, but after compiling the student logs, students had logged more than 534 hours on their service-learning projects (RJC26, 7).

Intentions Lead to Actions

Awareness is Fundamental

As projects were explained and class content was reviewed and discussed, students noted their lack of knowledge on international and Indigenous issues through multiple data sources. Without knowledge of issues, action is impossible. Once students heard speakers, watched documentaries, and learned about situations, students often noted feeling compelled to spread the new awareness that they had gained. This message was reinforced by 21 students in 76 units from three data sets.

This awareness needs to be heard to every citizen in America. This percentage makes me want to scream, "20% of Africa has AIDS! Let's do something!" (Louisiana, S1-3 3)

Many people in the U.S. today do not feel as though AIDS is something that directly affects them and therefore, they ignore it. I will try to make people more aware of AIDS, how they will be affected by it and how it is a massive problem that needs attention. (Massachusetts, S2-3)

Motivation, Energy, and Desire to Take Action

Students found their motivation and energy in different ways. Twenty supporting units from the first set of focus groups contain statements from students noting they were interested in their topic and or their desire to learn more fueled their selection and participation.

I never really knew about what was happening so I chose it to learn more. (Michigan, FF3-A 24-25)

I chose this project because it seems different than all the others and sounded very interesting. I wanted to learn more about something that people don't ever hear about. (Maryland, FS1 6)

For me it is on a personal level to find out more about Native Americans. My grandmother just finally admitted that she is part Native American and I am doing this as a way to also find out about my own history, to find out what was important. (Maine, FF2-A 42-45)

In addition, after studying the service-learning issues, seventeen units emerged from the first set of focus groups in which students commented that they wanted to help the people that they would be working with. Students demonstrated a desire to contribute. Students illustrated in various ways from multiple sets of data, how they did, in fact, care. In addition and possibly more importantly, they articulated that they wanted to take action about what they had learned.

I had never heard about 50 Lanterns until this semester in HURL 102. It grabbed my attention right away. I can't imagine what it must be like to live without electricity and I wanted to help. (Georgia, FS1 10)

I chose this project because I would like to help children who have been abused and raped. HIV/AIDS has affected many children and I would like to do something about it. (Colorado, FS3-A 8)

I feel strongly about Native American issues. Bear Butte is something in the here and now that I can help save for people in the future. (Maine, FS2-A 9)

Contributions and Impacts

Inability to Conceptualize the Role

Although the desire to help was evident among many students, the actuality of how this might happen remained elusive. A feeling or belief of not possessing the capacity to help was a theme that appeared during the beginning of the service-learning projects from group discussions through two focus groups. Although many students noted in the pre-assessment that they thought the service-learning projects were a good way to learn about international and Indigenous communities, some were skeptical that any difference could be made. The distance was cited as a reason and many students commented on not believing that something could be done so far away to actually make a difference.

Answers to a question from one of the pre-assessment surveys support this feeling from students as 11 students marked that they either disagreed or were uncertain about the statement: My involvement in the world community improves the lives of others. However, data from the same question in the post-assessment showed that 25 out of 26 students agreed or strongly agreed that their involvement in the world community improves the lives of others.

Understanding Roles and Goals

Throughout the semester, some projects ran into multiple snags while others were able to capitalize on what was already being planned on campus to add to the implementation of their service-learning projects. In addition, because of the emergent process of some of the projects, some students found themselves unclear as to how they would contribute. Understanding roles and goals in concrete terms for the overall project was important. When noting their "ah-ha" moments, 19 units support that students moments centered around seeing concrete examples of their work: "When my group and I finished my poster" (Missouri, FS8 37). Missouri's statement illustrates how this student had difficulty conceptualizing her contribution until the completion of her group's poster, which carried the purpose of educating others on the issue. In addition to seeing tangible examples of efforts, understanding the role each student played on the team also became an issue. Teams began to form and some quickly became cliquey as demonstrated by sitting in groups and excluding others. Students noted in the second set of focus groups with nine supporting units that they would have liked to have known or understood their roles better. It wasn't until near the end of the semester when some students finally figured out how to contribute: "When we've been working on the S-L [service-learning] projects I haven't really known what to do.

But when the silent auction came up, I knew I could do that!" (Hawaii, FS8 36).

Tangible, Concrete Results

A prominent theme that emerged through multiple stages of the data collection process was the importance of tangibility in efforts and outcomes when working on service-learning projects. Comments from each group emphasized the importance of seeing the *results* of their work or knowing in tangible terms where their efforts were going (e.g., $50 buys one lantern, one family benefits from each lantern bought). This tangibility seemed to be just as important for those who were working in the direct local community as it was for those who were working with groups located on other continents. However, the groups who found themselves in the predicament of not being able to see the results of their work at the beginning stages were two of the three projects focusing their efforts overseas. The importance of "seeing the results" appeared in both sets of focus groups with 15 and 19 supporting units respectively.

> There are tangible results—working on the HIV/AIDS project seems like trying to stop a freight train with a cinderblock, but with this [50 Lanterns International Project], you can count each person you help. (Kentucky, FF1 16-18)

Implications for Participation

Distance and ambiguity of roles and responsibilities were culprits of the skeptical and hesitant beginnings to some students' service-learning projects. Both at the beginning of their service-learning projects and upon or near completion of their projects students pointed to the significance of understanding their ability to contribute and make an impact as a factor in their participation. Students demonstrated the importance of this factor clearly through: (a) ultimately conceptualizing how one or many can make a difference internationally, (b) the stated importance of understanding both goals of the projects, (c) the stated importance of roles of each group and individual, (d) and the significance of having tangible outcomes as factors in their participation. Five supporting units in the second set of focus groups positively affirming understanding roles, goals, and their ability to contribute were factors in their involvement.

> To me it is the fact that we're actually working to make a difference in people's lives. (Nebraska, FS8 3)

> Yes, this is a project I feel extremely strong about and the chance to educate others about it is amazing. (Nevada, FS6 5)

Yes, I think that our organization is unique and stands out and I actually feel like I am making a difference. (Georgia, FS5 9)

Connections

Connections are generally easier to create when they are developed in person and more likely to occur or strengthen when there is a longer period of time to work alongside people. As a researcher and a person with an extensive service-learning background, *connections* was the area that I was most concerned about. My understanding of the vital role that connections play within the success or impact of service-learning prompted the creation of the second guiding research question for this study: Is it possible to set up meaningful service-learning that does not necessitate participation onsite with the international community?

Empathy/Sympathy

Students demonstrated finding connections in a variety of ways. An emotional connection was forged by some early on as a theme emerged in the first set of focus groups in which students demonstrated through their statements empathy or sympathy for the people and communities with which they were slated to work. Specific stories of those who organizations had worked with in the past along with photographs were venue referenced by the students.

I guess the part that really moved me was when the question was asked about not being able to do homework and daily activities because of the no light issue was proposed to us. I felt passionate in helping this. (Arkansas, FS1 7)

Speakers, Site Sponsors, Documentaries

Many outside speakers came to class or to sessions held before class, called *preclass*, to speak to students about topics that the service-learning teams covered. More than 12 guest experts (some came as teams) came to speak to the students in the service-learning class about their project topics. Two of the speakers, founders of the organizations with which the students worked, came with many pictures, stories of the realities people face, and statistics connected to the projects. For the group that worked on-site with tutoring Somali youth, they noted their site supervisor and team leader as helping them understand situations and make the connections. Five units included in this category note that documentaries used in class or before class were also an avenue to make an impact or spark a connection: "Watching visually about what Botshabelo [orphanage] is going through—that started the spark" (Colorado, FF8 51-52).

Students noted that speakers, site sponsors, and documentaries were factors in their involvement in their service-learning projects.

Although not enough units were available for a rule of inclusion in any one category, another venue for making connections that was given by students who engaged in their service locally. Students noted or illustrated making personal connections and learning from students with whom they were working (RJC13, 43; FS4 30). The Service-Learning Background Survey supports this as two students mention in their most meaningful experience as working with the students at the respective sites: "Tutoring the 2 year told Somali children. They are so cute and give me a different outlook on life" (Alaska, S-LBPP 12).

Involvement in Group

A strong and somewhat surprising discovery that emerged was the power of group work. Because 21 out of the 26 students in class did not work on site with the people from the communities they were partnered with, students found alternate ways of making connections. Students noted, documented by 14 supporting units, they found connections and were encouraged or inspired by other group members as well as other groups in class. Students commented that other people who were excited about the work that they were doing encouraged them and made them want to become more involved. They noted in their statements that these factors played a significant role in their participation.

> Yes—this group pulled me in. I am now better informed and like to help spread awareness, but I wish we could have had more group on group interaction during the process. (Connecticut, FS7 7)

> What made a difference in my involvement was the group members—they were awesome! (California, FS5 5)

> In addition, I witnessed community within the classroom increasing with the beginning of the service-learning projects. As early as class 10 (of 26 classes), students began sitting in their service-learning groups and attendance at sessions provided for students before class including invited guest speakers, additional videos and documentaries, and service-learning meeting time, labeled pre-class, began increasing (RJC10, 2).

Solidarity

Students illustrated in multiple ways that many moved from lack of knowledge which facilitated no action to active involvement in solidarity. A theme that supports the shift in thinking is the fact that students noted the benefit and how they have changed their habits because of this course. Students noted that they learned from this type of education; it afforded a different impact, a different way for learning to occur: "I have learned so much and look at things so differently because of this" (Delaware, FF5 52).

Opening the Door

The movement toward solidarity is also evident from the data that suggested that students were moving away from *othering* and judging. When focusing on international issues and collaborating with new cultures, especially working on international and global initiatives locally with distance as a factor, a common response for people is to *Other*. *Othering*, a concept discussed earlier in this chapter, facilitates *working for* and prevents opportunities for solidarity whereas moving away from othering facilitates *working with* and the opportunity to work in solidarity. The comments that support this movement can be found with a proposition from the second written analyzed assignment in which students stated that they were waiting to get to know people before making judgments about them. By doing this, students opened themselves up to possibility of connecting with others and thus the opportunity to work in solidarity.

As mentioned earlier in the disposition postassessment, out of 26 students in the class, 25 agreed or strongly agreed that their involvement in the world community improves the lives of others. In addition to the recognition of their role in the world community, all of the 23 students who were present at the second set of focus groups affirmed that it is important to be involved in the international/Indigenous community.

> Yes, I think that its important to get involved so that you can get a better understanding of how other people live and living in the richest country I think that its important for Americans to become active. (Georgia, FS5 26)

> Yes! It is super important to be active in the international and Indigenous communities because these groups are part of our society and issues that involve these groups affect everyone of us in some way. (California, FS5 30)

Got Privilege?

A premise that was carried out throughout the semester by the instructor and me as the teaching/research assistant stemmed from a shared vision. We both took the position of challenging our students to consider what privileges they possess and what they do with those privileges. In stating the importance of involvement with international/indigenous communities, many students indicated their privilege when stressing the importance of working with international/Indigenous communities. Thirteen units that emerged from the second set of focus groups contained statements that indicated student recognition of privilege and a duty to help.

> I believe (it is important to be involved in Indigenous/international communities) there are so many people out there in the world that benefit from others. (Michigan, FS8 25)

> Yes, I think that it is important to get involved so that you can get a better understanding of how other people live and living in the richest country, I think it is important for Americans to become active. (Georgia, FS5 26)

In understanding their privilege, students demonstrated that they felt the need to do something with it. Possibly the last significant marker that these projects made an impact on students and that solidarity is possible was the reality that multiple students, some of whom were originally skeptical, noted wanting to spend or devote more time and work more on their initiatives. One student even noted, when asked what she would have done differently,

> (I would have gotten) to know what the other groups were doing and more about what they were doing to help so I could be more informed going into the exhibits (support others groups). (Connecticut, FS7 12)

IN SUMMARY— SEEKING SOLIDARITY

Integral to developing critical consciousness is the shift from a charity model to a solidarity model; a critical and stressed aspect of this service-learning implementation. Students demonstrated their shift from personal, local, and national thinking to globally-oriented thinking toward the end of the course as was illustrated by their movement to unanimously agreeing, by noting on their surveys, that it was important to be involved in international and Indigenous communities. In addition, that the entire class, with the exception of one student, felt their involvement in the world community improves the lives of others. This shift supports the statement by Eyler and Giles (1999) that this type of "learning is transforming in the sense that as students move along in their service they shift from working with a charity focus to one of social justice" (p. 19).

Monard-Weissman (2003) found that through service-learning, once students were engaged and focusing on social justice issues, "students could not turn away after coming across poverty, abandonment, illness, and ignorance. They examined ways they ought to act in order to strive for social change" (p. 167). Data from this inquiry also support this finding as students demonstrated this through their (a) committed language,

(b) recognition of privilege, (c) commitment to take a stand against discrimination, and (d) actions taken. It is important to also note that with fundraising efforts, it is easy to slide into a charity-based doing-for model, so it is vital that team leaders and instructors are prepared to frame non-Western forms of reciprocity and understanding in addition to the crucial contextualization western dominance currently and historically.

Evidence of a Beginning

The data show that the connection to the global community, for the majority of students, is at least in the beginning stages. The director for the Center for International Studies from the university where the study took place spoke at the celebration ceremony during the final class meeting and noted the importance of facilitating the global connection as the reality is that many students and people in the area and in the United States will never make it to another country (RJC26, 16-20). Although this study calls attention to the importance of being surrounded by others who are aware or involved in the global community, one can hope that students will carry this experience with them and build from it. The results of this study supports Monard-Weissman's (2003) finding that stated "service-learning helped them reiterate their commitment to be agents of change, not only locally but globally" (p. 168).

It is important to note that although it appears that as if these projects, for the most, part did begin or strengthen a global connection where there wasn't one before; most students were just beginning the process of critical consciousness. Although there was a shift from biased to unbiased language, committed language by many students still utilized unequal language of *helping* instead of a larger shift to *working with*. It is important to remember that change and critical consciousness does not occur immediately, but rather, is a process that requires education, reflection, self-reflection, and contextualization.

The Future of Service-Learning

Although the term service-learning is relatively new, the ideals of experiential education, service, and civic responsibility are not. The historical background of service-learning has seen a range of foci: reinforcement of the status quo, charity, and solidarity. The future of service-learning is still being determined. Where do we go from here—creating and nurturing equal partnerships, offering options and responsibility, providing guided reflection, contextualizing and connecting to course content, taking what we have learned from the research of the past 20 years? How do we continue to help facilitate change and interest in students who are increasingly facing a world where partitions are being solidified within communities all across the United States and the globe? I believe it possible to look to service-learning to bring about connections within our global family.

The research presented here illustrates a possible method of how to forge seemingly difficult connections globally. More research is called for in the area of globally-focused international and indigenous service-learning. My positionality influences not only how I do research but also how I teach. With this, it is important to note that within the social responsibility/social justice framework, it is integral to introduce and consciously reinforce the framework of reciprocity and equality. With fundraising efforts, it is easy to slide into a charity-based model, so it is vital that team leaders and instructors are prepared to frame and contextualize non-western forms of reciprocity, understanding in addition to western dominance historically and currently. My hope is that we use this powerful and meaningful learning tool toward the ideal goal in social justice work: to engage students and to reach the point where they will continue to examine systems and work in solidarity for social justice beyond their courses, classrooms, and educational experiences.

ACKNOWLEDGMENTS

Grateful acknowledgement is made to Douglas F. Warring (2007), author, for permission to reprint this chapter from *Understanding and Applying Human Relations and Multicultural Education: Teaching~Learning in a Global Society* (6th ed., Rev., pp. 246-262). Modifications have been made for the purposes of this publication. The original study was published as my thesis in social responsibility, master of science, St. Cloud State University, St. Cloud, Minnesota (see Weiley, 2007b).

REFERENCES

Barber, Benjamin R., & Richard Battistoni. (1993). A season of service: Introducing service learning into the liberal arts curriculum [Electronic version]. *Political Science and Politics, 26*(2), 235-240.

Brown, Elinor L. (2004). What precipitates change in cultural diversity awareness during a multicultural course: The message or the method? *Journal of Teacher Education, 55*(4), 325-340.

Brown, Elinor L., & Bobby R. Howard II. (2005). Becoming culturally responsive teachers through service-learning: A case study of five novice classroom teachers. *Multicultural Education, 12*(4), 2-8.

Cipolle, Susan. (1994). Service-learning as a counter-hegemonic practice. *Multicultural Education, 11*(3), 12-23.

Cohen, David K. (1998). Dewey's problem. *The Elementary School Journal, 98*(5), 427-446.

Daniel, Beverly-Jean. (2005). Researching African Canadian women: Indigenous knowledge and the politics of representation. In George J. Sefa Dei & Gurpreet Singh Johal (Eds.), *Critical issues in anti-racist research methodologies* (pp. 52-78). New York: Peter Lang.

Dei, George J. Sefa. (2005). Critical issues in anti-racist research methodologies: An Introduction. In George J. Sefa Dei & Gurpreet Singh Johal (Eds.), *Critical issues in anti-racist research methodologies* (pp. 1-27). New York: Peter Lang.

Denzin, Norman K., & Yolanda S. Lincoln, (1998). Introduction: Entering the field of qualitative research. In Norman K. Denzin & Yolanda S. Lincoln (Eds.) *Collecting and interpreting qualitative materials* (pp. 3-4). Thousand Oaks, CA: SAGE.

Dewey, John. (1930). *Construction and criticism*. New York: Columbia University Press.

Durkheim, Emile. (1951). *Suicide*. New York: The Free Press.

Elyer, Janet, & Dwight E. Giles Jr. (1999). *Where's the learning in service-learning?* San Francisco: Jossey-Bass.

Francis, Marc (Director/Producer), & Nick Francis (Director/Producer). (2007). *Black gold* [Motion picture]. (Available from California Newsreel: www.newsreel.com)

Freire, Paulo. (1970). *Pedagogy of the oppressed*. New York: Continuum International.

Grossman, Lev. (2005, January 16). Grow up? Not so fast. *TIME Magazine*. Retrieved April 2, 2007, from http://www.time.com/time/magazine/article/0,9171,1018089,00.html

Harkavy, Ira, & Lee Benson. (1998). De-Platonizing and democratizing education as the basis of service learning. *New Directions for Teaching and Learning, 73*, 11-21.

Hollis, Shirley A. (2004). Blaming me, blaming you: Assessing service learning and participants' tendency to blame the victim [Electronic version]. *Sociological Spectrum, 24*(5), 575-600.

Holst, John D. (2006). Paulo Freire in Chile, 1964-1969; *Pedagogy of the Oppressed* in its sociopolitical economic context. *Harvard Educational Review, 24*, 243-270.

Howard, Jeffrey. (1993/2003). Community service learning in the curriculum. In Campus Compact (Ed.), *Introduction to service-learning toolkit* (pp. 101-104). Providence, RI: Campus Compact.

Huber, Tonya, & James F. Nolan. (1989). Nurturing the reflective practitioner through instructional supervision: A review of the literature. *Journal of Curriculum and Supervision, 4*(2), 126-145.

Huber-Warring, Tonya. (2006). Developing critical self-reflection in teachers: Understanding our own culture in international contexts. *International Journal of Curriculum and Instruction, 6*(1), 41-61.

Huber-Warring, Tonya. (2007a). *Human relations and race, HURL 102.* Unpublished syllabus, St. Cloud State University, St. Cloud, MN.

Huber-Warring, Tonya. (2007b). STEPS guidelines. In Douglas F. Warring, *Understanding and applying human relations and multicultural education: Teaching~learning in a global society* (6th ed., Rev., pp. 284-287). Scottsdale, AZ: Leadership.

International Partnership for Service-Learning and Leadership. (2003). *Declaration of principles & an invitation to join.* Retrieved November 11, 2006, from http://www.ipsl.org/pdfs/Declaration.pdf

Institute for International Education. (2006). *U.S. students abroad top 200,000, increase by 8 percent.* Retrieved August 26, 2007, from http://opendoors.iienetwork.org/?p=89252

Jacoby, Barbara. (1996). *Service-learning in higher education: Concepts and practices.* San Francisco: Jossey-Bass.

Jacoby, Barbara. (Ed.). (2003). *Building partnerships for service-learning.* San Francisco: Jossey-Bass.

Johnson-Hunter, Paige, & Michael T. Risku. (2003). Paulo Freire's liberatory education and the problem of service learning [Electronic version]. *Journal of Hispanic Higher Education, 2*(1), 98-108.

Kendall, Jane C., & Associates. (1990). *Combining service and learning: A resource book for community and public service.* Raleigh, NC: National Society for Internships and Experimental Education.

Kraft, Richard J. (1996). Service learning: An introduction to its theory, practice, and effects [Electronic version]. *Education and Urban Society, 28*(2), 131-159.

Krain, Matthew, & Anne M. Nurse (2004). Teaching human rights through service learning [Electronic version]. *Human Rights Quarterly, 26*(1), 189-207.

Leonard, Gavin. (2007). Rethinking volunteerism in America. In Paula S. Rothenberg (Ed.), *Race, class, and gender in the United States: An integrated study* (7th ed., pp. 730-733). New York: Worth.

Marlin-Bennett, Renee. (2002). Linking experiential and classroom education: Lessons learned from the American university-amnesty international USA summer institute on human rights [Electronic version]. *International Studies Perspectives,* 384-395.

Max, Karen. (2005). Anti-colonial research: Working as an ally with Aboriginal peoples. In George J. Sefa Dei & Gurpreet Singh Johal (Eds.), *Critical issues in anti-racist research methodologies* (pp. 79-94). New York: Peter Lang.

Maybach, Carol Wiechman. (1996). Investigating urban community needs: Service learning from a social justice perspective [Electronic version]. *Education and Urban Society, 28*(2), 224-236.

Maykut, Pamela, & Richard Morehouse. (1994). *Beginning qualitative research: A philosophical and practical guide.* Philadelphia: Routledge Falmer.

Minnesota Campus Compact. (2001). *America Reads Tutor Evaluation II: Outcome Evaluation.* Unpublished survey.

Moely, Barbara E., Megan McFarland, Devi Miron, Sterett Mercer, & Vincent Ilustre. (2002). Changes in college students' attitudes and intentions for civic involvement as a function of service-learning experiences. *Michigan Journal of Community Service Learning, 9*(1), 18-26.

Monard-Weissman, Kathia. (2003). Fostering a sense of social justice through international service-learning [Electronic version]. *Academic Exchange Quarterly, 7*(2), 164-169.

Morton, Keith, & Sandra Enos. (2002). Building deeper civic relationships and new and improved citizens. *Journal of Public Affairs, 6*, 83. Retrieved August 20, 2007, from Academic Search Premier database.

National and Community Service Act of 1990. (1990). Retrieved September 14, 2006, from www.americorps.gov/pdf/cncs_statute.pdf

National Center for Public Policy and Higher Education. (2002). *Losing ground: A national status report on the affordability of American higher education.* Retrieved April 2, 2007, from http://www.highereducation.org/reports/losing_ground/affordability_report_final_bw.pdf

O'Grady, Carolyn R. (Ed.). (2000). *Integrating service learning and multicultural education in colleges and universities.* Mahwah, NJ: Erlbaum.

Porter, Maureen, & Kathia Monard. (2001). *Ayni* in the global village: Building relationships of reciprocity through international service-learning. *Michigan Journal of Community Service Learning, 8*(1), 5-17.

Putnam, Robert D. (2000) *Bowling alone: The collapse and revival of American community.* New York: Simon & Schuster.

Roberts, Bill. (2000). Good guidance on the ground: Mentoring international service learning programs. *Metropolitan Universities: An International Forum, 11*(1), 45-52.

Rosenberger, Cynthia. (2000). Beyond empathy: Developing critical consciousness through service learning. In Carolyn R. O'Grady (Ed.), *Integrating service learning and multicultural education in colleges and universities* (pp. 1-19). Mahwah, NJ: Erlbaum.

Schniedewind, Nancy, & Ellen Davidson. (2006). *Open minds to equality: A sourcebook of learning activities to affirm diversity and promote equity.* Milwaukee, WI: Rethinking Schools.

Smith, Linda Tuhiwai. (2006). *Decolonizing methodologies: Research and indigenous peoples* (9th ed.). London: Zed Books.

Stoecker, Randy. (2003). Community-based research: From practice to theory and back again. *Michigan Journal of Community Service Learning, 9*(2), 35-46.

Tevlin, Jon. (2007, March 11). Going abroad: An ode to international travel. *Star Tribune*, p. G1.

Ward, Kelly, & Lisa Wolf-Wendel. (2000). Community-centered service learning moving from *doing for* to *doing with* [Electronic version]. *American Behavioral Scientist, 43*, 767-780.

Warren, Karen. (1998). Educating students for social justice in service learning [Electronic version]. *The Journal of Experiential Education, 21*(3), 134-139.

Warring, Douglas F. (2007). *Understanding and applying human relations and multicultural education: Teaching~learning in a global society* (6th ed., Rev.). Scottsdale, AZ: Leadership.

Weah, Wokie, Verna Cornelia Simmons, & McClellan Hall. (2000, May 1). Service-learning and multicultural/multiethnic perspectives [Electronic version]. *Phi Delta Kappan, 81*, 673.

Weiley, Kelly C. (2007a). Indigenous, international service-learning. In Douglas F. Warring, *Understanding and applying human relations and multicultural education: Teaching~learning in a global society* (6th ed., Rev.; pp. 246-262). Scottsdale, AZ: Leadership.

Weiley, Kelly C. (2007b). *Uniting in solidarity through globally-focused service-learning.* Unpublished master's thesis, St. Cloud State University, St. Cloud, MN.

CHAPTER 18

HELPING BEGINNING TEACHERS SHAPE THEIR PERSONAL PRACTICAL KNOWLEDGE

An Essential Process in Teacher Education

Chun-kwok Lau, Wai-ming Yu, and Francis Nai-kwok Chan

Personal practical knowledge has been a part of the teacher education discourse for over 20 years in Europe and North America, but it is just entering the educational field in Hong Kong. In this study, we document our initial attempt in helping student teachers reflect on their experiences by telling stories from their teaching practice. In the process of helping teachers shape their personal practical knowledge, we are at the same time helping them become more reflective practitioners. This process is essential in teacher education because it helps teachers reflect and, when this is built into their daily practice, will enable them to meet the demands of the educational goals of all-round development and lifelong learning in education reforms worldwide.

INTRODUCTION

From our experiences in teacher education over the past 10 years, we have noticed the phenomenon of *apprenticeship of observation* (Lortie, 1975) in our student teachers. Unlike novices entering other professions, such as those of doctors or lawyers, most student teachers already have preconceptions and partial knowledge about teaching when they enroll for their teacher training courses. As argued by Lortie, these preconceptions and partial knowledge primarily come from the thousands of hours they spent observing their teachers in action as schoolchildren. While these preconceptions and partial knowledge are easily recognized, they are seldom explored directly in teacher education programs that often emphasize imparting various educational theories, pedagogical knowledge, and subject matter knowledge instead. This, as we argue in this paper, is an undesirable situation. When the partial understanding of student teachers is not analyzed, it remains "intuitive and imitative" (Lortie, 1975) and merely provides teachers with "ready-made recipes for action and interpretation" (Buchmann, 1987) or "default options" (Tomlinson, 1999) *that* they resort to in times of indecision or uncertainty in their teaching practice. The period of apprenticeship of observation is so long and influential that teacher education courses are said by many to have a relatively weak effect on student teachers (Borg, 2004). Once they have joined the profession, teachers often teach as they have been taught in their school days, abandoning much of their training in the teacher education programs (Richards & Pennington, 1998).

In this chapter, we report on a study that taps into the intuitive knowledge and experience of a group of student teachers in their teaching practice. We argue that becoming more aware of the intuitive or implicit aspect of our knowledge is a crucial part of teachers' professional development.

CONTRASTING TEACHER KNOWLEDGE AND KNOWLEDGE FOR TEACHERS IN HONG KONG AND NORTH AMERICAN LANDSCAPES

Teaching is a practical activity. Teachers possess a kind of knowledge that is not purely objective, conceptual, or academic (Connelly & Clandinin, 1988). This knowledge is a blend of the theoretical and the practical. Teachers hold and use this special knowledge to guide their teaching. For over 20 years, the literature in education in Europe and North America has begun to recognize this knowledge as *teacher knowledge* in contrast to *knowledge for teachers* (Clandinin & Connelly, 2000), and in more specific terms as *practical knowledge* (Elbaz, 1981) or *personal practical knowledge* (Clandinin, 1985).

Teacher knowledge refers to the knowledge that is held by teachers and is enacted in professional practice while *knowledge for teachers* refers to a core knowledge base that is researched, developed, and conferred as essential by researchers in universities. In many traditional teacher education programs, knowledge for teachers usually includes subject matter knowledge, general pedagogical knowledge, and foundation knowledge related to teaching, such as psychology, sociology, and the philosophy of education (Connelly & Clandinin, 2000a, 2000b; Grossman, 1990; Sharples, 2002). Knowledge for teachers is regarded as more objective and provides generalized guiding principles across different contexts. In contrast, because of its idiosyncratic and contextualized nature, teacher knowledge remains implicit and unexamined by researchers until recently.

We regard knowledge for teachers as a necessary but insufficient component in a teacher education program; it should be complemented by and integrated into teacher knowledge. While knowledge for teachers can be learned from books and lectures, teacher knowledge has to be discovered, developed and refined through the active engagement of the individual teachers in their own learning process. Personal experiences and stories are critically explored in this process of understanding of self and others. From our personal experiences of studying in different countries, we notice that narratives, teacher memoirs, biographies, and autobiographies (e.g., Ayers, 2001; Carger, 1996; Johnson, 1995; Miller, 2005; Paley, 1989; Phillion, He, & Connelly, 2005; Rodriguez, 1983) are more likely to be used as teaching materials in teacher education programs in North America than in Hong Kong. Narrative inquiry is one approach to help teachers reflect on their own teaching experiences through studying narrative texts and telling stories of their own experiences (Clandinin, Davies, Hogan, & Kennard, 1993; Conle, 2003; Lyons & LaBoskey, 2002). It contributes to the construction of teacher knowledge through a process of *re-storying* personal practical knowledge. Through telling and retelling stories of experience, the participants are able to examine their implicit values and assumptions as they live and relive their personal and professional lives from a different perspective (Connelly & Clandinin, 1988, 1990). In some preservice teacher education programs, for example, students are invited to explore the connections between personal and professional knowledge of teaching through different narrative activities: responses to practicum experiences, responses to reading, group discussions, and reflective papers (Olson, 2000). Olson argues that if preservice teachers are unable to connect the formal professional knowledge of teaching with their own unexamined narrative knowledge of teaching, "professional knowledge presented in courses remains decontextualized theory; their personal narrative knowledge of teaching remains implicit and unexamined; and they teach as they believe they were taught" (p. 109).

In the past 20 years, there has been a notable development of narrative approach in educational research and professional practice in North America, and "narrative researchers no longer need to argue for the legitimacy of their methods with every new study" (Elbaz, 1997, p. 77). In Hong Kong, however, the discussion of the potential of using narratives in the education field has begun only recently (D. W. Chan, 2003, 2004) and many local educators remain skeptical about narrative work.[1] The design of most current teacher education programs in Hong Kong is still giving most credit to knowledge for teachers, but very little attention to teacher knowledge. The view that teachers should be receivers of formal professional knowledge remains dominant. The narrative knowledge of teaching, gained from their many years of experiences as students or from their practical experiences, is rarely acknowledged or explored.

In this paper, we discuss the significance of teacher knowledge, and more specifically, personal practical knowledge in the context of Hong Kong. We try to show that it is an essential but much neglected component in our local teacher education programs. We have documented our attempt in studying the personal practical knowledge of a group of student teachers. In our study, we organized eight weekly meetings with 18 student teachers during their teaching practice. There were also follow-up interviews with eight participants. Our experience in working with this group of student teachers, our own discussions in researcher meetings, as well as the transcribed interviews, provided useful data and insight into the knowledge held by student teachers during their teaching practice.

In the following sections, we examine the concept of personal practical knowledge, the context of local teacher education, and our attempt to introduce narrative activities in Hong Kong. We conclude by discussing the outcomes and implications of our work.

CONCEPT OF PERSONAL PRACTICAL KNOWLEDGE

In his review of the concepts of knowledge in research on teaching, Fenstermacher (1994) observed that research programs were based on two different notions of teacher knowledge: *formal knowledge* that is gained from studies of teaching that use conventional scientific research and *practical knowledge* that is generated by the teachers from their experience and embedded in their practice.

The origin of valuing teachers' practical knowledge can be traced to Schwab's (1969, 1971, 1973) *theory of the practical* in understanding curriculum. Within this concept, the work performed by teachers is viewed as a complex activity connecting four commonplace concerns to classroom practice—the students, teachers, subject matter, and social milieu. Following this understanding, Elbaz, Clandinin, and Connelly have conducted in-depth and long-term studies on teacher knowledge and discussed its significance in teacher professional development (Clandinin, 1985, 1986; Clandinin & Connelly, 2000; Connelly & Clandinin, 1988; Elbaz, 1981).

Elbaz (1981) observed a high school teacher for 2 years in order to gain an understanding of what she called the teacher's practical knowledge. She contended that teachers held and used this special kind of knowledge in guiding their teaching practice. She conceptualized this practical knowledge as a set of understandings that "encompasses first hand experience of students' learning styles, interests, needs, strengths and difficulties, and a repertoire of instructional techniques and classroom management skills" (Elbaz, 1983, p. 5).

With reference to Elbaz's concept, Clandinin (1985) further pointed out the importance of adding the *personal* element in defining teacher knowledge. In Clandinin's words, "personal" means "all that goes to make up a person" (p. 362). The use of *personal* recognizes "the individual local factor which helps to constitute the character, the past, and the future of any individual" (p. 362).

In Clandinin's (1985) elaboration, academics own a better knowledge of the theoretical, in theories of learning, teaching, and curriculum, while parents and others own a better knowledge of the practical, in knowing children. And teachers own a special kind of knowledge blending both. "A teacher's special knowledge is composed of both kinds of knowledge, blended by the personal background and characteristics of the teacher and expressed by her in particular situations" (p. 361). From this understanding, personal practical knowledge is neither theoretical, nor merely practical.

Our study was informed by the concept of personal practical knowledge developed by Connelly and Clandinin (1988), which states that experiences are felt, valued, and appreciated. Teachers develop through experiences their own personal practical knowledge which is a "moral, affective, and aesthetic way of knowing life's educational situations" (p. 59). This knowledge is found in "the person's past experience, in the person's present mind and body, and in the person's future plans and actions" (p. 25) and is a way of "reconstructing the past and the intentions for the future to deal with the exigencies of a present situation" (p. 25).

THE PREVAILING CONTEXT OF LOCAL TEACHER EDUCATION IN HONG KONG

Although research in teacher knowledge and narrative curricula practices are no longer marginal experiments in the West (Conle, 2003), similar discussion is still limited in Hong Kong. Being involved in the development of various teacher education programs in Hong Kong, we have seen very little change in the prevailing view of teachers as receivers of formal knowledge over the past 10 years in teacher education institutions. Such view, we believe, is limiting the development of local teacher education. Teaching is often understood as a linear and one-way process of applying theoretical knowledge to a practical situation. Teachers put into practice the theoretical and specific content knowledge developed by other experts. They are commonly viewed as practitioners and receivers of knowledge but not developers of knowledge (Cole & Knowles, 2000). This concept of knowledge was labeled *rhetoric of conclusions* by Schwab (1962), as *technical rationality* by Schön (1983), as knowledge for teachers by Clandinin and Connelly (2000), and as *knowledge-for-practice* by Cochran-Smith and Lytle (1999). These scholars doubt the usefulness of such knowledge as it neglects the practical situations teachers encounter. The kind of knowledge these scholars argue for is knowledge generated from and for teachers' own practice. Such an understanding of teacher knowledge, as we have pointed out earlier, has little circulation in Hong Kong until recently.

There has been an increasing number of studies on topics such as teacher stories (Chiu-Ching, 2005; Li, 2002), autobiographical or self studies (N. Chan, 2004; Lau, 2004), and teacher narratives (Eng, 2005; Lam, 2005). These works give teacher knowledge more visibility and the voices of teachers more value. In this paper, we report our study aiming to raise the teachers' awareness of the significance and importance of personal knowledge in the local context.

HELPING TEACHERS SHAPE THEIR PERSONAL PRACTICAL KNOWLEDGE THROUGH STORY TELLING

For many years, we have worked in different departments in the same teacher education institute and have witnessed our student teachers encountering tremendous difficulties in their teaching practice. The formal knowledge we equipped the students before the practicum did not seem to give them enough confidence and preparation for the challenges in their teaching. We began to ponder and experiment with alternative ways to bridge the gap between theory and practice. We found a common interest in adopting narrative inquiry in our teaching. We tried to help our student teachers integrate the formal professional knowledge they learned as student teachers in the lecture halls with the personal practical experiences they were likely to gain in their own classrooms.

In early 2005, we pulled our puzzles together and decided to support our student teachers in a different way. A few weeks before teaching practice, we advertised our plan of forming a teaching practice support group among the students we taught. Eighteen students agreed to participate in our project. We arranged meetings at a convenient location in town to accommodate as many of the student teachers as possible. Each meeting lasted for approximately one and a half hours. In our meetings, the three of us encouraged students to tell stories about their teaching practice. A roster was introduced to ensure we could have two to three story-telling sessions each time. In order to encourage their participation, we created simple routine duties for members, for example, they took turns to prepare snacks and drinks for the evening meetings.

We focused on telling stories in our meetings since we believed that telling stories is one of the best ways for people to unpack their personal practical knowledge (Clandinin & Connelly, 2000). As Bolton (2006) remarked, all professional and personal experience is naturally storied. By story telling, people start to organize their personal experiential narratives in an inquiry mode (Conle, 2000) and reflect on their experience. We also intended that the telling and retelling of stories of experience can help the student teachers discover and make explicit their taken-for-granted narrative knowledge of teaching and learning (Olson, 2000) in order to construct a more informed personal practical knowledge.

The basic notion guiding this study is that the practical knowledge of a teacher is personal in nature. In order to understand how a teacher teaches, it is important to take into account the personal dimension. The knowledge for teachers, which has been erroneously believed to be universally applicable, fails to meet the personal needs of individual teachers. Instead, we have to recognize the personal experience of a teacher which has constituted a crucial part of his practical knowledge. There are three distinctive qualities in personal practical knowledge as reflected from story telling: moral, affective, and aesthetic. The first story retold by Lau, "The Duster Story" (see Table 18.1), at the first meeting exhibits all three qualities and served as an example of what story telling is about for the participants.

Lau's story shows clearly how the moral, affective, and aesthetic qualities are weaved together in this teaching episode. In the latter part of this paper, we make use of two stories student teachers told to illustrate how far the participants were aware of the role their personal practical knowledge plays in informing their practice.

METHODOLOGY AND DATA SOURCES

We adopt a narrative inquiry approach in our work, which employs story telling as a means to understand experiences (Clandinin & Connelly, 2000). In our study, we followed 18 student teachers for 2 months during

Table 18.1. The Duster Story

It was 1983. I was in my first year of teaching. Kenny was sitting at the front row near the teacher's desk. He kept talking back and making funny noises. I warned him several times but was not successful. I was annoyed but took no further action. I went on teaching and writing on the chalkboard. Then I reached a point when I could tolerate it no more. I turned round suddenly, holding a duster in my hand and slapped the duster right on his face. He was wearing no glasses.

I could see the chalk mark of the duster on his face. Chalk dust was flying in the air in front of him. There was absolute silence. Everybody in the classroom was astonished by my sudden outburst. It was dead air. No one dared to utter a word. No one in the classroom knew what I was going to do next. I did not know either.

I could feel my heart beating heavily. I knew I had done something unacceptable of a teacher. But what should I do next? What should be the next words I said to the class? I could choose to defend my teacher ego, and go on to tell the class how naughty Kenny was and that he received the punishment he deserved. And anybody who dared to break the classroom rules would receive the same punishment. I knew I could gain control in this way. My words were backed up by my forceful action and the boys were just a class of 12-year olds anyway. Another action I could take was to admit that I was wrong, say sorry to the poor boy and apologize for what I had done.

I did not know what to do next. I kept pondering during these two minutes of absolute silence. My mind kept switching back and forth between these two opposite lines of action.

I finally made up my mind. I explained to the class that although Kenny's behavior in the class was unruly, he did not deserve such a punishment, which was a violent act. And violence could never solve problems. Then, in front of the whole class, I asked Kenny to accept my apology. I asked him to go and wash his face and come back for the lesson.

After this incident, I found that instead of "losing face" in my class, I seemed to have earned the students' respect and had a better relationship with the students. And more importantly, I learned to respect my students, no matter how they behaved in class. One year later, Kenny left the school and went to study in the United States. And I received Christmas cards from him for a few more years (Lau, 1998).

their teaching practice. We held regular meetings and student teachers were asked to share their experiences in schools during their teaching practice. Each week, we scheduled two to three of them to tell their stories. After each telling, other participants responded by sharing similar experiences, giving comments or suggesting solutions to problematic situations. We did not explicitly teach narrative inquiry to the participants, but intended to help them experience what narrative inquiry is by encouraging them to tell their own stories, share other people's experiences, and reflect upon the stories and experiences.

Our Participants

Our participants are student teachers who had received their undergraduate qualifications from universities elsewhere. They came to our Institute to do a 1-year, full-time program of training in both teaching methodologies and professional studies in education. Several of them had short-term work experiences as social workers or teaching assistants. All participants had taken one or more of the modules we taught in the first semester of the year. They joined our project on a voluntary basis.

Data Sources

The data was mainly collected in three ways: meeting records, project-end evaluations, and follow-up interviews.

Meeting records. A research assistant came to the weekly meeting as an observer. He kept notes and prepared summaries of the key contents of the stories. These notes provided a documentation of the stories we shared and the progress of the meetings.

Project-end evaluation. A short, open-ended questionnaire was filled out by each participant at the end of the final meeting to collect individual feedback. The questionnaire focused on their experience in telling stories and listening to other people's stories and the influences, if any, of the meetings to their professional learning.

Follow-up interviews. Interviews with eight of the student teachers were conducted to gather more in-depth personal experiences on the weekly meetings. Those who had attended more than 70% of our meetings were selected for the follow-up interviews. Apart from their experiences of being a story teller and a listener, their further reflection after the meetings were explored. These interviews were conducted by researchers and the research assistant during the summer months before they started teaching as qualified teachers.

The methodological significance of this inquiry project lies in its attempt to broaden the research tradition in Hong Kong from a mostly formal and positivistic orientation to one which acknowledges and values the narrative knowledge of people. We hope to achieve this by burrowing into the stories of the facilitators and the participants. With enlightened understanding of our experiences, we can re-story our personal and professional lives so as to "imagine and live new stories of practice rather than just unconsciously teach as [we] believe [we] were taught" (Olson, 2000, p. 125).

STUDENT TEACHERS' STORIES

As reflected in the stories our participants shared, the most pressing concerns of this group of student teachers included: teacher-student relationship, collegiality, development of student subculture, and classroom

Table 18.2. Samuel's Story: Student Smokers

I was invited by a group of students to lunch. After lunch, we went to a park near the school. As soon as we sat down on the bench, my teenage students started to smoke. They smoked heavily and chatted loudly. From time to time, they spoke to each other in foul language.
I reminded my students, "Hey! Behave properly. You are in school uniform."
"So what?" my students responded.
I was not offended as I did not consider myself old-fashioned. I had spent so much time trying to get closer to these kids. I had sacrificed all the spare time I had, and I really wanted to influence them. Having gained their trust, they came to invite me to their smokers' party. One of them told me that they had smoked less just because I was there, as a way of showing respect for me.
On one hand, I was glad to be invited. But on the other hand, I felt uneasy. I did not want to be seen in my role as a teacher chatting to a group of young students who were smoking in a park near the school. There was a chance that somebody from the school would bump into us. What if I was caught by the principal? (Meeting record, April 29, 2005)

---

management issues, with the issue of the teacher-student relationship being the most challenging for them. From these concerns we were able to understand the kind of personal practical knowledge they held. Two stories, "Samuel's Story: Student Smokers" (see Table 18.2) and "Catherine's Story: I Hate Being Called by My Full Name" (see Table 18.3), told by student teachers and the feedback participants gave, show how story telling and sharing could enhance understanding of the student teachers' problems, and its potentials of unpacking their personal practical knowledge.

In Samuel's story, we saw the dilemma a young teacher had in handling student-teacher relationship. When this story was told in one of the meetings, it stirred up vigorous discussion among the participants. There were diverse views. Some peers began to respond by telling their own stories of smoking and shared their experiences as smokers. Some found these behaviors to be absolutely unacceptable and suggested strict disciplinary punishments. Some held more lenient views and took a more empathetic stance with the students.

As the discussion continued, the group began to understand that their values and perceptions on smoking hinged on their personal experiences. Their responses to student smoking as in Samuel's story and the conflicts they might experience in similar situations provided good inroads into understanding the personal practical knowledge they held.

As can be seen in Samuel's case, he was faced with two conflicting principles in his personal practical knowledge in dealing with teacher-student relationship. Above all, he wanted to be as friendly as possible with his students. Yet at the same time, he was challenged by his moral standards

Table 18.3. Catherine's Story: I Hate Being Called by My Full Name

Something happened today when I was leaving the school and made me very upset.

There were three girls by the school gate when I was walking past it. They smiled in a very unfriendly way. I noticed that I taught one of them.

I nodded and walked down the slope to the entrance of the school. Before I reached the bottom of the slope, I heard someone call my full name[2] very loudly behind me. I turned and saw the three girls laughing mischievously.

I was furious and told them off.

They called my full name again, loudly.

I was embarrassed and I could not forgive them. I was a teacher and they were just students. How dare they! (Meeting record, May 6, 2005)

---

on smoking and his perceived role as a teacher to monitor and stop the inappropriate behavior of his students. When he was chatting with a group of student smokers near the school, he was at a crossroads and had to decide whether he should stop the students from smoking or maintain the positive relationship. Facing these difficult situations, novice teachers hoped to get an easy answer to the question—"what should I do?"—from their instructors. However, as the group discussion went on, they began to understand that there were no hard and fast rules to make decisions. They discovered that the decisions they made could only come forth when they had adequate knowledge of their own values, their personal experiences, and the contexts of their particular schools and students. This knowledge did not come from books or lectures but from the experience they gained from the particular stories they reflected on. "Catherine's Story" also showed how the process of story telling and sharing could change the way we pose our problems.

This was another story that was referred to many times by other participants in our follow-up interviews. This has reflected how much it impressed the peers. On the day that Catherine shared her story, some of us stayed behind wanting to know why Catherine was so upset and tried to console her. Some of the student teachers even invited her outside our meeting time to chat and comfort her (follow-up Interview, June 14, 2005).

In response to our queries during the meeting, Catherine said she felt that she had not been respected. She felt hurt. Catherine's story revealed the emotions involved in her personal practical knowledge. No matter how hard we tried to comfort her that her students might not be challenging her status, Catherine was still very upset and appeared to be more disturbed when our support group did not seem to stand on her side. In Catherine's own perception and moral standards, a teacher called by her full name was not respected. She was conscious of her image as a respected teacher and she held her own standard of appropriate behaviors between teachers and students. What she was not aware of at that time was that her students, and other fellow teachers as well, might hold different standards towards the same behaviors. When her students called her by her full name, she automatically saw it to be a lack of respect.

It can be seen from the stories above that when Samuel and Catherine faced problematic situations in teacher-student relationship, they could find no immediate solutions from the theoretical knowledge they gathered from the books and lectures. Instead, they drew from their own experiences as schoolchildren. Samuel was caught in the dilemma of wanting to be a friendly teacher but at the same time was challenged by his moral standard. In Catherine's case, she perceived the situation from what she believed about being a respected teacher. When she was called by her full name, she could not tolerate such behavior because her personal practical knowledge told her that she was not respected. Through the purposeful story-telling activities, the student teachers began to reflect upon and examined their experiences in a different light, providing a broader platform to think about and deal with similar situations in the future (follow-up interviews: June 20, 2005; July 12, 2005; August 23, 2005; August 29, 2005).

REFLECTION ON THE PROJECT

Feedback on the story-telling sessions was gathered from both the project-end evaluations and follow-up interviews. The participants found values in both telling their stories and sharing other people's stories: they learned to be more reflective from telling stories and gained insights by listening to other people's stories.

One major effect brought by our support group as reflected by several student teachers was the questions that the three of us, as facilitators, asked at critical points when their stories were told. In the example of Catherine's case, we asked her why she was so upset. This question encouraged Catherine to look inward to her own values and experiences as a student. This question stimulated many more questions that are related to other aspects of the story: for example, where was Catherine from? How was she brought up? What kind of family background did she have? What kind of school did she attend? All these questions helped Catherine explore how she became who she was and why she reacted in the way she did.

Most of them particularly enjoyed listening to other people's stories since they were at different schools during their teaching practice. Listening to other people's problems gave them a supportive feeling that they do not face the challenges alone (follow-up interviews: June 20, 2005; July 12, 2005; August 23, 2005). In several students' responses, they said that they felt like being reenergized in the meetings for the challenges they faced in the school the next week. They saw that the stories their peers told were authentic situations in the current school landscapes in Hong Kong. The value of such sharing lies in the specific context of the experiences, something that could not be found in books.

The rapport established among the group was regarded as valuable by most of the participants. Some student teachers compared our meetings to the friendly and trustworthy feeling they had in attending religious gatherings. Some of them described the discussion platform we created as the place where they could obtain fuel to revitalize their passion for teaching.

By telling stories, we successfully encouraged student teachers to explore their personal practical knowledge. This was revealed in the discussion of Samuel and Catherine's stories. However, the discussions were not vigorous enough and thus hampered the process of burrowing into the meanings embedded in the stories. The major impediment and challenge of this study was the limitation of time.

In our study, we hope to make use of story telling and sharing to unpack the experience of student teachers and to discover some aspects of the personal practical knowledge held by these young teachers. However, we achieved only partial success in this aspect. Much more time and effort and reflection are needed in this path of personal and professional development. The continuation of Lau's story illustrates this point (see Table 18.4).

Lau's reflection did not come forth in hours or days or weeks. His story was retold and reflected upon a long time after the episode—when he was working on his thesis. He added the following note to illustrate how one's experiences, though small or insignificant at the time, could find its meaning and its way of surfacing later.

> I would usually retell this story to my student teachers when I was teaching modules like "classroom management" or "teacher-pupil relationship" in my teacher training courses. But now I have discovered a deeper meaning in this story: it is a story of a young teacher who did not know how to express his emotions and regulate his actions properly. This story has its beginning in the boyhood of the teacher, or even before he was born. (Lau, 2004)

As Connelly and Clandinin (1995) argued, "If one remembered something with passion, then it was important to one's education though one might not know the reasons why. If something affected one profoundly, it was of educational importance." Schön (1983) also described the practice of the practitioner as a process that allowed him to experience surprise, puzzlement, or confusion in uncertain or unique situations. In other

Table 18.3. Lau's Story Continues

Like many traditional Chinese families, the family atmosphere in my childhood was determined by the eldest man in the family—my grandfather. He was a tall and stern man. As far as I could remember, he seldom talked or played with us. Many years later, my mother told me that when we were young, we could play at home only when our grandfather was out. When he came back, everyone in the family had to go back to "normal" as quickly as possible—silence. He seldom talked at the dinner table, and we were not allowed to talk. We had learned this saying since we were very young: "Do not talk over dinner. Do not talk when going to bed." Bedtime stories were obviously out of the question.

Growing up in this family, I became a quiet and shy boy with great self-restraint, hiding feelings within myself. I did not know how to express my emotions and I was tactless in initiating or responding to social interactions. I had not learned these social skills when I was small but did not find any problem with it since everybody in the family seemed to behave in the same way. My sister and brothers did not talk much either. Or maybe I was too young to join them when they talked or played with each other. I don't know.

I remembered one day when I was 4 or 5 years old, a little boy in my neighborhood annoyed me (maybe he just wanted to play with me) by standing next to me and repeatedly calling my name, hitting me lightly in my stomach again and again. I did not know how to react until I could no longer hold my temper: I punched him hard in his stomach. He cried and ran away. This incident found its reverberation 20 years later in my classroom (Lau, 2004).

---

words, the essence of this process of professional development is the discovery of meanings. This process is important because it assists us to gain deeper self-understanding.

When we started our project, we had two aims. First, we wanted to provide some support to our student teachers during teaching practice, which could be a very frustrating time for inexperienced teachers. Second, we wanted to use story telling as a vehicle for narrative inquiry, to help the student teachers reflect on and explore their experiences. We argue that teacher knowledge comes from making sense of and learning from experiences. It is a process of integrating theory and practice in action in a conscious way.

Our study provided us with opportunities to look into one's experiences as an essential process in teacher development. In telling stories, student teachers posed unsolved puzzles from their teaching practice. We did not expect solutions to be found immediately from telling stories, but the telling process served to provide the story tellers with insights into different possibilities as to how they can go about solving their problems. Catherine's story is a good example as it has aroused discussion and stimulated reflection among participants although we have not yet succeeded in helping Catherine crack her personal experience. We understand that this process of self understanding takes time—much longer time than we could allow in our project.

We hope that, in the future, the story telling could be broadened and burrowed into deeper understandings through guidance from more experienced narrative inquirers. Providing student teachers with more guidance on how to make meaning from their storied experience is the next step in our future inquiry.

THE CHALLENGES

In this chapter, we presented our initial attempt at introducing a narrative mode of teacher education, and the tensions we experienced in the process. In this section, we reflect on the implications of this study. There are several tensions we experienced in promoting personal practical knowledge as an essential element for teacher education in Hong Kong. We hope these implications will shed light for other narrative inquirers who share similar interests.

Tensions of new Practices Bumping Against the Traditions

From our experience as teacher educators in Hong Kong, a narrative approach to teacher development might not be easily accepted in the formal teacher education curriculum in the near future. From our experiences in arguing for a space for narratives in the formal teacher education curriculum, we found ourselves bumping into boundaries (Connelly & Clandinin, 1995) or edges (Elbaz, 1997). In this particular study, the boundary could be between teacher's knowledge and knowledge for teachers. We, as teacher educators, however, have learned about the potential and practical constraints of such an approach in the preparation of teachers. This has presented us with a new possibility in educating our teachers.

Moreover, in the local context of teacher education, our student teachers were not the only ones who were not familiar with the narrative approach. As teacher educators ourselves, we are still puzzling how this could be fitted into our teacher education curriculum. Our experience in running a kind of support group could be seen as a small experiment in the initial stage of integrating narrative inquiry into the current curriculum of local teacher education in Hong Kong.

Tensions of Cultural Difference in Deep Rooted Beliefs

From the review we made about the prevailing understanding of teacher knowledge in the local field, we experienced cultural tensions when deeply held beliefs, such as those from the knowledge for teacher tradition, are challenged by the introduction of teachers' personal practical knowledge. We realize that the introduction of the notion of personal practical knowledge is an uphill process similar to what Schön (1987) experienced in the professional landscape in North America when he started to promote his ideas about educating students to be reflective practitioners in the 1980s. From our research, we understood the importance of helping our teachers to become aware of the personal practical knowledge they held. We learned from Schön's passion that "we must work against the doctrine that teachers are to be taught the results carried out by researchers which accounts for a widespread sense of irrelevancy of courses in faculties of education" (Schön, 1987). We see this as a difficult, but definitely not impossible, challenge.

Tensions of Learning Alongside with Participants in Making Sense of Storied Experiences

From this study, we see that student teachers already possess and employ their own personal practical knowledge in their teaching practice. Telling their stories from teaching practice can help them to reflect on and refine this knowledge. Our study has enabled us to explore the personal practical knowledge being held by participants from the stories they shared. However, from our observations and their feedback, we found that not many of the participants were adequately aware of the influence of personal practical knowledge on their practice. Very often, in telling the critical incidents, they failed to see that some incidents were perceived as "problems" due to their personal practical knowledge. As we see in Catherine's case, the incident might not be considered problematic if it was viewed from other perspectives.

We are not satisfied with students loosely sharing their experiences. We want to help them to reflect upon their experiences and through this reflection, gain further understanding of themselves and thus grow from accumulating experiences. A further step is needed to unpack and burrow into the stories told. In this study, however, we were learning alongside with our student teachers about how such unpacking could be done.

CONCLUDING REMARKS

In the current educational reform in Hong Kong and elsewhere, the call for lifelong learning and all-round development necessitates a different kind of teaching which is far more demanding than transmitting factual knowledge to the students (Education Commission, 2000). In this context, we advocate that it is not enough to rely on theoretical knowledge alone in expecting our teachers to accomplish the curricular changes in the reform. We consider that personal practical knowledge should have a more significant role in teacher preparation. Our study could be seen as a practical exploration in this direction and a contribution to the understanding of the struggles and the possible solutions in teacher education issues around the globe.

ACKNOWLEDGMENTS

We acknowledge the trust of our students in sharing their stories with us in the study. This work is supported by the Research Grant Council through the Hong Kong Institute of Education's Internal Research Grant.

NOTES

1. In winter, 2003, the Hong Kong Educational Research Association published a special issue on "Narratives of Teaching and Learning in the Time of SARS" in one of its major journals. This is possibly the first time narrative approach has received wider attention in the local education field (D. W. Chan, 2003).
2. In Chinese culture, students usually greet their teachers by giving their surnames a title, such as Mr., Mrs., or Miss. Seldom do students call teachers by their full names. This is considered very rude and impolite.

REFERENCES

Ayers, William. (2001). *To teach: The journey of a teacher.* New York: Teachers College Press.
Bolton, Gillie. (2006). Narrative writing: Reflective enquiry into professional practice. *Educational Action Research, 14*(2), 203-218.
Borg, Michaela. (2004). The apprenticeship of observation. *ELT Journal, 58*(3), 274-276.
Buchmann, Margaret. (1987). Teaching knowledge: The lights that teachers live by. *Oxford Review of Education, 13*(2), 151-164.
Carger, Chris Liska. (1996). *Of borders and dreams: A Mexican-American experience of urban education.* New York: Teachers College Press.
Chan, David Wai-ock. (Ed.). (2003). Special issue: Narratives of teaching and learning in the time of SARS. *Educational Research Journal, 18*(2). Hong Kong: Hong Kong Educational Research Association.
Chan, David Wai-ock. (2004). Narrative means to educational ends: Introducing the narrative approach to Hong Kong schools. *Educational Research Journal, 19*(1). Hong Kong: Hong Kong Educational Research Association.

Chan, Nai-kwok. (2004). *Crossing the border: Identity and education—A narrative self study.* Unpublished doctoral dissertation, University of Toronto.

Chiu-Ching, Rosa Tak-Lan. (2005). *Teachers who make a difference: A narrative inquiry into three teachers' professional journeys into special education and their conception of special education in Hong Kong.* Unpublished doctoral dissertation, University of Toronto.

Clandinin, D. Jean. (1985). Personal practical knowledge: A study of teachers' classroom images. *Studies in education.* Ontario, Canada: John Wiley & Sons.

Clandinin, D. Jean. (1986). *Classroom practice: Teacher images in action.* London: Farmer Press.

Clandinin, D. Jean, Annie Davies, Pat Hogan, & Barbara Kennard. (Eds.). (1993). *Learning to teach, teaching to learn: Stories of collaboration in teacher education.* New York: Teachers College Press.

Clandinin, D. Jean, & F. Michael Connelly. (2000). *Narrative inquiry: Experience and story in qualitative research.* San Francisco: Jossey-Bass.

Cochran-Smith, Marilyn, & Susan Lytle. (1999). Relationships of knowledge and practice: Teacher learning in community. *Review of Research in Education, 24,* 249-305.

Cole, Ardra L., & J. Gary Knowles. (2000). *Researching teaching: Exploring teacher development through reflexive inquiry.* New York: Allyn & Bacon.

Conle, Carola. (2000). Narrative inquiry: Research tool and medium for professional development. *European Journal of Teacher Education, 23*(1), 49-63.

Conle, Carola. (2003). An anatomy of narrative curricula. *Educational Research, 32*(3), 3-15.

Connelly, F. Michael, & D. Jean Clandinin. (1988). *Teachers as curriculum planners: Narratives of experience.* New York: Teachers College Press.

Connelly, F. Michael, & D. Jean Clandinin. (1990). Stories of experience and narrative inquiry. *Educational Researcher, 19*(5), 2-14.

Connelly, F. Michael, & D. Jean Clandinin. (1995). Narrative and education. *Teachers and Teaching: Theory and Practice, 1*(1), 73-86.

Connelly, F. Michael, & D. Jean Clandinin. (2000a). Narrative understandings of teacher knowledge. *Journal of Curriculum and Supervision, 15*(4), 315-31.

Connelly, F. Michael, & D. Jean Clandinin. (2000b). *Teacher education: A question of teacher knowledge.* In John Freeman-Moir & Alan Scott (Eds.), *Tomorrow's teachers: International and critical perspectives on teacher education.* Christchurch, New Zealand: Canterbury University Press.

Education Commission. (2000). *Learning for life, learning through life: Reform proposals for the education system in Hong Kong.* Hong Kong: Author.

Elbaz, Freema. (1981). The teacher's *practical knowledge*: Report of a case study. *Curriculum Inquiry, 11,* 43-71.

Elbaz, Freema. (1983). *Teacher thinking: A study of practical knowledge.* London: Croom Helm.

Elbaz, Freema. (1997). Narrative research: Political issues and implications. *Teaching and Teacher Education, 13,* 75-83.

Eng, Betty C. (2005). *Exploring teacher knowledge through personal narratives: Experiences of identity, culture and sense of belonging.* Unpublished doctoral dissertation, University of Toronto.

Fenstermacher, Gary D. (1994). *The knower and the known: The nature of knowledge in research on teaching*. In Linda Darling-Hammond (Ed.), *Review of research in education* (Vol. 20, pp. 3-56). Washington, DC: American Educational Research Association.

Grossman, Pamela L. (1990). *The making of a teacher: Teacher knowledge and teacher education*. New York: Teachers College Press.

Johnson, LouAnne. (1995). *Dangerous minds*. New York: St. Martin's Press.

Lam, Tak-sing. (2005). Teachers' narratives: Teacher professional development and school development. In King-fai Hui & Wai-sing Li (Eds.), *Teacher leaders and professional development* [in Chinese]. Hong Kong: Infolink.

Lau, Chun-kwok. (1998). *Emotional development and multiple intelligences: A rediscovery of my own stories*. Unpublished manuscript.

Lau, Chun-kwok (2004). *Moving back and forth between Hong Kong and Toronto: A narrative inquiry into a family's cultural and educational experiences*. Unpublished doctoral dissertation, University of Toronto.

Li, Wai-sing. (2002). *Understanding lived experience and professional development: The life history of a Chinese migrant teacher*. Doctoral dissertation, University of Nottingham.

Lortie, Dan C. (1975). *Schoolteacher: A sociological study*. Chicago: University of Chicago Press.

Lyons, Nona, & Vicki Kubler LaBoske.y (Eds.). (2002). *Narrative inquiry in practice: Advancing the knowledge of teaching*. New York: Teachers College Press.

Miller, Paul Chamness. (Ed.). (2005). *Narratives from the classroom: An introduction to teaching*. Thousand Oaks, CA: SAGE.

Olson, Margaret R. (2000). Linking personal and professional knowledge of teaching practice through narrative inquiry. *Teacher Educator, 35*(4), 109-127.

Paley, Vivian Gussin. (1989). *White teacher*. Cambridge, MA: Harvard University Press.

Phillion, JoAnn, Ming Fang He, & F. Michael Connelly (Eds.). (2005). *Narrative and experience in multicultural education*. Boston: SAGE.

Richards, J. C., & M. C. Pennington. (1998). The first year of teaching. In J. C. Richards (Ed.), *Beyond training*. Cambridge, England: Cambridge University Press.

Rodriguez, Richard. (1983). *Hunger of memory: The education of Richard Rodriguez*. New York: Bantom Books.

Schön, Donald A. (1983). *The reflective practitioner: How professionals think in action*. New York: Basic Books.

Schön, Donald A. (1987). *Educating the reflective practitioner*. Paper presented at the annual meeting of the American Educational Research Association, Washington, DC.

Schwab, Joseph Jackson. (1962). *The teaching of science as enquiry*. Cambridge, MA: Harvard University Press.

Schwab, Joseph Jackson. (1969). The practical: A language for curriculum. *School Review, 78*(1), 1-23.

Schwab, Joseph Jackson. (1971). The practical: Arts of eclectic. *School Review, 79*(4), 493-542.

Schwab, Joseph Jackson. (1973). The practical 3: Translation into curriculum. *School Review, 81*(4), 501-522.

Sharples, Donald K. (2002). *Advanced educational foundations for teachers: The history, philosophy and culture of schooling.* New York: Routledge Falmer.

Tomlinson, P. (1999). Conscious reflection and implicit learning in teacher preparation. Part II: Implications for a balanced approach. *Oxford Review of Education, 25*(4), 533-544.

CHAPTER 19

PROMISE AND PERILS OF STUDY ABROAD

White Privilege Revival

JoAnn Phillion, Erik Malewski, Eloisa Rodriguez, Valerie Shirley, Hollie Kulago, and Jeff Bulington

Universities in the United States and elsewhere are offering study abroad programs for students in order to meet the requirement that graduates have an international perspective in their discipline. Teacher education students are increasingly provided with study abroad opportunities to receive credit for course work and field experiences. The promise of the programs lies in the belief that as students experience a diverse environment and a language other than English and work with students unlike themselves, they will be better prepared to work with historically underserved students in the future. The Esperanza School (pseudonym) has been the setting for this Midwestern university's Honduran study abroad program for 5 years. Predeparture orientations are offered, followed by immersion in a field experience in the school and visits to rural schools and cultural sites, in addition to course meetings, readings, and assignments. Research has been conducted on the program for 4 years. A case

Growing a Soul for Social Change: Building the Knowledge Base for Social Justice
pp. 365–382
Copyright © 2008 by Information Age Publishing
All rights of reproduction in any form reserved.

study approach was used to examine preservice teachers' perceptions of the program and its implications for their self-conceptions as future teachers. The results indicate that preservice teachers collectively view the program as an opportunity to grow academically and socially. The research also demonstrated potential perils of the program as participants' feelings of White privilege were reinforced rather than questioned. This reinforcement was revealed in the emergent themes found: *comfort zones, externalizing poverty out of the United States,* and *blessedness.*

INTRODUCTION

Study abroad is a key component of U.S. universities' efforts to both create and solidify their commitments to international education, and to prepare graduates who have a global perspective in their disciplines (Dolby, 2007; Open Doors, 2003). According to Engle and Engle (2005), the goal of all education, particularly education abroad, should be to encourage a more complex view of the self and the world. Colleges of education are developing study abroad programs with these general goals in mind and more specific goals related to concerns in how to prepare preservice teachers for classrooms of the present and future. A key concern for teacher educators is how to prepare predominantly White preservice teachers for the increasingly diverse cultural, ethnic, and socioeconomic student populations (Sleeter, 2001b). Another concern is how to raise preservice teachers' awareness that education takes place in a global context and that social justice issues are played out on a world stage (see Bigelow & Peterson, 2002). In a review of research on the epistemological foundations of various forms of research and findings related to how to prepare White preservice teachers to work with historically underserved populations of students, Sleeter (2001a) noted that field experiences in diverse settings, including study abroad field experiences, demonstrate promise in meeting these goals. Completing field experiences through study abroad programs offers preservice teachers opportunities to venture beyond their own particular culture by involving them in cross-cultural experiential learning encounters that have the potential to broaden their horizons in ways that could never be achieved on their college campus or their home town environments (Mahan & Stachowski, 1990; Mahon & Cushner, 2002).

In this chapter we discuss these potential promises and what we term the potential *perils* of study abroad programs focused on offering preservice teachers field experiences in cross cultural settings. While the promise of these programs is well documented in the literature (Kitsantas, 2004) and while there is an ever-increasing proliferation of programs and undergraduate students who seek these experiences (Kinzie, 2006; Open Doors 2003), little work has been done to examine students' experiences with these programs through the lenses of race, identity, and representation, and none to date that we could locate that address White privilege in particular. Rather, the primary focus has been on language acquisition, program duration, career goals, oral communication skills, and citizenship competences, with less attention to issues of multiculturalism and how students' perceptions of race, identity, and representation are impacted by study abroad experiences. Accordingly, in this chapter we address preservice teachers' understanding of who they are in relation to those they encounter in the Honduran study abroad program.

In response to a university-wide mandate to create more globally aware graduates with a deeper understanding of international issues, a Midwestern university's college of education has developed a study abroad program to facilitate students' interaction in multicultural environments with the broad goals that they develop the ability to work with diverse students and the ability to recognize the implications of social justice issues for teaching. The program has been in place for five years and will continue in the future; to date, 37 undergraduates and seven graduate students, mostly White females, have completed the 5-week program. We have engaged in research on the program for 4 years; in general we have examined what happens to our participants in a study abroad experience in a developing country, Honduras. In particular, we have looked at the effects of this short-term study abroad program on White preservice teachers' awareness of White privilege. Due to the economic and cultural realities that participants encountered in Honduras, specific themes emerged. To some extent, these undermine the program's intention and limit the impact of the experience in terms of an opportunity for a deeper realization of White privilege—the unacknowledged capital accrued by virtue of being White (McIntosh, 1990). There is a well documented tendency of White preservice teachers toward resistance to recognizing White privilege (Horton & Scott, 2004; Sleeter, 2001b; Solomona, Portelli, Daniel, & Campbell, 2005), and in an experience like this, where local communities perceive the participants as holders of power and knowledge, notions of White privilege are reinforced. This reinforcement of White privilege, for us, is of concern, and is a peril of such programs currently undocumented in the literature.

Malewski (2006) suggests that reinforcement of White privilege originates in subjugation where "identities are not tied to legacies of symbolic and material inequities" but "a sense of self and community severed from history ... linked to a dreamt up past" (p. 322). We found in interviews with preservice teachers that they held a decontextualized sense of self and the world and were resistant to notions of both White privilege and a racialized past that is also classed, gendered, and sexed. They tended to view themselves as originators of their own identities and fully in control of their positions in the world, positions shaped less by social forces than the capacity to make wise decisions ("I stayed focused on my goals"). Even as we encouraged them to engage in critical consciousness raising examinations of the links between ignorance, knowledge, and their own sense of who they were given their experiences studying in another country, they focused on comfort zones, externalizing poverty out of the United States, and blessedness in interviews. Regardless of our intentions, the resurgence of White privilege was particularly prevalent in follow up interviews once we returned to the United States as students focused primarily on their own development and what they were able to take from the program.

The majority of participants in the program agreed to participate in our research efforts. Although the experiences of many preservice teachers might be used to explore issues raised in this chapter, the perceptions of two participants serve as examples. Both preservice teachers are White, female, middle to upper class students who have completed their first year at the university.

PROGRAM DESCRIPTION

The Honduras study abroad program takes place during the summer semester which allows the preservice students to be immersed in the setting for 3 weeks. In the 2 weeks prior to departure, students partake in two course meetings where expectations are reviewed; lessons are given on the historical, political, and economic dimensions of Honduras; and a series of logistical concerns are addressed. While the program has multiple goals, the primary aim is to develop students' understanding of diversity and social justice issues. This focus is of paramount importance to a teacher education program located in a predominately White and rural area, such as ours; study abroad provides an opportunity to prepare preservice teachers to work in diverse settings not readily available in our local public schools. Beginning preservice teachers' who participate in the program enroll in two courses: exploring teaching as a career and multicultural education. These two courses, along with a shared field experience, fulfill the requirements for completing block I, the first semester in the teacher education program.

The setting for the program is the Esperanza School located in a small town in Honduras. It consists of nursery through sixth grades. Students who attend this school primarily come from rural areas; some are bused in from Tegucigalpa, the capital city. Students experience a bilingual education (essentially English immersion after the first 2 years) and are provided with resources to fulfill their academic goals. Forty percent of the student population is on scholarship funded by donations from international organizations and private donors; the remainder pays fees on a sliding scale. The school's personnel consist of Honduran and U.S. teachers.

In an effort to expose the preservice teachers to the Honduran culture and educational system, the college of education faculty encouraged the students to immerse themselves in the school environment, to work closely with teachers and students, and to interact with parents and other community members. After initial observations of each classroom, they identify which grade level they want to be placed in for the remainder of the program. Once they have made their choice, they act as a teacher assistant in the classroom and have the opportunity to work closely with teachers and students. During their time in the school, the preservice teachers are introduced to the Honduran educational system, teaching methodologies and school and classroom activities, and become involved in planning sessions and teacher development workshops. In addition to their work in the school, in evening course meetings the preservice teachers are expected to read and discuss assigned texts related to multicultural issues and second-language learners. These texts are intended to promote discussions about the field experience and to help develop an understanding of race, class, gender, and bilingual/second language education. As part of the preservice teachers' coursework, they are also required to complete written assignments consisting of daily reflective journals, an autobiographical narrative, an educational philosophy paper, and a school-teacher portrait that together offer a montage of their experiences in the Honduras study abroad program. On weekends, students visit local historical sites; they also travel to the nearby city of Copan where they explore Mayan archeological sites. They write reflections on these visits as well. At the end of the study abroad experience, they compile all the material, as well as digital photographs, and prepare electronic portfolios that house the artifacts from their block I experiences.

While goals of developing understanding of diverse students and social justice issues permeate the overall philosophy of the program and while discussion of these issues is promoted, most preservice teachers tend to write about themselves and their personal feelings, and focus on their personal comfort or discomfort in specific situations. Some students also engage in social justice oriented activities; however, the deep causes of social problems, particularly poverty, are seldom discussed. For example, over the years, preservice teachers have raised funds for impoverished local schools; one group raised funds to sponsor a child in the Esperanza School. This aspect of the program, for us, is part of the promise of study abroad in what is termed a *developing country*, as preservice teachers begin to recognize public education is inherently concerned with issues of social justice. Ironically, it is also part of the peril as they see themselves as the benefactors of poor children. Yet, even with the probing reflective questions embedded in the curriculum, preservice teachers are largely unable, and possibly unwilling, to examine personal and national culpability for and complicity with the structures and practices that maintain the contemporary political, economic, and social conditions in Honduras.

In addition to the field experience in Esperanza School and the structured academic activities, preservice teachers also visit two rural schools in the area and an orphanage in which Esperanza school teachers do volunteer work. The orphanage is for boys only; most of the children have been found on the streets of the capital city and brought to live there. The public schools are situated in impoverished communities where there is an apparent lack of resources. While nearly all the students who attend these schools speak exclusively Spanish, only 20% of our preservice teachers have basic Spanish speaking abilities and therefore there were few opportunities for dialogue between preservice teachers and students. Instead, they engaged students in art projects, taught songs in English, and participated in other activities that do not require fluency in Spanish. The intention of the visits is to provide a contrast between a school with substantial resources by Honduran standards, the Esperanza School, and a more *typical* public school that has few resources, including basic necessities the preservice teachers take for granted, such as running water, bathrooms, electricity, books, paper, and so on. The aim of these visits is, again, to draw links between poverty in a developing country and what is happening around the world with global interdependence. The goal, as is demonstrated in remaining sections of this analysis, is seldom achieved.

METHODOLOGY

As a research group, we feel it necessary to explain who *we* are. We are a diverse group of two professors and four graduate students from a large Midwestern university. We are made up of one Honduran female, two Native American females, one White female, and two White males. During the summer semester we focus on in this chapter, the two faculty members codirected the program, along with support from a Honduran graduate student who served in the role of program coordinator. Each of us has our own varying knowledge and interests in teacher education, multicultural education, social justice, and study abroad programs and, more specifically, the Honduras study abroad program. We believe that these varying aspects that constitute who we are, and the various perspectives we bring to this issue, are what makes our analysis useful and multi-layered. We view this diversity as a strength.

For the purpose of this chapter, we discuss two individuals as case studies in order to illustrate problematic outcomes, what we term the perils of a study abroad program. The generalizations that we make are generalizations that regularly occur all along the way (Stake, 1995, p. 7) and therefore constitute a pattern in the data. The program we discuss has been classified by Engle and Engle (2005) as a level two short-term study abroad program. Specifically, this includes programs that last three to eight weeks, provide an orientation session that addresses cultural customs and guidelines for interaction, and offer limited opportunities for experiential learning and critical interactions due to time constraints (p. 11).

As a form of data collection, we interviewed the preservice teachers in focus groups during the study abroad experience and then individually twice after they returned to the United States. All interviews were transcribed by an outside transcriber and coded for developing themes. Transcripts were not returned to interviewees; they were reviewed for accuracy by the interviewers who listened to tapes and edited the transcripts. The responses used in this study came from typical preservice teachers—White, females from homogenous communities (Cushner & Mahon, 2002). We started the initial individual interviews with seven participants who had completed the study abroad program the prior year. There were six females and one male, all of whom were White. Interview questions were similar to those used by Cushner and Mahon:

1. What specific circumstances from your [Honduras] experience influence you today?
2. What have you learned about yourself as a result of your [Honduras] student teaching experience?
3. What did you learn about others as a result of your [Honduras] experience?
4. In what ways are you different from those teachers who did not have [a Honduras] experience?
5. What aspects of your international experience do you think other teacher education students could learn from?

Prominent themes that emerged from the initial individual interviews were used to generate a second round of individual interview questions specific to each participant. Together with the two individual interviews, we reviewed and analyzed the journals and other assignments the students wrote while in Honduras and reread focus group transcripts of interviews done on site. In this way the second interviews were used as a type of "member check" (Lincoln & Guba, 1985) in which we asked the students to comment on the themes we had discovered in the first interviews.

We identified four students who we thought were different from each other based on their different experiences and personalities. What we found interesting from interviews with our four participants was that two of them had almost the same responses to the interview questions. These students claimed that they were changed by the experience. We decided that this shift in our focus would benefit the Honduras study abroad program in terms of identifying real-life significant experiences that affected the participants in their everyday experiences abroad as they understood them.

The themes that emerged were what we termed comfort zones, externalizing poverty outside the United States, and blessedness. We then analyzed these themes through a lens of White privilege as defined by McIntosh (1990) to be "an invisible package of unearned assets ... like an invisible weightless knapsack of special provisions" (p. 31). Our discussion of the preservice teachers' responses through this lens focused mainly on the preservice teachers wanting to help others be more like them, and also the gratitude that the Honduran people expressed at the arrival of the group. This unearned capital is described as blessedness by several participants who comment on the privileges of being a U.S. American. These interrelated themes emerge through the two cases that we selected to illuminate the failure of preservice teachers to identify and name their White privilege and how this privilege shaped their experiences and outlooks in Honduras. We begin with Julie and then move on in a comparative fashion to Sophie's accounts [pseudonyms].

Julie

Julie is a shy, 19-year-old, White, elementary education student who grew up in a small, middle-class rural Midwestern community which she described as not having "a lot of diversity or anything." She directly linked her interest in study abroad to her desire to "experience something different" and increase her level of comfort "in an unfamiliar territory." Reflecting back on her experiences in the Honduras program, Julie portrayed them as having had a lasting positive impact on her self-confidence and her interest in exploring the world. In her eyes, the program "really made me step out of my comfort zone" and she reported that she felt transformed and empowered by the ways in which she had demonstrated her ability to thrive in a foreign environment.

In spite of her perceptions of having gotten out of her *comfort zone*, however, there were salient ways in which Julie's study abroad experience did not disrupt her perceptions (or lack thereof) of her privileged status as a White American. For instance, when it came to choosing between programs in Russia, South Africa, and Honduras, Julie's decision to go to Honduras was largely influenced by her father's sense of which location would offer her the most security.

> My dad thought Honduras sounded the safest of the three, because, you know, with all the terrorist things that have been going on lately [sic]. So I respected his choice and went to Honduras.

This approach to choosing a study abroad program suggests the parameters under which Julie was interested in stepping out of her comfort zone. Encountering the unfamiliar was acceptable; the potentially hostile was another matter. Just the same, Julie's encounters with unfamiliar living circumstances while in Honduras were both real and trying for her. When asked to recall how her time there had taken her out of her comfort zone, Julie focused on the various ways in which her everyday living routines were interrupted.

> Probably the biggest thing was the language barrier since I didn't speak any Spanish at all. That was definitely a challenge. And like I said, I've always been kind of a shy person, so like going on a trip with a bunch of people I didn't know, for three weeks ... being away from family. I'm a really family oriented-person. So, I mean, that was tough. Knowing that I wouldn't be able to call home or talk to my boyfriend for three weeks. That was hard. Oh, going to experience another culture when I really haven't traveled a whole lot. So, I mean there were just so many things that were out of the ordinary for me.

Julie's idea of exploring unfamiliar territory was limited. Perhaps this explains why, for instance, she subsequently showed little inclination to pursue critiques of privilege which were indicated in course readings, such as *Of Borders and Dreams* (Carger, 1996). Instead, Julie chose to focus on how her experiences abroad functioned to improve her self-esteem and awareness such that she could function in cross-cultural settings. In this sense, Julie, like the other participants, noted gains in personal development and expanded outlook on the world while failing to exhibit awareness of or the capacity to articulate a deeper understanding of the political, economic, or social structures that helped shape her experiences or the differences between Honduras and her country of origin. Accordingly, as she focused on her experience searching for self-understanding within a new setting, the identity she seemed to settle on was one of an altruist.

One particularly striking way in which Julie found comfort in Honduras involved her interactions with poor children at the rural schools, an orphanage, and the Esperanza School.

> I don't understand how children can learn in such an environment! They were all dripping with sweat, so there is no way that they could be completely focused on learning. I felt really bad for them, but I hope that we brought some cheerfulness to their day! We donated all of the leftover supplies to the school, so the teachers were excited as well! It feels so great to be able to help people and provide them with materials they desperately need. While I really enjoy my time spent at Esperanza School, I feel like these other schools need us more.

In her journals and in poststudy abroad interviews, Julie described experiences like these as "the highlight of our trip." Her journals, in particular, are interspersed with euphoric accounts of the thrill associated with receiving "the appreciation of the students and the teachers when this [giving gifts and teaching lessons] happens." From within the context of their poverty, Julie applied her religious conviction that "everybody serves a purpose and for some reason or other God wanted me to be where I am" to assert her spiritual identity as a steward of others. The children's combination of openly expressed gratitude with apparent helplessness aligned naturally with her senses of Christian caring and charity.

Rather than leading her to investigate—or even recognize—the sociopolitical circumstances which undergird such realities (and her own favored place within them), Julie's encounters with child poverty in Honduras became an opportunity to fashion a familiar position of privilege in a new context, that of a benevolent caretaker. Paradoxically, a rather profound opportunity to see oneself in an entirely new and potentially disturbing light, instead, became a routine point of reassurance. In short, Julie's religious perspective served as a release valve which allowed her to keep a handle on just how far she would stray from her comfort zone.

Even with this ideological buffer, however, Julie's more mundane struggles with daily living were wearying and she felt relief when her time in Honduras ended. When asked how she would have fared had the program lasted the entire summer, Julie expressed her doubts.

> You know 3 weeks I think is the perfect amount of time because I wasn't really missing my family too horribly. I think you should leave still wanting more. You know, leave when you're still having a lot of fun, still really into it so that you'll always remember the good things and the things you learned as opposed to, "Oh, I was so stressed out," "I was so sick," cause I was start-

ing to get a little queasy from the food. So, you know, it was the perfect amount of time, I think.

Having the experience end on a positive note was central to her sense of accomplishment, and the shorter duration of the program made that manageable for her. Her perception of having proved "that I can be thrown in a situation that's totally unfamiliar for me and survive" appears to have impacted Julie's sense of self. In terms of her status in her family, her participation in the program served as a rite of passage. When asked if her experiences had affected her father's concern for her safety, Julie reported that "my dad says I'm a lot more street smart now." Beyond that, her family has come to recognize and respect her continued commitment to doing philanthropic work.

> I think they realize how much this trip meant to me, and they see that I want to help people. So I think they'll support me no matter where I end up. They'll always worry about me, but that's what I want to do with my life.

These were big steps for Julie toward self-determination and stretching her domain somewhat beyond the control of family members.

Her time in Honduras became a defining moment for Julie, and it has led her to pursue similar experiences in the United States. Unlike several other program participants who seemed to think of "real poverty" as a "Third World problem," Julie recognized that "there are a lot of things we need to do in our own country, too." Although she appears to still be operating with the understanding that poverty is best (or perhaps only) addressed through some form of charitable gift-giving, Julie has extended the work she saw herself having begun in Honduras to her life now that she has returned to the United States.

> Well, it's made me want to do more to help out. I joined Habitat for Humanity this year so we go around and help build houses, and I'm really looking forward to being part of that and just helping around the United States. Like the hurricane in New Orleans, we're probably going to go down and help out with that.

In this light, we can say that Julie's encounter with poverty in Honduras struck a genuine chord with her and left her with the understanding that she has the power and inclination to do something about it with her life. However, this seems to have happened without her having developed an accompanying sense of the political dimensions of poverty's origins and her place of privilege within them.

Sophie

Sophie is a White, female, undergraduate, preservice teacher from a small, conservative, homogenous community in the Midwest. She reported that she did not plan to teach in the community she grew up in because "there was still racism there" and said she will teach in a "diverse suburban school in a small city." Sophie considered herself outgoing and "open to other cultures." She expressed her joy in traveling and always knew she wanted to study abroad in order "to gain new experiences that would be eye-opening."

Sophie expressed how her study abroad trip to Honduras had a lasting effect on her life. For instance, she stated that she "has an insight into the world" of a disabled child because she viewed her lack of speaking Spanish as a disability. In addition to the language barrier where she "felt very handicapped," she was also immersed in a different culture where the level of poverty had an immediate and profound impact on her; this led her to feel like she was taken out of her "comfort zone." Sophie expressed vehemently throughout the interview how "it was so hard" for her to witness the conditions in Honduras and that she "felt sorry for them" [Honduran students].

> How can they have like nothing, and survive on so little? Especially at the orphanage. That was my hardest day. I met this little boy and everyone went back but I couldn't go back because I cried so hard when I had to say goodbye to him. I was like, "he just has to be here by himself. Why isn't someone helping him?"

Sophie's dismay at the poverty in Honduras can be found in other responses as well. For example, in reference to a visit to a poor rural school, she described,

> They were so malnourished. Their necks were so skinny and it was so hot in the classroom. If I was a child, I know I can't concentrate when I'm hot or when I'm hungry. I can't imagine going to school on an empty stomach and then have to sit there and be hot and have flies flying around your head.

Similar to Julie's reaction to the level of poverty and lack of assistance, while she was troubled by what she saw in her new setting, Sophie found comfort in giving. In contrast to her feeling of helplessness, she brightened up when she spoke of how she and the other preservice teachers resembled Santa Claus.

> When we were down there we looked like Santa Claus when we went to this very small school. We came in with a suitcase and a big trash bag full of supplies and things for our art [project]. And they're clapping for us and they were so excited and knowing that they didn't have food and stuff, we donated money and brought them food.

A sense that she had contributed to the social good of Hondurans surfaced many times in Sophie's responses. She happily spoke of how the students clapped for her and the other preservice teachers as they handed out supplies.

This experience with altruism as a self-identity while in Honduras, similar to Julie's, moved Sophie to join such programs as the Big Brother/Big Sister Program and to help with food and clothing drives through her sorority once she returned to the United States. She left the study abroad program committed to the belief that once she had "financial stability" she would adopt "a child of a different culture."

Like Julie, Sophie used her experience in Honduras to rethink her everyday living practices once she returned home. She stated, "before I left [to Honduras], I just really took everything I had for granted." She also spoke of how she is "a more well-rounded person" now because of her experiences in Honduras. This changed sense of self and the contributions she had to make to the world in turn resulted in a noticeable change in the ways she interacted with peers, friends, and family. She proudly stated,

> When I came back [from Honduras], people were like, "Wow you're a little different." I [proudly said], "Thank you, thank you, thank you!"

Although, the small things that Americans take for granted are not always explicitly where study abroad programs set out to raise awareness—at such a personal level—Sophie claimed that this was where she was impacted the most. She frequently made general statements such as, "we should be grateful for everything." In one response, she elaborated, "We don't appreciate all the little things that we have. Comforts I guess. You know like Thanksgiving is coming up and I'm super excited because I always get to go see my family and have this huge meal. But a lot of places where there's poverty, they don't have a Thanksgiving." Upon further questioning in regards to who constituted the "we" in the previous quote, she stated that "society as a whole, takes things for granted, Americans" which—while it seemed to indicate that she believed that all Americans were as well off as she was—also suggested that she was more aware of the unearned symbolic and material advantages of many U.S. Americans.

Although Julie displayed *blessedness* by asserting her religious convictions, Sophie did not mention religion but spoke of privileges that go unrecognized. Both individuals discussed the importance of caring and charity within the context of poverty in Honduras. Sophie differentiated between degrees of poverty and described real poverty as a Third World problem. In a follow up response she further clarified her thoughts about the difference between poverty in the United States and Honduras, "We have a lot of poverty in our own country, and well, they [U.S. Americans] think they have it bad, but I really feel they [Hondurans] have it a lot worse." Although Sophie knew poverty existed in the United States, she explained that she had only viewed it at a distance and was uncertain what to make of it,

> Well I guess we do have a lot, especially with the hurricane victims and they're kind of just like forgotten about.... There are definitely more spots than that, I know that, but they're more widespread. [She lowered her voice and mumbled her words.] But in every major city, there's a lot of poverty. I didn't see much; there is poverty in like the town I grew up in, but I don't think it was as dramatic as in other places.

Like Julie, Sophie's perception developed without an understanding of the economic, political, and social relationship that shaped her own privilege and Honduran poverty. Instead of offering a critical analysis of structures and practices that maintain poverty, educational or otherwise, both concluded that poverty can be best addressed through charitable gift-giving and philanthropic work.

When asked if she would encourage others to study abroad in Honduras, she replied,

> I would definitely tell them to go because I wouldn't take back any of that. Just because I didn't have comfort on some days and I didn't like the food—the last 5 days I was miserably ill because I could not keep anything in me (laugh).... All of that I wouldn't take back because I got to meet new people and I got to go out and experience the night life like dancing and I love dancing. I was so excited that they took us out to salsa. And all of that I wouldn't take back. You can go to the mall and call home it's really cheap. I could've stayed there longer and gone to a few more schools and all that. A few weeks is like good for the program I think.

Sophie's exposure to living within a different culture and being outside her comfort zone challenged her thought processes by illuminating differences between privileged societies and underdeveloped countries, such as Honduras. Like Julie, Sophie's encounter with poverty left a lasting effect and triggered a strong emotional response that left her feeling like she had the ability to do something about it. Again, this occurred without acknowledgement the political, economic, and social dimensions of racism, or economic differences in general, and did not result in any indicators that she had gained an increased sense of her own privileges as a White U.S. American.

IMPLICATIONS

The three interrelated themes throughout the case studies were comfort zones, externalizing poverty out of the United States, and blessedness. Through the three themes, we have shown how two participants reinforced their privileged positions. Our case studies illustrate something more complex than the literature suggests with its emphasis on the promise of such programs. Short-term study abroad experiences can create perils; in this study on a short-term program, we identified the potential to reinforce White privilege.

As both instructors and researchers in this study abroad program, we have witnessed our preservice teachers struggle with feelings of comfort and discomfort as they made sense of their new surroundings: they found security in familiar elements of a new culture, including malls and fast food restaurants, but also were shocked, dismayed and distressed in their confrontations with poverty, disease, and hunger. In interviews, participants noted numerous experiences which resulted in more moderate forms of discomfort, including language barriers, new foods, and being seen as *other*. They also had difficulties making connections between the poverty in Honduras and poverty in their home country, often reducing images of the United States to their experiences as relatively privileged citizens and describing highly publicized examples of poverty, such as Hurricane Katrina, as exceptions and less extreme than those they witnessed during the program. Lastly, the theme of blessedness had both material and religious connotations where participants felt guilty for having more than others and cited it as their duty as practicing Christians to provide for those less fortunate. In each of these cases, the participants were unable, and possibly unwilling to recognize their Whiteness, and therefore unable to associate it with privilege. Whiteness was seen by them as morally neutral, normative, average and, especially, ideal.

We believe that following McIntosh's suggestion (1990), we need to work to question unearned advantages which serve to reinforce the contemporary structures that perpetuate social inequity. However, we continuously grapple with how to go about doing this. Through ongoing reconfigurations of the formal on-site curriculum, incorporating work such as that done by Zinn (2003), we hope to further challenge some of the fixed, unquestioned notions that the preservice teachers seem to possess. In particular, through an examination of Whiteness, we aim to shift their perspectives from a focus on self with blinders in place, a modern self, disconnected from the world, to a more critical and organic self developed in relation to others. We hope that our preservice teachers begin to question how they fit into societies, and begin to question the economic relationships and social consequences of global dominance and interdependence among nations.

As we plan experiences that will foster this kind of critical global consciousness, we also recognize that there are limits to what we can and want to do. In our observations over the past 5 years we have witnessed our preservice students distressed by what they have seen, close to reaching saturation point in being able to absorb the meaning of daily life for some people in Honduras, and in tears at the realization of world conditions they have never before seen or discussed.[1] Confronted with what we believe are the limits as to what our preservice teachers can bear, we are unwilling to push too hard or too far, and yet, we aim without compromise at moving beyond pity or sympathy for others who are oppressed economically, politically, or socially. What to do, what to discuss, what to read to reach a balance is a challenge. The challenge is on-going.

Study abroad and cross-cultural research often takes on the position that the experience is culturally enlightening. We suggest that a critical analysis, such as we used in this study, is needed to explore in more complex and context-specific ways how students come to understand their experiences while studying abroad. In the rush to create these kinds of programs that meet the call for international experiences, we need to also reflect on ways we can foster more critical awareness, outlooks that engender deeper understanding of the social, political, and economic forces that shape the contexts in which study abroad programs such as this one take place. The implications of research on the promise and perils of study abroad for teacher education are immense: for program development, for understanding preservice teacher identity, for ways to develop a more global consciousness in preservice teachers, and for ways to facilitate preservice teacher understandings of how to work with diverse populations of students. At this stage of our research, however, as we continue to engage in studies of Whiteness and race, identity, and representation, in particular, and turn our focus to understanding the Honduran community's response to our program, we are left with more questions and puzzles than answers and certainties.

NOTES

1. This excerpt is taken from our field notes: "It was clear that at certain points during the program preservice teachers were reaching the limits of what they felt they could discuss and still maintain their composure. In one example, we were on a bus ride returning from the mall and had to travel on a disintegrated road through a particularly distressed community on the outskirts of town. Right outside our window young children were filling the holes with handfuls of dirt and begging for money. Many of the preservice teachers stopped talking, turned their heads away from the windows, and remained silent. When one of the two faculty asked students what they were thinking about, one preservice teacher said, 'I just can't look or talk right now' and many of the others nodded their heads. We didn't talk for the next 20 minutes."

REFERENCES

Bigelow, Bill, & Bob Peterson. (Eds.). (2002). *Rethinking globalization: Teaching for justice in an unjust world*. Milwaukee, WI: Rethinking Schools.

Carger, Chris. (1996). *Of borders and dreams: A Mexican American experience of urban education*. New York: Teachers College Press.

Cushner, Kenneth, & Jennifer Mahon. (2002). Overseas student teaching: Affecting personal, professional, and global competencies in an age of globalization. *Journal of Studies in International Education, 6*(1), 44-58.

Dolby, Nadine. (2007). Reflections on nation: American undergraduates and study abroad. *Journal of Studies in International Education, 11*(2), 141-156.

Engle, Lilli, & John Engle. (2005). Study abroad levels: Toward a classification of program types. *Frontiers: The Interdisciplinary Journal of Study Abroad, 9*(2), 1-20.

Horton, Julie, & Dominic Scott. (2004). White students' voices in multicultural teacher education preparation. *Multicultural Education, 11*(4), 12-16.

Kinzie, Susan. (2006, August 8). The world is calling: Area college students join those hitting the books overseas in record numbers. *Washington Post*, p. B01.

Kitsantas, Anastasia. (2004). Studying abroad: The role of college students' goals on the development of cross cultural skills and global understanding. *College Student Journal, 38*(3), 441-454.

Lincoln, Yvonna, & Egon Guba. (1985). *Naturalistic inquiry*. Newbury Park, CA: SAGE.

Malewski, Erik. (2006). Naming a Latino/a curriculum. In Lourdes Diaz Soto (Ed.), *The Praeger handbook of Latino education in the U.S.* (pp. 319-329). Westport, CT: Praeger.

Mahan, James M., & Laura L. Stachowski. (1990). New horizons: Student teaching abroad to enrich understanding of diversity. *Action in Teacher Education, 12*(3), 13-21.

Mahon, Jennifer, & Kenneth Cushner. (2002). The overseas student teaching experience: Creating optimal learning. *Multicultural Perspectives, 4*(3), 3-8.

McIntosh, Peggy. (1990). White privilege: Unpacking the invisible knapsack. *Independent School, 49*(2), 31-36.

Open Doors. (2003, November). American students study abroad in growing numbers: Despite economic and security concerns post-Sept 11, numbers continue to rise. *IIE Network*. Retrieved June 10, 2004, from http://opendoors.iienetwork.org/?p=36524

Sleeter, Christine. (2001a). Epistemological diversity in research on preservice teachers preparation for historically underserved children. *Review of Research in Education 25, 2000-2001* (pp. 209-250). Washington, DC: American Educational Research Association.

Sleeter, Christine (2001b). Preparing teachers for culturally diverse schools. *Journal of Teacher Education, 52*(2), 94-106.

Solomona, Patrick, John Portelli, Beverly-Jean Daniel, & Arlene Campbell. (2005). The discourse of denial: How white teacher candidates construct race, racism, and *white privilege*. *Race, Ethnicity and Education, 8*(2), 147-169.

Stake, Robert E. (1995). *The art of case study research*. Thousand Oaks, CA: SAGE.

Zinn, Howard. (2003). *A people's history of the United States*. New York: Harper Collins.

CHAPTER 20

SOWING SEEDS OF SOCIAL JUSTICE THROUGH PERFORMATIVE PEDAGOGY

Middle School Students Explore Genocide

Mary Ann Reilly and Rob Cohen

This chapter chronicles the work of a teacher of eighth-grade students and a college researcher who, together, engage middle school students in art conversations, independent study, and collage in order to build understandings of social justice (in)formed by a close examination of genocide. Through performative pedagogy, the authors occasion students' examination of genocide. Specifically, students compose and intermix various key notions in a series of performances intended to develop an awareness of power, domination, and resistance while transmediating some of these compositions and readings in multimedia hypertexts, performance, and finger painting.

Growing a Soul for Social Change: Building the Knowledge Base for Social Justice
pp. 383–397
Copyright © 2008 by Information Age Publishing
All rights of reproduction in any form reserved.

INTRODUCTION

We, the coauthors, Mary Ann Reilly, an associate professor in New York, and Rob Cohen, a teacher of eighth-grade students in northeast New Jersey, have been investigating the uses of collage as an organizing force for teaching social justice in Cohen's language arts class. Together, we have been wondering in what ways the use of collage might influence students to engage in double-voiced readings of texts (Bakhtin, 1981, 1984) and how such readings might influence their composing processes as well as their sense of social justice. Bakhtin defines double-voiced discourse as the presence of two voices, dialogically interrelated. Bakhtin (1984) writes, "Two embodied meanings cannot lie side by side like two objects—they must come into inner contact; that is, they must enter into a semantic bond" (p. 189). In thinking about Bakhtin's understanding of double-voiced discourse, we wondered if collage might act as a conduit occasioning inner contact. Brockelman (2001) says postmodern collage "produces a kind of *tension* between the specificity of its signifiers and the truth they represent" (2001, p. 14, emphasis in original). We wondered what tensions might be produced as economically privileged students investigated poverty and genocide and did so through performance. The text that follows focuses on the students' performances with Wilkes's (1994) *One Day We Had to Run: Refugee Children Tell Their Stories in Words and Paintings* and locates the students' responses to Wilkes's text within a larger study of genocide.

CONVERSING THROUGH PAINT: *ONE DAY WE HAD TO RUN*

It is an unusual day in January insomuch as beyond the windows of this middle school classroom the weather hints at the coming of spring—almost as if February and March have been neatly folded into the last few days of January. But warm weather in January in New Jersey is an anomaly for certain, and winter will reassert itself within the week. Inside the classroom, less certainty resides. Twenty-one eighth graders and their teacher, Rob Cohen, are settling in—readying themselves for their 90-minute language arts class. The students have recently concluded writing an I-Search paper (Macrorie, 1980). In these texts, the students recounted the information they had learned about a particular genocide and also provided more detailed information about the searching process they undertook. Each student in this class has selected a different genocide to research. On this day, the students are eager to get started, knowing that they will be doing some finger painting.

"Each pair should get one sheet of paper," explains Cohen as he holds up a 12" × 18" sheet of glossy, heavyweight paper. "The threesome here," he says pointing to a group of three students, "needs to tape together two sheets."

Seated at tables, the 21 students are arranged in pairs, with one group of three. Students sit opposite their respective partners. Before them on tables covered with newspaper, are cups of gloppy finger paint. Their sleeves are rolled and they are restless, anxious in some ways to get started. They retrieve paper; return to their seats and listen as their teacher further explains what they will be doing.

For the next 6 minutes, Cohen reads aloud the narrative, "Something Like an Accident," written by Chol Paul Guet, a 14-year-old Sudanese boy. It is his story of survival and loss collected by Wilkes (1994) and included in her stunning and moving text, *One Day We Had to Run: Refugee Children Tell Their Stories in Words and Paintings*. The text is a compilation rendered by refugee children in Kenya. Interspersed throughout the 64-page text are photographs of the children and the refugee camps.

"It was something like an accident when I ran away from my village. We were playing at about 5 o'clock when these people, the soldiers, came," says Cohen, as he reads the opening to Guet's four-page narrative. Throughout the reading, the students remain quiet, shifting in their seats as they listen. Some appear bored, impatient to play with the paint, others appear to listen with more acuity, especially as they get rooted in the story of how Guet at the age of 9 had to run for his life; a journey that would take 4 years to complete and cover 1,200 miles.

"I don't know whether my mother or father are dead or alive. I was 9 when I left Sudan. I am 14 now. I am an olde man now. My mother will not know me," says Cohen, reading the conclusion of Guet's narrative. At the end of the story, images of the paintings created by the refugee children and photographs from the Wilkes text are projected onto a screen at the front of the classroom.

Alongside this, *Spem in Alium* (Sing and Glorify) performed by the Kronos Quartet (Trallis, 1990, track 4), can be heard. Cohen has directed the students to converse about what they heard and what the images being projected suggest. Their conversation, however, will not be verbal. Paint will be the medium they use. For the next 20 minutes, students converse with their partner(s) in silence, using the single piece of paper and paint.

Interpreting the Conversation

As the students' paintings are drying, Cohen asks them to reflect on the process they have gone through and the images they have created and viewed.

Figure 20.1. Students engaged in art conversation.

"I want you to take a couple of minutes and reflect on what you put in your painting, what you were thinking, what this whole process meant," prompts Cohen. "Take a few minutes to really go through what you were doing, what thoughts were in your head." The students spend the next ten minutes writing, before Cohen gathers the class.

"Let's start with the easy stuff. What stands out?" asks Cohen.

"Color," Selma says. "Red and black."

"Red and black?" queries Cohen.

Kelly looks at the painting she and Selma have done and adds, "Well, like for me it started out as like just a painting, like a fun activity. What our painting evolved into was just so surprising." Kelly pauses here and gathers her next thought. "I don't know. I really didn't expect it to turn into what it did," she adds, shifting in her seat.

"What did it turn into?" asks Cohen.

"Well, I don't know. I think I could sorta tell a story from ours and say this is what everything represents," explains Kelly. "But I didn't plan it that way. That's just how it," she pauses as if looking for the next word and resumes slowly, "That's just how it happened in the end."

The students' first comment on the colors they selected while painting. This leads them to begin to interpret what they have created.

Sowing Seeds of Social Justice Through Performative Pedagogy 387

Figure 20.2. Students completed art conversation.

"This side is more like hectic and crazy," Sam says as she gestures to the painting before her.

"This side is where the main genocide is going on," adds Kerry, Sam's partner. She points to the darkened portion of the painting. "And then like the line down is like the paths the people were taking or trying to get to the safe land. Like they kept getting to places but the places kept being invaded by other people."

Gesturing to a sweep of lighter shades of tan on the opposite edge of the paper, Kerry adds, "This is like happier, but not as happy and the red is like, there is still destruction and suffering where it was supposed to be safe. And it says," Kerry stops and points to the center of the painting. "We wrote *help* and then we crossed it out because they asked for help and they didn't get any."

"It's just, basically it's about trying to get to safety," concludes Sam.

"And even when they got to safety, it wouldn't be 100% safe," adds Kerry.

As the students talk, it becomes clear that their paintings have become vehicles through which they retell Guet's story of literally having to run for his life. The students struggle to express that which seems only to be expressed through a language of starts and stops; for with what voice might grief and sorrow and outrage and despair and complicity be uttered? In some ways Guet's story is the story of the inexpressible; the inhumane absence of global and individual response to a young child's most desperate needs; a child who finds himself at 14 to be an "olde man" who his mother would not recognize. By telling and retelling Guet's story, will the students begin to give voice to challenging feelings?

"I was also just drawing stuff in the paint and I ended up doing, rubbing my fingers along the edge with red," explains Kelly as she rubs her finger across the table where she is sitting. "And like now that I, well, it kinda feels like almost like it's cloudy and you can't really tell what's on the outside. But it's cloudy for us to look in. Like we don't really know what's going on over there and so that's what the edges (of the painting) represent on mine."

"How does this hook up with what we just finished; the genocide unit?" prompts Cohen. "How clear is the connection between what's going on in one and the other?"

"Well now that you said that, it kinda makes me realize something," says Sam. "How it (the art conversations) started off as really nothing. We were just having fun, fooling around. And then slowly we kept doing things and we would wash it," she says motioning with her hands. "And then we would do some more things. And that's kind of what genocide is. It starts as something little and slowly gets bigger and bigger, and wipes things out and does more and more things."

"Can you explain that a little more?" Reilly asks. "I'm not sure I understand that."

"Well, like before the genocide starts, before people start dying, they're not really doing anything big. And so they just do something small that doesn't really seem to mean anything," she continues, stressing the word *seem*. "Like how we started the painting. And slowly like more people got into it, and so you got more colors and more paint and you would wash off that level and okay we're done with that. Let's move on to something new. And they would do more things to hurt the people. You just keep wiping out things and adding more, until the whole page is covered. And you have this full scale plan of what you're going to do."

"So the violence escalates?" Reilly queries.

"Yeah. In the painting and in the genocide," she says, turning her head away and down.

"What do you think about that?" Reilly asks.

"I think it's just crazy that something like that," says Sam, "Like with all these genocides like so many people can be killed and no one would do anything about it. My project was all about genocides in general. So I just basically studied the topic. One of the main reasons people didn't go in to try to help was because the United Nations said that they couldn't for some reason and they kept making up different excuses."

"Did you know about genocides before the I-Search?" Reilly asks.

"We didn't know a lot about genocides because we only focused on the Holocaust, but we knew a little bit about it, but not the details," adds Kerry. "I worked on the Armenian genocide. And what surprised me the most was that the only reason the Turks tried to kill the Armenians was so they could expand their country and the Armenians were just in their way. And when World War I started it was like a perfect alibi for them to start to kill the Armenians. So I think it just surprised me so much that the only reason they killed the Armenians was so they could create the Pan-Turanian Empire."

"Did you see any patterns across the genocides?" Reilly asks.

"Well one pattern I read," Sam begins, "Like this guy wrote about the eight steps of genocide. It starts with people saying these people are bad and then there's the dehumanization where like people will make the people they are trying to kill like stupid and one man to clean the street with a tooth brush. And it slowly emerges from small pranks to mass killings."

Inherent in the language that Kelly and Sam use to make sense of their art conversation and Guet's story is their research about genocide. When Cohen asks about the connections between the genocide unit and the art conversations, the students use their prior knowledge as a lens to help them interpret their abstract painting. Bakhtin's double-voiced discourse can be heard in the borrowing of language the students use to make sense of their art conversation.

LEARNING AS COLLAGE: SEPTEMBER TO JANUARY

Well before students begin finger painting in response to Guet's narrative, they have been engaged in learning through multiple perspectives, reflection, and performance. One could understand Cohen's class as performative pedagogy (Ellsworth, 1997; hooks, 1994; Pineau, 1994) instruction that combines performance methods and theory with critical pedagogy. As such the students learn through performance, but it is performance designed to help students recognize relations of power, domination, and resistance (Giroux, 2000; Giroux & Shannon, 1997).

Beginning in September, Cohen asks his students to create a general class rubric, scaling what they consider important reading and writing skills to focus on across the school year. Cohen helps inform these students' views by having them participate in a series of brief teacher-selected evaluatives, snapshots of student reading and writing performances. For this purpose, Cohen uses *headline poems* and *found poems* (Dunning & Stafford, 1992) composed in response to read text. Cohen then asks students to examine their work and the class rubric in order to make any adjustments needed with regard to what they believe is important to learn. This rubric highlighting (most important to least important) content and establishing a basic initial criteria for excellence also informs the curricular path the class will walk (Pinar & Grumet, 1976). The rubric is revised throughout the year as needed. Because teaching for social justice requires intellectual understanding and praxis (Freire, 1968/1970; Giroux, 2000; Giroux & McLaren 1994; hooks, 1994), this collaborative work seeds the idea of collage as a curricular construct and provides information about Cohen and the students for the entire class while initiating conversations about power and negotiation in the classroom.

During the time the students are engaged in rubric making, they are also learning how to compose list poems, recipe poems (Dunning & Stafford, 1992), and two types of collage poems. In the first, Cohen asks students to collect ten ideas for poems and record each on a separate index card. This work occurs across several weeks, students bring their ten cards to class, partner and flip the cards onto the rug in front of them. Based on a coin toss, one student in each partnership chooses either the three nearest or the three most distant cards and uses the ideas on each of the chosen cards to compose a single poem. Cohen also has students write cento poems, a patchwork poem composed entirely from lines or phrases from other authors' works.

Alongside these learning experiences, Cohen engages students in ongoing conversations about postmodern collage (Brockelman, 2001). He and his students discuss how collage is an assemblage of related images used to create a larger image. Unlike modern collage where theme remains constant, postmodern collage privileges counterpoint. The students' study the wall in the classroom where they have displayed their poetry, paintings, and other texts they have assembled as hypertext, and begin to consider how they might use the work of the class in a detailed and arranged manner to represent their learning in a mid-year, self-assessment essay.

Contemporaneous with all this is a reading of Cisneros' (1981) *The House on Mango Street*, which produces a kind of narrative disorientation for eighth-grade readers since it does not follow a traditional chronological plot sequence. Cohen and his students approach the text as a visual collage, cataloguing and piling up images students see repeated in the text, such as the repeated image of women who lean elbows on window ledges and by mapping Cisneros' fictional neighborhood on large drawing paper. Cohen prepares the city grid, and students add details, such as homes, businesses, schools, and parks as they read. They continue this practice until students indicate they can visualize the neighborhood while reading. Cohen explains that the coalescence from disparate and seemingly unrelated images and vignettes in Cisneros into a coherent sows the seeds for the kind of thinking that will be needed later in the year for the genocide research project.

After Cisneros and before the genocide study is formally introduced, students transmediate fiction using MediaBlender, a hypermedia software. Here, students are given envelopes with five random sentences culled from a Ray Bradbury (2003) short story, "The Pedestrian." There are 25 sentences in play in various random five-sentence configurations across the classroom. Students first work to order *their* sentences as they see fit and write a linking narrative using all five of the sentences they each have been given. Then Cohen asks students to work in small groups to illustrate one of the student narratives using MediaBlender. Students view each group product prior to reading the entire story as Bradbury wrote it and then write and then discuss Burroughs' (2001) notion that "a *functioning* police state needs no police" in response (p. 31, italics in original). Again, the work here serves several purposes: it is collage-like in its construction, it deepens reading skills, and the conversations extend and begin to germinate ideas of social justice. Further, the work also serves to introduce the idea of a police state, something that most of the students living in this economically advantaged northeast suburb indicate to Cohen that they have little or no relevant prior knowledge of despite their annual study of the Holocaust.

STUDYING GENOCIDE: WRITING THE I-SEARCH ESSAY

Alongside the other learning that has taken place during the school year, the students are beginning to piece together a sense of the world that is far larger than the more intimate place where they live. This broadening of perspectives is essential when teaching for social justice as Kumashiro (2001) explains,

> All students come to school with partial knowledge. In some ways they may not know much about marginalized groups in society, but even when they do know about the *Other*, that knowledge is often a mis-knowledge, a knowl-

Table 20.1. Genocides Researched by the Students

Armenia
Australian Aborigines
Brazilian logging
Cambodia
Chernobyl (former USSR)
Hernando Cortez
The Crusades (emphasis on The Children's Crusade)
Deseparacidos (the Disappeared)
East Timor
Ecuador (oil)
Hiroshima & Nagasaki
Iraq (the Kurds)
Iraq (2 Gulf Wars and the UN/US sanctions between them)
Irish Potato Famine
Ghengis Khan
Maylaysian logging
Middle Passage
Nanking
Native Americans (Trail of Tears)
Nigeria (oil)
Rwanda
Sierra Leone
Former Soviet Union under Josef Stalin
Sudan
Former Yugoslavia (Bosnia)

edge of stereotypes and myths learned from the media, families, peer groups, and so forth. (p. 4)

In early December, students begin their study of genocide. On the first day of the project, students receive an introductory handout that defines what genocide is in accordance with the United Nations and informed by Cohen's review of literature (Gellately & Kiernan, 2003; Hinton, 2002; Power, 2002). The genocides studied are listed in Table 20.1.

The name of each genocide is placed on a separate index card; each index card is then folded up so that it cannot be read and all the cards are put into a bowl. A student volunteer distributes one folded card to each student and that student then gets to choose from the remaining topics for himself or herself. As students unfold their cards, cries immediately go up: "Where's *East Timor*?" "Who's *Sierra Leone*?" "What's *Middle Passage*?"

Once the distribution of topics is complete, a period of trade and negotiation begins. For about 15 minutes, students use laptop computers to gather cursory information about their topics and can trade assignments with a willing partner; often the trades are initiated by students interested in studying genocides related to their ethnicity or race.

Throughout the school year, students have been engaged in *workshop* (Atwell, 1998; Ernst, 1997; Fletcher, 1992; Graves, 2003; Lensmire, 1994; Willinsky, 1990) and use the same structure during the I-Search essay. In writing the I-Search, students' compositions are divided into four sections: introduction, searching, finding, and conclusion (Macrorie, 1980). Each section tells a part of the research process. Cohen tells his students that it might be easiest if they think about the I-search as four separate, but related essays. The completed I-search is a record of students' thinking, as it is the story not only of *what* students' learned, but also of *how* they learned. Students track their thinking through a double-entry notebook, and they track their searching through an activity log. They keep drafts of their work, confer with Cohen and external experts where available, and maintain a bibliography of works cited.

The written I-Search essay, however, is only the first part of the work. Although students share their essays with one another, they also use them to inform the design and content of a virtual museum. In spring of the school year, the class creates a virtual museum related to genocide and social justice. Students compose the virtual museum using MediaBlender. Each wing of the museum is designed and created by student work groups, and students are grouped according to the studied genocides. Each room in the wing is dedicated to a particular genocide and contains images and information pertaining to that genocide. There is one additional room in each wing for memorials, poetry, and other compositions generated in response to the genocide studies and/or genocide in general.

Through MediaBlender, students can include images, text, sounds, animation, and video. TJ and Carlos used Guet's narrative, their painting, I-Search compositions, and notes to create a multivoiced poem that they performed in front of their peers (see Table 20.3). Videos of student performances, such as TJ and Carlos' poem, are included in the museum. The museum is shared with other students and faculty via the school's intranet and through invitation to the classroom.

SOWING SOME SEEDS

In articulating the benefits of performative pedagogy, Thompson (1997) states

> the idea is not to build on existing personal experiences but to create a counterpoint to ordinary experience.... The educative value of such experiences is that they shift our connections to the world, not only providing the occasion for seeing and feeling in ways perhaps not ordinarily available to

Table 20.3. Student's Poem

We Just Walked
A Poem for Two Voices
by TJ and Carlos

The soldiers.	
	The shooting.
The screaming.	
	The bombing.
Nothing.	Nothing.
Feet burned	
	No water.
We just walked.	We just walked.
	Nothing we could do.
Not our country.	
We just walked.	We just walked.
Went to Kenya	
	to be safe.
We just walked.	We just walked.
	Took so long
Wanted to	
	Wanted to
die.	die.
We just walked.	We just walked.
	We made it.
We're safe.	
No more walking.	No more walking.
We have	
shoes.	
	shoes.
	We have
shirts	shirts.
We live	
freely.	freely.
No more walking.	No more walking.

us, but specifically illuminating experience as framed by expectations and conventions. (p. 33)

Through writing an I-Search essay, finger painting, composing and performing multivoiced poems, and constructing the virtual museum, performative space is created in the classroom. It is within such spaces that students' beliefs about genocide and the culture they live in are unsettled.

Thirteen-year-old Kevin studied the genocide in Sierra Leone. "I didn't have any idea what my project was about," he writes in the introduction to his I-Search essay.

> I felt really lost, because I had never heard of my topic before. I wanted to find out what happened there. By the end of all my research, I wanted to be able to tell people about the genocide that happened in Sierra Leone.

In conducting his I-Search, Kevin read *Glitter and Greed* (Roberts, 2003) and *Blood Diamonds* (Campbell, 2004). He collected information through internet searches learning more about Sierra Leone, DeBeers diamond mining, the Revolutionary United Front, progovernment militia, and the financing of Osama Bin Laden's terror through diamond purchases with the Revolutionary United Front. In addition, he also interviewed a local jeweler to understand more of the business of diamonds. Concluding his study, Kevin wrote,

> I learned how greed and power lead to horrible and unimaginable things. The diamonds we love and adore so much here in America are called *blood diamonds* in the places that they come from. Our happiness is costing someone somewhere an arm, a hand, a life. I have finally taken off my training wheels and opened my eyes to the world around me.

Kevin's conclusion may be read as an example of double-voiced discourse, one that "is half-ours and half-someone else's" (Bakhtin, 1981, p. 345). As Kevin researched the genocide in Sierra Leone he came to understand that diamonds are not neutral baubles. The texts he read and wrote informed his emerging understanding. Juxtaposing his reading of the book-length texts alongside his interview of the diamond merchant, Kevin was also able to "make use of someone else's discourse for his own purposes" (Bakhtin, 1984, p. 189). His new understanding now included the human costs associated with diamonds.

In doing each of these projects and then (re)positioning their learning within a hypertextual environment, it is Cohen's hope that students will begin to stretch the borders that bracket their lives and consider how they come to (re)name their life actions through multiple perspectives. Cohen recognizes that social justice is both a process and a skill (Adams, Bell, & Griffin, 1997) and as such provides opportunities across a school year for his students to learn about others in the world and to (re)affirm their abilities and obligations to respond.

Some years ago we chanced on a recording of Studs Terkel reading, "Oh, Sacred World" (Appleseed Recordings, 1998, disc 2, track 18). In thinking about this classroom work and the genocide project, we found ourselves throughout the project repeatedly returning to listen to the 23-second recording. With a deep, gravelly voice, Terkel intones:

> Oh sacred world, now wounded, we pledge to make you free.
> Free of war, free of hate, of selfish cruelty.
> And here in our small corner, we plant a tiny seed,
> And it will grow in beauty to shame the face of greed.

Perhaps, on that almost spring-like day in late January, when students began learning about the refugees in Africa and connecting that learning to their studies of genocide, some seeds were sown.

REFERENCES

Adams, Maurianne, Lee Anne Bell, & Pat Griffin. (1997). *Teaching for diversity and social justice, a sourcebook.* New York: Routledge.

Atwell, Nancie. (1998). *In the middle: New understanding about writing, reading, and learning.* Portsmouth, NH: Heinemann.

Bakhtin, Mikhail M. (1981). Discourse in the novel. In Michael Holquist (Ed.), *The dialogic imagination: Four essays* (Caryl Emerson & Michael Holquist, Trans). Austin: University of Texas Press.

Bakhtin, Mikhail M. (1984). Problems of Dostoevsky's poetics. In Caryl Emerson (Ed. & Trans.), *Theory and history of literature* (Vol. 8, pp. 3-325). Minneapolis: University of Minnesota Press.

Bradbury, Ray. (2003). The Pedestrian. In *Bradbury stories: 100 of his most celebrated tales* (pp. 600-603). New York: William Morrow.

Brockelman, Thomas. (2001). *The frame and the mirror: On collage and the postmodern.* Evanston, IL: Northwestern University Press.

Burroughs, William. S. (2001). *Naked lunch: The restored edition* (James Grauerholz & Barry Miles, Eds.). New York: Grove Press.

Campbell, Greg. (2004). *Blood diamonds.* Cambridge, MA: Westview Press.

Cisneros, Sandra. (1981). *The house on Mango Street.* New York: Vintage.

Dunning, Stephen, & William Stafford. (1992). *Getting the knack: 20 poetry writing exercises.* Urbana, IL: National Council Teachers of English.

Ellsworth, Elizabeth. (1997). *Teaching positions: Difference, pedagogy, and the power of address.* New York: Teachers College Press.

Ernst, Karen. (1997). *A teacher's sketch journal: Observations on learning and teaching.* Portsmouth, NH: Heinemann.

Fletcher, Ralph. (1992). *What a writer needs.* Portsmouth, NH: Heinemann.

Freire, Paulo. (1968/1970). *Pedagogy of the oppressed* (Myra Bergman Ramos, Trans.). New York: Continuum. (Original Portuguese work published 1968)

Gellately, Robert, & Kiernan, Ben. (2003). *The specter of genocide: Mass murder in historical perspective.* New York: Cambridge University Press.

Giroux, Henry A. (2000). *Impure acts: The practical politics of cultural studies.* New York: Routledge.

Giroux, Henry A., & Peter McLaren. (Eds.). (1994). *Between borders: Pedagogy and the politics of cultural studies.* New York: Routledge.

Giroux, Henry A., & Shannon, Patrick. (1997). *Cultural studies and education: Towards a performative practice.* New York: Routledge.

Graves, Donald. (2003). *Writing: Teachers and children at work (20th anniversary ed.).* Portsmouth, NH: Heinemann.

Hinton, Alexander Laban. (2002). *Annihilating difference: The anthropology of genocide.* Berkeley: University of California Press.

hooks, bell. (1994). *Teaching to transgress: Education as the practice of freedom.* New York: Routledge.

Kumashiro, Kevin K. (2001). "Posts" perspectives on anti-oppressive education in social studies, English, mathematics, and science classroom. *Educational Researcher, 30*(3), 3-12.

Lensmire, Timothy J. (1994). Writing workshop as carnival: Reflections on an alternative learning environment. *Harvard Educational Review, 64*(4), 371-391.

Macrorie, Ken. (1980). *Searching writing.* Rochelle Park, NJ: Hayden.

Pinar, William F., & Madeleine R. Grumet (1976). *Toward a poor curriculum.* Dubuque, IA: Kendall Hunt.

Pineau, Elyse Lamm. (1994). Teaching is performance: Reconceptualizing a problematic metaphor. *American Educational Research Journal, 31*(1), 3–25.

Power, Samantha. (2002). *A problem from Hell: America and the age of genocide.* New York: Basic Books.

Roberts, Janine. (2003). *Glitter and greed: The secret world of the diamond cartel.* New York: The Disinformation Company.

Tech4Learning. (2007). *MediaBlender* (Version 3.0) [Computer software]. San Diego, CA: Author.

Terkel, Studs. (1998). Oh, sacred world. On *Where Have All the Flowers Gone: The Songs of Pete Seeger* [CD]. Washington, DC: Appleseed Recordings.

Thompson, Audrey. (1997). For anti-racist education. *Curriculum Inquiry 27*(1), 7-44.

Trallis, Thomas. (1990). *Spem in alium* (Sing and glorify). On *Black Angels* [CD Recorded by Kronos Quartet]. Nonesuch Records.

Wilkes, Sybella. (1994). *One day we had to run: Refugee children tell their stories in words and paintings.* Brookfield, CT: Millbrook Press.

Willinsky, John. (Ed.). (1990). *The new literacy: Redefining reading and writing in the schools.* New York: Routledge.

ABOUT THE CONTRIBUTORS

ABOUT THE EDITORS

Lisa A. Holtan serves as the editorial assistant in the publication of this book series *Teaching<~>Learning Indigenous, Intercultural Worldviews: International Perspectives on Social Justice and Human Rights*. She came to this position after a year of working as a technical assistant to the editor of the scholarly publication of the World Council for Curriculum and Instruction. Lisa is currently a graduate student at St. Cloud State University in St. Cloud, Minnesota, where she recently successfully defended and completed her thesis, *The Experiences of Students with Disabilities at a United States Public Higher Education Institution*, for the master of science in social responsibility. She earned a bachelor of arts in criminal justice studies with a human relations and multicultural education minor. Lisa has worked to make a difference in the world anywhere she has been.

Aneesh Joshi served as the volume associate editor for this premier edition of *Teaching<~>Learning Indigenous, Intercultural Worldviews: International Perspectives on Social Justice and Human Rights* book series. He has been with the series from its initial venture as a journal issue in August 2006 to its transformation and culmination as a book series. He has been associated with Huber-Warring's publication endeavors since July 2002, and served as the managing editorial assistant of the *Journal of Critical Inquiry Into Curriculum and Instruction* (JCI<~>CI) and as an editorial assistant with her on a guest-edited issue of *Journal of Thought*. He holds a bachelor's degree in industrial and production engineering from Karnatak University, Dharwar, India, and master of science degree in industrial engineering from Wichita State University, Kansas. His interests include English translations of Russian literature, British literature, movies, stage plays, and documentaries from any part of the globe, Sufi poetry, and Urdu ghazals. He has been writing on a small scale and, so far, has only dreams of writing something of high accomplishment.

Tonya Huber-Warring, PhD, founding editor of this book series, *Teaching <~>Learning Indigenous, Intercultural Worldviews: International Perspectives on Social Justice and Human Rights*, is passionate about meaningful inquiry that informs the challenge of global human rights. Huber was founding editor of the *Journal of Critical Inquiry Into Curriculum and Instruction* (1998-2004, Caddo Gap Press, San Francisco), an international, scholarly, refereed journal committed to publishing the research of graduate students focused on representing meaningful ways of exploring multicultural education and critical pedagogy in teaching<~>learning dynamics, particularly through narrative inquiry and arts-based educational research. She has also worked as an associate literary editor for *Multicultural Education* since the first issue in 1993.

As one of the 13 founding members of the National Association for Multicultural Education in 1990, Huber worked diligently to build the organization. She served more than a decade on the executive board of officers and the board of directors, chartering the first state chapter (Kansas, 1995), hosting the first national leadership institute (New Mexico, 1996), and chartering the first university chapter (Wichita State University, Kansas, 2003).

She served on the International Overseas Program Faculty, College of New Jersey, Trenton (1997 to 2005), teaching courses required for the master of education for teachers working in American international schools around the world. Her teaching and research focus on culturally responsible pedagogy, education for world citizens, Huber has presented, consulted, taught, and/or researched in more than half of the 50 states in the United States, and in England, Cyprus, Vietnam, Canada, Spain, Venezuela, Côte d'Ivoire, West Africa, South Africa, China, Australia, and Kuwait. She is the author of *Quality Learning Experiences (QLEs) for all Students* (2002), *Teaching in the Diverse Classroom* (1993), and more than 140 articles and chapters.

Huber-Warring teaches research courses for the critical pedagogy doctoral program and the master of arts in curriculum and instruction at the University of St. Thomas, Minneapolis, Minnesota. Committed to culturally responsible pedagogy, she serves as the education coordinator of the social responsibility master of science, St. Cloud State University, St. Cloud, Minnesota, where she teaches courses in human relations and antiracist research.

ABOUT THE AUTHORS

John Abell is a professor of economics at Randolph College in Lynchburg, Virginia. He received his masters and PhD degrees from the University of Kentucky. Although his formal training was in the areas of macroeconomics, monetary economics, and finance, years of experience in the central highlands of Guatemala have shifted his research and teaching focus to the topic of sustainable economic development. The economic development programs of the parroquia of San Lucas Tolimán have been particularly influential. Professor Abell has published several articles describing these programs and their impacts on the community. His other published research has focused on poverty, unemployment, military spending, budget deficits, and distributional effects of monetary and fiscal policy.

Patricia Ann Horton Aceves received her master's degree in vocational education from Montana State University-Northern, with an emphasis in adult learning and technologies. She has taught in social service agencies working with adults on employment and computer skills. With a desire to teach at the university level, Ms. Aceves has pursued her doctorate of education in leadership from Saint Mary's University of Minnesota, and is currently working on her dissertation. Her dissertation research focuses on the impact of internationalization and technology on the creation of distance education degree programs between the United States and China. She currently works as the director of distributed learning at St. Cloud State University and is responsible for the distance learning initiatives of the University. Her additional research interests include correctional education and restorative justice.

Deborah A. Adeyemi is a lecturer in the Department of Languages and Social Sciences Education at the University of Botswana, Gaborone. She has published articles in international refereed journals including *New Horizons in Education* and *the Journal of International Society for Teacher Education*. Her area of specialization is English education.

Richard G. Berlach, PhD, is an associate professor in the School of Education at the University of Notre Dame Australia. Research interests include multiple intelligences, self-concept in education, assessment and evaluation, outcomes-based education, social and personal development, and pastoral care in education.

Kevin H. Brockberg, EdS, is a doctoral candidate in educational leadership at Oakland University in Rochester, Michigan. His career spans experience in public, parochial, and international schools in early childhood, K-12, and higher education. He believes discourse initiates personal and professional insight into both learning theory and inclusive school cultures leading to social justice; these are his primary research and leadership interests.

Jeff Bulington is a doctoral graduate student in Curriculum Studies at Purdue University. His research interests include equity issues in school mathematics, philosophy of education, and sociology of knowledge.

Danielle Celermajer, PhD, is currently director of global studies and postgraduate human rights at the University of Sydney, Australia. She was director of indigenous social justice policy at the Human Rights and Equal Opportunity Commission in Australia before moving to New York, where she completed her doctorate in political theory and human rights law at Columbia University, where she also taught human rights and ran an international program on human rights and religion. She is currently exploring the influence of Jerusalem or revelation traditions on Western political and philosophical thought and seeking to link this project with the reemergence of religion as a significant social and political vector in the human landscape of the twentieth century. Critically, she hopes this work will contribute to the potentials of religious tradition to equip us to face our unprecedented social, political, ethical and environmental challenges.

Elaine Chan, PhD, is an assistant professor of diversity and curriculum studies in the Department of Teaching, Learning, and Teacher Education at the College of Education and Human Sciences, University of Nebraska, Lincoln. Her research interests are in the areas of curriculum, ethnic identity of Chinese immigrant students, narrative inquiry, educational equity policies, and multicultural education.

Francis Nai-kwok Chan is a senior lecturer at the Hong Kong Institute of Education. He received his BA, certificate of education and MA from the University of Hong Kong, MEd from the University of Bristol and EdD from the Ontario Institute for Studies in Education of the University of Toronto. His teaching and research interests lie in teacher professional development in the areas of history education, citizenship education and moral and religious education. He is also the head of the Religious and Moral Education Curriculum Development Centre of the Hong Kong Catholic Diocese.

Melinde Coetzee, Dlitt et Phil-industrial and organizational psychology, is a professionally registered industrial psychologist and an associate professor in personnel and career psychology in the Department of Industrial and Organizational Psychology at the University of South Africa. She has published extensively on various topics in the fields of emotional intelligence, skills development and career psychology. She is extensively involved in research projects on the topic of emotional intelligence in the South African school environment.

Rob Cohen is the curriculum coordinator and an English teacher at Franklin Avenue Middle School in Franklin Lakes, New Jersey. He earned a graduate degree in English and is currently working on a doctorate.

Judy Davison is an assistant professor in curriculum and instruction at Western Kentucky University. Her specialty is in curriculum and program design for diverse student populations. Davison also has served as a Bureau of Indian Affairs contract monitor for Indian schools across the United States. She is a Senior Fulbright Scholar and conducted presentations, research and seminars in Eastern and Western Europe, Morocco, and Paraguay.

Eno Edem, PhD, is a senior lecturer in the Department of Curriculum Studies at University of Uyo, Nigeria. She holds a doctorate degree in science education from the University of Lagos. Edem taught instructional techniques at Naval Training School, Naval Base, Lagos. In addition to her research interest in educational instruction, she is an educational consultant specializing in training and human capacity building and has worked for many years with families in military and police barracks in Nigeria.

Betty C. Eng is an assistant professor at the City University of Hong Kong in the Department of Applied Social Studies. Her teaching responsibilities include teaching in educational psychology and counseling. Previously, she was a teacher educator for over 10 years at the Hong Kong Institute of Education, a major teacher education institute, and a counselor with an international school. Before coming to Hong Kong, she was a faculty member at California State University, Sacramento, and the University of California, Davis. Her teaching departments included Asian American Studies, Women's Studies, and Counseling. Her research interests include narrative inquiry, cross-cultural studies, counseling, and gender. Eng obtained her EdD at the Ontario Institute of Studies for Education of the University of Toronto. Her doctoral research was an exploration of teacher knowledge through personal narratives of identity, culture, and sense of belonging.

Ming Fang He is an associate professor of curriculum studies, Georgia Southern University. She currently advises doctoral students, directs doctoral dissertations, and teaches graduate courses in curriculum studies, multicultural education, and qualitative research methods. *A River Forever Flowing: Cross-Cultural Lives and Identities in the Multicultural Landscape* (2003) and *Narrative and Experience in Multicultural Education* (2004) are her significant works. She is also an associate editor of *Handbook of Curriculum and Instruction* (under contract with Sage). She was an editor of *Curriculum Inquiry* and is an associate editor of *Multicultural Perspectives*. Currently she is engaged in a program of research on language, culture, and identity development of Chinese immigrant children and their mainstream schooling in-between Black and White tensions in the South. She coordinates an international educator training program sponsored by United States Department of State Bureau of Educational and Cultural Affairs, Office of Global Education Programs.

Larry Hufford has degrees in education, social work and political science. He received his PhD in political science from The London School of Economics and Political Science, England. He is a professor of international relations at St. Mary's University, San Antonio, Texas and has published books on nonviolence, bicultural and peace education. Hufford has served as an official election observer in Guatemala and Nicaragua, and has worked with grassroots organizations promoting participatory democracy in Central America and Asia. His current research and activism is promoting peace and democracy education curricula in inter-faith settings. He is a past president of the World Council for Curriculum and Instruction.

Ilene L. Ingram, EdD, is an assistant professor in the Department of Educational Leadership at Oakland University in Rochester, Michigan. She teaches graduate courses in educational administration and coordinates the on campus education specialist degree program. From both the micro (classroom and school) and macro (national and world) levels her work in education demonstrates an ongoing commitment to moral leadership development as a fundamental aspect of education, and to making visible the intersections between education, ethics, diversity, social justice praxis, and educational outcomes from the multiple and synergistic viewpoints of teacher, researcher, and world citizen. Her interest in all things connected to the challenges of preparing educational leaders committed to equity and social justice has taken her to the national stage, Canada, China, and

South Africa where she has presented her work, ensuring a broader dissemination of her beliefs, ideas, and commitment. She has published in these areas.

Cecelia A. Jansen, DEd, is an associate professor in psychology of education in the Department of Teacher Education at the University of South Africa. She has coauthored the book *Emotional Intelligence in the Classroom: The Secret of Happy Teachers* with Melinde Coetzee. They are also copresenters of the *"Short Course in the Dynamics of Classroom Climate"* which is presented through the Centre for Community Training and Development, University of South Africa. Dr. Jansen is extensively involved in research projects on the topic of emotional intelligence in the South African school environment.

Hollie Kulago is a doctoral student in curriculum studies at Purdue University. Her research interests are in the ways Navajo students define community and the implications this could have on teacher education cross-cultural experiences for student teachers who do their practicum on the Navajo reservation.

Chun-kwok Lau is working as an assessment consultant in the Education and Manpower Bureau of the Hong Kong Government. Previously he has been a secondary school teacher and a lecturer at the Hong Kong Institute of Education. He received his education in Hong Kong and Canada. His research interests involve narrative inquiry and teachers' personal and professional development.

Erik Malewski, PhD, is assistant professor of curriculum studies at Purdue University. His research interests include study abroad, social justice issues, and the ways that poststructuralist and critical theory can inform curriculum studies and educational practice. His most recent research has involved a long-term study of preservice teachers' experiences studying abroad in Honduras and a critical examination of cross-cultural suicide prevention and intervention policies. In 2005 he hosted a national state of the field conference entitled *Articulating Present (Next) Moments in Curriculum Studies: The Post-Reconceptualization Generation(s)*. Currently, he giving a series of invited lectures in India and completing an edited book on the state of the field of curriculum studies.

Terrence McCain is currently an assistant professor in curriculum and instruction at Western Kentucky University. He is a former Peace Corps volunteer in Honduras and has extensive experience with multicultural/

diversity issues in public schools and at the university level. His expertise is in ESL strategies and bilingual education. McCain is presently involved with several educational and environmental projects in Central America and Spain.

JoAnn Phillion is an associate professor of curriculum studies at Purdue University. Prior to pursuing her doctorate she was an ESL teacher in Japan for 6 years and in Canada for 3 years. Her research interests are in narrative approaches to multiculturalism, teacher knowledge, and teacher education. She teaches graduate courses in curriculum theory and multicultural education, and an undergraduate course in preservice teacher development. She is involved in international teacher development in Honduras and Hong Kong. She was the recipient of the AERA Division B's Dissertation of the Year Award in 2000, the Purdue Faculty of Education Outstanding Teaching Award in 2002, and Purdue University Teaching for Tomorrow Award in 2003. She published *Narrative Inquiry in a Multicultural Landscape: Multicultural Teaching and Learning* (Ablex Publications, 2002) and *Narrative and Experience in Multicultural Education* (Sage Publications; 2005). She served on the editorial board of *Curriculum Inquiry* since 1999 and was editor from 2003 to 2005.

Mary Ann Reilly, EdD, is an associate professor in the Department of Literacy at Manhattanville College in Purchase, New York. She has previously worked as an assistant superintendent for urban public school districts and as the director of literacy for Newark Public Schools in New Jersey. She earned a doctorate in English education from Teachers College/Columbia University.

Eloisa Rodriguez is a doctoral student in curriculum studies at Purdue University. She earned a MEd from Purdue University in 2003 as a Fulbright scholar and a BA in pedagogy from the National Autonomous University of Honduras. Her research is focused on a critical ethnographical study of grass roots community schools in Honduras. She has presented at AERA and NAME conferences. She currently serves as the codirector of the Study Abroad Program in Honduras for Purdue University's College of Education. She also serves as the curriculum development committee chairperson for BECA-Bilingual Education for Central America—a nonprofit 501(c) (3) grassroots organization focused on realizing the hopes and dreams through education for the children and families of Cofradia, Honduras.

Annette Sanders is the associate principal at Cooloongup Government Primary School, Australia. She is a broadly experienced educator specializing in areas related to the social and emotional dimensions of learning. As an accredited Tribes trainer, she has been instrumental in developing a school-based Tribes approach at Cooloongup.

Valerie Shirley is Navajo from Ganado, Arizona. She has taught in two Native American reservation elementary schools. She received her masters from the University of Wisconsin, Madison in curriculum and instruction. She is currently pursuing her doctoral degree at Purdue University in curriculum studies where she also teaches multiculturalism in education in the preservice teacher education program.

Clay M. Starlin is an American educator. He received his bachelor's degree in sociology and his master's and doctoral degrees in special education and educational psychology, all from the University of Oregon. Starlin has worked in public school, university and human service settings. These experiences have involved teaching children in clinical settings, public school supervision, university research & teaching, self-employed educational consulting and coordinating a state office program. He is professionally interested in individualizing education for the diversity of students, educational measurement, international literacy and human relation's curriculum. He is currently a senior consultant for the International Educational Systems Project which provides curriculum and services to support educational systems throughout the world.

Douglas Warring, PhD, is a professor in the School of Education, chair of teacher education and director of continuing education at the University of St. Thomas. His area of focus for teaching, writing, and consulting include diversity, critical reflection, identity development, and accreditation. Doug has been a high school teacher, coach, and official and was a licensed psychologist. He also serves as a member of the board of examiners of the National Council for the Accreditation of Teacher Education and is a former member of the board of directors for the Association of Teacher Educators and the Minnesota Association for Supervision and Curriculum Development. He is the author of *Understanding and Applying Human Relations and Multicultural Education: Teaching~Learning in a Global Society* (2007, Rev., 6th ed.).

Kelly C. Weiley earned her masters in social responsibility from St. Cloud State University in St. Cloud, Minnesota, where she is an adjunct instructor in the Department of Human Relations and Multicultural Education. Ms. Weiley received her bachelor of music degree from Northwestern University, Evanston, Illinois. Through AmeriCorps*National Civilian Community Corps, she worked in solidarity completing 10 projects over 2 years with communities throughout the United States. She recently collaborated with a former AmeriCorps colleague to design and implement diversity training for team leaders and corps members. In addition to working with youth from various communities within the United States, Kelly has had the opportunity to work with youth from the Dominican Republic, Cape Verde, Haiti, Somalia, and Lesotho, South Africa. Her thesis, *Uniting in Solidarity through Globally-Focused Service-Learning* is the basis for several publications, an opportunity for Kelly to share her passion for working with youth to facilitate global learning through experiential education.

Barbara Wind, director of the Holocaust Council, United Jewish Communities of MetroWest, Whippany, New Jersey, has been sharing the Paper Clips Project in Whitwell, Tennessee, with other Holocaust survivors, serving as tour director, program planner, and speaker, where she epitomizes Linda Hooper's motto: "Changing the world one class at a time." A former journalist for the *New York Times* and the *New Jersey Jewish News*, she is also widely published as a poet with her work appearing in the *Journal of the American Medical Association* and the chapbook *Jacob's Angels*. EOS Verlag published a book of Holocaust poems in Germany *Auf Asche Gehen/Walking on Ash*, translated into German by Marlen Gabriel, whose father was a soldier in the German Army. Barbara was born to parents who were the sole survivors of the Holocaust in each of their families.

Wai-ming Yu is an assistant professor in the Department of Curriculum and Instruction at the Hong Kong Institute of Education. She received her EdD from the Ontario Institute for Studies in Education of the University of Toronto in 2005, following the completion of BEd from the University of Liverpool, and MA from the University of London. Her teaching and research interests lie in curriculum, assessment, and teacher education. She has been involved in research and published in the areas of assessment, curriculum reform, and teachers' professional development.

RECOGNIZING REVIEWERS' CRITICAL FEEDBACK

The editorial policy of *Teaching <~> Learning Indigenous, Intercultural Worldviews: International Perspectives on Social Justice and Human Rights* provides for a series editor (serving as the lead editor) to work closely with the author(s) of each chapter accepted for publication. In issues featuring an invited guest editor, the guest editor assists in this role. Each manuscript published as a chapter in this volume has been reviewed by the series editor, the volume's associate editor, and three to five external refereed reviewers. The editorial assistant provides both the technical and editorial inputs required for each chapter. The editors extend sincere appreciation to the following professionals for their critical feedback on the authors' manuscripts. Ultimately, final decisions are the responsibility of the editor, but her work could not be accomplished without the selfless, dedicated expertise of the reviewers.

Chanda Abdul-Quddoos
Doctoral Student in Critical Pedagogy, University of St. Thomas, Minneapolis, Minnesota, USA
Teacher, North Community High School, Minneapolis, Minnesota, USA

Patricia Aceves
Director of Distributed Learning, Center for Continuing Studies, St. Cloud State University, St. Cloud, Minnesota, USA

Abalo F. Adewui
Associate Professor, Undergraduate Faculty, Teacher Education and Professional Development, Central Michigan University, Mount Pleasant, Michigan, USA

Mara Alagic
Associate Professor, Department of Curriculum and Instruction, Wichita State University, Wichita, Kansas, USA

Peter Appelbaum
Associate Professor, Department of Education, Arcadia University, Glenside, Pennsylvania, USA

Tamara Arnott
Assistant Professor, Higher Education Administration, College of Education, St. Cloud State University, St. Cloud, Minnesota, USA

Dinorah Azpuru
Assistant Professor, Department of Political Science, Wichita State University, Wichita, Kansas, USA

Timothy Benson
Spanish Instructor, Lake Superior College, Duluth, Minnesota, USA

Monica Byrne-Jiminez
Assistant Professor, Department of Foundations, Leadership, and Policy Studies, School of Education and Allied Human Services, Hofstra University, Hempstead, New York, USA

Tak Cheung Chan
Professor, Educational Leadership, Kennesaw State University, Kennesaw, Georgia, USA

Julie Condon
College ESL Coordinator, Department of English, St. Cloud State University, St. Cloud, Minnesota, USA

Dean Cristol
Associate Professor of Education, College of Education and Human Ecology, The Ohio State University, Lima, Ohio, USA

Larry Cross
Professor, Division of Education, Governors State University, University Park, Illinois, USA

Michele Dahl
Doctoral Student in Critical Pedagogy, University of St. Thomas, St. Paul, Minnesota, USA
Teacher, Oak Knoll Lower School, New Jersey, USA

Judith Davison-Jenkins
Associate Professor, Department of Teacher Development, St. Cloud State University, St. Cloud, Minnesota, USA

Ilka Dunne
Actions Speak Educational Design, Rand Afrikaans University, Johannesburg, Gauteng, South Africa

Joseph Edelheit
Associate Professor, Department of Philosophy, St. Cloud State University, St. Cloud, Minnesota, USA

Betty Eng
Assistant Professor, Department of Applied Social Studies, City University of Hong Kong, Kowloon, Hong Kong

Richard Farber
Chairperson, Professor, Educational Administration and Secondary Education, College of New Jersey, Ewing, New Jersey

Doug Feldmann
Assistant Professor, College of Education and Human Services, Northern Kentucky University, Kentucky, Highland Heights, USA

Victor Forrester
Professor, Department of Education Studies, Hong Kong Baptist University, Kowloon Tong, Hong Kong

Kerry Frank
Associate Professor, Graduate School of Professional Psychology, University of St. Thomas, St. Paul, Minnesota, USA

Belinda Gimbert
Assistant Professor, Educational Administration and Higher Education, School of Educational Policy and Leadership, The Ohio State University, Columbus, Ohio, USA

Kimberly Goebel
Third Grade Teacher, St. Mary of the Lake, White Bear Lake, Minnesota, USA

Phyllis Greenburg
Associate Professor, Community Studies, St. Cloud State University, St. Cloud, Minnesota, USA

Heather Hackman
Associate Professor, Human Relations and Multicultural Education, St. Cloud State University, St. Cloud, Minnesota, USA

Leonita Herrera
Associate Professor III, Eastern Visayas State University, Ormoc City, Leyte, Philippines

Michael Higgins
Professor, Foreign Language Center, Yamaguchi University, Yamaguchi, Japan

William Howe
Education Consultant for Multicultural Education and Gender Equity, Connecticut State Department of Education Bureau of Certification and Professional Development, Hartford, Connecticut, USA

Alex Jassen
Assistant Professor, Department of Classical and Near Eastern Studies, Center for Jewish Studies, University of Minnesota, Minneapolis, Minnesota, USA

Kathryn Johnson
Assistant Professor of Special Education, College of Education, St. Cloud State University, St. Cloud, Minnesota, USA

Leeann Jorgenson
Associate Professor, Educational Leadership and Community Psychology (ELCP), College of Education, St. Cloud State University, St. Cloud, Minnesota, USA

Khyati Joshi
Assistant Professor, School of Education, Fairleigh Dickinson University, Teaneck, New Jersey, USA

Maya Kalyanpur
Assistant Professor, Department of Reading, Special Education and Instructional Technology, Towson State University, Towson, Maryland, USA

Frances Ann Kayona
Associate Professor, Department of Educational Leadership and Community Psychology College of Education, St. Cloud State University, St. Cloud, Minnesota, USA

Terrie Keilborn
Adjunct Professor, Department of Curriculum and Instruction, University of West Georgia, Carrollton, Georgia, USA

David Lee Keiser
Associate Professor, Director, Agenda for Education in a Democracy, Montclair State University, Montclair, New Jersey, USA

Polly Kellogg
Associate Professor, Human Relations and Multicultural Education, St. Cloud State University, St. Cloud, Minnesota, USA

Michalis Koutsoulis
Assistant Professor of Education, Intercollege, The University of Nicosia, Acropolis, Cyprus

Jason Royce Lindsey
Assistant Professor, Department of Political Science, St. Cloud State University, St. Cloud, Minnesota, USA

Gregory Martin
Lecturer, School of Education and Professional Studies (Gold Coast), Griffith University, Southport, Queensland, Australia

Matthew Maruggi
Director of the Tutor/Mentor Program, University of St. Thomas, St. Paul, Minnesota, USA

Rebekah McCloud
Associate Director, Office of Diversity Initiatives, University of Central Florida, Orlando, Florida, USA

Joseph Melcher
Associate Professor of Psychology, Psychology Department, St. Cloud State University, St. Cloud, Minnesota, USA

Ismail Hakk Mirici
Assistant Professor, Faculty of Education, Akdeniz University, Antalya, Turkey

Linda Mitchell
Associate Professor, Department of Curriculum and Instruction, Wichita State University, Wichita, Kansas, USA

Mumbi Mwangi
Assistant Professor, Women's Studies Program, St. Cloud State University, Minnesota, St. Cloud, USA

Su Oteme
Teacher, International University of Grand Bassam, Abidjan, Côte D'Ivoire, West Africa

Christopher T. Pears
Social Studies Teacher, Minnetonka High School, Minnetonka, Minnesota, USA

George Perrault
Professor, Department of Educational Leadership, School of Education, University of Nevada, Reno, Nevada, USA

David Petkosh
Professor, Reading, Harrisburg Area Community College, Harrisburg, Pennsylvania, USA

JoAnn Phillion
Associate Professor of Curriculum Studies, Department of Curriculum and Instruction, Purdue University, West Lafayette, Indiana, USA

Michael Philson
Executive Director, Office of International Programs, Old Dominion University, Norfolk, Virginia, USA

Larry Ramos
Director, Educational Talent Search/Project Discovery, Wichita State University, Wichita, Kansas, USA

David Rigoni
Associate Dean, School of Education, University of St. Thomas, St. Paul, Minnesota, USA

Teresa Rishel
Assistant Professor, Teaching, Leadership, and Curriculum Studies, Kent State University, Kent, Ohio, USA

Michael Round
Retired Headmaster, Croydon, United Kingdom

Michael Shaffer
Assistant Professor of Philosophy, Department of Philosophy, St. Cloud State University, St. Cloud, Minnesota, USA

Patricia Shaw
Associate Professor, Department of Curriculum and Instruction, University of Wisconsin, Whitewater, Wisconsin, USA

Lalita Subrahmanyan
Professor, Teacher Development, St Cloud State University, Minnesota, USA

Piyush Swami
Professor, Science Education and Curriculum and Instruction, University of Cincinnati, Cincinnati, Ohio, USA

Julius Tangwe
Teacher/Soccer Coach, Saint Thomas Academy, Mendota Heights, Minnesota, USA

Kristof Van Assche
Assistant Professor of Community Studies, St. Cloud State University, St. Cloud, Minnesota, USA

Christine van Halen-Faber
Principal, Covenant Canadian Reformed Teachers College, Hamilton, Ontario, Canada, and Independent Scholar at the Centre for Teacher Development, OISE/University of Toronto, Toronto, Ontario, Canada

Margaret Villanueva
Professor of Community Studies, St. Cloud State University, St. Cloud, Minnesota, USA

G. Vishwanathappa
Reader, Regional Institute of Education (NCERT), Manasagangothri, Mysore, Karnataka State, India

Douglas Warring
Educational Psychologist, Multicultural Studies, University of St. Thomas, St. Paul, Minnesota, USA

Kelly Weiley
Adjunct Instructor, Department of Human Relations and Multicultural Education, College of Education, St. Cloud State University, St. Cloud, Minnesota, USA

Janet Wozenski
Registrar and Director of Student Services, International University of Grand-Bassam, Bassam, Cote d'Ivoire

Printed in the United States
108097LV00001B/12/P